$35.00

10·4·83

Photo of François Truffaut by Jacques Grenier

François TRUFFAUT

a guide to references and resources

A
Reference
Publication
in
Film

Ronald Gottesman
Editor

François TRUFFAUT

a guide to references and resources

EUGENE P. WALZ

G.K.HALL&CO.

70 LINCOLN STREET, BOSTON, MASS.

Library of Congress Cataloging in Publication Data

Walz, Eugene P.
  François Truffaut: a guide to references and
resources.

  Includes indexes.
    1. Truffaut, François.   2.   Truffaut, François—
Bibliography.   I.   Title.
PN1998.A3T76   791.43'0233'0924   82-6201
ISBN 0-8161-8337-6   AACR2

This publication is printed on permanent/durable acid-free paper
MANUFACTURED IN THE UNITED STATES OF AMERICA

To Kathryn Manix Walz

Contents

The Author   x

Preface   xi

   I.   Biographical Background   1

  II.   Critical Survey   17

 III.   The Films: Synopses, Credits, Notes, and Reviews . .   37

  IV.   Writings about François Truffaut   91

   V.   Writings by François Truffaut   153
            Scripts and Books   153
            Reviews, Essays, and Interviews by Truffaut . . .   161
            Undated Reviews and Essays   246
            Programs and Bulletins to which Truffaut
               Contributed   247

  VI.   Interviews with François Truffaut   249

 VII.   Other Film-Related Activity   287

VIII.   Archival Sources   291

  IX.   Film Distributors   295

   X.   Appendix   299

Author Index   303

Film-Title Index   309

Auteur Index   317

The Author

Gene Walz earned a bachelor's degree from St. John Fisher College and advanced degrees in literature and film from Indiana University and the University of Massachusetts. He has taught at Frostburg State College, worked for educational television, and written for a variety of journals. He currently teaches in the Film Studies Programme at the University of Manitoba, where he is a member of the editorial board of The Canadian Review of American Studies and the executive board of The Film Studies Association of Canada.

Preface

He was once notorious for being France's most fractious critic; now he is the most familiar of all the "New Wave" directors of the sixties, the one whose film career has been the most continuous and successful. But François Truffaut was also France's most prolific critic, as he is now probably its most thorough filmmaker, not only writing, directing, acting in, and closely supervising the editing of his films, but also spearheading the publicity for them through numerous articles and interviews. The resources available on Truffaut, therefore, are very extensive, so extensive that certain modifications of the usual format for books in this series were necessary.

These modifications are most evident in Chapter III (The Films: Synopses, Credits, Notes, and Reviews). Since scripts are readily available on most of Truffaut's films and the films themselves are more accessible in North America than those by many other European directors, the synopses have been considerably shortened to provide a functional outline of the plots. Notes have been limited to the most essential. For instance, although there are often discrepancies between the running times for Truffaut's films listed in newspaper credits and distributors' catalogs (usually only a few minutes, but as many as seven), I have not referred to these discrepancies in the notes; where possible I have used the running times listed in the publicity material provided by Les Films du Carrosse, Truffaut's production company.

The most dramatic change in format in Chapter III has to do with the Reviews section for each film. Almost all of these were originally annotated entries from Chapter IV (Writings about Truffaut). To keep the book from being unwieldy, I made a distinction between "reviews" on the one hand and "critical articles," "essays," or "analyses" on the other. The line of distinction is fairly commonly used, though not very firmly established. Often the same person writing for the same journal or newspaper on successive films by Truffaut would write in one case a "review" and in the next a "critical article." For instance, Vincent Canby, who writes well on almost all of Truffaut's movies and is very receptive to them, is often relegated to the "Reviews" sections of Chapter III. (Two exceptions are his articles on L'Enfant Sauvage (The Wild Child) and La Nuit américaine (Day for Night)--see entries 206 and 264.) The "Reviews" are simply not as thorough, systematic, original, or insightfully analytical as the "critical articles," "essays," or "analyses" (which have been re-tained and annotated in Chapter IV).

The "Reviews" as listed in Chapter III are arranged by language: English first (both for the United States and Great Britain), then French (France and Quebec), and German. For brevity's sake I have eliminated the titles of the reviews and the page numbers--including simply the title of the journal or newspaper, the author, and the issue number and/or date. And the reviews are arranged neither alpha-betically nor chronologically, as is usually the case, but by my own order of importance. What I felt were the more useful reviews were put at the beginning of each language section. Thus someone wanting to find the more representative or valuable reviews of a particular film (the ones, frankly, that I had the most trouble distinguishing from "critical articles") would only have to consult the first four or five entries for each language. Everything written about a par-ticular film at the time of its release will not necessarily be found in the "Reviews" sections. Those interested in finding everything written about a particular film should check the title index for the relevant annotated entries in Chapter IV.

Again to conserve space, some modifications were also made in Chapter IV (Writings about Truffaut). Rather than repeat the phrase "Reprinted in Les Films de ma vie (The Films of My Life), see entry 465" over 100 times, I have simply written "In FMV" after those arti-cles that Truffaut reprinted in his book. Special issues devoted to Truffaut by some film journals have been listed by the title of the journal; individual articles have been cited and commented upon in this one entry and not individually by author as is the usual case (see entries 83, 87, 145, 189, 308). Articles on larger issues or controversies that involved Truffaut have been restricted to the most important ones. (For the auteur controversy in America, see entries 86, 158, 226, 263, 268-269, 274, 293, and 312; for "the Langlois affair" and the closing of the French cinémathèque, see entries 168, 171, and 176; for the shutting-down of the Cannes Film Festival, see entries 161-162, 165, 170, 174, 178, 180, and especially 183.) Among the items annotated in Chapter IV are eleven books on Truffaut (see entries 220, 239, 245, 249, 284, 291, 330, 365, 371, 380, 397) and four dissertations (see entries 325, 347, 378, and 401a). An aster-isk to the left of an entry indicates that I have not had first-hand access to it.

Chapter V (Writings by Truffaut) is divided into two sections. The first part contains all the published scripts and script-extracts for Truffaut's films, plus all the books he wrote, compiled, or edit-ed, and excerpts from them. The second part is the first published list of Truffaut's enormous output as a critic. It includes not only

his reviews and essays for Cahiers du Cinéma and Arts, but also his
interviews with other directors, his incidental comments and anecdotal
contributions to the "Intimate Journal" section of Cahiers, and his
"Ten-Best" lists. More importantly, it lists, for the first time
anywhere, all the work he wrote anonymously and pseudonymously (using
the names Robert Lachenay, Louis Chabert, and François de Monferrand
--his mother's maiden name). Because the list was compiled with the
assistance of Truffaut, it is as complete a list as can be expected.
The major omissions from the bibliography are from Le Temps de Paris,
an ephemeral journal to which Truffaut contributed articles in the
spring of 1956 on François Mauriac, Kazan's Baby Doll, Laughton's
Night of the Hunter, Resnais' Night and Fog, Robson's The Harder the
Fall, Charles Vidor's Love Me or Leave Me, Preminger's Man with the
Golden Arm, de Sica's Il Tetto, and Germi's Man of Iron. His files
in Paris also indicate that Truffaut wrote about twenty articles in
the early 1950s that were published in journals which cannot be lo-
cated or ascertained (on, for instance, Fellini's Variety Lights and
La Strada, Cukor's Born Yesterday and The Marrying Kind, Nick Ray's
Run for Cover and The True Story of Jesse James, and Lang's Clash by
Night, Rancho Notorious, and The Blue Gardenia). Articles on Alfred
Hitchcock and the Marx Brothers in Arts in May and August of 1954
were mentioned to me too late to include, as was one signed "Robert
de la Chesnaye" entitled "Feu Mathias Pascal" in Arts in February of
1956. At the end of Chapter V (beginning with entry 1184) are grouped
six films about which I could not obtain complete information. Entry
1189a refers to those articles that Truffaut wrote for special events
whose transcripts or programs were unobtainable.

The articles in Chapter V are listed alphabetically by title for
each year. Where Truffaut used a pseudonym or his initials, or left
the article unsigned, this has been indicated in square brackets after
the title of the article.

Chapter VI (Interviews with Truffaut) marks another departure
from the usual format for books in this series. It is a departure
dictated by both the sheer magnitude of these printed interviews
(Truffaut himself was startled when I told him the number I had
found) and their uniqueness and value. The list of interviews (arranged alphabetically according to the last name of the interviewer)
is taken only from those periodicals that have some claim to national
prominence and/or international circulation. Some of them are disguised as articles or career overviews; that is, they are based on
interviews and are composed of extensive quotations from the interview
with an introduction, conclusion, and comments that serve merely to
place the quotations in context. See especially in this regard Sanche
de Gramont's "Life Style of Homo Cinematicus" (entry 1303).

Although the list of printed interviews here is extensive, it is
by no means exhaustive. On the day that I met Truffaut in Montreal
during the Canadian premiere of Le Dernier Metro (The Last Metro), as
many as ten interviewers had been granted private sessions with the

filmmaker. This was evidently typical of Truffaut's promotional tactics for the opening of his films. Those who are interested in expanding the list are advised to check local newspapers and magazines in the cities in which Truffaut has appeared. The Washington, D.C. and Los Angeles papers, for instance, are said to contain several valuable interviews on the occasion of the American Film Institute (AFI) retrospectives on Truffaut in these two cities in 1979.

The section devoted to Archival Sources (Chapter VIII) was compiled from responses to questionnaires sent to the archives listed. I was only able to visit and verify the statements of the archives in New York City, Toronto, and Montreal. Perhaps the most valuable address in this regard has not been included in Chapter VIII as it is, technically speaking, not an archive; this is the address of Truffaut's production company, through which he can be contacted: Les Films du Carrosse, 5, rue Robert-Estienne, Paris (8e), France.

The distributors cited in Chapter IX are current to December 1980. Only the main offices of companies in the United States and Canada are listed. Since the distribution side of the film industry is in a constant state of change, however, and the videotape and videodisc markets are expanding so rapidly, it is advised that James L. Limbacher's Feature Films on 8 mm and 16 mm and the latest videotape catalogs be consulted for more up-to-date information.

When the AFI did its retrospective in 1979, it included not only all of Truffaut's films but also those films that he has acknowledged as having influenced his career. The list of these films is included in an Appendix.

Since Truffaut has written so much more than any other filmmaker and his films have been so extensively reviewed, the indexing of this book is somewhat different than others in this series. The Author Index contains the names of all the critics and essayists from Chapter IV who have written about Truffaut or his films, all the interviewers from Chapter VI, but only the major reviewers from the "Reviews" part of Chapter III (people whose names appear more than three times, who have also written articles or essays, or who have achieved some international prominence). The Film Title Index lists all Truffaut's films --by both French and English titles. Whoever has trouble with the titles in any other section of the book is advised to check the Film Title Index. This index also lists the major films that Truffaut has reviewed since 1950. American and British films are included by their English titles only. The Auteur Index, another new feature in this book, includes the names of approximately one hundred directors, two stars (Bogart and James Dean), one novelist (Henri-Pierre Roché) and one mentor (André Bazin). These are the movie personalities who were the prominent subjects of Truffaut's work as a critic. To be included in this index a director had to have been the subject of at least two articles by Truffaut or been included in his anthology, Les Films de ma vie. Some of the names that are included in the Author Index are also in the Auteur Index (Bazin's, for instance, and Godard's). There are separate entries for them as writers and as the subjects of Truffaut's writing.

No convenient place could be found to index the various film festivals that Truffaut was notorious for criticizing. Those who wish to discover quickly everything that Truffaut wrote about the Cannes Film Festival should see entries 644, 720, 804, 816, 833, 902, 912-913, 926, 960, 981, 987-990, 992, 1024, 1047, 1138. For articles on the Venice Film Festival, see entries 630, 643, 687, 753, 887-889, 985, 1002, 1013, 1033.

There were times, as the number of pages in this book grew to more than twice the original projections and unanticipated complications arose, that the words of Ferrand, the director played by Truffaut in La Nuit américaine, would haunt me with their appropriateness. Comparing the making of a movie to the crossing of the old American West in a stagecoach, he says: "At first you hope to have a good trip. But very soon, you start wondering if you'll even reach your destination." I had similar feelings about this book, and it was only because of the help I received that I have been able to reach my "destination."

Four people should be singled out for their special assistance. First of all, my sincere thanks go to the subject of this study, François Truffaut, who provided me with books, articles, lists, and answers to anxious questions, and who not only read the biographical section of this study to check for errors, but also arranged to meet with me in Montreal in the middle of a very busy schedule to clear up some last-minute concerns. Thanks to Lou-Ann Layton, who aided me immeasurably in my annotations of the Arts material; to Barbara Bennell and her coworkers in the Interlibrary Loan Department of the University of Manitoba's Dafoe Library, whose tenacity and resourcefulness in securing literally hundreds of articles were truly inspiring; to Ron Gottesman for his patience and expert advice.

Others whose assistance should also be acknowledged are Professors Graham Petrie of McMaster University, Seth Feldman of Western Ontario, Peter Harcourt of Carleton University, Annette Insdorf of Yale, Leo Braudy of Johns Hopkins, George Toles of the University of Manitoba, and Blaine Allan of Queens. Also to Karen Kiewra at G. K. Hall, to Pierre Allard and his staff at Le Centre de Documentation Cinématographique, to my sister Margaret Mary Sofalvi, and to my father, Paul Walz, to John MacKinnon, John Kozak, Lynne Marie Gray, to my typists, Gwen McKenzie and Lynne Dobbs, and to the University of Manitoba Research Council. Finally, to my wife, Kathy, whose love and quiet understanding sustained me through all of this.

I. Biographical Background

Although the American Film Institute held a unique retrospective in 1979 to celebrate the twentieth anniversary of his work as a film-maker, the film career of François Truffaut is actually closer to forty years long. Its outlines are perhaps familiar: he was a lonely, unsettled child and a delinquent teenager who became an insatiable moviegoer; befriended by André Bazin, the young cinéphile then became a notoriously outspoken and passionate film critic; within ten years he was a celebrated filmmaker whose first three films had thrust him into the international spotlight as an energetic "New Wave" director; since then he has continued to produce warm, distinctive, polished films at the steady rate of almost one per year, while supplementing his directorial work with interviews, books, articles, and performances in his own films and those of others. Despite his very public film career, however, Truffaut is a man who keeps to himself; in a word, he is "reserved."

CINÉPHILE

François Roland Truffaut was born in Paris on 6 February 1932, the only child of Roland Truffaut, a draftsman for an architectural firm, and Janine de Montferrand, a secretary. Because his parents worked and spent their spare time pursuing Roland's passion for hiking, camping, and mountain climbing, François was given immediately at birth to a wetnurse and was shifted from one grandmother to the other until he was about eight. At that time his maternal grandmother (whom he remembers gratefully for her love of books) became too sick to tend him.

There is barely a ripple of happiness in Truffaut's memory of childhood. Home during the war was a small, cramped apartment in the Pigalle district of Paris at 33, rue de Navarin. His parents were not bad people--"just nervous, busy, and in love." He felt unwanted at home, not mistreated but simply not treated at all, particularly by his mother. She did not like children and was especially sensitive to any noise he might make; so he often had to sit, absolutely quiet and still, reading a book. Punished for petty transgressions at home

1

and counseled, above all, to be honest, he was one of many children sent by their parents to exchange counterfeit tickets for food from gruff merchants who would never have accepted them from adults. This "paradox" and others (going hungry because a camp counselor sold the camp's food) made him long for the impunity that came from not being a child. His "profound wariness of all certitudes" is the adult residue of this period.

Truffaut considers himself to have been a good student up to the age of nine or ten. After flunking the exam to get into the upper grades of Lycée Rollin, however, he began a series of moves from one public school (école communale) to another, always an outsider, never settling down long enough to work himself into the educational or social fabric.

By 1943 he was a confirmed truant, often skipping school with his only friend, Robert Lachenay (who was later to work as an assistant on Les Mistons (The Mischief Makers) and whose name Truffaut was to adopt as one of his pseudonyms as a critic). He was absent so often, pretending to be sick, that his mother was told by the director of one school that he was too sickly to remain there. Once when he needed a good excuse, he claimed that his father had been arrested by the Germans. Truffaut was unable to face his parents when they discovered this lie and spent the night in the Jules-Joffrin metro station. (During the Occupation, the Paris subway stations were used as dormitories--air raid shelters from overnight bombings.) Instead of going to school, he spent his time in the library reading (Balzac was a particular favorite) or at the movies.

Movies, "the life of spectacles," Truffaut believes, were very important to people during the war. His first clear memory of the cinema involves going to the Gaieté Rochechouart in 1939. The film was Abel Gance's Paradis perdu. Because of the palpable rapport between the audience, mainly composed of military personnel, and the war-related scenes in the film, it was an emotionally-charged experience. Le Corbeau by Clouzot provided another memorable experience for Truffaut, as did the first screening in France of Citizen Kane on 6 July 1946--despite the fact that he understood not a bit of the dialogue. As a teenager Truffaut was seeing upward of fifteen movies per week, sitting through some of them twice and returning to others with his parents to disguise the fact that he had skipped school to see them already. From the age of twelve he kept a movie diary, starring those films he saw more than once. Renoir's La Regle du jeu, Carné's Le Visiteur du soir, and Guitry's Roman d'un tricheur, among others, eventually received twelve stars each. He also kept an alphabetical file on over 300 directors (later given to the cinémathèque in exchange for a lifetime pass). Very early he was attracted to "artistic" or "difficult" films. He would argue violently with schoolmates and was openly hostile to a teacher who happened to ridicule a Cocteau film. His tastes also ran to love stories, policiers, and psychological films; he did not like period films, or ones about boxing and wrestling. He identified with modern characters--Bogie, cops, assassins, and criminals--but not with pirates or cowboys. In many ways he was a typical teenage moviegoer, except that he was much more serious and systematic about it.

Upon quitting school for good at age fourteen, Truffaut embarked on a series of jobs (messenger boy, office worker, welder), each of which he abandoned or was fired from in a matter of months. In the winter of 1946-47, because of his irregular work habits, he lost his job as stockboy for a seed exporter. He used his severance pay to form a ciné-club with Robert Lachenay, with whom he was now boarding. Le Cercle cinémane met on Sunday morning at ten o'clock at the Cluny Palace and was in trouble right from the start. Some films did not arrive when they were scheduled; others arrived in poor condition. André Bazin's Ciné-club de la Chambre Noire, which met at the Broadway theater, had much better luck. In early 1947 Truffaut went to discuss the matter with his competitor. Bazin was apparently so impressed by the youth's passion and knowledge that he invited Truffaut to speak before his own club. Their almost legendary friendship dates from this initial meeting.

Le Cercle cinémane was a short-lived venture. Stealing and sell-ing copper doorknobs was one of the dubious methods to which Truffaut resorted to cover the losses incurred when a swindler promised him a print of Metropolis and then disappeared with his money. When a com-plaint was eventually lodged against the youth because of his mount-ing bills, his father, already angered by an advertisement for the ciné-club in L'Écran Français, found Truffaut and brought him to the police. After two nights in the central jail in a cell with thieves and prostitutes, the boy was sent to le Centre d'Observation des Mineurs Delinquants (C.O.M.) at Villejuif, part insane asylum, part house of correction.

"I was never a delinquent at heart--I only became delinquent in order to get to see films," Truffaut said in 1972. Presumably this is one of the things that André Bazin realized in the correspondence ini-tiated by Truffaut from Villejuif and what prompted him to work for the youth's release (although Bazin's natural beneficence is legen-dary). After a brief investigation around his parents' neighborhood "turned out unfavorably for them" and Bazin promised to get him a job, Truffaut was freed in March 1948 after five months in Villejuif. By order of the court, his parents forfeited their rights over him.

For a while Truffaut was Bazin's assistant at Travail et Culture, a left-wing, trade union organization financed by the French govern-ment as a cultural program. He worked as a projectionist, showing movies in factories. Because of his association with Bazin and his interest in movies, he met many other cinéphiles, including Alain Resnais and Chris Marker. This period, as he notes in Les films de ma vie, was "the first happy time of my life . . . watching films, talking about them, and to top it off, I was getting paid for it!"

But when Bazin's health deteriorated and he was confined to a sanatorium, Truffaut was fired.

Working in a factory as a welder and then for a while rewriting articles for Elle (an editor hired him because he was impressed by the way he attacked some filmmakers he disagreed with at the Ciné-club du Faubourg), Truffaut continued his insatiable moviegoing. He became adept at gate-crashing preview screenings set up for distributors. With Jacques Rivette, Eric Rohmer, and Jean-Luc Godard, he frequented the many ciné-clubs and smaller moviehouses of Paris as well as the Minotaur (a film bookshop) and Henri Langlois' cinémathèque. At the first Festival du Film Maudit, organized by Bazin in August of 1949 as an anti-Cannes celebration of alternative cinema (featuring neglected or "accursed" films, mainly from the United States), the four young cinéphiles were enthusiastic participants, sleeping on floors and eagerly joining discussions.

At about the same time Truffaut became enamored of a young woman named Liliane, whom he met at the cinémathèque. He impetuously moved into a hotel across the street from the yard goods shop in which she worked. Though her parents favored him, Liliane soon grew tired of him, and so, two days after Christmas in 1950, Truffaut abruptly joined the French Army of the Occupation in Germany. "The unbalanced things I did were always in December, my bad month," he once explained.

Enlistments meant three years of service. They also included, inevitably, Indochina. Although he had hoped to join the cinematography branch of the army, he was assigned to the artillery and trained in Coblenz for the war. But on the eve of his departure for Indochina, he went AWOL. Wandering around Paris without lodgings, money, or civilian clothes, he met Chris Marker who, with Alain Resnais, packed him off to Bazin's house in Bry-sur-Marne outside Paris.

On the advice of his mentor, Truffaut reported back to the army and went on sick call. The army did not fall for his fake illness, but it did not send him to the Far East. Instead he was reassigned to Germany. While returning some books lent to him by friends, he decided to desert a second time. He was quickly arrested and sent to Germany in handcuffs. Robert Lachenay eventually discovered his whereabouts and put Bazin back in touch with him. For the next year, while Truffaut was moved from military prison to hospital to madhouse, reading constantly and filling scraps of paper and the margins of books with notes, Bazin worked indefatigably to secure the prisoner's release; he even tried posing with his wife Janine as Truffaut's real parents to try to get to see him in the prison at Dupleix Barracks in Paris. Through Bazin's efforts Truffaut was eventually discharged, just after his twentieth birthday, for "instability of character."

Truffaut spent the next year living in the Bazins' attic in Bry-sur-Marne, serving a kind of informal apprenticeship to Bazin, the master critic. Janine's meals were occasions for extended film discussions. Sometimes points raised at breakfast escalated into heated arguments, continuing throughout the day uninterrupted by travels to and from Paris for Bazin's editorial work or the regular screenings they attended together. During this time Truffaut worked (again as a projectionist) for the Ministry of Agriculture; he was discharged shortly after he asked the head of his unit, who made movies, if he could be his assistant director.

CRITIC

Before he joined the army, Truffaut was published only occasionally: an interview with Antonioni in La Gazette du Cinéma and articles on Renoir, Chaplin, and René Clair in the bulletin of the Film Club of the Latin Quarter. While he was in the army, Bazin founded Cahiers du Cinéma (Truffaut read the third issue while being transported to Germany in handcuffs) and before he was released his friends had already started writing for it (Godard wrote for the January 1952 issue under the pseudonym of Hans Lucas). Tutored and restrained by Bazin, Truffaut was not allowed to break into Cahiers until March 1953.

His first review, entitled "Les Extremes me touchent" (see entry 496), is a catalog of future Truffaldian issues, tactics, and concerns that is uncanny in its presumably unpremeditated completeness. The contemporary French cinema is ridiculed for being polished and effete, especially in comparison to the more forceful and spontaneous American movies. Truffaut notes that the audience has been conditioned by movies--for the worse. He praises the film being reviewed, Sudden Fear, by invoking other films by its director, David Miller, and by comparing him to Renoir, Bresson, Hitchcock, and other masters. He singles out the natural performance of Gloria Grahame, a star but also a character whose physical mannerisms can be appreciated from one film to the next. All of these matters--antagonism to mainline French cinema, attraction to low-budget American films, the role of the audience, auteurs, the directorial pantheon, and natural acting--will be the major issues throughout Truffaut's six-year career as a film critic.

Truffaut's rise to prominence in the pages of Cahiers was meteoric, not only fast but fiery. In the June 1953 issue (see entry 507) he criticized the special issue of the rival film journal, Télé-Ciné, for its "curious homage" to Jean Renoir. The article was deemed inflammatory enough by the Cahiers editors to rate a prefatory paragraph by "A.B." (Bazin) that was complimentary to Télé-Ciné in light of the "sincere but perhaps excessively severe" piece to follow. One month later Truffaut contributed reviews of five films and an essay on cinemascope to Cahiers. In the back pages of the next two issues of the journal (numbers 26 and 27; see entries 487 and 488) Truffaut's notoriety as a "demolisher" begins to emerge. In the August-September issue's correspondence section is an exchange of letters prompted by

Truffaut's passing remarks on Queval's book about Marcel Carné in a
June book review. Queval accuses Truffaut of having the "sympathetic
arrogance of a one-year-old" and of being "a venomous iconoclast."
Truffaut responds with heavy irony. One month later, not unexpect-
edly, Jean d'Yvoire writes a letter of protest on behalf of Télé-Ciné
against the "venomous" treatment of his journal. Truffaut again resorts to irony, confessing to "the extreme harshness of confining myself to citing your own phrases." Refusing to prolong "this boring
dialogue," Truffaut abruptly leaves it to the readers to decide the
matter.

At about the same time, Cahiers received a potentially more inflammatory submission from the young writer. Bazin and his coeditors
evidently held the essay for some time before deciding to publish it
in their January 1954 issue and were nervous enough about it to include a brief editorial in an attempt to mollify their critics. Five
years later, in anniversary issue number 100, editor Jacques Doniol-
Valcroze was to look back at this essay, "Une Certaine Tendance du
cinéma français," as the single most important one in the journal's
eight-year history, the one that crystalized things for the entire
staff of Cahiers, and gave purpose and direction to its editorials,
interviews, and reviews.

In the preface to The Cinema of Cruelty, Truffaut praises Bazin
as "the cinema's best critic" because he dedicated himself to "analyzing films and describing them more than judging them." In "Une
Certaine Tendance . . ." (see entry 530) Truffaut is primarily the
judge; the essay is his indictment of postwar French cinema, those
films that were adapted from novels and/or reliant on plot and dialogue and psychological realism (termed by Truffaut "la tradition de
la qualité" and, derisively, "le cinéma de papa"). Especially criticized was the successful writing team of Jean Aurenche and Pierre
Bost--for "being contemptuous of the cinema by underestimating it"
(that is, for failing to exploit its visual and intellectual possibilities). Against these "littérateurs" Truffaut proposes "un cinéma
d'auteurs"--praiseworthy directors like Renoir, Bresson, Cocteau,
Gance, Ophuls, and Tati, who write or create what they film.

As his "intimate movie journal" in the July 1954 issue of Cahiers
indicates (see entry 588), Truffaut was at this point totally immersed
in everything to do with the film industry. Not only was he seeing
scores of movies every month, he was meeting directors, visiting sets,
reading, it seems, virtually every film journal and book, and writing
constantly--under his own name and a series of pseudonyms (Robert
Lachenay, François de Monferrand, Louis Chabert) for Cahiers, La
Parisienne, Radio-TV-Cinéma, and especially for Arts, a weekly that
hired him on the strength of "Une Certaine Tendance." He worked
anonymously for Arts for about six months; after this his names
(Truffaut and Lachenay) appeared regularly. (He even arranged to
have Godard, Rohmer, and Rivette write.) From the fall of 1954 until
he made the transition to feature-film directing in 1959, he was

rarely absent from its pages, building a reputation there as "the
gravedigger of French cinema." (Although many of the essays later
collected into Les Films de ma vie are taken from Arts, this anthology
contains little evidence of the often devastating work done by "the
young critic with the sharp canines.")

Almost nothing connected with the French film industry escaped
Truffaut's critical eye. Producers, directors, writers, actors,
technicians, distributors, other critics, festivals, even the audience
felt his lash. His most famous attacks, however, are his criticisms
of the "untouchables" of French cinema (in Cahiers--December 1957;
see entry 919) and of René Clement, who "stands for films against
which we at Cahiers fight" (issue number 84 for June 1958; see entry
1031), and his repeated assaults on the Cannes Film Festival and
Claude Autant-Lara, a well-known French director of scripts by Aurenche
and Bost, who also happened to be president of the film technicians'
trade union and thus an almost-too-perfect bête-noir for everything
that Truffaut hated in the "French tradition of quality." His contin-
ual denouncements of Cannes resulted in his being the only writer
banned from the festival in 1958. (He attended and wrote about it
anyway, his expenses paid by Arts.) His antagonism to Autant-Lara
produced more than one heated exchange after film club screenings.

Truffaut often protested, however, that a critic had to be imper-
sonal. And, in fact, he did write some positive reviews of Autant-
Lara films, and he did return to Cannes as a jury member after his
success there with Les Quatre Cents Coups (The 400 Blows), a decision
he was to regret. He also was, alternately, to pillory Ado Kyrou for
his work for the film journal Positif and later praise him for his
book on love and eroticism in the cinema (a topic he himself showed
some interest in, especially under his "Lachenay" pseudonym). He admitted, however, that he was not as "generous" a critic as his mentor
Bazin.

As his anthology Les Films de ma vie attests, Truffaut was by no
means an entirely ungenerous or negative critic. His generosity mani-
fests itself in many ways, nowhere more so than in the series of interviews he did for Cahiers (in collaboration with Jacques Rivette,
Eric Rohmer, and Claude Chabrol) in the year or so following his "Une
Certaine Tendance" polemic. In the preface to an interview with Abel
Gance (issue 43, January 1955; see entry 679), Truffaut articulates
his and Cahiers' policy. He points out that he and his cohorts are
careful to choose "only directors we love" and to let them "express
themselves in their own way without ever asking embarrassing questions." The directors he interviewed and obviously loved were
Jacques Becker, Jean Renoir, Roberto Rossellini, Alfred Hitchcock,
Gance, and Howard Hawks. During that same period he also wrote
lengthy, appreciative essays on the work of Fritz Lang, Max Ophuls,
and Sacha Guitry. These directors continue to be important to him.

Truffaut's devotion to certain films and filmmakers was sometimes

idiosyncratic, and in retrospect it was sometimes misplaced. His repeated championing of Robert Aldrich and Otto Preminger seems particularly misguided now (as he himself will admit). Even at the time,
though Cahiers was a close-knit group, his opinions were not shared
by everyone. In the March 1956 issue of Cahiers (see entry 810), for
instance, the editor appended a note to his review of Si Paris nous
était conte pointing out that Truffaut was the only defender of this
Sacha Guitry film. His opinions in Cahiers' "Council of Ten" film
appraisals (a feature he now regrets having instituted) were more
emphatically laudatory or damning than anyone else's. And his arguments periodically took the form of simple assertions such as "there
are no good or bad films, only good or bad directors," or "it is not
what an artist makes that counts but what he is."

   Whatever the shape or focus of his arguments, he was not a critic
without clear and consistent standards. The central statement of his
concerns as a critic is contained in an article he wrote for Arts
(number 621, May 1957; see entry 952) entitled "Nous sommes tous des
condamnés." Critics are acknowledged to be more intelligent than
most filmmakers, but they are advised to be "humble and respectful"
toward the 10 percent of works that surpass them. On the other hand,
they must "denounce vulgarity, stupidity, and baseness of inspiration
in all insincere films." As a list of the words most often repeated
in his reviews will attest, Truffaut especially disliked insincerity.
But he also disliked timidity, banality, and pretense. He valued invention, verve, and audacity or aesthetic ambition--all based on not
underestimating the audience and defended with an almost moralistic
fervor (for the moral dimension, see "Le Règne du cochon de payant
est terminé," Arts, number 643; see entry 964).

   By the middle of 1957 it was clear that Truffaut's real ambitions
lay beyond full-time film criticism (Arts, number 626; see entry
903). Six months later he was offering advice to young filmmakers
(Arts, numbers 652 and 682; see entries 1029 and 1003). Once he became a director, his regular contributions to Cahiers and Arts ceased.
He continues, however, to be a critic--in print, in interviews, and
in his films. But, as a result of his experiences in filmmaking,
Truffaut has admitted that he no longer feels a compulsion to reform
the cinema. Nor does he need to write about almost every film, good
or bad, that is released. Filmmaking has allowed him to return to the
ideals he expressed while at Cahiers--to write only about those films
and filmmakers that he loves and to serve as an intermediary between
various chosen filmmakers and the audience.

CINÉASTE

   Looking back on his critical work in the 1950s, Truffaut once
noted that writing for Arts helped him develop some of the skills
needed to become a good scriptwriter. In revising each essay he
wrote, he often eliminated up to one-third of it so as to require

attentive reading and substituted short words for longer ones to give
each essay "punch." His critical work, however, prepared him in many
ways. In his review of <u>Destination Gobi</u> (<u>Arts</u>, number 506; see entry
667), for instance, he was already talking about "breaking out of
genres." Edgar Ulmer's <u>The Naked Dawn</u> (<u>Arts</u>, number 559; see entry
770) made him aware of the possibility of filming the novel <u>Jules et
Jim</u>. Not only did writing about film allow him the opportunity to
formulate ideas, it also gave him access to the production side of
the industry. Although he says he decided to become a movie director
at age twelve and doubtless talked about it and planned and even wrote
scripts in the early 1950s, the usual means of access to the movie
industry were unavailable to (and likely not considered seriously by)
Truffaut. As a critic he was able to visit sets, watch and question
directors both formally and informally, and observe and absorb the
techniques of filmmaking.

In 1955 Truffaut worked very briefly as an assistant to Max Ophuls
during the making of <u>Lola Montès</u>, quitting after a disagreement with
the production manager. He then began a two-year working relationship
with Roberto Rossellini. Although none of their projects (an adaptation of <u>Carmen</u> by Prosper Merimée and an original screenplay for
Ingrid Bergman titled <u>La Decision d'Isa</u>) were ever filmed, Truffaut
readily admitted his debts to Rossellini, from whom he learned, among
other things, "clarity, simplicity, and coherent and logical dis-
course."

At the same time that he was assisting Rossellini, he was also at
work on two more personal projects: a sixteen-millimeter silent short
film called <u>Une Visite</u>, which used the daughter and the apartment of
Jacques Doniol-Valcroze (one of the editors of <u>Cahiers</u>), and was done
in the manner of a George Cukor comedy, and a feature-length film
script, <u>A bout de souffle</u> (Breathless), which he tried to sell to
Philippe Lemaire, a popular French actor of the time. <u>Une Visite</u> was
shot, edited by Alain Resnais, and quickly forgotten. <u>A bout de
souffle</u> was considered by several people, including Gerald Blain and
Edouard Molinaro, but became a viable project only with the success
of <u>Les Quatre Cents Coups</u>, when Godard used it as the basis for his
first feature film.

Jacques Rivette, who assisted Truffaut with the photography on
<u>Une Visite</u>, was involved in various filmmaking schemes at the time
and is credited by Truffaut with providing the inspiration for his
first successful film venture. Rivette, Resnais, Truffaut, Alexandre
Astruc, and some others came up with a plan for making several films
for the price of one and for reassuring producers wary of bankrolling
novice directors. All that ever resulted from this was a lengthy
script, <u>Les Quatres Jeudis</u>, on which Rivette, Truffaut, Claude Chabrol,
and Charles Bitsch collaborated. It made the rounds of directors,
but was never filmed. Meanwhile Rivette succeeded in making a shorter, cheaper film--<u>Le Coup de berger</u>. Its successful completion encouraged many of his friends, among them Truffaut, who decided to

commit himself to one of the short films based on childhood that he had been planning.

During August of 1957 Truffaut went to Nimes to shoot Les Mistons. Using money from an indemnity from the daily newspaper Le Temps de Paris, which had fired him in response to pressure from publicity and advertising people, Truffaut formed the production company he still maintains--Les Films du Carrosse, named after his favorite Renoir film, Le Carrosse d'or (The Golden Coach)--to give the venture some credibility. It was during the editing of this film, his first adaptation (which used elements from other works by the same author--a practice he still follows) and the first to use voice-over narration, that Truffaut learned much of what he knows about filmmaking. In the midst of the editing he married Madeleine Morgenstern, the daughter of a prominent movie producer. (They were divorced in 1964. The marriage produced two daughters, Laura and Eva, born in 1959 and 1961, who were, contrary to some opinions, not named after movie characters.)

The flooded French countryside gave Truffaut the idea for his third film in the spring of 1958. He convinced producer Pierre Braunberger to provide him with enough footage to shoot it. No matter what he did, however, he could not edit it into satisfactory shape and was ready to abandon the project when Godard stepped in to salvage the film. Though Une Histoire d'eau is listed as a mutual effort, it fits more neatly into Godard's career than Truffaut's.

In the fall of the same year, partly in response to a challenge from his father-in-law, producer Ignace Morgenstern, Truffaut began filming his first feature-length film. The idea for the film, as with many of his films, began with a single incident, an incident that was to have been the central one in a short autobiographical film called La Fugue d'Antoine (Antoine's Flight). Although he felt himself to be very much the nervous amateur, Truffaut was assured enough to choose the experienced Marcel Moussy to do the dialogue, to film in Dyaliscope (the French equivalent of cinemascope), and to alter his concept of the main character and the story in accordance with the talents of a remarkable youth chosen after elaborate auditions--Jean-Pierre Léaud. As a critic he had recommended to young filmmakers that they shoot cheaply. He followed his own advice scrupulously, avoiding big-name stars, shooting on location, sticking to the legal minimum in the technical crew, and using postsynchronized sound, no process shots, and fewer takes. Les Quatre Cents Coups cost thirty-seven million francs or about seventy-five thousand dollars.

Filming began on 10 November 1958. After an exhausting first day, Truffaut rushed to the bedside of his mentor, André Bazin, who died the following morning. When the film opened on 18 May at the same Cannes Festival that the year before had barred Truffaut as a critic, it was dedicated to Bazin. With the support of Jean Cocteau, a festival judge, the neophyte director was honored for his direction of Les Quatres Cents Coups. And what he had expected to be "a little

film . . . likable and gently encouraged by the press, but a film
that people wouldn't go to see" turned out to be an international
phenomenon. Since it was one of two dozen films made by first-time
directors in 1959 (the next year there were twice as many), it became
one of the most celebrated films in what was christened by L'Express
as the "nouvelle vague"--the French New Wave. Truffaut quickly used
the proceeds of the film to coproduce Paris nous appartient (1959) by
Jacques Rivette and Le Testament de'Orphee (1959) by Jean Cocteau.

For his second film Truffaut chose an entirely different subject
and approach: a genre film full of surprises and experimentation,
based on a crime novel by David Goodis and starring Charles Aznavour.
He had originally planned to shoot Tirez sur le pianiste (Shoot the
Piano Player) in a studio in late 1959, but then opted for location
shooting. It was released at the end of 1960 to favorable critical
response but a cool public. Truffaut, who had frequently distinguished between directors who were sensitive to audience response and
those who were not and placed himself in the former camp, was stung
by the reception into criticism of his own film.

After this he assisted his friend, Claude de Givray, in making
his first film, Tiré au flanc (1962). Truffaut produced the film,
offered advice on the direction, and even agreed to play a small role
in front of the cameras. He also worked on his own project, a film
called Bleu d'outre-tombe, but abandoned it in favor of adapting a
novel that he had wanted to film since at least 1955: Henri-Pierre
Roché's Jules et Jim (Jules and Jim). Truffaut had befriended Roché
and gotten his support for the project. The author died, however,
just after arranging to meet with Jeanne Moreau, a perfect choice, he
agreed, for the role of Catherine. Truffaut was granted the film
rights to the book on the strength of a short film on insects made
for Roché's son. Shooting took place in the spring of 1961; the editing, never a simple or fully finished task for Truffaut, was especially difficult on Jules et Jim and convinced him to simplify future
films. The effort paid off, however, as the film was released to almost universal acclaim and is still considered by many to be Truffaut's
masterpiece.

Years later Truffaut was to say of his initial film work: "Your
first film is always a great adventure. Your second film is always
a violent reaction against your first. Your third film is usually a
synthesis of the first and second. After that you should probably
retire for a few years. That's probably why I've tended to do trilo-
gies and then put myself out to pasture for a while" (see entry 1455).
Truffaut did not temporarily retire, however. Before Jules et Jim
was even released he had finished shooting Antoine et Colette, a short
film that was the centerpiece of an international anthology on young
love. It allowed him to collaborate again with Jean-Pierre Léaud on
an autobiographical incident. During 1962 he cowrote Mata-Hari,
Agent H-21 for Jeanne Moreau and her husband, Jean-Louis Richard, one
of the many directors whose practical advice and blunt criticism

Truffaut has solicited in preparing all of his own scripts for production. (Eric Rohmer, Marcel Ophuls, Jacques Rivette, and Jean Aurel are some of the others.) Once Richard's film was finished, he and Truffaut retired to Cannes to coscript La Peau douce (Soft Skin) when it became obvious that Truffaut's pet project, an adaptation of Ray Bradbury's Fahrenheit 451, could not begin production until at least 1964.

His filmmaking activities during this period reflect Truffaut's lifelong compulsion to keep busy. He does not take vacations, is not interested in sports or hobbies, and finds little of interest except movies. "I relax from one film," he claims, "by exhausting myself in a different way, by work that represents a contrast or counterpoint to the previous one." La Peau douce is one of the best examples of this practice of contrasts or alternation. It originated partly as a response to Jules et Jim, as a film, antiromantic in both style and content, intended to counter some of the excesses of its predecessors. In contrast to the lyrical style of Jules et Jim, La Peau douce is almost clinical; and it is not a literary adaptation but a realistic, adult portrait based on actual stories and anecdotes (Truffaut keeps a dossier of newspaper clippings) and on autobiographical material (the hero's name is Lachenay, the pseudonym most often used by Truffaut the critic). Although it treated a cliché-ridden story in a surprisingly original way, on its release at Cannes in 1964 La Peau douce was viewed as a departure and a disappointment and was the occasion for many critical reassessments of the New Wave.

When the production of Fahrenheit 451 had to be postponed again, Truffaut devoted himself to a book-length interview with the director he has acknowledged as one of his masters, Alfred Hitchcock. The book, Le Cinéma selon Hitchcock, was released in 1965; its influence can be seen in Fahrenheit 451, which was finally filmed in England in early 1966, and in La Mariée était en noir (The Bride Wore Black) (1968), a film based on a mystery-thriller by William Irish (a Cornell Woolrich pseudonym), which Truffaut used as an opportunity to work again with Jeanne Moreau, but in a different vein. He used the filming of Fahrenheit 451, a traumatic affair because he was shooting in a foreign tongue with an unfamiliar crew and surroundings and a balky star, as the occasion for a uniquely thorough behind-the-scenes diary, which was published serially in Cahiers du Cinéma and has often been reprinted. (These experiences have since led him to turn down all offers to make English language films in Hollywood. Among the projects turned down are: Bonnie and Clyde, The Strawberry Statement, Is Paris Burning?, The Day of the Locust, and Hammett.) That same year (1967) he was the subject of a special tribute at the Annency Film Festival, for which occasion he re-edited Les Mistons and Les Quatre Cents Coups.

Although he has often maintained that he is apolitical, Truffaut did become actively engaged in the events of 1968. Early in the year the de Gaulle government attempted to replace the founder and longtime

head of the French cinémathèque, Henri Langlois. Truffaut and several
other members of the council of the cinémathèque protested. A defense
committee was created, with Jean Renoir as honorary president and
Truffaut as treasurer. Many French directors agreed to withdraw from
the cinémathèque the rights to screen their films; other foreign directors joined them. When the cinémathèque was closed, demonstrations
ensued. All of this began four days after Truffaut had begun shooting
his second feature and third film with Jean-Pierre Léaud.

"L'Affaire Langlois" consumed his mornings with its meetings,
phone calls, interviews, pamphleteering, and money raising; Baisers
volés (Stolen Kisses) was fitted into his afternoons. What had begun
as the least scruprlously prepared of all of his films became even
less rigorous. But Truffaut had learned from Renoir to trust improvisation, and the film was to be the ultimate test of this method, gaining from it a lightness and spontaneity missing from some of his previous work. Shooting was finished at the end of March, the Langlois
controversy was resolved a month later, and three weeks after this
Truffaut was again caught up in politics. He and Godard and several
other members of the Committee for the Defense of the Cinémathèque
were instrumental in closing down the Cannes Film Festival, in sympa-
thy with the strikes and agitation taking place across France as a
result of the May uprisings.

Baisers volés, which won for Truffaut the prestigious Prix Delluc
in December of 1968, is the first of a cluster of films that Truffaut
made in two very productive years. In that film Antoine at one point
is seen reading a William Irish thriller, La Sirène du Mississipi
[sic] (Mississippi Mermaid), on which Truffaut was to base his next
film. Sirène was as different from its predecessors as it was from
its successor: L'Enfant sauvage (The Wild Child). While Baisers
volés is improvisational, with a large ensemble cast and a modest
budget, Sirène is a glossy superproduction starring two international
stars, Catherine Deneuve and Jean-Paul Belmondo, and shot at picturesque locations--all of which demanded more rigorous preparation and
less improvisation. With L'Enfant sauvage Truffaut returned to low-
budget filmmaking. It is a low-key, black-and-white film that is not
overly audience-conscious. To cut down on the intermediaries between
himself and the novice teenage actor who took the title role, the
director himself played the other lead role. Both Sirène and L'Enfant
Sauvage are based on previously printed materials; typical of Truffaut,
however, who does not believe in a single rule for adaptations, their
translations to the screen are markedly different. The former is "a
choice of scenes" from the novel, the latter a transcription of a
scientific diary. Truffaut ended this prolific two-year period with
a return to the character who started it--Antoine Doinel--in a light
comedy based on an original script: Domicile conjugal (Bed and Board).

Exhausted by this flurry of activity, Truffaut attempted to take
a brief leave from filmmaking. But within a year he was back at work,
this time on a second novel by Henri-Pierre Roché, Les Deux Anglaises

et la continent (Two English Girls, or Anne and Muriel). The film
was based not only on Roché's novel but on his diaries and notebooks
as well, and strongly echoes Jules et Jim and the lives of the Brontë
sisters. It afforded Jean-Pierre Léaud his first serious, non-Doinel
role in collaboration with Truffaut, who took pains to emphasize that
the film was a "physical film about love." One year later he reteamed
with Bernadette Lafont (who played the woman in Les Mistons) in another adaptation--Une Belle Fille comme moi (Such a Gorgeous Kid like
Me), based on the book by Henry Farrell. This black comedy and Les
Deux Anglaises seem to have been made partly to challenge the conventional notion about Truffaut the "reserved" or "modest" filmmaker.

The abandoned set for The Madwoman of Chaillot on the lots of the
Victorine Studies in Nice (where he was relaxing and editing Les Deux
Anglaises) provided Truffaut with the idea that was to unite the notes
he had been gathering since the filming of Jules et Jim. La Nuit
américaine (Day for Night) was conceived as a behind-the-scenes look
at the production of a film and returned to the ensemble casting of
Baisers volés and his decision to play a lead role in L'Enfant sauvage.
La Nuit américaine marked a turning point of sorts in Truffaut's career. It was a deliberate challenge to the by-now popular notion of
the auteur theory and "a kind of farewell to my previous films. There
are ten to twelve important parts in the picture and in many cases
they are based on parts from old films. It is as if these characters
had all met in Day for Night to say goodbye" (see entry 1377).

Buoyed by an Academy Award for the Best Foreign Film for La Nuit
américaine, Truffaut took a two-year sabbatical from filmmaking to
edit three books of Bazin's writings on film, to prepare his own collection of film criticism, Les Films de ma vie, and to collect his
thoughts and develop some more of his own screenplays.

Although he claimed that the success of La Nuit américaine had
convinced him of the necessity to make only personal films, based on
his own ideas and not adaptations, Truffaut returned to directing in
1975 with an adaptation of the diaries, recently translated (from
code), of the eccentric daughter of Victor Hugo. The film, L'Histoire
d'Adèle H. (The Story of Adèle H.), featured the tour de force acting
of Isabel Adjani in the lead role and was as confined in its emphasis
on one character as its predecessor and its successor were broadly
focused on an ensemble. L'Argent de poche (Small Change), released
early in 1976, was a return by Truffaut to the characters and concerns
with which he began his career: children and the trials of growing
up. Both films, in very different ways, were compared to L'Enfant
sauvage. The former was a great critical success, the latter became
one of Truffaut's most popular box office successes.

As soon as L'Argent de poche was released, Truffaut agreed to
play a French scientist in Steven Spielberg's Close Encounters of
the Third Kind. During the shooting in Wyoming and Alabama, he wrote
the script for the film that was to begin his latest cluster of works.

The first of these four films, L'Homme qui aimait les femmes (The Man Who Loved Women), made in 1977, is calculated to do for books what Truffaut had done for movies in La Nuit américaine. The most recent, Le Dernier Metro (The Last Metro) (1980), does the same for theater. Both films afforded Truffaut the opportunity to work with people he had worked with previously (a not unusual practice for the director): Charles Denner, whom he had wanted to use again ever since the actor's memorable secondary roles in La Mariée était en noir and Une Belle Fille, and Catherine Deneuve, for whom he wanted to provide a good role as "a responsible woman."

Although these two films have their autobiographical overtones (the former shows the young Bertrand being punished much like the young Truffaut, and the latter focuses on the German occupation of Paris, a period of strong personal resonances for the director), the two films sandwiched between them are more overtly personal. In La Chambre verte (The Green Room), a film based on his readings of Henry James and his own musings on death, Truffaut again plays the lead role—to make the film more personal, "like a handwritten note." L'Amour en fuite (Love on the Run) is a final look at Antoine Doinel, a character initially created from the combined autobiographies of the director and the star (and from whom the director had become in- creasingly distanced) in a film using footage from all of the films on which the two had collaborated.

The AFI tribute on the twentieth anniversary of Les Quatre Cents Coups, coupled with the release of the intensely personal La Chambre verte and the laying to rest of Antoine Doinel in L'Amour en fuite, seemed to signal a major turning point in the film career of François Truffaut. With the successful release of La Dernier Metro, it now seems that this convenient "crisis point" was more apparent that real. There is no question, however, that Truffaut has adjusted his perspec- tive recently. He has always gratefully acknowledged awards (his most recent being the prestigious Luchino Visconti career award for film- making presented in Florence, Italy in September, 1981) and pointed to their importance in terms of "extending the life of" a film. The ten "Cesars" garnered by Le Dernier Metro in France and its nomination for a Hollywood "Oscar" have prompted him to talk now about the op- portunities the success of this film will provide him for the remain- der of his career. He assumes that there are perhaps only "eight to ten" more films that he can reasonably expect to make. The first of these is La Femme d'à coté (The Woman Next Door), a modern love story reminiscent of Soft Skin, which afforded him the opportunity to work again with Gérard Depardieu and to work for the first time with Fanny Ardante whose film career, in fact, commences with this film.

II. Critical Survey

Toward the end of The Last Metro, Truffaut abridges time to conclude his film with indications of the postwar fates of his characters. Bernard Granger, who gave up acting after his initial success and joined the French Resistance, lies wounded in the hospital. Marion Steiner, the actress and theater manager with whom he had a brief affair, comes to visit. He tells her that their relationship is over, that it never meant much anyway. Marion is hurt by his blunt declaration. Suddenly the camera pulls back: the hospital is shown to be a stage set, and the two characters are performing together in a play. Marion's husband, Lucas Steiner, the play's writer and director, then comes out on stage. He and his wife and Bernard join hands, and all three bow to acknowledge the audience's enthusiastic applause.

At first glance this "trick" looks like a mere contrivance, arranged to give the film a speciously happy ending along with a hackneyed thematic (illusion-versus-reality) dimension. It is more than this. Its subtlety, resonance, and ambiguity get to the heart of Truffaut's aesthetic; its meaning is at the center of his weltanschauung.

The device is not a new one for Truffaut. It was used, among other places, in Shoot the Piano Player, where what first appears to be a direct shot of Edouard/Charlie turns out to be his reflection in a mirror; it was used most notably at the beginning of Day for Night, where a street scene is shown to be part of the shooting of a movie. What is new in The Last Metro (and this is important for everything in the filmmaker's career) is not the device but the use to which the device is put. Here the momentary deception should crystalize some specific questions about the characters. How accepting is Lucas Steiner, the man who monitored all of the theater's rehearsal activities from his below-stage hiding place, of the love affair between his wife and Bernard? Didn't he overhear their lovemaking in the young actor's dressing room? Didn't his wife realize he might? How aware are the lovers that the play is at least an oblique comment on their "real lives"? In any event, isn't the triple hand-holding ironic and somewhat chilling?

Critical Survey

These are questions that Truffaut chooses not to raise directly. The implications are there to color the seemingly rosy conclusion. These questions also serve to strengthen the associations between Steiner and two characters from Day for Night (associations that help to undermine the criticism leveled at Truffaut for supposedly being unable to create mature characters). Lucas Steiner combines the cool, all-for-art detachment of Ferrand, the writer-director who could appropriate the words and experiences of others (specifically, Julie Baker) for the purposes of his film, with the tolerance and understanding of Doctor Nelson, the patient husband who could overlook his wife's sexual indiscretion with a young and impetuous fellow actor. The dominant impression of the ending of The Last Metro is thus modified—by Truffaut's allusiveness, his use of undertones, irony, and implication, and his willingness to leave some things unresolved. These are quintessentially Truffaldian qualities.

In addition to specific questions about the characters, the concluding device (which shows the hospital to be a stage) should also raise general questions about the reliability of appearances and the distinction between the public and private selves. Appearances are seductive yet deceiving. They remain valid only up to the point where some other image or incident replaces or contradicts them or a new role is called for. What the device says as device, in other words, is that perspective is everything, that our understanding of things is relative, that is, determined by our point of view. And this is at the center of Truffaut's world view.

Point of view accounts for Truffaut's attitude toward character ("everyone has his reasons"), his presentation of character (a privileged intimacy, which allows the audience to share a character's point of view), and his fascination with characters rather than stories. It is related to his cinematic style (mise-en-scène qualifies action, words or sounds modify images). And it helps to explain his return to the same character, Antoine Doinel, or similar characters, his practice of alternation, and even the overall progress of his filmmaking career.

Truffaut has acknowledged that he established his artistic terrain in his first three feature films and that each film he has made since then is "a kind of mixture of the ones that [he] made before." He has frequently pointed out that his characters are quite similar. Camille Bliss, the title character in Such a Gorgeous Kid like Me, for instance, is "the female replica" of Victor, the title character in The Wild Child. Victor is like Montag in Fahrenheit 451 and Antoine Doinel in The 400 Blows (they each lack something). Julien Davenne of The Green Room is "the little brother of" Adèle H. Bertrand Morane of The Man Who Loved Women resembles a forty-year-old Antoine Doinel. Furthermore, Les Mistons, The Bride Wore Black, and Such a Gorgeous Kid like Me, as Annette Insdorf notes, all "explore the adoration of one woman by five males" (see entry 397). In Jules and Jim the number is reduced, and in The Man Who Loved Women the sexes are reversed. Even names recur throughout Truffaut's works, most notably Jules/Julie/Julien: Julien Doinel (Antoine's father) in The 400 Blows, Jules of Jules and Jim, Julie Kohler in The Bride Wore Black, Julie Roussel in Mississippi Mermaid, Julie Baker in Day for Night, Julie and Julien Davenne in The Green Room, and the young Julien in Small Change. The same basic ingredients offer further possibilities for development because Truffaut continually sees that there is another way of looking at things, another perspective or point of view. He works dialectically, each new film proposing antitheses for previous theses. As he has said, "My critical tendency leads me to work always 'in reaction against'" (see entry 1203). The conclusions he reaches in each film, therefore, no matter how vivid and convincing, are conditional. Truffaut sees alternatives. Perhaps this is one of the reasons that Citizen Kane struck such a resonant chord. The film, with its six different versions of the Charles Foster Kane story, provides the archetypal pattern for Truffaut's entire career.

CHARACTERS: SOLITARY, IMMATURE, MYOPIC

When Truffaut noticed that audiences responded much more negatively than he had expected to Antoine's parents in The 400 Blows, he set about planning his approach to characterization much more carefully for his second feature film. Although the main character in the book he was adapting was more like a Sterling Hayden type, he chose Charles Aznavour to star in Shoot the Piano Player and emphasized his vulnerability and timidity. And he made the thugs who chase the main character's brothers and kill Lena more inept and less single-minded than most shadowy antagonists. For, as he said, he did not wish "to have a division between the sympathetic and the unsympathetic characters in a film" (entry 1219). With the exception of Daxiat in The Last Metro and perhaps the fleetingly glimpsed mother and grandmother of the battered child in Small Change, this practice of presenting neither heroes nor villains has been followed since Shoot the Piano Player.

Truffaut focuses his attention on the characters in his films; his first concern is to make them believably human. He does not reduce them to stereotypes or caricatures, nor does he elevate them to heroic proportions. Jean-Paul Belmondo and Gerard Depardieu, for instance, two stars with larger-than-life reputations as screen lovers or adventurers, are carefully diminished in their Truffaut films Mississippi Mermaid and The Last Metro, the former by uxoriousness and the latter by immaturity. In this regard, Robin Wood's complaint that Truffaut's films never "achieve the stature of tragedy" and that "the fate of his heroes is often poignant and pathetic, but it stops short of the tragic" (entry 201) is a classic case of accurate description but faulty appraisal. Truffaut has never aspired to the lofty realms of tragedy. His characters are flawed, but not tragically so. He has consistently eschewed heroics, opting for characters

ordinary enough to be recognizable and sympathetic, but eccentric
enough to be fascinating. He places his emphasis on what Annette
Insdorf calls "the primacy of the imperfect individual" (entry 397).
Truffaut himself characterized them as being "on the edge of society.
I want them to testify to human fragility" (entry 1303).

What is most recognizable about the characters in Truffaut's
films is the fact that they are such solitary creatures. Lena's description of Charlie in Shoot the Piano Player can be applied to all
of Truffaut's characters: "Even when he's with somebody, he walks
alone." The ultimate expression of this condition is presented in
The Story of Adèle H., a film about love involving only one person.
Adele is a woman without a last name, who flees from her family and
their refuge on one island (Guernsey), slowly detaches herself from
any personal relationships on another (Nova Scotia), wanders oblivious of everything on a third (in Barbados), and eventually lives out
her days isolated in an asylum. She is not the exception in Truffaut's
oeuvre, merely the extreme. From Antoine Doinel's lonely flight to
the sea, Charlie Kohler's numb withdrawal into honky-tonk piano playing, and Jules' walk through the cemetery, to Genevieve's detached
view of Bertrand Morane's funeral, Julien Davenne's single-minded
dedication to his dead, and Lucas Steiner's enforced retreat below
stairs, all of Truffaut's characters are at one time or another alienated from the people around them. Leo Braudy, in his introduction
to Focus on "Shoot the Piano Player", has noted that Truffaut has created "a palpable space around his central character" in this film, "a
space that it is difficult to penetrate" (entry 239). Most of
Truffaut's characters are surrounded by a similar kind of space,
whether it be enforced by the device of a hearing aid, as it is with
Ferrand in Day for Night, or, more amusingly, by an apartment wall,
as it is by the recluse in Bed and Board, who has not ventured outside
since the Liberation to insure that Petain will not be buried at
Douaumont. In many of his films there is a kind of emptiness or hol-
lowness around all of the characters--as if everyone involved in the
particular story exists in a vacuum into which no one from beyond the
edge of the screen or from the world outside the immediate purview of
the characters can intrude.

Often the isolation that invariably occurs in a Truffaut film
occurs at the end (which gives the isolation a more ominous sense of
being "ground zero"). Even when attachments are formed or reinforced
at the end of a Truffaut film, however, there is little genuine reas-
surance. Some element has usually been introduced to call the relationship into question. Thus the ironies at the end of The Last Metro.
Thus the sense of fragility and precariousness at the conclusion of
the "adult" Doinel films (Stolen Kisses, Bed and Board, and Love on
the Run), where the bonds between Antoine and Christine, Antoine and
Sabine, are subtly undercut by the presence of another character or
couple. The most salient example of the uncertain resolution occurs
in Mississippi Mermaid. Here Louis Mahe and his wife are once more
reconciled, at the end of the film. Louis forgives Marion/Julie

again, this time for trying to kill him slowly and surreptitiously
with rat poison, and she vows to renew her love. Then they trudge
off through the snows of Switzerland, fleeing the authorities, with
little money, Marion dressed incongruously in an elegant black fur
and feather-trimmed coat.

Not only are love relationships uncertain, but friendships and
family ties are rare or nonexistent. Friendships seem to be available
only to young people: the teenage Antoine, the youthful Jules and
Jim, the kids in Small Change. Antoine enjoys the companionship of
of René in The 400 Blows and Antoine and Colette; but when his wife
has a baby in Bed and Board, there is evidently no one close enough
for him to share his news with. He is typical, and Bertrand Morane
an extreme. As Delphine says to this most exaggeratedly amusing of
all Truffaut's self-enclosed characters: "You have no friends, only
mistresses or old girlfriends."

Antoine Doinel's family life is at best a tenuous matter, which
is abruptly dissolved at the end of The 400 Blows when his mother
coldly informs him that he is on his own. After this, except for some
instances in Small Change when children and both parents remain together, families exist in Truffaut's works only in fragments or as
contrivances. If a parent is in evidence, it is usually a mother,
and her "parenting" is inadequate--for instance, Claude's mother in
Two English Girls, Bertrand's in The Man Who Loved Women. Jules and
his daughter are left at the end of Jules and Jim, though the little
girl disappears from the film once Jim and Catherine try to have a
child. Siblings survive. Sabine (another significant name duplica-
tion) commiserates with her brother in Love on the Run. Julie Kohler
has a solicitous sister in Mississippi Mermaid. Charlie has two trou-
blesome brothers in Shoot the Piano Player. He also acts as father
to his youngest brother, Fido, with the prostitute next door function-
ing as surrogate mother. This parody of a family recurs in slightly
different form in The Wild Child and The Green Room, where a young-
ster's upbringing by an emotionless man and his elderly housekeeper
emphasizes the inadequacy of the arrangement. And, of course, Antoine
finds substitute parents in Colette's and then Christine's mother and
father. These family-parodies demonstrate the need for sustaining
family life, while at the same time reinforcing the inadequacies of
that life. Characters searching for father-figures or mother-figures
or both are common in Truffaut's films.

The closest approximation in Truffaut's films to the satisfying
family unit is the work unit. As Bertrand, the producer in Day for
Night, says: "We movie people are one big family." He is quickly
reminded of the House of Atreus, however, and Severine earlier has
pointed out how transitory the entire set-up is: "Phfft!--it's no
longer there!" Beyond the family and the temporary community of the
workplace (and perhaps the movie theater and, for children, the
schoolyard), there is nothing. Interaction between an individual
and society is nonexistent, except in negative terms in Fahrenheit

451. Even under the pressure of war and the occupation in The Last Metro, people are not united by a common cause or a common enemy. Politics, if anything more than the "intimate politics" of two or three people, is irrelevant in Truffaut's films as in his life. Despite the fact that The 400 Blows makes a "political" statement about child welfare, The Wild Child can be seen as a firm denial of the noble savagery of the counterculture, The Story of Adèle H. and The Man Who Loved Women (to cite only two) take on added significance in the context of the feminist movement, the films are about personal concerns rather than political gestures. As Arlene Croce contends, Truffaut "protests in terms of the transcendent values; he protests the inhumanity of man" (entry 45).

What counts more for Truffaut is what he singled out for praise in 1954 in Fritz Lang's work: "moral solitude, a man struggling alone against a half-hostile, half-indifferent universe" (entry 511). What stands out in his work are, to use James Monaco's phrase, "images of separation," those "visual tropes which summarize Truffaut's own feelings about the human condition" (entry 349), like couples sitting in bed with each person absorbed in a book, which only serves to emphasize the distance between them.

If Truffaut has a special regard for the alienated, he has an even more demonstrable affinity for children, those outsiders par excellence. Children are the specific focus in four of his films: Les Mistons, The 400 Blows, The Wild Child, and Small Change. More revealingly, there is not one Truffaut film that is without at least one significant vignette involving a child. Just how significant children are and what their significance is can be discovered, paradoxically, from the ease with which they can be excised from many of Truffaut's films without doing irreparable damage to the story. Snip from the films the footage containing Sabine (Jules and Jim), or the scared children (Fahrenheit 451), or the child to whom Adèle reveals her real name, or the girl whom Bertrand consoles (The Man Who Loved Women), and virtually no one who had not seen these films would realize there was something missing. Yet their inclusion, as Dominique Fanne has shown in her chapter on Jules and Jim (entry 249), is orchestrated very precisely and usually underlines the film's central concerns. How the children are treated by others is generally more important than what they do. Their presence, and especially their vitality and vulnerability, reveal things about other characters and help to concretize the audience's emotional response to a situation or character.

Childhood has even broader implications in Truffaut's films, because it is a condition that many of his characters fail to escape. Antoine Doinel in particular is a character who has been growing older without growing up. He is no more mature and no less boyishly impulsive once he is discharged from the army at the beginning of Stolen Kisses than he was as a youth, when he stole a typewriter he could not peddle and blurted out that he was absent from school because his

22

mother had died. In Stolen Kisses he is not mature enough to master
any of the jobs he gets; in Bed and Board one of his jobs, characteristically, involves playing with toy boats in a miniature harbor; in
Love on the Run he impetuously jumps on a train to follow his former
girlfriend Colette. These are not isolated incidents. They are
pieces in an overall pattern of adolescent behavior, behavior that
Antoine shares with Claude Roc in Two English Girls and Alphonse in
Day for Night (both roles also played by the charmingly convincing
Jean-Pierre Léaud), with Bertrand Morane in The Man Who Loved Women
(whose childishness is also signaled by his occupation--playing with
toy planes), with Charlie Kohler and Bernard Granger, and in fact
with most of the male protagonists in between these two, including
Pierre Lachenay (whom Truffaut himself characterized as immature) and
Montag (who lives in a not-too-distant future world that itself has
not been allowed to grow up).

These characters exhibit all the narcissistic and erratic qualities of overgrown teenagers. Like Charlie Kohler, who cannot bring
himself to hold hands with Lena when she asks him to walk her home,
they are insecure and indecisive, with little sense of real direction,
identity, or personal worth. Thus Antoine in Stolen Kisses must repeat to the mirror his own name plus the names of the two women in
his life as if the incantation will somehow tell him something about
himself and what he should do. These characters generally tend to be
passive or inhibited (the two English girls do not call Claude Roc
"le continent" just because he is from mainland Europe; his continence,
or self-restraint, is like Charlie's or Montag's and that of others),
allowing themselves to be swept along by events and relationships and
acting only when the situation forces them to. But they can also be
willful, aggressive and single-minded in their dedication to something. This combination of active and passive tendencies is probably
best illustrated by Bertrand Morane in The Man Who Loved Women, who
can use every wily detective's methods to discover the identity of a
fetching pair of legs and even for a fleeting moment consider going
to Montreal to conclude his search, but who, once a relationship with
a woman has gone stale, will wait for the woman to force the issue to
its crisis. Other less amusing examples of characters who go to extremes, who overdo or overcontrol things, are Ferrand, Itard, and
Julien Davenne, each of whom cuts himself off from any emotional contact with people around him in his obsessive pursuit of an objective,
be it completing a film, educating a boy to prove a theory, or pre-
serving the memory of the dead. (For a discussion of existential
freedom and responsibility in Truffaut, of "how sudden seemingly gra-
tuitous decisions shape his characters' lives," see entry 384.)

Like the young Antoine who builds an altar to Balzac that almost
burns down his apartment, or Charlie Kohler who tries to break up an
argument between his boss and his girlfriend and ends up killing his
boss, Truffaut's characters are almost always well-intentioned in
their actions. The effects of their actions well outstrip their in-
tentions, however, and this is caused by their failure to stand back

and consider consequences or alternatives. They are curiously myopic, unwilling or unable to see beyond the immediate. And not only are they unaware of the implications of their actions, they also rarely seem to be aware of themselves. So, when Plyne tells Charlie Kohler that his problem is that he is afraid, Charlie can say "J'ai peur" as if it had never occurred to him before and he must try out how to say it right.

Truffaut's female characters, especially in the early part of his film career, possess many of the same qualities as his males. They too are alone, with no close friends and little meaningful connection to family or any other sustaining group. Catherine's jump into the river in Jules and Jim and Delphine's lovemaking in semipublic places in The Man Who Loved Women prove them to be as impulsive as any of Truffaut's male characters. Julie Kohler in The Bride Wore Black and Camille Bliss in Such a Gorgeous Kid like Me are more obsessed with their tasks than even Julien Davenne. And Adèle H. can only see her actions as "liberated" rather than self-destructive.

The difference between Truffaut's male and female characters has been succinctly expressed by Graham Petrie: "Truffaut's men tend to be shy and passive, allowing the women to take the initiative and to dominate. The women have vitality, energy, a desire for new experiences which the men usually lack" (entry 220). The result is that while Antoine and Charlie and Bertrand Morane and Bernard Granger seem absurdly amusing and Julien Davenne and Itard and Montag seem sadly pathetic, Catherine and Julie Kohler and Camille Bliss, Anne and Muriel, and even Adèle H., though sometimes magically attractive, seem nonetheless threatening and destructive. This has changed somewhat since Day for Night (1973). In this film and in The Man Who Loved Women (1977) and The Last Metro (1980), Truffaut has attempted to present a more balanced picture of women, providing a kind of spectrum of female possibilities. The implied danger associated with women nevertheless remains. It is evident in women's seeming obliviousness to or insouciance about their own sexuality, especially with regard to a mature woman, often a mother, and a young man or boy. This concern was established in Les Mistons, returned to most critically in The 400 Blows, and repeated recently in both Small Change and The Man Who Loved Women.

The traumatic influence of a woman on an impressionable boy takes on greater significance because the past plays such a determining role in Truffaut's films. Truffaut calls himself a nostalgic and claims that the things that influenced him most (the anecdotal and artistic fund that he draws from in creating his films) happened to him in his youth. As with him, so too with his characters. Most of his films contain brief incidents recollected from a character's past (either consciously or subconsciously) that take on added significance in light of present behavior. For Antoine Doinel there are many such moments in Love on the Run. So too for Julien Davenne (though these are only implied in the photographs he mounts in his sanctuary) and for Bertrand Morane. The films in which they appear are statements about the cumulative effects of the past. But even for them some incidents have a singular importance: Antoine's illegitimacy and abandonment, World War I and the death of Julien's young wife, the barely disguised hatred of Bertrand's mother. For many other characters similar influential moments resurface. Adèle H. has nightmares of the drowning death of her sister and brother-in-law. Camille Bliss recalls her rocky upbringing. For Julie Kohler there was the inexplicable death of her just-wed husband. Dr. Itard theorizes that Victor was abandoned. Charlie Kohler's brothers reminisce about his youthful rides with a wealthy patroness in a car being pelted by rocks thrown by them, and Lena recalls for him his wife's suicide. There is also the curious nightmare of Ferrand, involving the theft of publicity photos for <u>Citizen Kane</u>. None of these recollections explain away a character's present behavior. They are clearly meant to have some bearing, however, to indicate that characters are at least working from patterns of activity established some time ago. As the characters that Truffaut presents are generally ignorant of the consequences of actions, they also seem unaware of the full implications of the incidents from their past and unable therefore to control their own destinies.

THEMES: LOVE, DEATH, ART

Although each film has its own subthemes and peculiar angle of vision, certain major themes recur throughout his career. They are the "capital letter" themes, their recurrence perhaps a function of Truffaut's recognition of the need for movies to speak a universal language as well as to reflect his own personal philosophy.

Gilles Jacob has called Truffaut "the great poet of the amorous encounter" (entry 151). True as this description is, it is incomplete. For Truffaut's films are noteworthy for the quiet abundance and variety of their intimate moments. Charlie and Lena in bed, the camera crosscutting between sleep and hopeful conversation. Jules and Jim and Catherine opening their villa's windows to greet the morning. Julie/Marion stripping to the waist while standing in Louis Mahe's red car in the middle of a country road. Antoine playfully naming Christine's breasts Laurel and Hardy. Delphine holding her head out the window, fanning herself with her hand, and exclaiming to Bertrand Morane: "Oh, the things you make me do!" Through telling gestures, words, caresses, looks, Truffaut has compiled a great catalog of amorous epiphanies ranging from clumsy prelude, to encounter, tentative commitment, fragile harmony, joy, shared exhilaration and tenderness, through to inevitable dissolution. (Significantly lacking, it should be noted, are languorous kisses and erotic lovemaking.)

"There are very few films I like," Truffaut has admitted, "outside films about love in one form or another" (entry 128). His viewing preference is matched by his own output. For all of his films are

"films about love in one form or another." The 400 Blows is about
the denial of love between a mother and son. In Shoot the Piano
Player everyone talks about love. Jules and Jim is, according to
Truffaut, about love in the country, and Soft Skin about love in the
city. Fahrenheit 451 follows the love of a man for books. The Wild
Child pivots on the emotional response of a man and a boy to each
other in the midst of a scientific project. In Two English Girls,
the filmmaker attempted to "squeeze love like a lemon" (entry 1128).

Truffaut's development of the love theme is, typically, dialec-
tical: "If I could say there's one point all my films share in common, it's questioning love, and the question is: Is love provisional
(temporary) or definitive (permanent)?" (entry 1462). In his films
he is not so much interested in answering this question as in explor-
ing the varieties of human behavior that result from the coexistence
of these two attitudes toward love. For some people love is provisional, for others it is definitive. (Truffaut has also used the antithetical terms "relative" and "absolute.") For most, it is a curious mixture. Rarely do two people share the same attitude at the
same time. And if they do, circumstances often conspire against them.

Completely provisional love is rare in Truffaut's films. The
characters whose relationships lack any emotional commitment are limited to Therese, the footloose radical in Jules and Jim who flits
away from Jules and later lists her various lovers to Jim (and who
ends up wed to a mortician), various prostitutes (one of whom, again
revealingly, has a room full of empty bookshelves), and Camille Bliss,
the main character in Truffaut's least successful film, Such a
Gorgeous Kid like Me.

Completely definitive love is likewise rare, but more fascinating
to Truffaut. Its practitioners are almost otherworldly in their ex-
tremism. They are what might be called ex post facto absolutists--
characters who obsessively devote themselves to the preservation of
an inviolable ideal as embodied in a former partner. Adèle H. and
Julien Davenne, despite overtures by possible alternative partners
(the bookstore owner and Cecilia), remain in the thrall of an idée
fixe. Although they have passionately dedicated their lives to their
past loves, they are curiously emotionless. Yet their death-in-life
makes them oddly creative.

Two characters who seem to straddle the extremes, who hold definitive and provisional love in an almost perfect equipoise, yet in significantly different ways, are also fascinating to Truffaut. Julie
Kohler, like Julien Davenne and Adèle H., is absolutely devoted to
the memory of her deceased husband. Yet she enters into a series of
temporary relationships, admittedly with an icy detachment, for the
purposes of gaining her revenge. Bertrand Morane is also obsessed,
but his amour fou is collective. He is "in love with the idea of
love," as one of his women tells him; his pursuit of WOMAN, not just
one woman, translates the provisional into the definitive.

26

Truffaut's most common approach to the question of love pits the definitive against the provisional, absoluteness against relativity, in one relationship. Many of his characters are romantics like Tamino in The Magic Flute, who is inspired by a woman's picture in a locket; they have preconceived notions or images of ideal love or the perfect partner. Lena has a poster of Edouard Saroyan, the successful concert pianist version of Charlie Kohler, covering a wall in her bedroom. For Jules and Jim, Catherine is the living version of a mysterious and captivating statue, the incarnation of the eternal female. Before Claude Roc sees her, Muriel Brown is described to him in glowing terms by her sister. Louis Mahe first falls in love with a woman's picture, and arranges to marry her through correspondence. Antoine Doinel (in Love on the Run) likewise falls first for a photograph of Sabine. Other similar characters simply transform women into ideals. In Stolen Kisses Fabienne Tabard is "a vision" to Antoine Doinel, as is the mother of Patrick's schoolmate in Small Change. Julie Kohler is Fergus' Diana. Arthur the exterminator in Such a Gorgeous Kid like Me repeatedly calls Camille Bliss "mon pauvre petit oiseau." Like Lachenay in Soft Skin, who is constantly arranging his stewardess/mistress into various poses, these characters all attempt to "freeze" the object of their love, to make him/her conform to a static image of perfection. The discrepancy between this static ideal and the dynamic, imperfect reality produces the dramatic tension in Truffaut's films. The romantic idealists are often not aware of this discrepancy; the idealized characters cannot accomodate themselves to it. The conflict that results is rarely resolved.

Death in Truffaut's films, instead of emphasizing the temporary nature of love, often does just the opposite. In Jules and Jim a story is recounted about a soldier who, from the trenches of war, writes a letter to a woman acquaintance. As the correspondence continues, it builds in passion and intensity until a wedding date is set. Two days before the wedding, the soldier is killed. Death, it is implied, preserves what life would have destroyed. It is a pattern that recurs throughout Truffaut's films.

Death for Truffaut is unexpected, often accidental, not without an element of romantic fatalism, and profoundly disruptive in its effects on the living. This should come as no surprise to someone familiar with the filmmaker's life.

Truffaut's maternal grandmother, evidently the one stable element in his childhood, died when he was eight. His mentor and surrogate father, André Bazin, died during the night of the first day's shooting of The 400 Blows. When he was asked ten years later about the intervening years, Truffaut answered in the form of a litany of the dead: "Actors. Françoise Dorleac, the star of La Peau douce and Nicole Berger, who played the pianist's wife in Tirez sur le pianiste, and Albert Remy, who played the father in Les Quatre Cents Coups. Also Guy Decomble, who played the teacher in Les Quatre Cents Coups, and Catherine Lutz, who played the lady detective in Baisers volés.

And there were writers, William Irish, who wrote The Bride Wore Black, and David Goodis, the author of Tirez sur le pianiste. . . . And there are filmmakers whom I don't know but loved a great deal. Jacques Becker and Jean Cocteau" (entry 1316).

Death's presence is continually acknowledged and its perverse timing is emphasized. Death can happen in the middle of a telephone conversation, for example, as it does to the old detective in Stolen Kisses, or just as a commitment has been made to give a love relationship some sense of permanence. The anecdote in Jules and Jim confirms a pattern established in Les Mistons (when Bernadette's lover dies in a mountain climbing accident on the eve of their wedding) and often repeated. Lena dies just after Charlie has pledged his love; Julie Kohler's husband is shot leaving their wedding; Anne Brown dies of tuberculosis just after she becomes engaged (this is an addition by Truffaut to the film version of Two English Girls); Alexandre dies in a car wreck just after he decides to adopt Christian (Day for Night); Adèle H.'s sister and her husband die just after they are wed—as does Julien Davenne's wife, Julie. Thus death serves as a warning to the hopeful (the death of Colette's baby as recounted in Love on the Run perhaps fits in here), to those who take chances, to those who are impulsive (Bertrand Morane). Life is not only unpredictable, it is absurd—and absurdly vindictive. Even premeditated murders confirm this notion. Consider the timing of Franca Lachenay's shotgunning of her husband—just after he has tried to phone to arrange a reconciliation. Consider too the unexpectedness of the death of Lena, shot by a previously incompetent thug come to call Charlie's brothers to account.

Vengeance, especially as it is carried out, for instance, by the methodical and not easily distracted Julie Kohler, 'is a way of imposing a kind of order on the world. Likewise suicide, as it is practiced by Catherine. These calculated attempts at controlling things by an assertion of the will are usually satisfied by other, less drastic means in Truffaut's films. Work and art are the most common ways of making "purposeful and ordered" what is otherwise "inconsequential and accidental" (entry 372). This is another way of articulating what André Bazin called the "mummy complex" of art in his essay on "The Ontology of the Photographic Image" (What Is Cinema?, vol. 1 [Berkeley: University of California Press, 1967]). Art is a way of "providing a defense against the passage of time."

Truffaut's attitude toward art is characteristically ambivalent. He has been more self-conscious in his fascination with artists and the interpenetration of art and everyday life than any other filmmaker. Four of his films are extended homages to specific kinds of art: books—Fahrenheit 451 and The Man Who Loved Women; films—Day for Night; and theater—The Last Metro. Most of his major characters have some intimate connection to art, be it music (Charlie Kohler, Antoine Doinel in Antoine and Colette, and Camille Bliss), painting (Fergus), or literature, from criticism (Pierre Lachenay) to the writing of diaries (Adèle H. and Dr. Itard), obituaries (Julien Davenne), novels (Doinel and Claude Roc) and theses (Stanislas Previne), most of which are only slightly fictional. Even children are involved: the precocious filmmaker in Such a Gorgeous Kid like Me and the letter writing Martine, whose correspondence frames Small Change. But Truffaut's paying homage to art is counterbalanced by a simultaneous demystification. In illuminating the processes involved in producing a work of art, he also reveals the artifices, the omissions, the inadequacies of the renderings to the actual experiences. Making a film or writing a book can bring people together and deepen their understanding of themselves or of life in general. Dr. Itard's journal accomplishes this. Stanislas Previne's thesis, however, does not; Camille Bliss debases language, learns nothing, merely uses the process to manipulate the naive sociologist. Even if the artist does learn things, as Bertrand seems to, it does not necessarily mean that there will be an alteration of behavior. And these attempts at communication, at sharing experiences, can often, in fact, serve as barriers to communication, because the artists cut themselves off from others in their devotion to the completion of their work and because the audience, in responding to the artifact, can withdraw into themselves. Antoine Doinel in Bed and Board is a perfect example of both of these tendencies, alienating his wife by both his writing and his reading in bed. The book people at the end of Fahrenheit 451 are at the center of Truffaut's dialectic. They memorize their favorite books in order to preserve them, but their conversations consist of recitations of the books. Their noble endeavor seems to have been undertaken at the expense of their identity, understanding, and true communication.

In general, art is not presented by Truffaut in the lofty terms of creativity, inspiration, or imagination. Rather it is scaled down to the more mundane. Balzac, Renoir, Nicholas Ray are honored, but the artists presented in the films are neither heroic nor especially gifted or insightful. Their works are provoked by death, frustration, or loss, and are more the result of a compulsion than poetic revery or the invocation of a muse. Art fulfills psychological needs. At times, for instance, Adèle H. seems to forget about transcribing her thoughts and feelings into code and writing them down; she simply talks out her story as if its mere release is more important than its transmission to others. Reception is secondary. Although The Last Metro ends with a new play received well, Day for Night concludes with just the propman's hopes that the audience will enjoy it as much as did the people making it. And Bertrand Morane dies before his book is in print. His editor sums up Truffaut's dominant attitude toward art: Bertrand, for better or worse, will live on in his work. Ars longa, vita brevis.

People are mortal; life is fleeting. This is the bedrock of Truffaut's work. Stolen Kisses is about it: "the whole film turns on what escapes you, what can't last" (entry 1356). The Green Room is about an attempt to deny it. But signs of transience are

everywhere. Nowhere is it captured better than in a scene from <u>Jules</u>
<u>and Jim</u>. After a long separation, Jim comes to visit Jules and his
family at their chalet. They hug each other and then smile and survey
each other at arm's length. There is an almost imperceptable freeze
frame. They tell each other heartily that they have not changed.
Catherine adds a postscript: "In short, no one has changed." Then
the shot switches to inside the chalet, and they all are seen through
a window. The only sound is the quiet ticking of the clock.

THE TRUFFAUT TOUCH

"In relation to all the American filmmakers," Truffaut has ob-
served, "I think we French are all intellectuals, even me, and I am
the least intellectual of all my compatriots" (entries 1218 and 1235).
He has also pointed out that he is a man of sensations, not ideas,
and that his first priority in a film is not the themes but the emotional content. As he said in the introductory remarks to <u>The Story</u>
<u>of Adèle H.</u>, "I am primarily concerned with the affective domain"
(entry 468). As a child in movie theaters, Truffaut moved increasingly closer to the screen, the better to enter into the world of the
film. As a filmmaker he attempts the same process from the other
side of the screen, working to engage the audience's emotions, to
draw the audience closer.

In this regard Truffaut is obviously indebted to Hitchcock, whose
single-minded "determination to compel the audience's uninterrupted
attention" he so admires (entry 442). His tactics, however, are different from those of the master of suspense. He is warmer, gentler,
and his love of people aligns him more closely with his other avowed
mentor, Renoir. But he has been influenced by more than just these
two filmmakers--as he has been quick to acknowledge in his interviews
and eager to signal in his films. In fact, it is the mixture (a word
Truffaut has often used) of many disparate elements under the influence of many diverse sources that has produced "the Truffaut touch"
and is responsible for the "charm" that his films are so often said
to possess.

The major ingredients in this mixture are a love and respect for
all kinds of people ("les gens sont formidables!" [people are wonder-
ful]), which counterbalances his basic pessimism about essential lone-
liness and inevitable loss. It is manifested in several ways: his
careful attention to eliciting evocative and believable performances
from his actors and an insistence on an immediate rapport between
characters and audience through the manipulation of point of view;
an "acute sense of the moment," to quote David Thomson (entry 324),
which is based on a sensitivity to the nuances of human behavior; on
a flair for comic situations and expressions that counterpoints his
predilection for the serious, poignant, or melancholy; on an encyclo-
pedic awareness of the possibilities for cinematic vocabulary and
grammar; and on a gentle irony, which is as much the result of his

command of the medium as a reflection of his view of the human condition.

Casting is the key to characterization and its effect in Truffaut's work. Léaud as Doinel, Aznavour as Charlie Kohler, Jeanne Moreau as Catherine, Charles Denner as Bertrand Morane, even Truffaut himself as Dr. Itard—many actors seem born to their roles. They look right for the parts, and Truffaut's reputation for improvisation and last-minute dialogue-writing obviously accommodates the role to the character. Furthermore, many of the roles simply require that an actor underplay his or her part or be virtually expressionless, suppressing emotion or seeming to. Emotional range and physical activity called for are fairly narrow; scenes of heightened or extended emotion are minimized. In other words, characters conduct themselves within the normal limits of undemonstrative middle-class conduct, and the context often carries the emotion of a scene. Everything is carefully controlled in Truffaut's most effective films to allow the actors to connect with the audience through the apparent naturalness of their actions and the appropriateness of small gestures or facial expressions.

Truffaut also draws an audience to his characters through a precise control of what he calls "a first-person confidential tone," whose influence he traces back to Sacha Guitry and films with spoken commentaries like Les Enfants terribles, Roman d'un tricheur, and Journal d'un curé de campagne (entry 1452). He too resorts to spoken commentaries, especially in his darker, more homogeneous and linear "liturgical films" like The Story of Adèle H. Yet the tactic is evident in the use of direct address in everything he has done. During the detention camp interview in The 400 Blows, the psychologist is not shown, and Antoine confesses to the camera. In Day for Night, several of the characters address the camera personally as part of supposed television interviews. And in Love on the Run, Antoine appears in his own story about discovering a photograph and speaks in a kind of cinematic soliloquy.

Although this tactic makes his films more like personal, one-on-one encounters between character and audience than is the case with most other films, Truffaut's are not entirely subjective. No film can be, Lady in the Lake notwithstanding. (In fact, Truffaut's subjective camera is just the opposite of Robert Montgomery's, relying on close-ups of the character in question rather than filming a scene as he would see it.) For film is the art of multiple perspectives, and this is what most intrigues Truffaut. At times he provides the audience with first-hand, privileged access to certain intimate disclosures. At other times information is withheld; things are left unspoken or unrevealed. (This is the main source of his reputation for pudeur ["discretion" or "modesty"].) In The Man Who Loved Women, the film in which Truffaut has the most fun with point of view, the audience shares Bertrand's nightmare, hallucinations, and memories. There is even a shot from his perspective in the grave, dead but

still imagined to be ogling the shapely legs. But the sex scenes in
the film are all judiciously elliptical. What Truffaut employs is a
very calculated kind of limited omniscient narrator. Viewpoints are
shifted; subjective and objective points of view are alternated, in-
termingled, and may even overlap. In the famous helicopter shot in
Jules and Jim, for instance, the voice-over narrator is sober and detached, while the point-of-view camera shares the trio's still youthful exuberance. The most haunting examples occur, however, at the
end of Truffaut's first two feature films (The 400 Blows and Shoot
the Piano Player) and The Wild Child. In each of these films the
main character, who has been oblivious of the camera in the immediately preceding scenes, suddenly turns and looks at or just past the
camera, implicating the audience with his sad stare--half pleading,
half accusatory. Comfortable detachment is denied. At certain stra-
tegic points Truffaut's characters seem to reach out to the audience
for advice, comfort, or assistance--which the audience, of course,
cannot provide. The audience thus participates in the movie more in-
timately, by sharing the character's feelings of helplessness. This
is at the heart of what Jean-Pierre Lefebvre calls Truffaut's "subjective objectivity," the main tactic used to involve the audience
(entry 82).

Truffaut's emphasis on the affective also has an effect on his
plots. Although his relatively recent use of nightmares in Day for
Night (1973), The Story of Adèle H. (1975), and The Man Who Loved
Women (1977), and his frequent inclusion of flashbacks or simple
references to the past betray an unmistakable psychological dimension
in his work, he is not very much interested in analyzing motivation
or probing the psychological depths of a complex personality. In
The Man Who Loved Women, for instance, everyone analyzes Bertrand's
"problem" at one time or another. None of the theories--misogyny,
self-hatred, gerontophobia--adequately explains the man. Nor do they
alter his behavior, neither deepening, complicating, nor deflating
his obsession. In addition, conflicts are not intensified or sustained here, or elsewhere. And so the plots are episodic. Roger
Greenspun expresses it best: "I think it is fair to say that the
Truffaut films develop activity rather than an Aristotelian 'action,'
that they are concerned with making things happen rather than with
the disposing of events in a dramatic structure, that by their own
inner necessity they must at last center upon the actor--he who acts,
or causes things to happen--and that they do not so much end as run
down, or run on in what is pretty clearly to be mere repetition"
(entry 97). Rather than dealing with forces set in motion and building cumulatively to an inevitable climax, Truffaut focuses on a fascinating variety of discrete and often amusing or disheartening details. Plot, insofar as it is forward-looking, eventually turns on
simple suspense. Will the filming of Meet Pamela be disrupted, how,
by whom, and how will it recover? Will Antoine in Stolen Kisses set-
tle down? Will Julie Kohler be able to get her revenge on all five
miscreants, and how? Truffaut is far more interested in the strange
things people say and do because of their peculiar make-up and the

confluence of circumstances than in the causes or even the effects. His focus is on the here and now.

"What Truffaut loves best about cinema," according to James Monaco, is "its ability to capture the poetry of la vie quotidienne" (entry 349). Monaco goes on to list at some length examples of this poetry in the Doinel films in which, he claims, Truffaut "allows himself free reign in this respect." But freedom reigns in all the dramatic comedies, including Day for Night, Small Change, The Man Who Loved Women, and The Last Metro, films composed like "vibrant mosaic[s]" [Monaco's term] of "engrossing busyness" [Greenspun's term]. These are collections of the most vivid and affecting anecdotes about making movies, growing up, writing a book about love affairs, and preparing a play that Truffaut and his assistants could compile. And they have their equivalents in the darker films which, though not as densely packed, are nonetheless evocatively poetic and anecdotal.

These moments are captured and assembled by a filmmaker with a perennial student's love for and mastery of the medium. Graham Petrie, whose assessment of Truffaut's use of the cinema's grammar and vocabulary is the most thorough to date, even though it ends with The Wild Child, believes that Truffaut has the uncanny ability "to make the camera do exactly the right thing at the right time for the right purpose" (entry 220). Examples abound of his seemingly effortless invention and efficiency with camera placement and movement, composition, framing, lighting, and color. Aside from the sheer number of images that come to mind in this regard, two things stand out in Truffaut's use of the camera.

First, there is the remarkable consistency in the look of his films throughout his career. Although there are individual differences attributable to the personalities of the various cinematographers with whom he has worked—most evident in the childlike blaze of colors that Nicholas Roeg created in Fahrenheit 451—and there is an overall arc in his career from the more frenetic camerawork of Raoul Coutard to the more sedate work of Nestor Almendros, there is a distinctive Truffaldian look that cuts across all of his films regardless of the cinematographer. It is recognizable, for example, in the slow tracking shots through natural landscapes in Les Mistons, Jules and Jim, Two English Girls, and The Green Room and in the respectful medium to medium-long shots in all of his films.

Secondly, there is a discernible regard on Truffaut's part for not only the emotional content and narrative function of a shot but also its thematic dimension, the ideas that lenses, camera placement and motion, framing, and lighting can help to convey. No one uses doors, windows, walls, and stairways with quite the thoroughness of Truffaut. And Soft Skin was deliberately not filmed in cinemascope, for example, as his previous features had been, because the conventional size screen better reflected the world view of the main character: a city man with no sense of panorama or connectedness, whose impression of things was truncated, fragmentary, and superficial.

Truffaut's intellectual command of the cinema is further elucidated by noting his editing techniques, his use of sound, and his attention to mise-en-scène. All three are dependent on the filmmaker's particular sensitivity to contexts, to the fact that the cinematic experience is the result of a mixture or layering of effects. Mise-en-scène requires an attention to spatial contexts. Truffaut's use of it can be as simple and obvious as the medium close-up shot of Jim and Catherine gazing lovingly into each other's eyes while a bug (Jules is an entomologist) crawls noticeably across a windowpane between and behind them. Or it can be more complex, as it is in The Wild Child, where depth-of-focus shots bring a fuller range of information to bear: Victor working in the foreground, Itard at his writing stand in the background, behind him a wall covered with scientific prints and a window that lets in the bright sunshine and shimmering trees from the extreme background. Truffaut's use of sound qualifies or amplifies the visual by the aural: either music, sound effects, dialogue, voice-over narration, or silence. Again the examples vary widely, from the use of particular musical refrains for characters-- for instance, Catherine's theme in Jules and Jim; to the subtle overlay of a jet plane noise when Alexandre is on screen in Day for Night; to an ironic Christmas carol, "Silent Night," being sung on the radio in Bertrand's hospital room just before he dies; to the voice-over commentary about Claude Roc's "crazy idea of touching Anne's breast" when he first kisses her. And, as mise-en-scène provides a spatial context, editing provides a temporal one. Truffaut was early recognized for his abrupt and radical changes of tone through editing. Recently he has concentrated on the more classical and subtle blending of shots and scenes.

A fourth context most clearly demonstrates the gentle tension between involvement and ironic detachment that is implicit in the previous three and finally comes to distinguish Truffaut's films from those of his colleagues. This is the context of allusions--those elements from the personal life of the filmmaker or the history of the cinema that change the experience of each film for each viewer in accordance with his or her own powers of recognition. Throughout his career Truffaut has carefully constructed an intricate network of correspondences that both enrich and undercut the immediate experience of a shot, a scene, or the entire film. The Last Metro, for example, is a slightly different experience for someone who has seen Mississippi Mermaid, for the obvious reason that Catherine Deneuve has a role in both films and because some dialogue in the former was lifted entirely from the latter. Similarly for those who have seen other World War II films from To Be or Not to Be to The Sorrow and the Pity, or Hollywood backstage movies, or the Doinel films, or Day for Night, or films with Gerard Depardieu or Jean-Louis Richard. The more movie experience one brings to Truffaut's films, the more one participates in the cinematic game arranged by the filmmaker between himself, his film, and the audience, a game that recognizes the primacy of the individual and the value of emotion, but does not exclude the more sophisticated pleasures of art.

CONCLUSION: NOT JUST AN ARTIST

Just after completing his third feature film, Truffaut outlined the typical arc of a filmmaker's career. There are, he proposed, four stages: (1) the beginnings, when films are "impetuous, a bit experimental and often have virtuoso tricks," since filmmaking at this stage is "a sort of amorous game with the camera"; (2) a settling-down period during which "the camera gets more measured, what is in front of the camera becomes more important," and the films contain "invariably a large amount of provocation," which can prevent the filmmaker from being commercially successful; (3) a period of commercial success achieved when the director's age (thirty-five to forty) and preoccupations correspond with those of the "median age of the audience"; and (4) the decline from popularity when the filmmaker becomes "more abstract," though his films become "the most fascinating to study" (entry 1221). This is an outline that Truffaut has conformed to yet battled against throughout his career.

Truffaut's first three feature films constitute probably the most auspicious debut of any narrative filmmaker. Shoot the Piano Player and Jules and Jim were especially full of virtuoso tricks. He then went on to make three films--Soft Skin, Fahrenheit 451, and The Bride Wore Black--that pushed the "explosion of genres" theory begun with Shoot the Piano Player to new levels and experimented with visuals, color, and narrative development, all provocations that were not successful commercially. With Stolen Kisses (begun the day before his thirty-sixth birthday), Truffaut entered a period that contained some notable failures, but also his most popular commercial and critical successes--The Wild Child, Day for Night, The Story of Adèle H., and Small Change. Since then he has made three films (The Man Who Loved Women, The Green Room, and Love on the Run) that are indeed "more abstract" and have not fared well with either the critics or the public. The Last Metro is a most determined effort to win back both critical and popular support.

Commercial success is often a two-edged sword, however, as Truffaut himself is aware. His most popular films did not enhance his reputation in some quarters. The disarming ease of Stolen Kisses, Day for Night, and Small Change caused some to take him less seriously. Words like pudeur ("modesty"), "charm," and "humaneness," formerly honorific, were used derogatively against him. His own critical indictments of the shallow filmmakers of the fifties were turned against his own films. Criticized for being too "Hitchcockian" in the late sixties, he became too "Renoirian" in the seventies, or too derivative in general, even of himself. Theoretical heavyweights (the Marxists, semiologists, structuralists, and myth critics) have by and large refused to consider his work.

In an age that thrives on energetic newness and extremes of thinking and behavior, François Truffaut is an anachronism, though his debut as a filmmaker and his career as a critic might have seemed to indicate otherwise. As a result he has unfortunately been relegated by some to the fateful byways of the vaguely or perennially disappointing. For he is neither a radical thinker nor a technical innovator. His films have provided no revolutionary changes in traditional cinematic or narrative forms, nor any groundbreaking insights into human psychology or conduct. Rather he has made conscientious personal use of a medium not noted for either quality. His films have documented with clarity, affection, and humor the plight of the romantic, the meek, and the marginal. His originality is the originality of a uniquely gifted craftsman and humanist. His accomplishments--certainly Shoot the Piano Player, Jules and Jim, The Wild Child, and Day for Night, and perhaps The 400 Blows, Stolen Kisses, Two English Girls, and The Story of Adèle H.--entitle him to be considered among the best practitioners of his art.

In the same interview in which he set down what can be seen as a paradigm of his own career, Truffaut also distinguished between the fate of Alfred Hitchcock as opposed to Buñuel, Ophuls, Chaplin, and Welles. The latter four, while as venerable and valuable to Truffaut as Hitchcock, he characterized as filmmakers "who are only artists" (entry 1221, his emphasis). But Hitchcock was presented as a filmmaker more to be emulated because he used commercial success "as an additional discipline." Truffaut's career has revealed him to be a very disciplined and dedicated person. His goal has been nothing less than to combine the two words that seem antithetical to many of his critics: "popular artist." For him the term is not a compromise but a challenge.

III. The Films: Synopses, Credits, Notes, and Reviews

*1   UNE VISITE (1954)

Synopsis

Looking for a room, a young man scans the want ads, makes a phone call, and goes to a young woman's apartment. In the hall he trips and falls over his suitcase. The woman laughs. He rents a room. Later the woman's brother-in-law arrives and leaves his daughter for the weekend. In jest he flirts with his sister-in-law -- and in vain. The new tenant, perhaps more sincere, tries his luck, clumsily, and is rejected. He repacks his bags and leaves. Night falls. The woman puts her niece to bed, closes the curtains and sits pensively on her bed.

Credits

Director, Scriptwriter:	François Truffaut
Producer and Assistant:	Robert Lachenay
Director of Photography:	Jacques Rivette (16mm, b/w, silent)
Editors:	Alain Resnais, François Truffaut
Cast:	Florence Doniol-Valcroze, Jean-José Richer, Laura Mauri, Francis Cognany

Filmed in Jacques Doniol-Valcroze's apartment in Paris.
Running time: 7 minutes 40 seconds

Note

This "Cukor-type" comedy, long thought lost, was rediscovered by Truffaut in the Spring of 1982.

2   LES MISTONS (1957)

Synopsis

Bernadette bikes through village streets, into the country, and across a viaduct. A voice-over narrator says she "was too beautiful . . . was our awakening to a wondrous world of sensuality." After she parks her bike and goes for a swim, the brats arrive to inspect her bike. They decide "to hate her." Bernadette and her boyfriend, Gérard, are amorous in an old, open, sunlit amphitheater, while the brats stalk and harass them and then play cops-and-robbers. They ogle her at tennis, hoot during a furtive kiss at the movies, disrupt the lovers' woodsy dalliance. When Gérard departs after proposing marriage, the brats send Bernadette a mildly pornographic postcard. The paper announces Gérard's death. The lovers' kiss is recalled. The film ends with the brats playing, oblivious to Bernadette's passing by.

Credits

Production Company:	Les Films du Carrosse
Production Manager:	Robert Lachenay
Director:	François Truffaut
Assistant Directors:	Claude de Givray, Alain Jeannel
Script:	François Truffaut. Based on a short story by Maurice Pons contained in the collection Virginales (Paris: Éditions Julliard, 1955).
Director of Photography:	Jean Malige (1, 33; b/w)
Editor:	Cécile Decugis
Music:	Maurice Le Roux
Narrator:	Michel François
Cast:	Gérard Blain (Gérard), Bernadette Lafont (Bernadette), and "les mistons"

Filmed in and near Nimes, Aug. and Sept. 1957.

Running time:	26 minutes (later cut by Truffaut to 17 minutes)
First shown:	Tours Festival, Nov. 1957 (out of competition)
Premiere:	Paris, 3 Mar. 1961; G.B., 19 Jan. 1961
G.B./U.S. Title:	The Mischief Makers
Prizes:	Prix de la mise-en-scène (Brussels festival), Prix des jeunes spectateurs (Belgium), Gold Medal (Mannheim, Germany), Blue Ribbon Award (U.S.)

Note

The film contains several allusions to other films, the most noteworthy of which are the homage to Lumiere's L'Arrosseur arrosé and the implied criticism of Jean Delannoy's Chiens perdus sans colliers, whose advertising poster the brats rip in half on emerging from the movie theater.

Reviews

Louis Black, Cinema Texas Program Notes 14, no. 1 (2 Feb. 1978); BFI Monthly Film Bulletin 28, no. 326 (Mar. 1961); Jonag Mekas, Village Voice 4, no. 38 (15 July 1959); William Bernhardt, Film Quarterly 13, no. 1 (Fall 1959); David Robinson, Sight and Sound 27, no. 5 (Summer 1958); William Whitebait, New Statesman 61, no. 1558 (20 Jan. 1961).

Claude Beylie, Cahiers du Cinéma 16, no. 91 (Jan. 1959); Jean D'Yvoire, Télé-Ciné, no. 80 (Jan.-Feb. 1959); Cinéma 58, no. 24 (Feb. 1958); Jacques Rivette, Arts, no. 646 (23 Nov.-3 Dec. 1957).

3 UNE HISTOIRE D'EAU (1958)

Synopsis

A woman descends some stairs, and, discovering the floods, starts to sing. General flood shots are commented upon by a pretentious voice-over. The woman gets to dry land via planks and a row boat, and there she meets a man; they set off in his car. Stream-of-consciousness voice-over provides impressions and drops names. The car gets stuck twice, prompting voice-over remarks about digression and the lack of freedom in France and her wrongful perference of word over image. He quotes Baudelaire and she sings about a wolf seducing a girl. Relaxing by a tree, she recounts (in voice-over) the jokes and anecdotes he told her. They find a boat and return to the car. On the way to Paris she muses about not loving him, but admits she will probably sleep with him because she is happy France is flooded.

Credits

Production Company:	Les Films de la Pléiade
Producer:	Pierre Braunberger
Production Manager:	Roger Fleytoux
Directors:	François Truffaut, Jean-Luc Godard
Commentary:	Jean-Luc Godard
Director of Photography:	Michel Latouche (16 mm)
Editor:	Jean-Luc Godard
Sound:	Jacques Maumont
Narrator:	Jean-Luc Godard
Cast:	Jean-Claude Brialy (Man), Caroline Dim (Girl).

Filmed on location in and around Paris, early Spring 1958.

Running time:	18 minutes
First shown:	Paris, 3 Mar. 1961

Notes

Truffaut convinced producer Pierre Braunberger to supply

him with enough footage to film the floods. Truffaut could not do anything satisfying with it. Godard salvaged it with his editing and voice-over commentary.

The film's effect derives from the contrast between the documentary footage of the flood and the voice-over, which is at points serious and whimsical, direct and digressive, in the present and past tenses. Godard made it "in homage to Mack Sennet."

Review

BFI Monthly Film Bulletin 33, no. 388 (May 1980).

4   LES QUATRE CENTS COUPS (1959)

Synopsis

Antoine, a 13-year-old student, is caught penciling a mustache on a pinup being passed through class. His teacher makes him stand in a corner while the others continue their lesson and then have recess. After school in his crowded apartment, he is the object of his mother's grumpiness and animosity. His school troubles escalate. He skips, lies outrageously and gets caught at it, unconsciously plagiarizes Balzac. Seen by Antoine with a man besides his father, his mother tries twice to be reconciled to the boy. When he steals a typewriter and gets caught trying to return it, however, his father takes him to the police. He spends the night in jail and is then sent to reform school, a place of quick discipline and boyish camaraderie. He tells the story of his life in answer to questions by an inquiring psychologist. His friend René is not allowed in to visit him, but his mother does, only to tell him he's on his own. During a soccer game, Antoine makes good his escape from the reformatory. He runs and runs until he reaches the sea.

Credits

Production Company:	Les Films du Carrosse/SEDIF
Production Supervisors:	Robert Lachenay, Jean Lavie
Production Manager:	Georges Charlot
Director:	François Truffaut
Assistant Directors:	Philippe de Broca, Alain Jeannel, François Cognany and Robert Bober
Script:	François Truffaut
Adaptation:	François Truffaut, Marcel Moussy
Dialogue:	Marcel Moussy
Script Girl:	Jacqueline Parey
Director of Photography:	Henri Decaë (Dyaliscope, b/w)
Camera Operator:	Jean Rabier
Editor:	Marie-Josephe Yoyotte
Art Director:	Bernard Evein

Music: Jean Constantin
Sound: Jean-Claude Marchetti
Cast: Jean-Pierre Léaud (Antoine Doinel),
                     Albert Rémy (M. Doinel), Claire
                     Maurier (Mme Doinel), Patrick
                     Auffay (René Bigey), Georges
                     Flamant (M. Bigey), Yvonne
                     Claudie (Mme Bigey), Robert
                     Beauvais (School director),
                     Pierre Repp (Bécassine, the
                     English teacher), Guy Decomble
                     (Teacher), Luc Andrieux (Gym
                     teacher), Daniel Couturier,
                     François Nocher, and Richard
                     Kanayan (Children), Claude
                     Mansard (Judge), Jacques Monod
                     (Commissioner), Marius Laurey
                     (Police clerk), Henri Virlogeux
                     (Nightwatchman), Christian
                     Brocard (Man with typewriter),
                     Jeanne Moreau (Woman with dog),
                     Jean-Claude Brialy (Man in
                     street), Jacques Demy (Policeman),
                     François Truffaut (Man in fun-
                     fair), Bouchon.
Filmed on location in Paris and Honfleur, 10 Nov. 1958 to
5 Jan. 1959.
Running time: 94 minutes (reedited by Truffaut for
                     Annecy Tribute to him in 1967;
                     running time: 101 minutes)
First shown: Cannes Film Festival, May 1959
Premiere: Paris, 3 June 1959; G.B., 3 Mar.
                     1960; U.S., Dec. 1959.
G.B./U.S. Title: The 400 Blows
Prizes: Grand prix de la mise-en-scène
                     (Cannes, 1959), Joseph Burstyn
                     Prize--Best Foreign Film (U.S.,
                     1959), New York Film Critics'
                     Award--Best Foreign Film, Prix
                     Melies (France, 1959), Nominated
                     for an Academy Award--Best
                     Original Screenplay (Hollywood,
                     1959), Prix de l'Association de
                     la Presse Cinématographique
                     Suisse, Le Grand Prix de l'Office
                     Catholique internationale du
                     cinéma (Cannes, 1959), Plume
                     d'Or--Austrian Critics, David O.
                     Selznick Award, Grand Prize for
                     Human Values (Valladolid).

Reviews

Filmfacts 2, no. 47 (23 Dec. 1959); G. DeVita, Cinema Texas
Program Notes 14, no. 1 (2.Feb. 1978); Dwight MacDonald,
Esquire 53, no. 3 (Mar. 1960); Robert Vas, BFI Monthly Film
Bulletin 27, no. 315 (Apr. 1960); Stanley Kauffmann, New
Republic 141, no. 23 (7 Dec. 1959); Jonas Mekas, Village Voice
5, no. 5 (25 Nov. 1959); Isabel Quigley, Spectator, no. 6870
(26 Feb. 1960); A. W. Richardson, Screen Education Yearbook,
1963; Robert Hatch, Nation 189, no. 18 (28 Nov. 1959); Paul
Rotha, Films and Filming 6, no. 7 (Apr. 1960); Philip Hartung,
Commonweal 71, no. 9 (27 Nov. 1959); Dilys Powell, Sunday
Times (London) (6 Mar. 1960); Louis Marcorelles, Observer, no.
8758 (10 May 1959); Bosley Crowther, New York Times (17 Nov.
1959); Louise Corbin, Films in Review 10, no. 9 (Nov. 1959);
Martin Perier, Film Journal, no. 15 (Mar. 1960); Doré Silverman,
Films in Review 10, no. 6 (June–July 1959); Time 74, no. 24
(14 Dec. 1959); Hollis Alpert, Saturday Review 42, no. 40
(3 Oct. 1959); Peter John Dyer, Sight and Sound 29, no. 2
(Spring 1960); William Whitebait, New Statesman 59, no. 1512
(5 Mar. 1960); Variety (29 Apr. 1959); Hollywood Reporter
(15 Dec. 1959).

Jacques Rivette, Cahiers du Cinéma 16, no. 95 (May 1959)
and Jean-Luc Godard 16, no. 92 (Feb. 1959) and F. Hoveyda, 17,
no. 97 (July 1959); George Sadoul, Les Lettres Françaises,
no. 777 (11–17 June 1959); Jean-Louis Tallenay, Signes du
Temps, no. 6 (June 1959); J. Chevallier, Image et Son, no.
124 (Oct. 1959); Michel Flacon, Cinéma 59, no. 37 (June 1959)
and Yves Boisset, no. 33 (Feb. 1959); Michel Mardore, Le Nouvel
Observateur, no. 126 (12–18 Apr. 1967); Claude Mauriac, Le
Figaro Littéraire 22, no. 1096 (20 Apr. 1967); Jean de
Baroncelli, Le Monde (6 May and 10 June 1959); Jacques Michel,
Le Parisien (5 May 1959); Henry Magnan, Combat (5 May 1959);
Paul Guyot, France-Soir (5 June 1959) and Edgar Schneider
(6 May 1959); Maurice Ciantar, Paris-Journal (5 May 1959);
L'Aurore (5 May 1959).

Enno Patalas, Filmkritik, no. 10 (1959); Karena Niehoff,
Der Tagesspiegel (22 Oct. 1959); Alfred Paffenholz, Filmdienst
(22 Oct. 1959); Martin Ruppert, Frankfurter Allgemeine Zeitung
(11 Nov. 1959); Helmut Kauer, Die Zeit (8 Jan. 1960); H.-D.
Roos, Süddeutsche Zeitung (11 July 1960), and Wolfgang Ruf
(14 Apr. 1974).

5   TIREZ SUR LE PIANISTE (1960)

Synopsis

In the dark a fleeing man runs into a pole. Revived, he
talks to a stranger about love and marriage. He then resumes
his flight, seeking refuge with his estranged brother, Charlie,

a piano player in a small pub. Charlie reluctantly helps his brother escape, walks home shyly with a barmaid, and allows his neighbor, a prostitute, to spend the night with him. The next morning Charlie's younger brother, Fido, tricks two thugs, but they kidnap Charlie and the barmaid, Léna. After Charlie and Léna escape, they go to her apartment, where the story of his previous concert career and unfortunate marriage are recounted. The two of them make love and plan his return to concerts. An argument develops when they go to quit their jobs at the pub, and Charlie ends up stabbing his boss. Léna hides him from the police and then drives him to his brothers' mountain hideaway. Charlie reminisces sadly with his brothers. Léna returns just as the two kidnappers arrive with another hostage, Fido. Gunshots are exchanged. Léna is killed. The kidnappers and Charlie's brothers flee. Charlie returns to pounding a piano at the pub.

Credits

Production Company:	Les Films de la Pléiade
Producer:	Pierre Braunberger
Production Manager:	Roger Fleytoux
Director:	François Truffaut
Assistant Directors:	Francis Cognany, Robert Bober, Bjorn Johansen
Script:	François Truffaut, Marcel Moussy. Based on the novel Down There by David Goodis (New York: Fawcett, 1956).
Script Girl:	Suzanne Schiffman
Dialogue:	François Truffaut
Director of Photography:	Raoul Coutard (Dyaliscope, b/w)
Camera Operator:	Claude Beausoleil
Editors:	Cécile Decugis, Claudine Bouché
Art Director:	Jacques Mély
Music:	Georges Delerue
Songs:	
"Dialogues d'amoureux"	Félix Leclerc; sung by Félix Leclerc, Lucienne Vernay
"Framboise"	Bobby Lapointe; sung by Bobby Lapointe
Sound:	Jacques Gallois
Cast:	Charles Aznavour (Edouard Saroyan/ Charlie Kohler), Marie Dubois (Léna), Nicole Berger (Theresa), Albert Rémy (Chico Saroyan), Claude Mansard (Momo), Daniel Boulanger (Ernest), Michèle Mercier (Clarisse), Richard Kanayan (Fido Saroyan), Jean-Jacques Aslanian (Richard Saroyan), Serge Davri (Plyne), Claude Heymann (Lars Schmeel),

Alex Joffé (Stranger who helps
Chico), Catherine Lutz (Mammy),
Bobby Lapointe (Singer).

Filmed in Paris and Le Sappey near Grenoble, 30 Nov. 1959–
22 Jan. 1960 (some scenes reshot during Mar. 1960).

Running time:	80 minutes
First Shown:	London Film Festival, 21 Oct. 1960
Premiere:	Paris, 25 Nov. 1960; G.B., 8 Dec. 1960; U.S., 24 July 1962
G.B. Title:	Shoot the Pianist; U.S. Title: Shoot the Piano Player
Prizes:	Prix de la nouvelle critique (France), Best Photography (Germany)

Notes

The American version of the film is usually 80 minutes long;
other versions are 84 or 86 minutes.

Truffaut first met Suzanne Schiffman at the cinémathèque in
the late 1940s. She worked as script girl through Mississippi
Mermaid, except for Fahrenheit 451 where, because of British
union rules, she served, uncredited, as Truffaut's personal
assistant.

Many of the printed credits indicate that Jean Constantin
wrote the music. He signed a contract to do it, but was replaced when he refused because he did not like the film.

The novel was reprinted in 1963 with the movie's title:
Tirez sur le pianiste (Paris: Éditions Gallimard) and Shoot
the Piano Player (New York: Grove Press).

Reviews

Filmfacts 5, no. 28 (10 Aug. 1962); Andrew Sarris, Village
Voice 7, no. 40 (26 July 1962); V. Allmendarez, Cinema Texas
Program Notes 7, no. 41 (12 Nov. 1974); Stanley Kauffmann, New
Republic 147, no. 2 (9 July 1962); John Gillett, BFI Monthly
Film Bulletin, no. 324 (Jan. 1961); Jay Jacobs, Reporter 27,
no. 5 (27 Sept. 1962); Robert Hatch, Nation 195, no. 4 (25 Aug.
1962); Bosley Crowther, New York Times (24 July 1962); Dwight
MacDonald, Esquire 55, no. 3 (Mar. 1961); P. J. Dyer, Sight
and Sound 30, no. 1 (Winter 1961); Time 79, no. 5 (3 Aug.
1962); Edith Oliver, New Yorker 38, no. 24 (4 Aug. 1962);
William Whitebait, New Statesman 60, no. 1533 (17 Dec. 1960);
Louis Marcorelles, Sight and Sound 29, no. 4 (Autumn 1960);
Francis Wyndham, Encounter 25, no. 4 (Oct. 1965); Variety
(30 Aug. 1960); Paul Beckley, New York Herald Tribune (24 July
1962); Hollywood Reporter (18 Jan. 1963); Moviegoer (Winter
1964); Newsweek (6 Aug. 1962).

Marcel Martin, Cinéma 61, no. 52 (Jan. 1961); Alain Vargas, Cinéma 60, no. 44 (Mar. 1960); R. Lefevre, Image et Son, no. 138 (Feb. 1961); Jean Collet, Télérama (11 Dec. 1960); André Labarthe, France-Observateur (24 Nov. 1960); Louis Chauvet, Le Figaro (28 Nov. 1960); Jean de Baroncelli, Le Monde (29 Nov. 1960); Pierre Marcabru, Combat (29 Nov. 1960); Le Film Français (6 Dec. 1960); Objectif 60 (Nov. 1960).

Georg Ramseger, Die Welt (26 Dec. 1960); Paul Sakkarndt, Filmdienst (7 Dec. 1960); Frantz Vossen, Süddeutsche Zeitung (11-12 Dec. 1960) and H.-D. Roos (14 Feb. 1961); Günter Sevren, Deutsche Zeitung (27 Dec. 1960); Dietrich Kuhlbrodt, Filmkritik, no. 1 (1961); Karl Korn, Frankfurter Allgemeine Zeitung (13 Jan. 1961); Karena Niehoff, Der Tagesspiegel (2 Feb. 1961); Heinz Ungureit, Frankfurter Rundschau (13 Mar. 1961); Martin Schlappner, Neue Zürcher Zeitung (18 May 1961).

6   JULES ET JIM (1961)

Synopsis

Kickboxing, exchanging poems, talking philosophy in Parisian cafés, Jules, an Austrian, and Jim, a Frenchman, are inseparable friends. When they see the slide of an enchanting smile, they go to Greece to find the statue that bears it. Back in Paris they meet a woman (Catherine) with the same smile. The three of them go to the theater and to the sea until Jules proposes to her and, when Jim fails to meet her at a café, they return to Austria to be wed. War separates the friends, but they write to each other. At war's end Jim is invited to Germany to visit Catherine and Jules and their daughter. Jules informs Jim of Catherine's infidelities and his own unhappiness and invites his friend to love, to marry his wife. The love that develops is stormy. Catherine desires a child, but when Jim remains attached to his lover, Gilberte, Catherine returns to her earlier impetuosity. She spends a night with Albert, an old lover. She drives crazily through a park outside Jim's apartment and even pulls a gun on him. He returns to Gilberte. Months later Jules and Catherine meet Jim in a theater. Catherine invites Jim for a drive and instructs Jules to watch. She drives her car off a bridge into the Seine. Jules has their bodies incinerated, according to Catherine's wishes.

Credits

Production Company:	Les Films du Carrosse/SEDIF
Production Manager:	Marcel Berbert
Director:	François Truffaut
Assistant Directors:	Georges Pellegrin, Robert Bober
Script:	François Truffaut, Jean Gruault.
	Based on the novel by Henri-

	Pierre Roché (Paris: Éditions Gallimard, 1953).
Director of Photography:	Raoul Coutard (Franscope, b/w)
Camera Operator:	Claude Beausoleil
Editor:	Claudine Bouché
Music:	Georges Delerue
Song:	
"Le Tourbillon"	Boris Bassiak; sung by Jeanne Moreau
Costumes:	Fred Capel
Narrator:	Michel Subor
Cast:	Jeanne Moreau (Catherine), Oskar Werner (Jules), Henri Serre (Jim), Marie Dubois (Thérèse), Vanna Urbino (Gilberte), Sabine Haudepin (Sabine), Boris Bassiak (Albert), Kate Noëlle (Birgitta), Anny Nielsen (Lucy), Christiane Wagner (Helga), Jean-Louis Richard and Michel Varesano (Customers in café), Pierre Fabre (Drunk in café), Danielle Bassiak (Albert's friend), Bernard Largemains (Merlin), Elen Bober (Mathilde), Dominique Lacarrière (Woman).

Filmed in and around Paris, Alsace, and St. Paul de Vence, 10 Apr.-3 June 1961

Running time:	105 minutes
Premiere:	Paris, 23 Jan. 1962; G.B., 17 May 1962; U.S., May 1962.
G.B./U.S. Title:	Jules and Jim
Prizes:	Best Director (Mar del Plata Festival and Acapulco Festival), Cantaclaros Prize (Caracas, Venezuela, 1961-62), Prix de l'Academie du Cinéma (Etoile de cristal, meilleur film français, and best actress award to Jeanne Moreau), Critics' Prize (Carthagenia Festival), Danish Oscar ("Bodil, 1963"--Best European Film), Nastro Argento (Best Film--Italian Critics).

Reviews

    Filmfacts 5, no. 19 (18 June 1962); Pauline Kael, Partisan Review 29, no. 4 (Fall 1962); Richard Roud, Sight and Sound 31, no. 3 (Summer 1962); Andrew Sarris, Village Voice 7, no. 28 (3 May 1962); Joe Rape, Cinema Texas Program Notes 12, no. 3 (26 Apr. 1977); Dwight MacDonald, Esquire (Sept. 1962); Penelope Houston, BFI Monthly Film Bulletin, no. 342 (July 1962); Vernon Young, Hudson Review 15, no. 4 (Winter 1962);

Philip Hartung, Commonweal 76, no. 6 (4 May 1962); Stanley
Kauffmann, New Republic 146, no. 19 (7 May 1962); Isabel
Quigley, Spectator, no. 6987 (25 May 1962); Dilys Powell,
Sunday Times (London) (20 May 1962); Robert Hatch, Nation 194,
no. 19 (12 May 1962); Brendan Gill, New Yorker 38, no. 11 (5
May 1962); John Coleman, New Statesman 63, no. 1627 (18 May
1962); Bosley Crowther, New York Times (24 Apr. 1962); James
Breen, Observer (20 May 1962); Douglas McVay, Film, no. 33
(Autumn 1962); Arthur Schlesinger, Jr., Show (June 1962);
Time 79, no. 18 (4 May 1962); Hollis Alpert, Saturday Review
45, no. 19 (12 May 1962); W. Huyck, Cinema (Hollywood) 4, no.
1 (Spring 1968) and 1, no. 3 (1963); Peter Baker, Films and
Filming 8, no. 9 (June 1962); Variety (7 Feb. 1962); Shama
Habibullah, Cambridge Review, no. 2046 (23 Feb. 1963); K.
Murphy, Thousand Eyes, no. 11 (June 1976).

Raymond Jean, Cahiers du Sud, no. 366 (May-June 1962);
Georges Sadoul, Les Lettres Françaises (25 Jan. 1962); Robert
Kanters, L'Express (25 Jan. 1962); Jean de Baroncelli, Le Monde
(26 Jan. 1962); Claude Mauriac, Le Figaro Littéraire (27 Jan.
1962); René Gilson and Pierre Billard, Cinéma 62, no. 64 (Mar.
1962) and B. S., no. 65 (Apr. 1962); Jean-Louis Bory, Arts
(31 Jan. 1962 and 6 Feb. 1962); Bernard Dort, France-
Observateur (1 Feb. 1962); P. Bretigny, Image et Son, no. 149
(Mar. 1962); Pierre Marcabru, Combat (27 Jan. 1962); J.-L.
Tallenay and Charles Avril, Télérama (11 Feb. 1962); Guy
Allombert, Le Cinématographie Française (17 Feb. 1962); Le
Film Français (20 Apr. 1962); Unifrance Film, no. 208; Gilles
Colpart, Télé-Ciné, no. 212 (Nov. 1976).

Wilfred Berghahn, Filmkritik, no. 3 (1962); Heinz Ungureit,
Frankfurter Rundschau (2 Mar. 1962); Karl Korn, Frankfurter
Allgemeine Zeitung (5 Mar. 1962); Karena Niehoff, Der
Tagesspiegel (10 Mar. 1962); Günter Seuren, Deutsche Zeitung
(13 Mar. 1962); U. Seelmann-Eggebert, Filmdienst (14 Mar.
1962); H.-D. Roos, Süddeutsche Zeitung (12 July 1962) and
Wolfgang Ruf (8 May 1974); Martin Schlappner, Neue Zürcher
Zeitung (29 Sept. 1962); Martin Gies, Jugend Film Fernsehen 17,
no. 4 (Dec. 1973).

7   ANTOINE ET COLETTE (1962)
     (First episode in L'AMOUR A VINGT ANS)

Synopsis

   Antoine Doinel, now seventeen, lives alone in a small room
and works as a packer in a record factory. He and his friend
René go to young people's musical concerts together. It is
there that he notices Colette, a young girl with whom he falls
immediately in love. Although he tries, he is too shy to make
the first move. She asks to borrow his program notes. They
meet, walk together. He phones, writes, then moves into a

hotel across the street from her. Her parents invite him to dinner, but Colette is standoffish in person, not so in letters. He objects when she comes to his room to invite him to dinner with her parents. During the dinner a new boyfriend arrives; he and Colette go off while Antoine remains to watch television with her parents.

Credits

Production Company:	Ulysse Productions/Unitel
Producer:	Pierre Roustang
Production Manager:	Philippe Dussart
Director:	François Truffaut
Artistic Adviser:	Jean de Baroncelli
Assistant Director:	Georges Pellegrin
Script:	François Truffaut
Director of Photography:	Raoul Coutard (Franscope, b/w)
Camera Operator:	Claude Beausoleil
Editor:	Claudine Bouché
Music:	Georges Delerue, Yvon Samuel (lyrics)
Lyrics (between sketches):	Sung by Xavier Despras
Narrator:	Henri Serre
Cast:	Jean-Pierre Léaud (Antoine Doinel), Marie-France Pisier (Colette), Francois Darbon (Colette's father), Rosy Varte (Colette's mother), Patrick Auffay (René), Jean-François Adam (Albert Tazzi).
Filmed in Paris, Nov. 1971	
Running Time:	29 minutes. Total film: 123 minutes
First Shown:	Berlin Film Festival, 24 June 1962
Premiere:	Paris, 22 June 1962; G.B., 10 Sept. 1964; U.S., Mar. 1963
G.B./U.S. Title:	Love at Twenty--Antoine and Colette

Note

The other episodes were directed by Renzo Rossellini, Marcel Ophuls, Andrzej Wajda, and Shintaro Ishihara.

Reviews

Filmfacts 6, no. 11 (18 Apr. 1963); Tom Milne, BFI Monthly Film Bulletin, no. 369 (Oct. 1964); Jonas Mekas, Village Voice 8, no. 17 (14 Feb. 1963); Time 81, no. 8 (8 Mar. 1963); Ernest Callenbach, Film Quarterly 16, no. 4 (Summer 1963); Brendan Gill, New Yorker 38, no. 52 (16 Feb. 1963); Romano Tozzi, Films in Review 14, no. 3 (Mar. 1963); Moira Walsh, America 108, no. 12 (23 Mar. 1963); Bosley Crowther, New York Times (7 Feb. 1963); Stanley Kauffmann, New Republic 148, no. 10 (9 Mar. 1963); Newsweek 61, no. 7 (18 Feb. 1963); Robin Bean,

Films and Filming 11, no. 2 (Nov. 1964); Hollywood Reporter (4 Oct. 1963).

Jean Collet, Cahiers du Cinéma, no. 135 (Sept. 1962); Jean Collet, Signes du Temps, nos. 8-9 (Aug.-Sept. 1962); Pierre Billard, Cinéma 62, no. 69 (Sept 1962); J.-L. Bory, Arts (27 June 1962); J.-P. Lefebvre and Jacques Leduc, Objectif 64, no. 26 (Feb.-Mar. 1964); Louis Seguin, Positif, no. 49 (Dec. 1962); Georges Sadoul, Les Lettres Françaises (28 June 1962); Georges Charensol, Les Nouvelles Littéraires (28 June 1962); Pierre Marcabru, Combat (27 June 1962) Claude Garson, L'Aurore (June 1962).

Hilde Herrmann, Filmdienst (29 Aug. 1962); Hanspeter Manz, Neue Zürcher Zeitung (30 Sept. 1962); Frieda Grafe, Filmkritik, no. 7 (1965).

*8   LA PEAU DOUCE (1964)

Synopsis

Pierre Lachenay, a middle-aged and comfortable husband and father, is editor of a small literary magazine. On a trip to Lisbon to talk about Balzac, he has a brief but satisfying affair with a stewardess named Nicole. He continues the affair on his return to Paris when he finds the phone number she left him. Unsatisfied with their trysting places, Lachenay arranges a lecture in Rheims and takes Nicole along. The demands of his lecturing and the need for secrecy make their stay less than idyllic. Back in Paris he faces a suspicious and angry wife. They quarrel and he leaves, determined to divorce his wife in favor of his mistress. Nicole is not interested in marriage, however. Despondent, Lachenay tries to phone his wife; when he cannot reach her, he goes to the restaurant he frequents. His jealous wife meets him there, armed with a gun and proof of his infidelity. She kills him.

Credits

Production Company:	Les Films du Carrosse/SEDIF
Production Manager:	Marcel Berbert
Director:	François Truffaut
Assistant Director:	Jean-François Adam
Script:	François Truffaut, Jean-Louis Richard
Dialogue:	François Truffaut
Director of Photography:	Raoul Coutard (1, 66; b/w)
Camera Operator:	Claude Beausoleil
Editor:	Claudine Bouché
Music:	Georges Delerue
Cast:	Jean Desailly (Pierre Lachenay), Francoise Dorléac (Nicole Chomette), Nelly Benedetti

(Franca Lachenay), Daniel Ceccaldi (Clément), Laurence Badie (Ingrid), Jean Lanier (Michel), Paule Emanuele (Odile), Sabine Haudepin (Sabine), Gérard Poirot (Franck), Georges de Givray (Nicole's father), Carnero (Organiser at Lisbon), Dominique Lacarriere (Pierre's secretary), Philippe Dumat (Cinema manager), Maurice Garrel (Bookseller), Pierre Risch (Canon), Charles Lavialle (Night porter at Hotel Michelet), Mme Harlaut (Mme Leloix), Olivia Poli (Mme Bontemps), Catherine Duport (Young girl at Rheims), Thérésa Renouard (Cashier), Brigitte Zhendre-Laforest (Linen delivery woman), Jean-Louis Richard (Man in street).

Filmed in Paris, Orly, Rheims, and Lisbon, 21 Oct.-31 Dec. 1963

Running Time:	115 minutes
First Shown:	Cannes Film Festival, 10 May 1964
Premiere:	Paris, 10 May 1964; G.B., 5 Nov. 1964; U.S., Oct. 1964
G.B. Title:	Silken Skin; U.S. Title: Soft Skin
Prizes:	Danish Oscar ("Bodil, 1964"--Best European Film), Entry in film festivals at Cannes, Montreal, Karlovy-Vary, and San Sebastian.

Reviews

Filmfacts 7, no. 40 (6 Nov. 1964); V. Almendarez, Cinema Texas Program Notes 6, no. 37 (Apr. 1974); Tom Milne, BFI Monthly Film Bulletin, no. 371 (Dec. 1964); Vernon Young, Hudson Review 18, no. 1 (Spring 1965); Andrew Sarris, Village Voice 10, no. 3 (5 Nov. 1964); Gilles Jacob, Sight and Sound 33, no. 4 (Autumn 1964); Richard Roud, Manchester Guardian, no. 36807 (6 Nov. 1964); Robert Hatch, Nation 199, no. 17 (30 Nov. 1964); Penelope Houston, Sight and Sound 33, no. 3 (Summer 1964); Isabel Quigley, Spectator, no. 7115 (6 Nov. 1964); John Coleman, New Statesman 68, no. 1756 (6 Nov. 1964); I. D. MacKillop, Delta, no. 36 (Summer 1965); Gordon Gow, Films and Filming 11, no. 4 (Jan. 1965); Philip Hartung, Commonweal 81, no. 7 (6 Nov. 1964); Time 84, no. 16 (16 Oct. 1964); Newsweek (26 Oct. 1964); Peter Graham, Observer, no. 9020 (17 May 1964); Bosley Crowther, New York Times (13 Oct. 1964); Ian Cameron, Spectator, no. 7091 (22 May 1964); Judith Crist, New York Herald Tribune (13 Oct. 1964); Ann Guerin, Life 57, no. 17

(23 Oct. 1964); Saturday Review (21 Nov. 1964); Wanda Hale,
New York Daily News (13 Oct. 1964); Variety (13 May 1964);
Frederick Wellington, Film Comment 3, no. 3 (Summer 1965);
Cinema (Hollywood) 2, no. 3 (Oct.-Nov. 1964); Kenneth Tynan,
Observer, no. 9045 (8 Nov. 1964); Peter Graham, International
Film Guide 1965; P. Chamberlain, Film Society Review (Sept.
1966); Moviegoer, no. 3 (1966).

P. Sengissen, Jacques Siclier, and Charles Avril, Télérama
(5 June 1964); André Techine, Cahiers du Cinéma 27, no. 157
(July 1964); Georges Sadoul, Les Lettres Françaises, no. 1032
(4-10 June 1964); Claude Brulé, Elle (22 May 1964); Claude
Mauriac, Le Figaro Littéraire 19, no. 943 (14 May 1964);
Robert Benayoun, France Observateur 15, no. 732 (14 May) and
(21 May 1964); Pierre Billard, Cinéma 64, no. 87 (June 1964);
Gerard Legrand, Positif, nos. 64-65 (Dec. 1964); Pierre
Marcabru, Arts (27 May 1964); Roger Regent, La Revue des Deux
Mondes (15 June 1964); J. Lajeunesse, Image et Son, nos. 180-
181 (Jan.-Feb. 1965); Gilbert Salachas, Télé-Ciné, no. 116
(May-June 1964); Christian Rasselet, Objectif 64, nos. 29-30
(Oct.-Nov. 1964); F.-R. Bastide, Les Nouvelles Littéraires
(7 Jan. 1965); Jean de Baroncelli, Le Monde (9 May 1964);
J.-L. Bory, Arts (13 May 1964); Guy Allombert, Le Cinématogra-
phie Française, no. 5 (May 1964); Claude Miller, Télé-Ciné,
no. 117 (Oct.-Nov. 1964); Louis Chauvet, Le Figaro (8 May
1964); Claude Tarare, L'Express (28 May 1964); Freddy Buache,
Tribune de Lausanne (11 Oct. 1964); André Lafargue, Parisien
Libéré (22 May 1964); Robert Chazal, France-Soir (21 May 1964);
Michel Aubriant, Candide (13 May 1964); Henry Rabine, La Croix
(9 May 1964); Samuel Lachize, L'Humanité (8 May 1964); Le
Soleil (18 Apr. 1964); François Maurin, Humanité Dimanche
(10 May 1964).

Brigitte Jeremias, Frankfurter Allgemeine Zeitung (9 May
1964); H.-D. Roos, Süddeutsche Zeitung (19 Jan. 1965); René
Drommert, Die Zeit (27 Jan. 1965); Filmdienst (27 Jan. 1965);
Film (Velber), no. 2 (1965); Enno Patalas, Filmkritik, nos.
2-3 (1965); Klaus Hellwig, Frankfurter Rundschau (3 May 1965),
also in Filmstudio, no. 47 (Oct. 1965).

9   FAHRENHEIT 451 (1966)

Synopsis

In a future society firemen do not extinguish fires; they
burn books. One of them, Montag, lives passively with his
mindless, television-addicted wife, even though he has secretly read David Copperfield. Clarisse, a woman he meets who
looks uncannily like his wife, asks him why he obeys the laws
and burns books. Then a book-burning session during which his
captain gives a rabid speech and an old woman chooses to be incinerated with her library causes him to change. He starts

reading in secret. His wife, recovered from a pill-overdose, denounces him. Forced to burn down his own house, he turns a flamethrower on the captain. He flees with Clarisse into the forest, and there they meet up with a group of "book-people." These mild and amusing subversives each memorizes a book in order to preserve it. They walk around "reciting themselves." In the softly falling snow, Montag decides that he too will memorize a book.

Credits

Production Company:	Anglo Enterprise/Vineyard Films
Producer:	Lewis M. Allen
Associate Producer:	Michael Delamar
Production Manager:	Ian Lewis
Director:	François Truffaut
Assistant Director:	Bryan Coates
Script:	François Truffaut, Jean-Louis Richard. Based on the novel by Ray Bradbury (New York: Ballantine Books, 1953).
Additional Dialogue:	David Rudkin, Helen Scott
Director of Photography:	Nicolas Roeg (1, 66; Technicolor)
Camera Operator:	Alex Thompson
Editor:	Thom Noble
Design and Costume:	Tony Walton
Consultant:	Tony Walton
Art Director:	Syd Cain
Special Effects:	Bowie Films, Rank Films Processing Division. Charles Staffel
Music:	Bernard Herrmann
Associate Costume Designer:	Yvonne Blake
Sound Editor:	Norman Wanstall
Sound Recordists:	Bob McPhee, Gordon McCallum
Casting Director:	Miriam Brickman
Cast:	Oskar Werner (Montag), Julie Christie (Linda/Clarisse), Cyril Cusack (Captain), Anton Diffring (Fabian), Bee Duffell (Book-Woman), Gillian Lewis (Television announcer), Jeremy Spenser (Man with the apple), Ann Bell (Doris), Caroline Hunt (Helen), Anna Palk (Jackie), Roma Milne (Neighbor), Arthur Cox (First male nurse), Eric Mason (Second male nurse), Noel Davis and Donald Pickering (Television announcers), Michael Mundell (Stoneman), Chris Williams (Black), Gillian Aldam (Judoka woman), Edward Kaye (Judoka man),

Mark Lester (First small boy),
Kevin Elder (Second small boy),
Joan Francis (Bar telephonist),
Tom Watson (Sergeant instructor),
Alex Scott (The Life of Henry
Brulard), Dennis Gilmore (Martian
Chronicles), Fred Cox (Pride),
Frank Cox (Prejudice), Michael
Balfour (Machiavelli's The
Prince), Judith Drynan (Plato's
Republic), David Glover (The
Pickwick Papers), Yvonne Blake
(The Jewish Question), John Rae
(The Weir of Hermiston), Earl
Younger (Nephew of the Weir of
Hermiston).

Filmed at Pinewood Studios, London, and on location in Black
Park, Roehampton (near London) and at Chateauneuf-sur-Loire,
France, 10 Jan.–28 Apr. 1966.

Running Time: 112 minutes
First Shown: Venice Film Festival, Sept. 1966
Premiere: Paris, 16 Sept. 1966; G.B., 18 Nov. 1966; U.S., Nov. 1966.

Note

Because he was working in a foreign language with unfamiliar
technicians and surroundings, because it was his first color
film and his only film with unusual special effects, and because of his constant battles with former friend and star Oskar
Werner, this remains Truffaut's most difficult filming experience.

Reviews

Filmfacts 9, no. 23 (1 Jan. 1966); Penelope Houston, Sight
and Sound 35, no. 1 (Winter 1966-67); Andrew Sarris, Village
Voice 12, no. 6 (24 Nov. 1966); David Robinson, Sight and Sound
35, no. 2 (Spring 1966); Mike Grossberg, Cinema Texas Program
Notes 9, no. 2 (9 Oct. 1975); P. J. S., BFI Monthly Film Bulletin,
no. 396 (Jan. 1967); Patrick McFadden, Take One 1, no. 3 (Feb.
1967); John Coleman, New Statesman 72, no. 1863 (25 Nov. 1966);
Louise Corbin, Films in Review 17, no. 10 (Dec. 1966); Philip
French, Observer, no. 9150 (20 Nov. 1966); Wilfred Sheed,
Esquire 67, no. 3 (Mar. 1967); Judith Crist, New York World
Journal Tribune (15 Nov. 1966); Louise Sweeney, Christian
Science Monitor (26 Nov. 1966); Joseph Gelmis, Newsday (15 Nov.
1966); George Perry, Sunday Times (London), no. 7453 (27 Mar.
1966); Arthur Knight, Saturday Review 49, no. 49 (3 Dec. 1966);
Gordon Gow, Films and Filming 13, no. 4 (Jan. 1967); Richard
Corliss, National Review 19, no. 5 (17 Feb. 1967); Time 88,
no. 21 (18 Nov. 1966); Genêt, New Yorker 42, no. 32 (1 Oct.

1966); Dilys Powell, Sunday Times (London), no. 7487 (20 Nov.
1966); Penelope Gilliatt, Observer, no. 9140 (11 Sept. 1966);
Bosley Crowther, New York Times (15 Nov. 1966); Tom Milne,
Sight and Sound 35, no. 4 (Autumn 1966); Richard Schickel,
Life 61, no. 23 (2 Dec. 1966); Theophilus Lewis, America 115,
no. 24 (10 Dec. 1966); Brendan Gill, New Yorker 42, no. 40
(26 Nov. 1966); Vernon Young, Hudson Review 20, no. 2 (Summer
1967); R. Kotlowitz, Harper's 234, no. 1400 (Jan. 1967); Ian
Wright, Manchester Guardian, no. 37380 (13 September 1966);
The Times (London), no. 56791 (11 Nov. 1966); Variety (14
Sept. 1966); Archer Winsten, New York Post (15 Nov. 1966);
Wanda Hale, New York Daily News (15 Nov. 1966); Stephen Manes,
Focus!, no. 1 (Feb. 1967) and no. 2 (Mar. 1967); E. Jahiel,
Film Society Review (Feb. 1968); Hollywood Reporter (14 Nov.
1966).

Sylvain Godet, Cahiers du Cinéma, no. 183 (Oct. 1966);
Michel Mohrt, Les Nouvelles Littéraires 45, no. 2054 (12 Jan.
1967); Michel Cournot, Le Nouvel Observateur, no. 97 (21-27
Sept. 1966); Jean Delmas, Jeune Cinéma, no. 17 (Sept.-Oct.
1966); Claude Beylie, Midi Minuit Fantastique, nos. 15-16
(Dec. 1966); Pierre Billard, L'Express, no. 796 (19-25 Sept.
1966); Jean de Baroncelli, Le Monde, no. 6736 (9 Sept. 1966);
René Quinson, Combat (28 May 1966) and Henry Chapier (8 Sept.
1966); Michel Flacon, Cinéma 66, no. 110 (Nov. 1966); Roger
Regent, La Revue des Deux Mondes (1 Nov. 1966); Georges Sadoul,
Les Lettres Françaises, no. 1148 (15-21 and 22-28 Sept. 1966);
Claude Mauriac, Le Figaro Littéraire, no. 1066 (22 Sept. 1966);
Revue Generale Belge 103, no. 6 (June 1967).

Urs Jenny, Süddeutsche Zeitung (8 Sept. 1966); Karl Korn,
Frankfurter Allgemeine Zeitung (9 Sept. 1966); Klaus Hellwig,
Frankfurter Rundschau (10 Sept. 1966); Peter W. Jansen,
Filmkritik, no. 10 (1966); Elke Kummer, Film (Velber), no. 10,
(1966); Eckhart Schmidt, Süddeutsche Zeitung (28 Dec. 1966);
Erwin Schaar, Jugend Film Fernsehen, no. 1 (1967); U. Seelmann-
Eggebert, Filmdienst (4 Jan. 1967); Enno Patalas, Filmkritik,
nos. 2, 3, 5 (1967); Volker Baer, Der Tagesspiegel (16 Feb.
1967); Wolf Dresp, Frankfurter Rundschau (2 June 1967);
Brigitte Jeremias, Frankfurter Allgemeine Zeitung (2 June
1967).

10   LA MARIÉE ÉTAIT EN NOIR (1967)

Synopsis

Having failed at suicide, Julie Kohler goes to the ultra-
modern house of M. Bliss for a party. She lures him to the
balcony and causes him to plunge over it to his death. She
then flies to meet M. Coral, an aging and lonely concertgoer.
She stalks him at a concert. At his small apartment, she be-
witches him, poisons him, and watches coldly as he dies. She

then begins playing with the child of a politician, Morane, and poses as its nurse. Morane tells her of his election plans as she plots his murder. He is locked in a closet, where Julie tells him of the accidental murder of her husband on their wedding night by the politician and his friends. Morane is suffocated. When the police arrest a Miss Becker for his death, Julie phones and exonerates her. She then goes to the junk car lot of Delvaux and is about to shoot him when he is arrested. She becomes an artist's model for Fergus, a sad-faced painter who falls in love with her. He paints her nude portrait and hangs it over his bed. Posing as Diana the hunt-ress, Julie looses an arrow at Fergus. He ducks and she screams to cover the deed. At a party a friend of Bliss's recognizes her, but before Fergus can be warned, he is dead-- shot with an arrow. At the funeral Julie is recognized and arrested. She is sent to the same prison occupied by Delvaux, who actually pulled the trigger when her husband died. She goes after him with a knife.

Credits

Production Company:	Les Films du Carrosse/Artistes Associés (Paris)/Dino De Laurentiis Cinematografica (Rome)
Producer:	Marcel Berbert
Production Manager:	Georges Charlot
Director:	François Truffaut
Assistant Director:	Jean Chayrou, Roland Thenot
Script:	François Truffaut, Jean-Louis Richard. Based on the novel The Bride Wore Black by William Irish [Cornell Woolrich--also known as George Hopley] (New York: Simon & Schuster, 1940) and (Paris: Presses de la cité).
Director of Photography:	Raoul Coutard (Eastmancolor; 1, 66)
Camera Operator:	Georges Liron
Editor:	Claudine Bouché
Art Director:	Pierre Guffroy
Music:	Bernard Herrmann
Musical Director:	André Girard
Sound:	René Levert
Cast:	Jeanne Moreau (Julie Kohler), Claude Rich (Bliss), Jean-Claude Brialy (Corey), Michel Bouquet (Coral), Michel Lonsdale (René Morane), Charles Denner (Fergus), Daniel Boulanger (Delvaux), Serge Rousseau (David), Alexandra Stewart (Mlle Becker), Christophe Bruno (Cookie Morane), Jacques Robiolles (Charlie), Luce Fabiole

(Julie's mother), Sylvie Delannoy
(Mme Morane), Jacqueline Raillard
(Maid), Van Doude (Inspector
Fabri), Paul Pavel (Mechanic),
Gilles Quéant (Examining magis-
trate), Maurice Garrel (Plantiff),
Frédérique and Renaud Fontanarosa
(Musicians), Elisabeth Rey (Julie
as a child), Jean-Pierre Dey
(David as a child), Dominique
Robier (Sabine), Michèle Viborel
(Gilberte, Bliss's fiancée),
Michèle Montfort (Model), Daniel
Pommereulle (Fergus' friend).

Filmed in and around Paris and in Versailles, Chevilly-Larue,
Senlis, and Cannes, 16 May–24 July 1967.

Running Time:	107 minutes
Premiere:	Paris, 17 Apr. 1968; G.B., 1 Aug. 1968; U.S., June 1968
G.B./U.S. Title:	The Bride Wore Black
Prize:	Edgar Allan Poe Award (U.S.).

Reviews

Filmfacts 11, no. 13 (1 Aug. 1968); Andrew Sarris, Village
Voice 13, no. 45 (22 Aug. 1968); Eric Rhode, Listener 80, no.
2054 (8 Aug. 1968); Maurice Rapf, Life 65, no. 6 (9 Aug. 1968);
Jan Dawson, BFI Monthly Film Bulletin, no. 416 (Sept. 1968);
Penelope Houston, Sight and Sound 37, no. 4 (Autumn 1968);
Penelope Houston, Spectator 221, no. 7311 (9 Aug. 1968);
Penelope Gilliatt, New Yorker 44, no. 20 (6 July 1968); Renata
Adler, New York Times (26 June 1968); Allen Eyles, Films and
Filming 15, no. 1 (Oct. 1968); Dilys Powell, Sunday Times
(London) (4 Aug. 1968); W. Huyck, Cinema (Hollywood) 4, no. 1
(Spring 1968); Judith Shatnoff, Film Quarterly 22, no. 1 (Fall
1968); Tom Milne, Observer, no. 9238 (4 Aug. 1968); Peter Cowie,
International Film Guide 1969; Time 92, no. 1 (5 July 1968);
Marion Armstrong, Christian Century 85, no. 43 (23 Oct. 1968);
Jay Cocks, Take One 1, no. 11 (May–June 1968); John Coleman,
New Statesman 16, no. 1951 (2 Aug. 1968); Robert Hatch, Nation
207, no. 2 (22 July 1968); A. B. Clark, Films in Review 19, no.
7 (Aug.-Sept. 1968); Joseph Morgenstern, Newsweek 72, no. 1
(1 July 1968); Stanley Kauffmann, New Republic 159, no. 2 (13
July 1968); Vernon Young, Hudson Review 21, no. 3 (Autumn 1968);
Philip Hartung, Commonweal 88, no. 18 (9 Aug. 1968); Arthur
Knight, Saturday Review 51, no. 25 (22 June 1968); Leo
Seligsohn, Newsday (26 June 1968); Kathleen Carroll and Archer
Winsten, New York Daily News (26 July 1968).

Roger Regent, La Revue des Deux Mondes, no. 9 (1 May 1968);
Claude Beylie, Cinéma 68, no. 129 (Oct. 1968); Pierre Billard,
L'Express, no. 878 (15–21 Apr. 1968); Image et Son, no. 203

(Mar. 1967) and J.-L. Passek, no. 221 (Nov. 1968); Jean-Louis
Bory, Le Nouvel Observateur (17 Apr. 1968); Paul-Louis Thirard,
Positif, no. 97 (Summer 1968); Jean de Baroncelli, Le Monde,
no. 7238 (20 Apr. 1968), trans. in Atlas (June 1968); Tristan
Renaud, Les Lettres Françaises, no. 1231 (24 Apr. 1968); René
Quinson, Combat (13-14 Apr. 1968) and Henry Chapier (18 Apr.
1968); Celia Bertin, La Revue de Paris 75, ncs. 6-7 (June-
July 1968); M. D., Cahiers du Cinéma, no. 2C2 (June-July 1968);
Gilbert Salachas, Télé-Ciné, no. 141 (Apr. 1968) and S. Pesci-
Beaudoin, no. 215 (Feb. 1977).

Leo Schonecker, Filmdienst (2 Apr. 1968); J. von
Mengershausen, Süddeutsche Zeitung (29 Apr. 1968); Werner
Kliess, Film (Velber), no. 5 (1968); P. M. Ladiges, Filmkritik,
no. 5 (1968); Enno Patalas, Die Zeit (10 May 1968); Helmuth de
Haas, Die Welt (11 May 1968); Karena Niehoff, Der Tagesspiegel
(12 May 1968); Wolfgang Vogel, Frankfurter Rundschau (25 May
1968); Brigitte Jeremias, Frankfurter Allgemeine Zeitung (27
May 1968); Ulrich Kurowski, Jugend Film Fernsehen, no. 4 (Aug.
1968).

11   BAISERS VOLÉS (1968)

Synopsis

   Upon being released from prison and military life, Antoine
Doinel rushes to a brothel and then to the house of an old
girlfriend, Christine Darbon. Her parents feed him in her absence and get him a job as night clerk in a hotel. He loses
this job through the wiles of an old detective, who then gets
him hired by his agency. Antoine bungles several cases before
being assigned to find out why the employees of a shoestore
hate their employer, M. Tabard. Antoine becomes infatuated
with Tabard's beautiful wife, but a slip of the tongue sends
him fleeing from her presence. She comes to his apartment for
a "one-time-only" affair; as a result Antoine gets fired. He
then becomes a television repairman. When Christine's parents
leave for a weekend, she dismantles her television and calls
Antoine. He ends up spending the night (while his meter ticks).
The next day they talk of the future. In the park a mystery
man who has been trailing Christine for days abruptly declares
his love. Antoine and Christine walk off together.

Credits

Production Company:	Les Films du Carrosse/Les Productions Artistes Associés
Producer:	Marcel Berbert
Production Manager:	Claude Miller
Director:	François Truffaut
Assistant Directors:	Jean-José Richer, Alain Deschamps
Script:	François Truffaut, Claude de Givray,

	Bernard Revon
Director of Photography:	Denys Clerval (Eastmancolor, 1, 66)
Camera Operator:	Jean Chiabaut
Editor:	Agnès Guillemot
Art Director:	Claude Pignot
Music:	Antoine Duhamel
Song: "Que reste-t-il nos amours?"	Charles Trenet; sung by Charles Trenet
Sound:	René Levert
Cast:	Jean-Pierre Léaud (Antoine Doinel), Delphine Seyrig (Fabienne Tabard), Claude Jade (Christine Darbon), Michel Lonsdale (M. Tabard), Harry Max (M. Henri), André Falcon (M. Vidal), Daniel Ceccaldi (M. Darbon), Claire Duhamel (Mme Darbon), Paul Pavel (M. Julien), Serge Rousseau (Stranger), Catherine Lutz (Mme Catherine), Jacques Delord (Conjuror), Simono (M. Albani), Roger Trapp (Hotel manager), Jacques Rispal (M. Colin), Martine Brochard (Mme Colin), Robert Cambourakis (Mme Colin's lover), Marie-France Pisier (Colette Tazzi), Jean-François Adam (Albert Tazzi), Christine Pellé (Secretary at Blady Agency), Jacques Robiolles (Writer), François Darbon (Adjutant), Marcel Mercier and Joseph Merieau (Men at garage).

Filmed in and around Paris, 5 Feb.–28 Mar. 1968

Running Time:	90 minutes
First Shown:	Avignon Film Festival, 14 Aug. 1968
Premiere:	Paris, 6 Sept. 1968; G.B., 27 Mar. 1969, U.S., Feb. 1969
G.B./U.S. Title:	Stolen Kisses
Prizes:	Grand prix du cinéma français, Prix Melies, Prix Delluc (France, 1969), Prix Femina (Belgium, 1969), Nominated for an Oscar for Best Foreign Film (Hollywood).

Note

The film is dedicated to Henri Langlois, head of the Paris cinematheque. It was in production during the turmoil that arose over the de Gaulle government's dismissal of Langlois.

Truffaut took an active part in getting Langlois reinstated.

Reviews

Filmfacts 12, no. 3 (1969); Andrew Sarris, Village Voice 4, no. 20 (27 Feb. 1969); Gavin Millar, Sight and Sound 38, no. 3 (Summer 1969); Gary Carey, Film Quarterly 22, no. 4 (Summer 1969); Gilles Jacob, Atlas, no. 17 (Feb. 1969)--trans. from Les Nouvelles Littéraires; Gordon Gow, Films and Filming 15, no. 9 (June 1969); Vincent Canby, New York Times (4 and 16 Mar. 1969); Jan Dawson, BFI Monthly Film Bulletin, no. 424 (May 1969); Joseph Morgenstern, Newsweek 73, no. 10 (10 Mar. 1969); Richard Schickel, Life 66, no. 9 (7 Mar. 1969); Louise Corbin, Films in Review 20, no. 2 (Feb. 1969); Peter Cowie, International Film Guide 1970; Eric Rhode, Listener 81, no. 2088 (3 Apr. 1969); Time 93, no. 12 (21 Mar. 1969); Penelope Houston, Spectator 222, no. 7344 (28 Mar. 1969); Pauline Kael, New Yorker 45, no. 3 (8 Mar. 1969); Stanley Kauffmann, New Republic 160, no. 8 (22 Feb. 1969); Judith Crist, New York (3 Feb. 1969); Hollis Alpert, Saturday Review 52, no. 6 (8 Feb. 1969); Robert Hatch, Nation 208, no. 4 (27 Jan. 1969); Philip Hartung, Commonweal 90, no. 3 (4 Apr. 1969); Louise Sweeney, Christian Science Monitor (24 Mar. 1969); Kenneth Allsop, Observer, no. 9272 (30 Mar. 1969); Michael Pepiatt, Sunday Times (London), no. 7581 (15 Sept. 1968); John Coleman, New Statesman 77, no. 1985 (28 Mar. 1969); Archer Winsten, New York Post (4 Mar. 1969); Wanda Hale, New York Daily News (4 Mar. 1969); Variety (18 Sept. 1968); Rex Reed, Holiday (May 1969); Robert Kotlowitz, Harper's 238, no. 1427 (Apr. 1969); Michael Korda, Glamour (Apr. 1969); Dan Wakefield, Atlantic Monthly 224, no. 1 (July 1969); Hollywood Reporter (4 Feb. 1969).

Jean-Louis Comolli, Cahiers du Cinéma, no. 205 (Oct. 1968); Gérard Langlois, Les Lettres Françaises, no. 1248 (11-17 Sept. 1968); Michel Perez, Positif, no. 99 (Feb. 1968); Jean-Louis Bory, Le Nouvel Observateur, no. 201 (16-22 Sept. 1968); André Cornand, Image et Son, no. 221 (Nov. 1968); J.-A. Gili, Cinéma 68, no. 130 (Nov. 1968); Claude Mauriac, Le Figaro Littéraire (23 Sept. 1968); Pierre Billard, L'Express, no. 896 (9-15 Sept. 1968); Célia Bertin, La Revue de Paris 75, no. 11 (Nov. 1968); René Quinson, Combat (2-3 Mar. 1968); Luce Sand, Jeune Cinéma no. 33 (Oct. 1968); Jean de Baroncelli, Le Monde, no. 7362 (14 Sept. 1968); Roger Regent, La Revue des Deux Mondes (1 Oct. 1968); Michel Capdenac, Les Lettres Françaises no. 1245 (21-27 Aug. 1968).

Klaus Geitel, Die Welt (21 Sept. 1968); Klaus Hellwig, Frankfurter Rundschau (5 Oct. 1968), also in Filmkritik, no. 11 (1968); Leo Schonecker, Filmdienst (22 Apr. 1969); Karena Niehoff, Der Tagesspiegel (26 Apr. 1969); Enno Patalas, Filmkritik no. 5 (1969); Sebastian Franz, Film (Velber) no. 5 (1969); J. von Mengershausen, Süddeutsche Zeitung (23 May 1969);

Brigitte Jeremias, <u>Frankfurter Allgemeine Zeitung</u> (29 Aug. 1969); Erwin Schaar, <u>Jugend Film Fernsehen</u>, nos. 4-5 (1969); Wolfgang Ruf, <u>Süddeutsche Zeitung</u> (24 May 1974).

12   LA SIRÈNE DU MISSISSIPI (1969)

Synopsis

Having advertised for a wife and corresponded with a woman named Julie Roussel, Louis Mahé, wealthy owner of a cigarette factory, waits for the woman to disembark from the steamship "Mississipi." The woman who comes to the island of Reunion to meet him bears no resemblance to the pictures Mahé has from her. The striking blonde claims that she used a friend's photo to make sure Louis loved her for more than her beauty; Louis confesses a similar deception: he is the owner, not the fore-man, of the factory. Louis falls in love, and they are married. Louis starts to notice contradictions between her behavior and that of the woman to whom he wrote. His foreman sees Julie handled roughly by a strange man. Shortly after Louis has set up a joint bank account, a worried letter arrives from Julie's sister. That evening Julie disappears with all the money. Louis and Julie's sister hire a detective, Comolli, to find this imposter, and Louis heads for France. Sickness forces him to convalesce in Nice, where he discovers the imposter on a television program. Her name is really Marion, and she is now an entertainer. Louis goes to her room to kill her, but can't go through with it. She tells her life story, and Louis forgives her, believing her declaration of love. They enjoy life together until Louis meets Comolli, still tracking his prey. When not even a bribe will stop him, Louis kills the detective. The couple flees to Lyon; when their money begins to run out, Louis sells the cigarette factory. With the police closing in on them, they flee to Switzerland, leaving most of the money behind. Without money Marion wishes to flee, but is prevented by Louis. She slowly poisons Louis, who realizes it, yet still loves her. Marion begs for forgiveness, and they walk away hand-in-hand through the snow.

Credits

Production Company:	Les Films du Carrosse/Les Productions Artistes Associés (Paris)/ Produzioni Associate Delphos (Rome)
Producer:	Marcel Berbert
Production Manager:	Claude Miller
Director:	François Truffaut
Assistant Director:	Jean-José Richer
Script:	François Truffaut. Based on the novel <u>Waltz into Darkness</u> by William Irish [Cornell Woolrich

	--also known as George Hopley] (New York: J. B. Lippincott, 1947).
Director of Photography:	Denys Clerval (Dyaliscope; Eastmancolor)
Camera Operator:	Jean Chiabaut
Editor:	Agnes Guillemot
Art Director:	Claude Pignot
Music:	Antoine Duhamel
Sound:	René Levert
Cast:	Jean-Paul Belmondo (Louis Mahé), Catherine Deneuve (Julie Roussel/ Marion), Michel Bouquet (Comolli), Nelly Borgeaud (Berthe Roussel and, in the photo, Julie Roussel), Marcel Berbert (Jardine), Roland Thenot (Richard), Martine Ferrière (Landlady), Yves Drouhet.

Filmed in Reunion, Antibes, Aix-en-Provence, Lyon, and near Grenoble, 2 Dec. 1968-Feb. 1969.

Running Time:	123 minutes
Premiere:	Paris, 18 June 1969; G. B., 6 Sept. 1970; U.S., Apr. 1970
G.B./U.S. Title:	Mississippi Mermaid

Notes

By accident or by design, the French title has only one "p" in Mississipi. Truffaut cut the film to be released with a length of 123 minutes. United Artists cut the film to 109 minutes.

This film marks a return to cinemascope ("Dyaliscope"), for the first time since Antoine et Colette (1962), to allow space for both Belmondo and Deneuve to be on screen at once.

Reviews

Derek Elley, Films and Filming 20, no. 9 (June 1974); Vincent Canby, New York Times (11 and 26 Apr. 1970); Richard Combs, BFI Monthly Film Bulletin, no. 485 (June 1974); Village Voice, Letters to the editor (7 and 21 May 1970); P. D. Zimmerman, Newsweek 75, no. 18 (4 May 1970); Jan Dawson, New Statesman 87, no. 2249 (26 Apr. 1974); Richard Schickel, Life 68, no. 17 (8 May 1970); Penelope Gilliatt, New Yorker 46, no. 9 (18 Apr. 1970); Stanley Kauffmann, New Republic 162, no. 18 (2 May 1970); Derek Malcolm, Manchester Guardian (25 Apr. 1974); Mari Kuttna, Film 2, no. 2 (May 1973); Time 95, no. 17 (27 Apr. 1970); Charles Samuels, American Scholar 39, no. 4 (Autumn 1970); Dilys Powell, Sunday Times (London), no. 7872 (28 Apr. 1974); Mosk, Variety (2 July 1969); Gavin Millar, Listener 95, no. 2440 (15 Jan. 1976); Hollis Alpert, Saturday Review 53, no. 17 (25 Apr. 1970); Robert Hatch, Nation 210, no. 16 (27 Apr. 1970); Eunice Sinkler, Films in Review 21, no. 5 (May 1970); Judith Crist, New York (27 Apr. 1970); Louise Sweeney, Christian Science Monitor (27 Apr. 1970); Archer Winsten, New York Post (11 Apr. 1970); Colin Westerbeck, Manhattan Tribune (18 Apr. 1970); Hollywood Reporter (3 Aug. 1970).

Claude Veillot, L'Express, no. 937 (23–29 June 1969); Roger Regent, La Revue des Deux Mondes (1 Aug. 1969); Michel Capdenac, Les Lettres Françaises (25 June 1969); Guy Braucourt, Cinéma 69, no. 139 (Sept.–Oct. 1969); J.-L. Bory, Le Nouvel Observateur (30 June 1969); Michel Sineux, Positif, no. 109 (Oct. 1969); Jean de Baroncelli, Le Monde, no. 7600 (21 June 1969).

P. H. Schroder, Die Welt (12 July 1969); Klaus Hellwig, Frankfurter Rundschau (9 Aug. 1969) and in Film (Velber), no. 9 (1969); J. von Mengershausen, Süddeutsche Zeitung (22 Dec. 1969); Volker Baier, Der Tagesspiegel (23 Dec. 1969); Wolf Donner, Die Zeit (16 Jan. 1970); Paula Linhart, Filmdienst (27 Jan. 1970); Wim Wenders, Enno Patalas, Gerhard Theuring, Filmkritik, no. 2 (1970); H.-K. Jungheinrich, Frankfurter Rundschau (5 May 1970); Wolfgang Ruf, Süddeutsche Zeitung (27 Apr. 1974).

13   L'ENFANT SAUVAGE (1969)

Synopsis

In the forests of Aveyron in the early nineteenth century, a wild boy runs about on all fours. He is discovered by a mushroom picker and is quickly captured, imprisoned, and put on display. He comes to the attention of Dr. Jean Itard, who arranges to examine him. Itard decides to bring the boy to his own home to educate and observe him. He trains the boy in some basic activities of civilized society: walking, eating with utensils, playing. They walk together, but Itard remains scientifically detached throughout. Only the governess shows any emotion. Because he responds to "O" sounds, the boy is named Victor. He responds to increasingly more difficult tasks involving music, the alphabet, symbols, and words, but remains happiest outdoors, even bouncing up and down joyfully in the rain. After Itard subjects him to a test to teach him about injustice, Victor runs away. But he returns to resume his lessons.

Credits

Production Company:	Les Films du Carrosse/Les Productions Artistes Associés
Producer:	Marcel Berbert

Production Manager:	Claude Miller
Director:	François Truffaut
Assistant Director:	Suzanne Schiffman
Script:	François Truffaut, Jean Gruault. Based on <u>Mémoire et rapport sur Victor de l'Aveyron</u> by Jean Itard (1806).
Director of Photography:	Nestor Almendros (1, 66; b/w)
Camera Operator:	Philippe Théaudière
Editor:	Agnes Guillemot
Art Director:	Jean Mandaroux
Music:	Antonio Vivaldi; played by Michel Sanvoisin (recorder) and André Saint-Clivier (mandolin)
Musical Adviser:	Antoine Duhamel
Costumes:	Gitt Magrini
Sound:	René Levert
Cast:	Jean-Pierre Cargol (Victor de l'Aveyron), François Truffaut (Dr. Jean Itard), Françoise Seignier (Mme Guérin), Jean Dasté (Professor Philippe Pinel), Pierre Fabre (Orderly at institute), Paul Villé (Rémy), Claude Miller (M. Lémeri), Annie Miller (Mme Lémeri), René Levert (Gendarme), Jean Mandaroux (Doctor attending Itard), Nathan Miller (Lémeri baby), Mathieu Schiffman (Mathieu), Jean Gruault (Visitor at institute), Robert Cambourakis, Gitt Magrini, and Jean-François Stevenin (Peasants), Laura Truffaut, Eva Truffaut, Mathieu Schiffman, Guillaume Schiffman, Frédérique Dolbert, Eric Dolbert, Tounet Cargol, Dominique Levert, and Mlle Théaudière (Children at farm).

Filmed at Aubiat in the Auvergne and in Paris, 7 July–1 Sept. 1969

Running Time:	85 minutes
Premiere:	Paris, 25 Feb. 1970; G.B., 18 Nov. 1970 (London Film Festival) and 18 Dec. 1970; U.S., 10 Sept. 1970 (New York Film Festival).
G.B./U.S. Title:	<u>The Wild Child</u>
Prizes:	<u>Palme d'or</u> (Festival de Valladolid), Christopher Award, Prix Femina (Belgium)

The Films: Synopses, Credits, Notes, and Reviews

Reviews

David Wilson, Sight and Sound 40, no. 1 (Winter 1970-71); Richard Corliss, National Review 22, no. 5 (15 Dec. 1970); Stanley Kauffmann, New Republic 163, no. 14 (3 Oct. 1970); Colin Westerbeck, Commonweal 93, no. 1 (2 Oct. 1970); Andrew Sarris, Village Voice 15, no. 42 (15 Oct. 1970); Jan Dawson, BFI Monthly Film Bulletin, no. 444 (Jan. 1971); Harriet Polt, Film Quarterly 24, no. 3 (Spring 1971); Richard Schickel, Life 69, no. 16 (16 Oct. 1970); Tom Milne, Observer (20 Dec. 1970); Louise Sweeney, Christian Science Monitor (11 Sept. 1970); Margaret Tarratt, Films and Filming 17, no. 5 (Feb. 1971); David Denby, Atlantic Monthly 226, no. 6 (Dec. 1970); Vincent Canby, New York Times (11 and 13 Sept. 1970); Robert Hatch, Nation 211, no. 9 (28 Sept 1970); John Coleman, New Statesman 80, no. 2075 (25 Dec. 1970); Derek Malcolm, Manchester Guardian (17 Dec. 1970); Judith Crist, New York 3, no. 39 (28 Sept. 1970); James Morton, Contemporary Review, no. 218 (May 1971); Christopher Hudson, Spectator 225, no. 7435 (26 Dec. 1970); Roland Gelatt, Saturday Review (3 Oct. 1970); Ruth Goldstein, Film News 34, no. 1 (1977); Nat Hentoff, Evergreen Review 15, no. 87 (Feb. 1971); Gavin Millar, Listener 84, no. 2178 (24 Dec. 1970); Hubbell Robinson, Films in Review 21, no. 9 (Nov. 1970); Mosk, Variety (18 Feb. 1970); Kathleen Carroll and Archer Winsten, New York Daily News (11 Sept. 1970); K. Saviola, Women's Wear Daily (11 Sept. 1970); Moira Walsh, America 123, no. 9 (3 Oct. 1970); Stefan Kanfer, Time 96, no. 12 (21 Sept. 1970); Stanley Kauffmann, Film Comment 7, no. 4 (Winter 1971); Felix Bucher, International Film Guide 1971; R. M. Goldstein, Film News, no. 43 (Jan.-Feb. 1977); Hollywood Reporter (11 Sept. 1970).

Michel Capdenac, Les Lettres Françaises, no. 1323 (25 Feb. 1970); Jean Collet, Télérama, no. 1051 (7 Mar. 1970); Mireille Amiel, Cinéma 70, no. 146 (May 1970) and Claude Beylie, no. 147 (June 1970); Georges Charensol, Les Nouvelles Littéraires (5 Mar. 1970); J. Lajeunesse, Image et Son, no. 238 (Apr. 1970); Claude Mauriac, Le Figaro Littéraire, no. 1240 (23 Feb. 1970); Luce Sand, Jeune Cinéma, no. 46 (Apr. 1970); Yvonne Baby, Le Monde (27 Feb. 1970); Richard Gay, Cinéma Quebec 1, no. 4 (Oct. 1971); Claude Viellot, L'Express, no. 973 (2 Mar. 1970); Henry Chapier, Combat (28 Jan. 1970); Judith Weiner, France-Soir (4 Mar. 1970); Claude Garson, L'Aurore (27 Feb. 1970); D. A., Cahiers du Cinéma, no. 219 (Apr. 1970); Michel Aubriant, Le Journal du Dimanche (1 Mar. 1970); Pierre Dumayet, Pariscop (9 Mar. 1970).

Günter Metken, Frankfurter Allgemeine Zeitung, (6 Mar. 1970), also in Neue Zürcher Zeitung (4 Apr. 1970); Wim Wenders, Filmkritik, no. 7 (1970); Wolf Lepenies, Frankfurter Allgemeine Zeitung (8 July 1970); Jürgen Ebert, Filmkritik, no. 10 (1970); Martin Schlappner, Neue Zürcher Zeitung (10 Oct. 1970); Ulrich

Kurowski, Kirche und Film, no. 3 (1971), also in Filmkritik, no. 5 (1971); Franz Ulrich, Filmdienst (23 Mar. 1971); A. F. Schirmer, Der Tagesspiegel (8 Apr. 1971); Rainer Fabian, Die Welt (11 May 1971); Frieda Grafe, Süddeutsche Zeitung (24 May 1971); H.-K. Jungheinrich, Frankfurter Rundschau (24 May 1971); Wolf Donner, Die Zeit (28 May 1971); Frank Scurla, Jugend Film Fernsehen, no. 4 (Dec. 1971).

14 DOMICILE CONJUGAL (1970)

Synopsis

   Antoine Doinel and his wife Christine live upstairs in an old building full of neighborly eccentrics--a recluse, a mystery man dubbed "the Strangler," a flirtatious waitress, and an opera singer constantly annoyed by his tardy wife. Antoine tends a flower stand in the building's courtyard, where he experiments dyeing carnations red. Christine gives violin lessons; she is soon pregnant. Through a mix-up Antoine lands a new job operating toy boats in a miniature harbor for an American hydraulics firm. At work he gets news of the birth of his first son, whom he names Alphonse rather than his wife's choice, Ghislain. Some marital disharmony results. Later at work he meets Kyoko, a beautiful Japanese woman, who easily seduces him. Christine soon discovers the liaison through love notes in a bouquet of flowers. The Doinels quarrel and separate, disrupting Antoine's writing. He becomes increasingly uncomfortable with Kyoko, especially at meals, and is reattracted to his wife and their conversations together. When Antoine interrupts their restaurant meal with three phone calls to Christine, Kyoto drops him. One year later, the young Doinels are back together, behaving just like the opera singer and his tardy wife.

Credits

Production Company:	Les Films du Carrosse/Valoria Films (Paris)/Fida Cinematografica (Rome)
Producer:	Marcel Berbert
Production Manager:	Claude Miller
Director:	François Truffaut
Assistant Director:	Suzanne Schiffman
Script:	François Truffaut, Claude de Givray, Bernard Revon
Director of Photography:	Nestor Almendros (Eastmancolor; 1, 66)
Camera Operator:	Emmanuel Machuel
Editor:	Agnes Guillemot
Art Director:	Jean Mandaroux
Music:	Antoine Duhamel
Costumes:	Françoise Tournafond

The Films: Synopses, Credits, Notes, and Reviews

Sound:	René Levert
Cast:	Jean-Pierre Léaud (Antoine Doinel), Claude Jade (Christine Doinel), Hiroko Berghauer (Kyoko), Daniel Ceccaldi (Lucien Darbon), Claire Duhamel (Mme Darbon), Barbara Laage (Monique), Jacques Jouanneau (Cesarin), Daniel Boulanger (Tenor), Sylvana Blasi (Tenor's wife), Claude Vega (Strangler), Pierre Fabre (Office Romeo), Billy Kearns (M. Max, the boss), Daniele Gerard (Waitress), Jacques Robiolles (Sponger), Yvon Lec (Traffic warden), Pierre Maguelon (Bistro customer), Marie Irakane (Concierge), Ernest Menzer (Little man), Jacques Rispal (Old solitary), Guy Pierrault (SOS employee), Marcel Mercier and Joseph Merieau (People in courtyard), Christian de Tiliere (Senator), Nicole Félix, Jerôme Richard, and Marcel Berbert (Employees in American company), Marianne Piketti (Violin pupil), Annick Asty (Violin pupil's mother), Ada Lonati (Mme Claude), Nobuko Mati (Kyoko's friend), Iska Khan (Kyoko's father), Ryu Nakamura (Japanese secretary), Jacques Cottin (M. Hulot), Marie Dedieu (Marie).

Filmed in and around Paris, 22 Jan.-18 Mar. 1970.

Running Time:	100 minutes
Premiere:	Paris, 1 Sept. 1970; G.B., 8 July 1971; U.S., Jan 1971.
G.B./U.S. Title:	Bed and Board

Reviews

Filmfacts 14, no. 2 (1971); Andrew Sarris, Village Voice 16, no. 4 (28 Jan. 1971); Bill Nichols, Commonweal 94, no. 3 (26 Mar. 1971); Jan Dawson, Sight and Sound 40, no. 4 (Autumn 1971); Jan Dawson, BFI Monthly Film Bulletin, no. 444 (Jan. 1971); Margaret Tarratt, Films and Filming 17, no. 5 (Feb. 1971) and Gordon Gow, 17, no. 12 (Sept. 1971); David Brudnoy, National Review 23, no. 23 (15 June 1971); Vincent Canby, New York Times (22 and 24 Jan. 1971); Gavin Millar, Listener 86, no. 2208 (22 July 1971); Moira Walsh, America 124, no. 5 (6 Feb. 1971); John Russell Taylor, Times (London), no. 58220 (9 July 1971); David Robinson, Financial Times no. 25500 (9 July

1971); Richard Schickel, Life (22 Jan. 1971); Judith Crist,
New York (25 Jan. 1971); P. D. Zimmerman, Newsweek (25 Jan.
1971); George Melly, Observer, no. 9390 (11 July 1971); Dilys
Powell, Sunday Times (London), no. 7727 (11 July 1971);
Christopher Hudson, Spectator 227, no. 7464 (17 July 1971);
Pauline Kael, New Yorker 46, no. 51 (6 Feb. 1971); John Coleman,
New Statesman 82, no. 2104 (16 July 1971); Henry Hart, Films in
Review 22, no. 3 (Mar. 1971); Jacob Brackman, Esquire (June
1971); Stanley Kauffmann, New Republic 164, no. 7 (13 Feb.
1971); Robert Hatch, Nation 212, no. 9 (March 1971); Hollis
Alpert, Saturday Review 54, no. 4 (23 Jan. 1971); Gail Rock,
Women's Wear Daily (22 Jan. 1971); Kathleen Carroll, New York
Daily News (22 Jan. 1971); Archer Winsten, New York Post (22
Jan. 1971); Mosk, Variety (26 Sept. 1970); William Pechter,
Commentary 51, no. 6 (June 1971); Jay Cocks, Time 97, no. 6
(8 Feb. 1971); Ann Birstein, Vogue (15 Mar. 1971); Richard
Roud, Manchester Guardian (5 Jan. 1971); Marion Armstrong,
Christian Century 88, no. 26 (30 June 1971); Michael McNay,
Manchester Guardian (8 July 1971); Geoffrey Minish, Take One
2, no. 8 (9 Nov. 1970); Hollywood Reporter (20 Jan. 1971).

Mireille Amiel and Jean Gili, Cinéma 70, no. 150 (Nov. 1970);
Frederick Vitoux, Positif, no. 121 (Nov. 1970); Pierre Billard,
L'Express, no. 1000 (7 Sept. 1970); Alexandre Astruc, Paris-
Match, no. 1115 (19 Sept. 1970); Michel Mardoré, Le Nouvel
Observateur, no. 304 (7 Sept. 1970); Marcel Martin, Les Lettres
Françaises (16 Sept. 1970); René Prédal, Jeune Cinéma, no. 49
(Sept.-Oct. 1970); André Cornand, Image et Son, no. 243 (Nov.
1970); Jean de Baroncelli, Le Monde, no. 7982 (12 Sept. 1970),
reprinted in Atlas (July 1968); André Leroux, Cinéma Ouebec 1,
no. 1 (May 1971); Gilbert Salachas, Télé-Ciné 23, nos. 164-165
(Aug.-Sept. 1970); Henry Chapier, Combat (10 Sept. 1970);
Monique Pantel, France-Soir (3 Sept. 1970); Louis Chauvet, Le
Figaro (11 Sept. 1970).

Günter Metken, Neue Zürcher Zeitung (24 Oct. 1970) and Carlo
Revay, (28 Aug. 1971); Edgar Wettstein, Filmdienst (28 Dec.
1971); W. Schutte, Frankfurter Rundschau (4 Jan. 1972); Rainer
Fabian, Die Welt (6 Jan. 1972); Ulrich Greiner, Frankfurter
Allgemeine Zeitung (6 Jan. 1972).

15   LES DEUX ANGLAISES ET LE CONTINENT (1971)

Synopsis

Childlike Claude Roc is introduced to Anne Brown, the
daughter of an old friend of his mother. While Claude is es-
corting her through some art museums, Anne shows him a picture
of her sister Muriel and invites him to visit them in their
home on the picturesque Welsh coast. Claude makes the trip
via train and bike. Muriel is coyly withheld from his sight
until she makes a dramatic entrance at dinner with her eyes

bandaged to protect her frail eyesight. Claude, who is called "le continent" by the two girls, enjoys the company of both but is increasingly drawn (and subtly maneuvered by Anne) toward Muriel. Her mother gets suspicious and moves Claude to a neighbor's house. So Claude proposes and returns to France to plead his case to his mother. She and Mrs. Brown object, but allow Mr. Flint (a judicious neighbor) to arbitrate. He proposes a one-year separation. Claude studies art and has many affairs, something his mother approves of. After six months he sends Muriel a farewell note. Muriel pines, keeps a fervent diary, eventually writes a formal letter of rejection to Claude. When Anne comes to Paris to study art, she and Claude see each other often, but are, according to the narrator, "more resolute than in love." Despite her red flannel underwear, she loses her virginity to him after three days in a Swiss chalet. They fall in love and enjoy a passionate relationship until Anne decides to live by Claude's theories about free love and goes to Persia for a year with another man. Muriel writes a letter to Claude confessing youthful masturbation. Mme Roc dies. Muriel visits Claude in Paris; he confesses how much he loved her and tells Anne she must reveal all to her sister. Muriel gets sick, and Claude, in despair, writes a book. Anne dies of tuberculosis. Muriel loses her virginity to Claude on her way to be married in Brussels. Fifteen years later she is married to a teacher; Rodin is an acclaimed sculptor; and Claude is lonely and aging.

Credits

Production Company:	Les Films du Carrosse/Cinetel
Producer:	Marcel Berbert
Production Manager:	Claude Miller
Director:	François Truffaut
Assistant Director:	Suzanne Schiffman
Script:	François Truffaut, Jean Gruault. Based on the novel by Henri-Pierre Roche (Paris: Éditions Gallimard, 1956).
Director of Photography:	Nestor Almendros (Eastmancolor; 1, 66)
Camera Operator:	Jean-Claude Rivière
Editor:	Yann Dedet
Art Director:	Michel de Broin
Music:	Georges Delerue
Costumes:	Gitt Magrini
Sound:	René Levert
Narrator:	François Truffaut
Cast:	Jean-Pierre Léaud (Claude Roc), Kika Markham (Anne Brown), Stacey Tendeter (Muriel Brown), Sylvia Marriott (Mrs. Brown), Marie Mansart (Mme Roc), Philippe Léotard (Diurka), Irene Tunc

68

(Ruta), Mark Peterson (Mr. Flint),
David Markham (Palmist), Georges
Delerue (Claude's business agent),
Marcel Berbert (Art dealer),
Annie Miller (Monique de
Montferrand), Christine Pellé
(Claude's secretary), Jeanne
Lobre (Jeanne), Marie Irakane
(Maid), Jean-Claude Dolbert
(English policeman), Anne
Levaslot (Muriel as a child),
Sophie Jeanne (Clarisse), René
Gaillard (Taxi driver), Sophie
Baker (Friend in café), Laura
Truffaut, Eva Truffaut, Mathieu
Schiffman, and Guillaume
Schiffman (Children).

Filmed in Normandy, Vivarais, the Jura, and around Paris,
28 Apr.-13 July 1971.

Running Time:	108 minutes
Premiere:	Paris, 26 Nov. 1971; G.B., 3 Aug. 1972; U.S., 11 Oct. 1972 (New York Film Festival).
G.B. Title:	Anne and Muriel; U.S. Title: Two English Girls

Note

The French distributor trimmed the film from its original
132 minutes.

Reviews

Filmfacts 15, no. 19 (1 Nov. 1973); Gordon Gow, Films and
Filming 19, no. 1 (Oct. 1972); Colin Westerbeck, Commonweal 87,
no. 11 (15 Dec. 1972); Vincent Canby, New York Times (12 Oct.
1972); Penelope Houston, New Statesman 84, no. 2160 (11 Aug.
1972); Gavin Millar, Listener 88, no. 2263 (10 Aug. 1972);
Jan Dawson, BFI Monthly Film Bulletin, no. 464 (Sept. 1972);
Andrew Sarris, Village Voice (2 Nov. 1972); Mari Kuttna, Film
2, no. 2 (May 1973); Charles Samuels, American Scholar 41, no.
4 (Autumn 1972); Stanley Kauffmann, New Republic 167, no. 19
(18 Nov. 1972); Pauline Kael, New Yorker 48, no. 34 (14 Oct.
1972); Win Sharples, Jr., Filmmaker's Newsletter 6, no. 3
(Jan. 1973); Robert Hatch, Nation 215, no. 13 (30 Oct. 1972);
Richard Roud, Manchester Guardian (31 Jan. 1972) and Derek
Malcolm (3 Aug. 1972); William Pechter, Commentary 55, no. 3
(Mar. 1973); David Leach, Films in Review 23, no. 10 (Dec.
1972); David Denby, Atlantic Monthly 231, no. 1 (Jan. 1973);
Jonathan Cott, Rolling Stone (23 Nov. 1972); Dilys Powell,
Sunday Times (London) (6 Aug. 1972); Jay Cocks, Time 100, no.
16 (16 Oct. 1972); Bernard Weiner, Take One 3, no. 8 (1 Mar.

1973--issue of Nov.-Dec. 1971); Richard Schickel, Life 72, no. 20 (17 Nov. 1972); Sophie Baker, Manchester Guardian (19 July 1971); Thomas Meehan, Saturday Review 55, no. 45 (Nov. 1972); Hollywood Reporter (18 Oct. 1972).

Jacques Julia, Écran 72, no. 1 (Jan. 1972); Pierre-Louis Thirard, Positif, no. 136 (Mar. 1972); Roger Regent, La Revue des Deux Mondes, no. 1 (Jan. 1972); Fernand Dufour, Cinéma 72, no. 162 (Jan. 1972); Ginette Charest, Cinéma Quebec 1, no. 9 (May-June 1972); Tristan Renaud, Les Lettres Françaises, no. 1412 (1-6 Dec. 1971); François Nourissier, L'Express, no. 1064 (29 Nov.-5 Dec. 1971); Claude Mauriac, Le Figaro Littéraire, no. 1333 (3 Dec. 1971); Michel Delain, L'Express, no. 1042 (28 June-2 July 1971); Louis Chavet, Le Figaro (29 Nov. 1971); José Bescos, Une Semaine de Paris--Pariscop, no. 187 (24-30 Nov. 1971); Guy Teisseire, L'Aurore (8-9 May) and Claude Garson (29 Nov. 1971); Henry Chapier, Combat (29 Nov. 1971); Georges Charensol, Les Nouvelles Littéraires 49, no. 2306 (3-9 Dec. 1971); J.-L. Bory, Le Nouvel Observateur, no. 368 (29 Nov.-5 Dec. 1971); Jean de Baroncelli, Le Monde, no. 8356 (25 Nov. 1971); André Cornand, Image et Son, no. 256 (Jan. 1972); Janick Arbois, Télé-Ciné, no. 175 (Jan. 1972); Pierre Billard, Journal du Dimanche (Dec. 1971); Michel Duran, Le Canard Enchaîné (1 Dec. 1971).

Urs Jenny, Filmkritik 16, no. 7 (July 1972); Der Spiegel (5 Feb. 1973); Reto Müller, Filmdienst (6 Feb. 1973); W. Schobert, Frankfurter Rundschau (10 Feb. 1973); Uta Gote, Die Welt (13 Feb. 1973); Brigitte Jeremias, Frankfurter Allgemeine Zeitung (13 Feb. 1973); S. Schober, Süddeutsche Zeitung (13 Feb. 1973); Wolf Donner, Die Zeit (16 Feb. 1973); V. B. Burg, Jugend Film Fernsehen, no. 4 (Dec. 1973).

16   UNE BELLE FILLE COMME MOI (1972)

Synopsis

A naive sociologist, Stanislas Previne, conducts a series of interviews with Camille Bliss for a book on criminal women. His tape recorder captures her story in her own crudely colorful language, and it is presented in flashback. After the suspiciously accidental death of her father, she is put in an orphanage and then a reform school. Later she becomes involved with the loutish Clovis Bliss and gets him to marry her by pretending to be pregnant. When his miserly mother, Isobel, fails to die, they steal her money and head for Paris. Their car breaks down on the way, and she takes a job as a waitress. She soon attracts the attention of singer Sam Golden. The jealous Clovis is hit by a car and ends up in the hospital. Meanwhile Camille meets Murène, a duplicitous lawyer, and Arthur, a puritanical exterminator. She attempts to do away with husband and lawyer with Arthur's poison, but Arthur saves

them and orders her to commit suicide with him. He jumps from
a church tower, she does not. She is subsequently arrested
for his murder. Once he hears Camille's life story (it has
been shown in flashback thus far), the sociologist sets out to
get a film by a youthful auteur to prove her innocence. Camille
is set free and becomes a celebrated singer. Clovis is found
dead, and Stanislas ends up in jail for the murder. There he
hears of the death of Clovis' mother and the new partnership
of Camille and Stanislas's lawyer.

Credits

Production Company:	Les Films du Carrosse/Columbia
Executive Producer:	Marcel Berbert
Production Manager:	Claude Miller
Director:	François Truffaut
Assistant Director:	Suzanne Schiffman
Script:	Jean-Loup Dabadie, François Truffaut. Based on the novel, Such a Gorgeous Kid like Me, by Henry Farrell (New York: Delacorte Press, 1967).
Director of Photography:	Pierre William Glenn (Eastmancolor; 1, 66)
Camera Operator:	Walter Bal
Editor:	Yann Dedet
Art Director:	Jean-Pierre Kohut
Music:	Georges Delerue
"Sam's Song"	Guy Marchand, Jean-Loup Dabadie
"Une Belle Fille"	Jacques Datin, Jean-Loup Dabadie
"J'Attendrai"	Dino Olivieri, Nino Rastelli
Costumes:	Monique Dury
Sound:	René Levert
Cast:	Bernadette Lafont (Camille Bliss), Claude Brasseur (M. Murène), Charles Denner (Arthur), Guy Marchand (Sam Golden), André Dussollier (Stanislas Previne), Philippe Léotard (Clovis Bliss), Anne Kreis (Hélène), Gilberte Geniat (Isobel Bliss), Danièle Girard (Florence Golden), Martine Ferrière (Prison secretary), Michel Delahaye (M. Marchal), Annick Fougerie (Schoolmistress), Gaston Ouvrard (Old prison warden), Jacob Weizbluth (Alphonse).
Filmed in Beziers, Languedoc-Roussillon, 14 Feb.–14 Apr. 1972	
Running Time:	98 minutes
Premiere:	Paris, 13 Sept. 1972; G.B., 26 June 1973; U.S., Mar. 1973
G.B. Title:	A Gorgeous Bird like Me; U.S. Title: Such a Gorgeous Kid like Me.

Reviews

Judith Crist, New York 6, no. 10 (5 Mar. 1973); Richard
Combs, Sight and Sound 42, no. 4 (Autumn, 1973); Gabor
Brogyanyi, Films in Review 24, no. 6 (June-July 1973); Jan
Dawson, BFI Monthly Film Bulletin, no. 472 (May 1973); Arthur
Cooper, Newsweek 81, no. 12 (19 Mar. 1973); Eric Braun, Films
and Filming 19, no. 12 (Sept. 1973); Andrew Sarris, Village
Voice (3 May 1973); Colin Westerbeck, Commonweal 98, no. 9
(4 May 1973); Vincent Canby, New York Times (26 Mar. 1973);
John Coleman, New Statesman 86, no. 2207 (6 July 1973);
Penelope Gilliatt, New Yorker 49, no. 6 (31 Mar. 1973); Robert
Hatch, Nation 216, no. 17 (23 Apr. 1973); Stanley Kauffmann,
New Republic 168, no. 16 (21 Apr. 1973); Jay Cocks, Time, 101,
no. 18 (30 Apr. 1973); Louis Sweeney, Christian Science Monitor
(31 Mar. 1973); George Melly, Observer (1 July 1973); Mosk,
Variety (27 Sept. 1972); Howard Kissel, Women's Wear Daily
(26 Mar. 1973); Archer Winsten, New York Post (26 Mar. 1973);
Ann Guarino, New York Daily News (26 Mar. 1973); Hollywood
Reporter (28 Mar. 1973).

Jean Collet, Études, no. 337 (Nov. 1972); Michel Grisolia,
Cinéma 72, no. 169 (Sept.-Oct. 1972); Marcel Martin, Les
Lettres Françaises, no. 1451 (13-19 Sept. 1972); Michel Ciment,
Positif, nos. 144-45 (Nov.-Dec. 1972); Mireille Amiel, Cinéma
72, no. 170 (Nov. 1972); Jean-Louis Bory, Le Nouvel Observateur,
no. 412 (2-8 Oct. 1972); Georges Charensol, Les Nouvelles
Littéraires (18 Sept. 1972); Jacques Doniol-Valcroze, L'Express,
no. 1105 (11-17 Sept. 1972); Laurent Gagliardi, Cinéma Quebec
2, no. 10 (July-Aug. 1973); Unifrance, nos. 437 and 449 (Oct.
1972); Jean de Baroncelli, Le Monde, no. 8609 (19 Sept. 1972);
J. Chevallier, Image et Son, nos. 276-277 (Oct. 1973); Roger
Regent, La Nouvelle Revue des Deux Mondes, no. 10 (Oct. 1972);
Henry Moret, Écran 72, no. 8 (Sept.-Oct. 1972).

Edgar Wettstein, Filmdienst (30 Apr. 1974); Sigrit Schmitt,
Süddeutsche Zeitung (4-5 May 1974); Uta Gote, Die Welt (7 May
1974); H. C. Blumenberg, Die Zeit (10 May 1974); R. R. Hamacher,
Medium, no. 4 (1974).

17   LA NUIT AMÉRICAINE (1973)

Synopsis

Meet Pamela, an old-fashioned Hollywood romantic melodrama,
begins shooting in the Victorine Studios in Nice with a street
scene. Cast and crew assemble on the set and in the Atlantic
Hotel: Alphonse, who plays a young newlywed, brings his girlfriend, whom he has gotten hired as the scriptgirl; Séverine,
an aging actress once romantically involved with Alexandre,
the man who will play her husband and who awaits the arrival
of a mysterious companion; Ferrand, the slightly hard-of-hearing

director; Joëlle, the dedicated script girl. They all await Julie Baker, who is to play the young wife and who is just recovering from a nervous breakdown. Ferrand is beset by problems from the outset: interviewers and would-be producers besiege him; the lab delays prints; the producer worries; Severine, slightly unsettled by drink and various anxieties, repeatedly mistakes doors and ruins a scene; an actress objects to a swimsuit scene. Ferrand dreams of his youth and gets a delivery of film books. Julie arrives with her new husband, a distinguished doctor. Alphonse quarrels with Liliane and begins asking people if women are magic. Christian, Alexandre's companion, arrives to the surprise of all. Shooting continues, and the script is composed after hours by Ferrand and Joëlle. The shooting moves to a country road for a stunt scene. Joëlle invites Bernard into the bushes for sex after fixing a flat tire. Liliane runs off with the stuntman, something with which Joëlle disagrees. Ferrand dreams of stealing <u>Citizen Kane</u> posters as a boy. Because Alphonse is despondent, Julie spends the night with him. He impulsively phones and tells her husband. Julie becomes distraught, Alphonse flees, and it is only the return of Julie's husband and the discovery of Alphonse on a go-cart track that get things rolling again. But Alexandre dies in a car crash, and the film has to be simplified to be completed, with another actor standing in for Alexandre. As cast and crew plan and disperse, the propman sums up the shooting.

<u>Credits</u>

Production Company:	Les Films du Carrosse/PECF (Paris)/ Produzione Internazionale Cinematografica (Rome)
Producer:	Marcel Berbert
Production Manager:	Claude Miller
Director:	François Truffaut
Assistant Director:	Suzanne Schiffman
Script:	François Truffaut, Jean-Louis Richard, Suzanne Schiffman
Director of Photography:	Pierre-William Glenn (Eastmancolor; 1, 66)
Editors:	Yann Dedet, Martine Barraque
Art Director:	Damien Lanfranchi
Costumes:	Monique Dury
Sound:	René Levert
Music:	Georges Delerue
Cast:	Jacqueline Bisset (Julie/Pamela), Valentine Cortese (Séverine), Alexandra Stewart (Stacey), Jean-Pierre Aumont (Alexandre), Jean-Pierre Léaud (Alphonse), François Truffaut (Ferrand), Jean Champion (Bertrand), Nathalie Baye (Joëlle);

Dani (Liliane, the assistant
continuity girl), Bernard Menez
(Bernard, the property man),
Nike Arrighi (Odile), Gaston Joly
(Gaston), Jean Panisse (Arthur),
Maurice Séveno (Television re-
porter), David Markham (Dr.
Nelson), Zénaïde Rossi (Gaston's
wife), Christophe Vesque (Boy),
Graham Greene and Marcel Berbert
(Insurers).

Filmed at Victorine Studios and on location in Nice, 25 Sept.-
Dec. 1972.

Running Time:	115 minutes
First Shown:	Cannes Film Festival, 14 May 1973
Premiere:	Paris, 24 May 1973; U.S., 28 Sept. 1973 (New York Film Festival)
G.B./U.S. Title:	Day for Night
Prize:	Oscar--Best Foreign Film (Hollywood), Best Film, Best Director, Best Supporting Actress--National Society of Film Critics and New York Film Critics.

Reviews

Gabor Brogyanyi, Films in Review 24, no. 10 (Dec. 1973);
Stanley Kauffmann, New Republic 169, no. 15 (13 Oct. 1973);
Marjorie Rosen, Jump Cut, no. 1 (May-June 1974); Richard Combs,
BFI Monthly Film Bulletin, no. 480 (Jan. 1974); Charles Samuels,
American Scholar 43, no. 3 (Summer 1974); Peter Cowie,
International Film Guide (1974), Andrew Sarris, Village Voice
(11 Oct. 1973); Colin Westerbeck, Jr., Commonweal 99, no. 4
(26 Oct. 1973); Pauline Kael, New Yorker 49, no. 34 (15 Oct.
1973); Stuart Rosenthal, Focus on Film, no. 16 (Autumn 1973);
Vincent Canby, New York Times (29 Sept. and 7 Oct. 1973); Jay
Cocks, Time, 102, no. 16 (15 Oct. 1973); Judith Crist, New York
(1 Oct. 1973); Penelope Houston and Richard Roud, Sight and
Sound 42, no. 3 (Summer 1973); Richard Fisher, Filmmaker's
Newsletter 7, no. 2 (Dec. 1973); Christopher Hudson, Spectator
231, no. 7587 (24 Nov. 1973); Joseph Kanon, Atlantic Monthly
232, no. 5 (Nov. 1973); Derek Malcolm, Manchester Guardian
(15 Nov. 1973); Robert Hatch, Nation 217, no. 12 (15 Oct. 1973);
Gavin Millar, Listener 90, no. 2330 (22 Nov. 1973); David
Brudnoy, National Review 25, no. 49 (7 Dec. 1973); John Coleman,
New Statesman 86, no. 2226 (16 Nov. 1973); Gordon Gow, Films
and Filming 20 (Nov. 1973); Paul D. Zimmerman, Newsweek 82,
no. 18 (29 Oct. 1973); B. J. Demby, Filmmaker's Newsletter 6,
no. 12 (Oct. 1973); P. Hogue, Movietone News, no. 30 (Mar. 1974)
and J. Purdy, no. 31 (Apr. 1974); D. Robbeloth, Audience, no. 6
(Dec. 1973); Stephen Farber, Hudson Review 27, no. 2 (Summer
1974); Dilys Powell, Sunday Times (London) (18 Nov. 1973);

Louise Sweeney, Christian Science Monitor (29 Sept. 1973);
Don Lyon, Real Paper (17 Oct. 1973); Mosk, Variety (23 May
1972); Tom Milne, Observer, no. 9512 (18 Nov. 1973); Rex Reed,
New York Daily News (7 Oct. 1973) and Kathleen Carroll (8 Oct.
1973); Howard Kissell, Women's Wear Daily (28 Sept. 1973);
Archer Winsten, New York Post (8 Oct. 1973); E. Turk, French
Review 51, no. 5 (Apr. 1978); Hollywood Reporter (28 Sept.
1973).

Guy Braucourt, Écran 73, no. 17 (July-Aug. 1973); Laurent
Gagliardi, Cinéma Quebec 3, no. 2 (Oct. 1973); F. Gevaudan,
Cinéma 73, nos. 178-179 (July-Aug. 1973); A. Ruszkowski,
Séquences 19, no. 75 (Jan. 1974); Michel Perez, Positif, nos.
152-153 (July-Aug. 1973); F. Chevassu, Image et Son, no. 273
(June 1973); M. Zeleny and Michel Serceau, Télé-Ciné, no. 181
(Sept. 1973) Jean de Baroncelli, Le Monde, no. 8813 (16 May
1973); Roger Regent, Revue des Deux Mondes, no. 7 (July 1973);
A. Tournes, Jeune Cinéma, no. 72 (July-Aug. 1973); Michel
Capdenac, Europe, nos. 533-534 (Sept.-Oct. 1973); Claude
Mauriac, L'Express, no. 1141 (21-27 May 1973).

W. Limmer, Süddeutsche Zeitung (30-31 May 1973) and Peter
Bucka (22-23 Sept. 1973); E. Schmidt, Medium, no. 10 (1973);
W. Kliess, Kino, no. 7 (Oct.-Nov. 1973); Unsigned, Der Spiegel
(15 Oct. 1973); Edgar Wettstein, Filmdienst (16 Oct. 1973); H.
C. Blumenberg, Die Zeit (26 Oct. 1973); Karena Niehoff, Der
Tagesspiegel (4 Nov. 1973); F. Luft, Die Welt (12 Nov. 1973);
W. Buhler, Filmkritik, no. 11 (Nov. 1973) and J. Ebert and P.
Nau, no. 12 (Dec. 1973); W. Knorr, Jugend Film Fernsehen, no.
4 (Dec. 1973); H. Fischer, Frankfurter Rundschau (31 Dec.
1973); Brigitte Jeremias, Frankfurter Allgemeine Zeitung (4
Jan. 1974).

18   L'HISTOIRE D'ADÈLE H. (1975)

Synopsis

   1863. A young woman disembarks in the dark in Nova Scotia
and sneaks past the customs officials. She rents a room with
Mrs. Saunders, using the name Miss Lewly, and tries to contact
the Lt. Pinson she has followed to Halifax. After Pinson refuses to accept a letter from her, she begins to be tormented
by nightmares of her drowning sister and starts to write in her
diary. Pinson visits her and tells her he does not intend to
marry her even with the permission of her illustrious father,
Victor Hugo. Adèle, however, writes optimistic letters home
and collects the money reluctantly forwarded to her. She continues to pursue Pinson; she lends him money, sends him notes,
spies on him as he makes love, disguises herself to meet him.
Her nightmares and diary writing continue. When she tells her
family that she and Pinson have wed, a newspaper runs an announcement of it, and Pinson is called on the carpet by his

military superiors. A hypnotist Adèle hopes will help win
Pinson back to her turns out to be a fraud. Adèle then con-
vinces Judge Johnston, the father of Pinson's new fiancée,
that she is wed to and pregnant by the lieutenant. Her health
deteriorates further, and she is forced to move into a cheap
dormitory for women. When Pinson is transferred to Barbados,
Adèle follows him there. She wanders the streets, unkempt and
tattered, kept alive by Madame Baa, a friendly black woman.
Pinson decides to confront her, but she walks right past him,
completely oblivious. Madame Baa accompanies her back to
Europe, where she entered an asylum and stayed there until
her death in 1915.

Credits

Production Company:	Les Films du Carrosse/Les Productions Artistes Associés (Paris)
Producer:	Marcel Berbert
Production Manager:	Claude Miller
Director:	François Truffaut
Assistant Directors:	Suzanne Schiffman, Carl Hathwell
Script:	François Truffaut, Suzanne Schiffman, Jean Gruault, with the collaboration of Frances V. Guille, editor of Le Journal d'Adèle Hugo. English adaptation by Jan Dawson.
Director of Photography:	Nestor Almendros (Eastmancolor; 1, 66)
Camera Operator:	Jean-Claude Rivière
Editor:	Yann Dedet. Assisted by Martine Barraque-Curie
Art Director:	Jean-Pierre Kohut-Svelko
Costumes:	Jacqueline Guyot
Music:	Maurice Jaubert (1900-1940)
Musical Director:	Patrice Mestral
Musical Adviser:	François Porcile
Sound:	Jean-Pierre Ruh
Cast:	Isabelle Adjani (Adèle Hugo), Bruce Robinson (Lt. Pinson), Sylvia Marriott (Mrs. Saunders), Reubin Dorey (Mr. Saunders), Joseph Blatchley (Whistler), M. White (Colonel), Carl Hathwell (Pinson's footman), Ivry Gitlis (Hypnotist), Sir Cecil de Sausmarez (Lawyer), Sir Raymond Falla (Judge Johnstone), Roger Martin (Dr. Murdock), Madame Louise (Mme Baa), Jean-Pierre Leursse (Let-terwriter), Chantal Durpoix

(Young prostitute), Geoffrey
Crook (Judge Johnstone's valet),
François Truffaut (Officer).
Filmed on the Isle of Guernsey and on the Isle of Gorée
(Senegal)

Running Time:	110 minutes (French version); 98 minutes (English version)
Premiere:	Paris, 8 Oct. 1975 New York Film Festival, Oct. 1975
G.B./U.S. Title:	The Story of Adèle H.
Prizes:	Grand Prix du cinéma français, New York Film Critics Award--Best Original Screenplay and Best Actress

Note

Truffaut shot English and French versions simultaneously.

Reviews

William Pechter, Commentary 61, no. 5 (May 1976); Roger
Greenspun, Thousand Eyes, no. 2 (Oct. 1976) and Jo Ann Crawford,
no. 2 (Feb. 1977); John Simon, New York 9, no. 2 (12 Jan. 1976);
R. C. Cumbow, Movietone News, no. 49 (18 Apr. 1976); Tom Milne,
BFI Monthly Film Bulletin 44, no. 519 (Apr. 1977); Michael Wood,
New York Review of Books 23, no. 1 (5 Feb. 1976); Gavin Millar,
Listener 98, no. 2526 (15 Sept. 1977); Derek Elley, Films and
Filming 23, no. 7 (Apr. 1977); Robert Hatch, Nation 222, no. 2
(17 Jan. 1976); Julian Jebb, Sight and Sound 46, no. 2 (Spring
1977); Vincent Canby, New York Times (11 and 13 Oct. 1975) and
Mel Gussow (26 Oct. 1975)--Gussow reprinted in Cinema (USA),
no. 35 (1976); D. McVay, Film (London), no. 49 (May 1977); J.
Teegarden, Audience, no. 8 (Apr. 1976); D. Johnson, Times Literary
Supplement (London), no. 3845 (21 Nov. 1975); Jay Cocks, Time
107, no. 1 (5 Jan. 1976); Judith Crist, Saturday Review 3, no.
9 (7 Feb. 1976); H. Phillips, National Review 28, no. 13 (16
Apr. 1976); Harold Clurman, Nation 221, no. 14 (1 Nov. 1975);
Richard Roud, Film Comment 11, no. 5 (Sept.-Oct. 1975), Elliott
Stein, 11, no. 6 (Nov.-Dec. 1975), and Jonathan Rosenbaum, 12,
no. 4 (July-Aug. 1976); David Sherritt, Christian Science
Monitor (8 Jan. 1976); Mosk, Variety (24 Sept. 1975); Richard
Corliss, New Times (6 Feb. 1976); H. Kissel, Women's Wear
Daily (13 Oct. 1975); Frank Rich, New York Post (13 Oct. 1975
and 10 Jan. 1976); Kathleen Carroll, New York Daily News
(13 Oct. 1975); Derek Malcolm, Manchester Guardian Weekly 117,
no. 11 (11 Sept. 1977); Hollywood Reporter (4 Nov. 1975).

Film Bulletin (Zurich), no. 94 (Dec. 1975)--entire issue
on Adèle H; Jean Collet, Études, no. 343 (Nov. 1975); Claude
Beylie, Ecran 75, no. 41 (15 Nov. 1975); Georges Charensol,
Les Nouvelles Littéraires, no. 2053 (20-26 Oct. 1975); Michel

Capdenac, <u>Europe</u>, nos. 561-562 (Jan.-Feb. 1976); Maurice Elia,
<u>Séquences</u> 21, no. 84 (Apr. 1976); G. Colpart and R. Lefevre,
<u>Image et Son</u>, no. 301 (Dec. 1975); Dominique Rabourdin, <u>Cinéma
75</u>, no. 203 (Nov. 1975); Patrick Thevenon, <u>L'Express</u>, no. 1265
(6-12 Oct.) and J.-L. Douin, no. 1267 (20-26 Oct. 1975);
Ginette Gervais, <u>Jeune Cinéma</u>, no. 90 (Nov. 1975); Alain
Garsault, <u>Positif</u>, no. 176 (Dec. 1975); Roger Regent, <u>La
Nouvelle Revue des Deux Mondes</u>, no. 12 (Dec. 1975); Annie
Oliver, <u>Cinéma Quebec</u> 5, no. 1 (1976); J.-L. Bory, <u>Le Nouvel
Observateur</u>, no. 570 (13-19 Oct. 1975); R. Chazal, <u>France-Soir</u>
(9 Oct. 1975) and Elizabeth Cadot, (24 Apr. 1978); Michel Mohrt,
<u>Le Figaro</u> (9 Oct. 1975) and Pierre Montaigne (23 Oct. 1975);
Guy Braucourt, <u>Les Nouvelles Littéraires</u>, no. 2500 (29 Sept.-
5 Oct. 1975); Jean de Baroncelli, <u>Le Monde</u>, no. 1409 (23-29
Oct. 1975); Gilles Colpart, <u>Télé-Ciné</u>, no. 203 (Nov.-Dec. 1975);
<u>Unifrance Film</u>, no. 496 (Dec. 1974); Maurice Tassart, <u>Carrefour</u>
(23 Oct. 1975); Pierre Billard, <u>Le Journal du Dimanche</u> (26 Oct.
1975); Janick Arbois, <u>Télérama</u> (11 Oct. 1975).

Peter Handke, <u>Der Spiegel</u>, no. 44 (27 Oct. 1975); G. Metken,
<u>Stuttgarter Zeitung</u> (27 Nov. 1975) and in <u>Der Tagesspiegel</u> (30
Nov. 1975); G. Waeger, <u>Neue Zürcher Zeitung</u> (26 Feb. 1976);
Edgar Wettstein, <u>Filmdienst</u> (27 Apr. 1976); Brigitte Jeremias,
<u>Frankfurter Allgemeine Zeitung</u> (20 Dec. 1976); A. F. Schirmer,
<u>Der Tagesspiegel</u> (8 Apr. 1977); F. Luft, <u>Die Welt</u> (13 Apr.
1977); H. Fischer, <u>Frankfurter Rundschau</u> (7 May 1977); N. Grob,
<u>Medium</u>, no. 7 (1977).

19   L'ARGENT DE POCHE (1976)

<u>Synopsis</u>

Martine sends a postcard from the center of France to her
classmates at home. It is confiscated by the teacher, M.
Richet. Instead of meting out punishment, he uses it for a
geography lesson. The teacher, students, and their activities
in and out of school become the focal point of the rest of the
film. Patrick memorizes an excerpt from Molière, while others
recite it in class, and Julien, a quiet and shabby newcomer,
joins the school. Patrick, who tends a wheelchair-ridden
father, develops a crush on Mme Riffle, the mother of a school
chum. In class he delays with an answer until saved by the
bell. A woman and her two-year-old son visit the teacher's
pregnant wife. When the mother and son return to their own
apartment, she discovers her wallet is missing; she leaves the
boy alone and goes to find it. He tumbles out a window, seven
stories to the ground, and lives. Two boys prepare a unique
breakfast. When a willful girl's parents leave her alone, she
uses her father's bullhorn to complain that she is locked in
and hungry; neighbors rig up a pulley to feed her. On Sunday
students, teachers, and parents go to the movies. After Julien
is punished in class, he sneaks out and rifles coat pockets.

The Films: Synopses, Credits, Notes, and Reviews

Two boys give another a bad haircut. Patrick embarrasses himself with a slip-of-the-tongue "thank-you" to Mme Riffle. He
has a double date to the movies with his friend Bruno, who ends
up with both girls because of Patrick's shyness. Richet's wife
gives birth to a boy; the day's lessons are altered. Patrick
gives red roses to Mme Riffle, who says to thank his father.
A school medical exam reveals that Julien is a battered child;
his mother and grandmother are arrested. Richet lectures his
class on Julien's case and the resilience of children. At summer camp Patrick, through the trickery of others, gets to exchange his first kiss--with Martine.

Credits

Production Company:	Les Films du Carrosse/Les Productions Artistes Associés
Producer:	Marcel Berbert
Production Manager:	Roland Thenot
Director:	François Truffaut
Assistant Directors:	Suzanne Schiffman, Alain Maline
Script:	François Truffaut, Suzanne Schiffman
Director of Photography:	Pierre-William Glenn (Eastmancolor; 1, 66)
Editors:	Yann Dedet, Martine Barraque-Curie, Jean Gargonne, Stephanie Granel, Muriel Zeleny
Art Directior:	Jean-Pierre Kohut-Svelko
Costumes:	Monique Dury
Makeup:	Thi-Loan N'Guyen
Music:	Maurice Jaubert
Musical Director:	Patrice Mestral
Musical Adviser:	François Porcile
Song: "Les enfants s'ennuient le dimanche":	Charles Trenet
Sound:	Michel Laurent, Michel Brethez
Cast:	ADULTS: Jean-François Stevenin (Jean-François Richet), Virginie Thevenet (Lydie Richet), Chantal Mercier (Mlle Petit), Nicole Félix (Nicole), Tania Torrens (Mme Riffle), Francis Devlaeminck (M. Riffle), Jean-Marie Carayon (Commissioner, Sylvie's father), Christian Lentretien (Richard's father), Marcel Berbert (School director), Roland Thenot (Librarian), Thi Loan N'Guyen (His wife), Christine Pellé (Mme Leclou), Jane Lobre (Julien's grandmother), Monique Dury (Florist), René Barnerias (Patrick's father), Helene

79

Jeanbrau (Woman doctor), Annie
Chevaldonne (Nurse), Vincent
Touly (Caretaker), Michel Dessart
(Cop), Paul Heyraud (M. Deluca),
Michèle Heyraud (Mme Deluca),
Yvon Boutina (Oscar as an adult).
CHILDREN: Geory Desmouceaux
(Patrick Desmouceaux), Bruno
Staab (Bruno Rouillard), Philippe
Goldmann (Julien Leclou), Corinne
Boucart (Corinne), Eva Truffaut
(Patricia), Sylvie Grezel (Sylvie),
Laurent Devlaeminck (Laurent
Riffle), Frank Deluca (Frank
Deluca), Claudio Deluca (Mathieu
Deluca), Richard Golfier (Richard
Golfier), Pascale Bruchon
(Martine), Laura Truffaut
(Madeleine Doinel), Sebastien
Marc (Oscar as a boy), and little
Gregory (Little Gregory).

Filmed in and around Thiers, July-Aug. 1975
Running Time: 105 minutes
Premiere: Paris, 17 Mar. 1976
G.B./U.S. Title: Small Change

Reviews

James McCourt and Elliott Stein, Film Comment 12, no. 6
(Nov.-Dec. 1976); Andrew Sarris, Village Voice (11 Oct. 1976)
and Molly Haskell (1 Nov. 1976); Verina Glaessner, BFI Monthly
Film Bulletin, no. 523 (Aug. 1977); Roger Greenspun, Thousand
Eyes (Oct. 1976); John Coleman, New Statesman 93, no. 2413
(17 June 1977); Vincent Canby, New York Times (1 and 10 Oct.
1976); Annette Insdorf, French Review 51, no. 3 (Feb. 1978);
L. Gerst, Audience (Apr. 1977) and C. Canham (May-June 1977);
Jack Kroll, Newsweek 88, no. 13 (27 Sept. 1976); John Simon,
New York (18 Oct. 1976); Will Aitken, Take One 5, no. 4 (Oct.
1976); Stanley Kauffmann, New Republic 175, no. 16 (16 Oct.
1976); Judith Crist, Saturday Review 4, no. 3 (30 Oct. 1976);
Harold Clurman, Nation 223, no. 13 (23 Oct. 1976); Marsha
McCreadie, Films in Review 27, no. 10 (Dec. 1976); Russell
Davies, Observer, no. 9697 (19 June 1977); Jay Cocks, Time (11
Oct. 1976); David Sterritt, Christian Science Monitor (4 Oct.
1976); Sylvia Feldman, Psychology Today 10, no. 8 (Jan. 1977);
Alan Brien, Sunday Times (London), no. 8035 (19 June 1977);
Rex Reed and Kathleen Carroll, New York Daily News (1 Oct.
1976); Frank Rich, New York Post (1 Oct. 1976); H. Kissell,
Women's Wear Daily (1 Oct. 1976); Derek Malcolm, Manchester
Guardian Weekly 116, no. 26 (26 June 1977); E. Perchaluk,
Independent Film Journal, no. 78 (11 Oct. 1976); D. Bartholomew,
Film Bulletin, no. 46 (Jan.-Feb. 1977); Hollywood Reporter

(5 Oct. 1976).

Henri Behar, Image et Son, no. 306 (May 1976) and Gilles Colpart, nos. 309-310 (Oct. 1976); F. Vitoux, Positif, no. 181 (May 1976); Pierre Maraval, Cinématographe, no. 18 (Apr.-May 1976); Claude Beylie, Écran 76, no. 45 (15 Mar. 1976); F. Forestier, L'Express, no. 1288 (15-22 Mar. 1976); Jacques Siclier, Le Monde, no. 9691 (20 Mar. 1976); Michel Mohrt, Le Figaro (19 Mar. 1976); J.-C. Guiguet, La Nouvelle Revue Française 47, no. 282 (June 1976); Joel Magny, Télé-Ciné, no. 208 (May 1976).

V. Baer, Der Tagesspiegel (29 June 1976); Brigitte Jeremias, Frankfurter Allgemeine Zeitung (29 June 1976); A. Nemeczek, Stern (1 July 1976); M. Walder, Neue Zürcher Zeitung (1 July 1976); W. Schutte, Frankfurter Rundschau (2 July 1976); F. Hanck, Film und Ton, no. 22 (Sept. 1976); Edgar Wettstein, Filmdienst (7 June 1976); N. Grob, Medium, no. 6 (1977).

20   L'HOMME QUI AIMAIT LES FEMMES (1977)

Synopsis

On the day after Christmas in a Montpellier cemetery, a funeral is taking place. Bertrand Morane, an engineer for the Institute for Fluid Mechanics, is being buried. Among the many mourners, there is not a single male. His story, the story of a man obsessed by women, unfolds. He spies a pair of attractive legs, crashes his car trying to follow them, thinks he has found them in a nearby town only to discover they are really in Montreal. He beds a rental car worker who helped him, instead. When he is rejected by a woman interested only in younger men, he starts to write a novel. He includes his prostitute mother; Fabienne, a woman who cannot penetrate his defenses; Liliane, a waitress who fails to attract him sexually; Delphine, a doctor's wife, who graduates from love in a car to murder for love. His typist is appalled by the book, and it is rejected by publishers until a female editor, Geneviève Bigey, champions it. She meets with Bertrand, pushes his book through publication, even has a brief affair with him. And she prevents him from adding a chapter on his one unfulfilled love. With the book about to be released, he returns home, gets hit by a car while pursuing another woman, and dies when he falls out of bed trying to get a better look at a shapely nurse.

Credits

Production Company:	Les Films du Carrosse/Les Productions Artistes Associés
Producer:	Marcel Berbert
Production Manager:	Roland Thenot

Director:	François Truffaut
Assistant Directors:	Suzanne Schiffman, Alain Maline
Script:	François Truffaut, Michel Fermaud, Suzanne Schiffman
Director of Photography:	Nestor Almendros (Eastmancolor; 1, 66)
Editor:	Martine Barraque-Curie
Art Director:	Jean-Pierre Kohut-Svelko
Costumes:	Monique Dury
Music:	Maurice Jaubert
Musical Director:	Patrice Mestral
Sound:	Michel Laurent
Cast:	Charles Denner (Bertrand Morane), Brigitte Fossey (Geneviève Bigey), Nelly Borgeaud (Delphine Grezel), Geneviève Fontanel (Hélène), Nathalie Baye (Martine), Leslie Caron (Vera), Jean Dasté (Dr. Binard), Roger Leenhardt (M. Betany), Sabine Glaser (Bernadette), Valerie Bonnier (Fabienne), Martine Chassaing (Denise), Roselyne Puyo (Nicole), Anna Perrier (Baby-sitter), Monique Dury (Mme Duteil), Nella Barbier (Liliane), Frederique Jamet (Juliette), M. J. Montfajon (Bertrand's mother), Michel Marti (Young Bertrand).

Filmed in Montpellier, Dec. 1976

Running Time:	115 minutes
Premiere:	Paris, 27 Apr. 1977
G.B./U.S. Title:	The Man Who Loved Women

Reviews

Andrew Sarris, Village Voice (3 Oct. 1977); Molly Haskell, New York 10, no. 42 (17 Oct. 1977); Vincent Canby, New York Times (1 and 7 Oct., 9 Dec. 1977); Gavin Millar, Listener 99, no. 2552 (23 Mar. 1978); Harold Clurman, Nation 225, no. 13 (22 Oct. 1977) and Robert Hatch, 225, no. 16 (12 Nov. 1977); Stanley Kauffmann, New Republic 177, no. 17 (22 Oct. 1977); John Simon, National Review 30, no. 1 (6 Jan. 1978); David Ansen, Newsweek 90, no. 18 (31 Oct. 1977); David Sterritt, Christian Science Monitor (6 Oct. 1977); Clancy Sigal, Spectator 240, no. 7811 (18 Mar. 1978) and John Wells, no. 7817 (29 Apr. 1978); Pauline Kael, New Yorker 53, no. 42 (5 Dec. 1977); Arthur Schlesinger, Jr., Saturday Review 5, no. 5 (26 Nov. 1977); Mosk, Variety (27 Apr. 1977); Judith Crist, New York Post, (1 Oct. 1977); Howard Kissell, Women's Wear Daily (27 Sept. 1977); Kathleen Carroll, New York Daily News (3 Oct. 1977); Frank Rich, Time 110, no. 15 (10 Oct. 1977); Richard

Roud, Film Comment 13, no. 5 (Sept.-Oct. 1977); and no. 6 (Nov.-Dec. 1977); Hollywood Reporter (5 Oct. 1977).

Claude Beylie, Écran 77, no. 59 (15 June 1977); Jacques Fieschi, Cinématographe, no. 27 (May 1977); Roger Regent, La Nouvelle Revue des Deux Mondes, no. 6 (June 1977); Claire Devarrieux, Le Monde, no. 10033 (3 May 1977); Guy Braucourt, Les Nouvelles Littéraires (28 Apr. 1977); J.-L. Tallenay, L'Express (20 Apr. 1977); Michel Mohrt, Le Figaro (28 Apr. 1977); F. Chevassu, Image et Son, no. 318 (June-July 1977); Jean Delmas, Jeune Cinéma, no. 103 (June 1977); S. Sorel, Télé-Ciné, no. 219 (June 1977); Robert Chazal, France-Soir (26 Apr. 1977); Henry Chapier, Le Quotidien de Paris (5 Apr. 1977); André Godin, Revue Nouvelle 68, nos. 7-8 (July-Aug. 1978); J. Montfort, Ciné Revue, no. 57 (28 Apr. 1977).

W. Schutte, Frankfurter Rundschau (27 June 1977); W. Wiegand, Frankfurter Allgemeine Zeitung (27 June 1977); Karena Niehoff, Der Tagesspiegel (28 June 1977); P. Buchka, Süddeutsche Zeitung (30 June 1977).

21   LA CHAMBRE VERTE (1978)

Synopsis

Documentary footage of battles from World War I is super-imposed over medium close-ups of a troubled Julien Davenne. He consoles his friend Gérard at the funeral of his wife. Julien's wife had also died, early in their marriage, and he recommends that Gérard dedicate his life to his wife's memory. Later when Gérard returns to introduce his new wife, Julien hides. For Julien has dedicated his life to the dead: he shows the mute boy who is his ward slides of dead soldiers; he is a virtuoso obituary columnist; he keeps a private sanc-tuary, a "green room" filled with mementos, where he communes with his dead wife. He even has a life-sized replica of his wife built; but he has it destroyed on seeing it. When light-ning starts a fire in his green room, Julien finds an abandoned cemetery chapel and gets permission from a priest to transform it into a new shrine to all his dead friends. He becomes in-creasingly attracted to Cecilia, a woman he met while looking for mementos for his wife, who shares his dedication to the dead. He shows her his chapel full of photos and candles and invites her to include her dead. When he realizes, however, that Massigny, a politician who was Julien's best friend until he mysteriously betrayed him, is the man whose memory she pre-serves, he ends things with her. Julien's health deteriorates; though gravely ill, he does finally respond to a letter from Cecilia. They meet at the chapel; he invites her to include a candle for Massigny and dies. Cecilia lights a candle in his name.

The Films: Synopses, Credits, Notes, and Reviews

Credits

Production Company:	Les Films du Carrosse/Les Productions Artistes Associés
Producer:	Marcel Berbert
Production Manager:	Roland Thenot
Director:	François Truffaut
Assistant Directors:	Suzanne Schiffman, Emmanuel Clot
Script:	François Truffaut; adapted by Jean Gruault from "The Altar of the Dead" by Henry James.
Director of Photography:	Nestor Almendros (Eastmancolor; 1, 66)
Editor:	Martine Barraque-Curie
Art Director:	Jean-Pierre Kohut-Svelko
Costumes:	Christian Gasc, Monique Dury
Music:	Maurice Jaubert
Sound:	Michel Laurent
Cast:	François Truffaut (Julien Davenne), Nathalie Baye (Cecilia Mandel), Jeanne Lobre (Mme Rambaud), Jean Dasté (Bernard Humbert), Patrick Maleon (Georges), Jean-Pierre Moulin (Gerard Mazet), Marcel Berbert (Doctor), Guy D'Ablon (Mannequin maker), Laurence Ragon (Julie Davenne), Jean-Pierre Ducos (Priest).

Filmed at Honfleur, Autumn 1976

Running Time:	94 minutes
Premiere:	Paris, Apr. 1978
G.B./U.S. Title:	The Green Room

Reviews

Vincent Canby, New York Times (14 Sept. 1979); Robert Hatch, Nation 229, no. 13 (27 Oct. 1979); Stanley Kauffmann, New Republic 181, no. 14 (6 Oct. 1979); Gilbert Adair, BFI Monthly Film Notes, no. 555 (Apr. 1980); Richard Roud, Sight and Sound 47, no. 3 (Summer 1978); Jack Kroll, Newsweek 94, no. 13 (1 Oct. 1979); Rob Edelman, Films in Review 30, no. 9 (Nov. 1979); Jonathan Baumbach, Partisan Review 47 (Spring 1980); David Sterritt, Christian Science Monitor (10 Oct. 1979); Mosk, Variety (29 Mar. 1978); Archer Winsten, New York Post (14 Sept. 1979); Kathleen Carroll, New York Daily News (14 Sept. 1979); Donald Barthelme, New Yorker 55, no. 32 (24 Sept. 1979); Harold Clurman, Nation 227, no. 13 (21 Oct. 1978); James McCourt and Elliot Stein, Film Comment 14, no. 6 (Nov.-Dec. 1978); Hollywood Reporter (26 Sept. 1978).

M. Devillers, Cinématographe, no. 37 (Apr. 1978) and L. Cugny, no. 38 (May 1978); Roger Regent, La Nouvelle Revue des

Deux Mondes (May 1978); Gilles Colpart, Image et Son, no. 327
(Apr. 1978); Jean Mambrino, L'Avant-Scène du Cinéma, no. 215
(Nov. 1978); Jean Delmas, Jeune Cinéma, no. 111 (June 1978);
P.-L. Thirard, Positif, no. 206 (May 1978); Robert Chazal,
France-Soir (14 and 23 Mar. 1978); Henry Chapier, Le Quotidien
de Paris (5 Apr. 1978); M. Péclet, Dimanche-Matin (3 Sept.
1978); Cinéma Français, no. 20 (1978); Revue Nouvelle 67, nos.
5-6 (May-June 1978); Jean-Louis Bory, Nouvelle Observateur,
no. 699 (3-9 Apr. 1978); Jean de Baroncelli, Le Monde, no. 1536
(6-12 Apr. 1978).

22   L'AMOUR EN FUITE (1979)

Synopsis

Antoine awakes next to a young woman, Sabine, and rises to
leave. They chatter and wrestle amorously. He goes to his
apartment, where a phone call from Christine reminds him of
their divorce proceedings. During the proceedings both muse
on details of their relationship. Once outside the courtroom,
he sees Colette, who recalls an incident with him, then buys
his novel in a bookstore run by her disinterested lover.
Antoine, who has broken a date with Sabine to do so, takes his
son to the train. Seeing Colette on another, he impulsively
jumps on. Colette reads several chapters of his book before
Antoine finds her. They reminisce. Struck by his naiveté,
she reveals the sad and sordid details of her life; she is a
struggling lawyer on her way to defend a child molester, and
she must resort to prostitution on the train to pay her bills.
Shattered, Antoine abruptly pulls the emergency cord and jumps
off the train. In the process he drops Sabine's photo, which
Colette recovers. Antoine races to Sabine to apologize for
breaking their date. She is cool at first, but they are reconciled. At work Antoine slowly recognizes his mother's old
lover. They go to a restaurant and reminisce; afterwards
Antoine is shown his mother's grave. This prompts him to begin
writing about his past. Meanwhile, Colette's client has attempted suicide, and she returns to Paris. On examining the
photo Antoine dropped, she realizes that her lover and Sabine,
the woman in the photo, share the same last name. Sabine joins
Colette's lover, secretly, at the movies--they are brother and
sister. Christine and Colette meet accidentally and reminisce
about Antoine. As they depart Colette asks Christine to return
the photo of Sabine to Antoine. She then meets and is reconciled with her lover. Antoine goes to Sabine's record store
where he tells her a story about how he first found her photo
and systematically tracked her down. She is convinced by this
that he is no mere "pick-up artist," and they embrace warmly.

Credits

Production Company: Les Films du Carrosse

Producer:	Marcel Berbert
Production Manager:	Roland Thenot
Director:	François Truffaut
Assistant Directors:	Suzanne Schiffman, Emmanuel Clot, Nathalie Seaver
Script:	François Truffaut, Marie-France Pisier, Jean Aurel, Suzanne Schiffman
Director of Photography:	Nestor Almendros (Eastmancolor; 1, 66)
Editor:	Martine Barraque-Curie
Art Directors:	Jean-Pierre Kohut-Svelko, Pierre Gompertz
Costumes:	Monique Dury
Makeup:	Thi Loan N'Guyen
Music:	Georges Delerue
Song:	
"L'Amour en fuite":	Music by Laurent Voulzy. Words by Alain Souchon
Sound:	Michel Laurent
Cast:	Jean-Pierre Léaud (Antoine Doinel), Marie-France Pisier (Colette), Claude Jade (Christine), Dani (Liliane), Dorothée (Sabine), Rosy Varte (Colette's mother), Marie Henriau (Divorce judge), Daniel Mesguich (Xavier), Julien Bertheau (M. Lucien), Jean-Pierre Ducos (Christine's lawyer), Pierre Dios (Revard), Monique Dury (Mme Ida), Alain Ollivier (Judge Aix), Christian Lentretien (Train traveler), Roland Thenot (Phonecaller), Julien Dubois (Alphonse Doinel).

Filmed in and around Paris, 1978

Running Time:	95 minutes
Premiere:	Paris, Feb. 1979
G.B./U.S. Title:	Love on the Run

Reviews

Andrew Sarris, Village Voice 24, no. 19 (9 Apr. 1979); Stanley Kauffmann, New Republic 180, no. 17 (28 Apr. 1979); Julian Jebb, Sight and Sound 49, no. 1 (Winter, 1979-80); Vincent Canby, New York Times (6 and 22 Apr. 1979); Penelope Gilliatt, New Yorker 55, no. 8 (9 Apr. 1979); Annette Insdorf, Take One (Mar. 1979); Arthur Schlesinger, Jr., Saturday Review 6, no. 12 (9 June 1979); Jeffrey Wells, Films in Review 30, no. 6 (June-July 1979); Robert Hatch, Nation 228, no. 16 (28 Apr. 1979); David Ansen, Newsweek 93, no. 15 (9 Apr. 1979); David Sterritt, Christian Science Monitor (6 Apr. 1979); Frank

Rich, Time 113, no. 17 (23 Apr. 1979).

Claude Beylie, Écran 79, no. 77 (15 Feb. 1979); Serge Daney
and Bernard Boland, Cahiers du Cinéma, no. 298 (Mar. 1979);
René Prédal, Jeune Cinéma, no. 117 (Mar. 1979); Michel Devillers,
Cinématographe, no. 44 (Feb. 1979); Michel Delain, L'Express
(20 Jan. 1979); Jean Collet, Études (Mar. 1979); C. M. Tremois,
Télérama (27 Jan. 1979); Michel Perez, Le Matin (25 Jan. 1979);
J. Michel, Télé-7-Jours (27 Jan. 1979); Elizabeth Ayala,
Liberation (24 Jan. 1979); Pierre Billard, Le Point (22 Jan.
1979)--reprinted in Atlas (Apr. 1979); Jacques Siclier, Le
Monde (25 Jan. 1979); Michel Marmin, Le Figaro (24 Jan. 1979);
Robert Chazal, France-Soir (25 Jan. 1979) and Monique Pantel
(27 Jan. 1979); Cinéma Français, no. 23 (1979).

23   LE DERNIER METRO (1980)

Synopsis

A young man, Bernard Granger, makes clumsy passes at an attractive woman before entering a theater, where he becomes
nervous about signing an acting contract when he overhears the
woman in charge rejecting another actor for being Jewish. The
woman, Marion Steiner, is amused by the young actor, especially
when full rehearsals for a new play begin, and the object of
the man's affections turns out to be the stage designer. One
evening while Bernard and an associate plot mysteriously in a
restaurant, Marion returns to the theater and proceeds through
a hidden trapdoor to the basement, where she meets her husband,
a German-Jewish director, actor, and writer, who is hiding there
from the Nazis occupying Paris. When escape plans fizzle, Lucas
Steiner begins to follow the progress of the rehearsals from
below the stage, eventually monitoring things from a hole he
makes in a heating duct and making copious notes on the production. He gives them to his wife, who has the director incor-
porate them into the play. When it opens, the play is praised
by the critics, except for Daxiat, a grasping and hypocritical
collaborator with the Germans, who has kind words only for
Granger. Granger confronts the critic in a restaurant, demands
an apology be made to Mrs. Steiner, and, when one is not prof-
fered, pummels and berates the critic outside in the rain.
Fearful of the consequences, Marion Steiner snubs Granger off-
stage and even during curtain calls. But when suspicious Nazis
wish to inspect the theater basement, she enlists Granger to
help disguise the hideout. There her husband informs the sur-
prised actor that his wife is in love with him. Later Marion
makes love to Granger as he clears out his dressing room, having quit the theater to devote himself entirely to the French
Resistance. During the liberation of Paris, Lucas Steiner
emerges from hiding and Daxiat is forced to flee through bomb-
scarred streets. Marion goes to comfort Granger in the hospi-
tal--this scene is actually part of a new play, at the end of

which the two of them join Lucas Steiner onstage to accept the audience's applause for their first post-Occupation production.

Credits

Production Company:	Les Films du Carrosse/SEDIF
Producer:	Marcel Berbert
Production Manager:	Jean-José Richer. Assisted by Roland Thenot
Director:	François Truffaut
Assistant Director:	Suzanne Schiffman. Assisted by Emmanuel Clot, Alain Tasma
Script:	François Truffaut, Suzanne Schiffman
Dialog:	Truffaut, Schiffman, Jean-Claude Grumberg
Director of Photography:	Nestor Almendros. Assisted by Florent Bazin, Emilio Pacull-Latorre, Tessa Racine (Eastmancolor; 1, 66)
Editors:	Martine Barraque; Marie-Aimée Debril, Jean-Francois Gire, assistants.
Art Directors:	Jean-Pierre Kohut-Svelko; Pierre Gombertz, Jacques Leguillon, Roland Jacob, assistants
Costumes:	Lisele Roos
Music:	Georges Delerue
Songs:	
"Bei Mir Bis Du Schon"	Music by Sholom Secunda. Words by Calin-Chaplin, Jacob Jacobs, Jacques Larue
"Priere a Zumba"	By A. Lara and Jacques Larue
"Mon Amant de Saint Jean"	By E. Carrara and L. Agel. Sung by Lucienne Delyle.
"Sombreros et Mantilles"	By J. Vaissalee-Chanty. Sung by Rina Ketty
"Cantique: Pitie Mon Dieu"	By A. Kunc
Sound:	Michel Laurent. Assisted by Michel Mellier
Cast:	Catherine Deneuve (Marion Steiner), Gérard Depardieu (Bernard Granger), Jean Poiret (Jean-Loup Cottins), Heinz Bennent (Lucas Steiner), Andrea Ferreol (Arlette Guillaume), Paulette Dubost (Germaine Fabre), Sabine Haudepin (Nadine Marsac), Jean-Louis Richard (Daxiat), Maurice Risch (Raymond), Marcel Berbert (Merlin),

Richard Bohringer (Gestapo member), Jean-Pierre Klein (Christian Leglise), Le Petit Franck Pasquier (Jacquot, or Eric), Renata (German singer), Jean-José Richer (René Bernardini), Martine Simonet (Martine), Laszlo Szabo (Lt. Bergen), Henia Ziv (Yvonne), Jessica Zucman (Rosette Goldstern), Alain Tasma (Marc), René Dupré (Mr. Valentin).

Filmed in and around Paris

Running Time:	130 minutes
Premiere:	Paris, Sept. 1980; U.S., New York Film Festival, Oct. 1980
G.B./U.S. Title:	The Last Metro
Awards:	Grand prix du cinéma français (plus nine other French awards); Oscar Nomination--Best Foreign Film (Hollywood).

Notes

The character Daxiat is based on a real Nazi collaborator named Alain Laubreauz, whom the actor Jean Marais once beat up outside a restaurant after the critic had insulted Jean Cocteau. Marais' memoirs served as the catalyst for the film script. As a boy Truffaut once had to undergo a shampoo when a relative saw a Nazi soldier tossle his hair. Suzanne Schiffman's father, a Polish-Jew, had to hide from the Nazis in Paris; she draped her scarf over her Jewish star when she ventured out.

Reviews

Peter Pappas, Cinéaste 10, no. 4 (Fall 1980); Robert Hatch, Nation (7 Mar. 1981); Steven Schiff, Atlantic Monthly (Apr. 1981); Elliott Stein, Film Comment 17, no. 6 (Nov.-Dec. 1981); Janet Maslin, New York Times (19 Oct. 1981); William Luhr, Wide Angle 4, no. 3; Village Voice 25, no. 44 (29 Oct. 1980); Richard Schickel, Time (23 Feb. 1981); Charles Michener, Newsweek (23 Feb. 1981); Variety (17 Sept. 1980); Vincent Canby, New York Times (12 Oct. 1980, reprinted 11 Feb. 1981); Stanley Kauffmann, New Republic (28 Feb. 1981); Richard Grenier, Commentary (Feb. 1981); Molly Haskell, Ms. (Jan. 1981); Judith Crist, New York (16 Feb. 1981); Horizon (Feb. 1981); Rolling Stone (30 Apr. 1981).

Yann Lardeau, Cahiers du Cinéma, no. 316 (Oct. 1980); Jean-Louis Cros, Image et Son (Oct. 1980); Jacques Fieschi and Jacques Grant, Amis du Film (Oct. 1980); Michel Perez, Le Figaro (17 Sept. 1980); Michel Mardore, Le Nouvel Observateur (13-19 Sept. 1980); C. M. Tremois, Télérama (17 June and 17

Sept. 1980); Michel Delain, L'Express (27 Sept. 1980); Les
Nouvelles Litteraires (18 Sept. 1980); J. Tonnerre,
Cinématographe, no. 57 (May 1980); Le Point, no. 417 (15 Sept.
1980).

*23a   LA FEMME D'À CÔTÉ (1981)

Credits

Production Company:	Les Films du Carrosse/TF 1 Films
Production Manager:	Armand Barbault. Assisted by Roland Thenot
Director:	François Truffaut
Assistant Director:	Suzanne Schiffman. Assisted by Alain Tasma
Script:	François Truffaut, Suzanne Schiffman, Jean Aurel
Director of Photography:	William Lubtchansky. Assisted by Caroline Champetier
Editor:	Martine Barraque
Costumes:	Michele Cerf
Music:	Georges Delerue
Sound:	Michel Laurent
Cast:	Gerard Depardieu (Bernard Coudray), Fanny Ardant (Mathilde Bauchard), Henri Garcin (Philippe Bauchard), Michele Baumgartner (Arlette Coudray), Roger Van Hool (Roland Duguet), Veronique Silver (Mme Jouve), Philippe Morier-Genoud (The Doctor).

Filmed in and around Grenoble, Apr.-May 1981.

Running Time:	106 minutes.
Premiere:	Paris, Sept. 1981; New York Film Festival Oct. 1981.
G.B./U.S. Title:	The Woman Next Door

ADDENDA (to all above credits)

Script Girl: Suzanne Schiffman (entries 6-8, 10-12); Christine
Pellé (entries 13-23a).
Make-up: Thi-Loan N'Guyen (entries 16-23a).
Ass't. Production Manager: Roland Thenot (entries 11-14,
16-17); Geneviève Lefebvre (entry 22).
Ass't. Director: Jean-François Adam (entries 6-7); Florence
Malraux (entry 6); Claude Othnin-Girard (entry 8); Jean-
François Stevenin (entries 12-14, 17); Jean-François Destrée
(entry 12); Olivier Mergault (entry 15); Bernard Cohn (entry
16).
Ass't. Art Director: Jean-Pierre Kohut (entries 12-15); Jean-
François Stevenin (entry 16); Pierre Gompertz (entries 20-21).

IV. Writings about François Truffaut

1957

24   MARCORELLES, LOUIS. "Journées du cinéma." Sight and Sound
       27, no. 3 (Winter):114-15.
          On the Tours short film festival, with remarks on The
       Mischief Makers.

1958

25   MARCORELLES, LOUIS. "French Cinema, the Old and the New."
       Sight and Sound 27, no. 4 (Spring):190-95.
          Singles out Astruc, Vadim, and others, but also mentions
       Truffaut to indicate new filmmaking climate in France.

1959

26   AUCUY, JEAN-MARC. "Evolution du cinéma français: Claude
       Bernard Aubert, François Truffaut, Alain Resnais." La
       Nouvelle Critique 11, no. 108 (July-Aug.):138-46.
          Truffaut gets the most space. Aucuy concentrates on the
       pitfalls Truffaut overcomes, such as getting a child actor
       to make spontaneity look natural, and presenting the world
       as an adolescent would confront it, yet penetrating into
       his or her character. The family and institutions are pre-
       sented, though, as melodrama and caricature.

27   BILLARD, GINETTE. "The Men and Their Work." Films and Filming
       6, no. 1 (Oct.):7-8.
          Brief descriptions of New Wave directors.

28   BURCH, NOEL. "Qu'est-ce que la Nouvelle Vague?" Film
       Quarterly 13, no. 2 (Winter): 16 ff.
          A scathing putdown of Rivette, Chabrol, Truffaut, Malle,
       and Vadim as "fake prodigies," preparatory to laudatory
       looks at Resnais' Hiroshima, mon amour and Marcel Hanoun's
       Une Simple Histoire.

1959

29   D[ONIOL]-V[ALCROZE], J[ACQUES]. "Les Quatre Cents Coups."
      Cahiers du Cinéma 16, no. 96 (June).
          The Cahiers editor puts the film in the perspective of
      the twelve-year history of the Cannes festival.

30   DONIOL-VALCROZE, JACQUES. "L'histoire des Cahiers." Cahiers
      du Cinéma 17, no. 100 (Oct.):62-68.
          One of the editors of the journal provides a brief ana-
      lytical history, citing Truffaut's "Une Certaine Tendance
      . . ." as "the real point of departure for what represents
      today, right or wrong, the Cahiers du Cinéma."

31   GODARD, JEAN-LUC. "Exclu l'an dernier du Festival Truffaut
      répresentera la France à Cannes avec Les 400 Coups." Arts,
      no. 719 (22-28 Apr.):1, 5.
          Not about Truffaut and his film but about the change
      that its acceptance at Cannes has signaled. "Today, victory
      is ours," Godard brags. He lists other Cahiers critics
      whose films will be just as important. Reprinted in Jean-
      Luc Godard par Jean-Luc Godard (see entry 172).

32   GRENIER, CYNTHIA. "The New Wave at Cannes." Reporter 21,
      no. 2 (23 July):39-41.
          News story with pertinent background information on
      Truffaut and the festival.

33   MARCORELLES, LOUIS. "Paris Notes." Sight and Sound 28, no.
      2 (Spring):66-67.
          Mentions Truffaut's (unrealized) plans.

34   ROUCH, JANE. "The Young Lions of the French Film Industry."
      Producers Guild of America Journal (formerly the Journal of
      the Screen Producers Guild) 8 (Dec.):16-18.
          Truffaut is given prime billing in this quick introduc-
      tion to nine directors. The 400 Blows is translated here
      as Hot-Headed.

35   SADOUL, GEORGES. "Notes on a New Generation." Sight and
      Sound 28, nos. 3 and 4 (Summer-Autumn):111-16.
          A report on the Cannes festival. Truffaut is included
      with Chabrol (Camus, Franju, Resnais, et al. are treated
      separately), though at the end Sadoul notes that he has
      "leapt to the front of his generation."

36   SALACHAS, GILBERT. "Les Quatre Cents Coups." Télé-Ciné, no.
      83 (June-July):1-11.
          Full plot summary, comments on the director and the ori-
      gin of the screenplay, analysis of the direction and the
      characters, plus a conclusion.

37 TAILLEUR, ROGER et al. "Quoi de neuf?" Positif, no. 31
    (Nov.):1-16.
        A roundtable discussion of the New Wave. Truffaut is
    pronounced "honest"--technically as well as intellectually
    and morally. Issue no. 33 (Apr. 1960) does a follow-up
    article, focusing on Breathless.

38 TALLENAY, JEAN-LOUIS. "Une Nouvelle Vague de réalisateurs."
    Signes du Temps, no. 2 (Feb.):35-37.
        New French cinema is subdivided into four sections:
    followers of Vadim, followers of Astruc, documentarians,
    and essayists/poets. Truffaut is included with Chabrol
    and Rivette in the Astruc circle not because they are his
    followers, but because they all oppose academic cinema and
    Vadim-style audacity.

39 WEBER, EUGEN. "An Escapist Realism." Film Quarterly 13, no.
    2 (Winter):9-16.
        Faults the New Wave (refers to films by Camus, Malle,
    Chabrol, and Resnais, but not Truffaut) for not being true
    to the complex interaction of general personal and social
    concerns.

1960

40 BILLARD, PIERRE et al. "Petit lexique de la nouvelle vague."
    Cinéma 60, no. 45 (Apr.):95-106.
        Alphabetical list of filmmakers with brief biographical
    sketches. Truffaut's is on page 105.

41 BORDE, RAYMOND. "Nouvelle Vague." Premier Plan, no. 10
    (June):1-33.
        A bracing tonic because of its unrestrained negativity
    about the New Wave in general and Truffaut in particular
    ("a sort of evil Bazin").

42 BUTCHER, MARYVONNE. "France's Film Renascence." Commonweal
    71, no. 15 (8 Jan.):414-16.
        Factors that contributed to the rise of the New Wave
    are presented. The 400 Blows lauded for the realism of its
    nonstudio setting.

43 CADIEUX, FERNAND; CASTONGUAY, PIERRE; CÔTÉ, GUY; and PILON,
    JEAN-CLAUDE. "Tirez sur le pianiste." Objectif 60 1, no.
    2 (Nov.):23-28.
        A round table discussion of the film's themes and style,
    plus certain scenes.

1960

44 COTET, JEAN. "La 'Nouvelle Vague' a-t-elle revolutionné les
   methodes de production?" and "La Nouvelle Vague et le
   marché mondial." Cinéma 60, no. 43 (Feb.):73-80 and no.
   44 (Mar.):14-17.
     The first pleads the case of the technicians' union and
   is mostly on Chabrol. The second is on the economic factors
   to be considered in marketing New Wave films worldwide.

45 CROCE, ARLENE. "The 400 Blows." Film Quarterly 13, no. 3
   (Spring):35-38.
     The film is a "genuinely un-neurotic work of public art"
   about freedom, with "the sadness of the universal estrange-
   ment," done in a "beautifully oblique style of commentary"
   that is both poetic and ambiguous. Reprinted in Great Film
   Directors; see entry 392.

46 CURTELIN, JEAN. "Nouvelle Vague." Premier Plan, no. 9 (May):
   1-40.
     "An ambiguous balance sheet" on Truffaut and others.

47 DARRACH, HENRY B. "The New Wave." Horizon 2, no. 5 (May):
   49-55.
     Background piece on the celebrated first films of
   Chabrol, Malle, Truffaut, Camus, and Resnais, which attrib-
   utes the New Wave to the twenty-year growth of "the first
   cinematically mature mass audience." Some of Truffaut's
   bluster is quoted. The 400 Blows is "painfully moving and
   amazingly wise."

48 GENÊT. "Letter from Paris." New Yorker 36, no. 26 (13 Aug.):
   87-88, 91-94.
     On the moral concern about the New Wave, plus description
   of its characteristics and filmmakers (mostly Godard and,
   oddly, Fellini).

49 GRENIER, CYNTHIA. "Renaissance of French Movies." New York
   Times Magazine (20 Mar.):44-45.
     More pictures than paragraphs. Reportage on "New Wave"
   and its "superficial homogeneity."

50 HOLLAND, NORMAN. "How New? How Vague?" Hudson Review 13,
   no. 2 (Summer):270-77.
     The 400 Blows reviewed with three other French films us-
   ing Freud's statement--mankind would be a lot happier with
   a little less concern for goodness and a little more for
   truth--as a motto. Holland believes that New Wave directors favor point of view approach, which is closer to a
   novelist's vision than to a cinéaste's.

1961

51 MARCORELLES, LOUIS. "Views of the New Wave." Sight and Sound
    29, no. 2 (Spring):84-85.
        A review of Breathless, with mistaken notion of Truffaut's
    role.

52 MARTIN, MARCEL. "Nouvelle vague: Tentative (raisonnée) de
    bilan (provisoire)." Cinéma 60, no. 44 (Mar.):4-13.
        In his initial appraisal of the New Wave phenomenon,
    Martin calls attention to its three essential characteris-
    tics, its heterogeneity, and the economic factors that con-
    tributed to its rise.

53 MEKAS, JONAS. "Cinema of the New Generation . . ." Film
    Culture, no. 21 (Summer):1-6.
        The New Wave "reflects new temperaments and new ideas:
    those of the cold-war generation." It is related to English
    and American new cinema.

54 RHODE, ERIC. "Les Quatre Cents Coups." Sight and Sound 29,
    no. 2 (Spring):89-90.
        In praising the film, Rhode notes its "Balzacian" irony
    and "Chaplinesque pathos." Truffaut's technique is con-
    trasted with Resnais'; Truffaut is said to have learned from
    Bazin how to "capture the ambiguity and multiple levels of
    meaning" in novels.

55 ROUD, RICHARD. "The French Line." Sight and Sound 29, no. 4
    (Autumn):166-71.
        Cahiers du Cinéma approach ("if driven to it, Cahiers
    will choose form") contrasted to that of Sight and Sound
    (content), with passing reference to Truffaut.

56 WEIGHTMAN, J. G. "New Wave in French Culture." Commentary
    30, no. 3 (Sept.):230-40.
        Beginning with an extended look at Breathless and con-
    tinuing through other recent films and the experimental
    novel, Weightman argues that the New Wave is part of a
    broader phase of sophisticated anarchism, within a frame-
    work of authority and prosperity in France, that can be
    traced back through Camus' work. The 400 Blows gets only
    one sentence.

1961

57 BORDE, RAYMOND. "The New French Cinema." Atlas 2, no. 5
    (Nov.):391-96.
        Reprint from Premier Plan (see entry 41).

1961

58   DURGNAT, RAYMOND. "Shoot the Pianist." Films and Filming 7,
        no. 5 (Feb.):29–30.
            An analysis that makes several unique points on the "new
        superficiality," the "creative use of reticence, ambiguity,
        and monotony," the stress on "style" and "spatial relation-
        ships."

59   HOUSTON, PENELOPE. "Uncommitted Artist." Sight and Sound 30,
        no. 2 (Spring):64–65.
            Using Truffaut's own attack on Stanley Kramer's big-
        issue films, Houston provides an articulate response to com-
        plaints of "left-wing critics" about Shoot the Piano Player,
        concluding that Truffaut is not an uncommitted artist. Re-
        printed in Braudy, Focus on "Shoot the Piano Player" (see
        entry 239).

60   KAST, PIERRE. "L'Âme du canon." Cahiers du Cinéma 20, no.
        115 (Jan.):44–46.
            Demonstrates the preeminence of the subject (timidity)
        over the development of the story in Shoot the Piano Player.
        Comments on its grace, charm, and gentleness. Truffaut's
        secret: he loves both the characters and the actors. Re-
        printed in Braudy, Focus on "Shoot the Piano Player" (see
        entry 239).

61   MARCORELLES, LOUIS. "Paris Notes." Sight and Sound 30, no.
        4 (Autumn):173.
            Production methods for Jules and Jim recommended as solu-
        tion to faltering industry.

62   PEARSON, GABRIEL, and RHODE, ERIC. "Cinema of Appearance."
        Sight and Sound 30, no. 4 (Autumn):161–68.
            Breathless and Shoot the Piano Player are used to indi-
        cate how a humanist can come to terms with the new cinema
        of discontinuity. Reprinted in Braudy, Focus on "Shoot the
        Piano Player (see entry 239).

63   SALACHAS, GILBERT. "Tirez sur le pianiste." Télé-Ciné, no.
        94 (Mar.):1–13.
            Plot description, preliminary remarks on the origin of
        the script and the dramatic construction, analysis of the
        direction and the characters, and a conclusion.

64   SICLIER, JACQUES. "New Wave and French Cinema." Sight and
        Sound 30, no. 3 (Summer):116–20.
            Premature criticism of the New Wave (with the exception
        of Truffaut), which has failed because the filmmakers "have
        resolutely turned their backs on authentic social reality
        and have immersed us in the complexes and obsessions of an

1962

intellectual world concerned primarily with preaching total disengagement."

65 _____. Nouvelle Vague? Paris: Les Éditions du cerf, 132 pp.
More journalistic than substantive introduction, divided
into three parts: background, catalog of filmmakers, and
general observations. Truffaut gets a long paragraph, which
is cool to his first film, but sees promise in his second.

66 TOROK, JEAN-PAUL. "Le Point sensible: Tirez sur le Pianiste."
Positif, no. 38 (Mar.):39-47.
An essential article, which contends that the film is a
faithful adaptation that destroys the original work ("honestly, in complicity with his author") and is a profoundly
autobiographical film. It is "a neurotic work" expressing
a fear of the world and a "Baudelairian obsession with wom-
en." Reprinted in Braudy, Focus on "Shoot the Piano Player"
(see entry 239).

1962

67 AUCUY, JEAN-MARC. "Jules et Jim: La Recherche de l'absolu."
La Nouvelle Critique, no. 136 (Apr.-May):130-41.
On Truffaut's faithfulness to the novel and the changes
he made. Extracts from the book are included.

68 BENAYOUN, ROBERT. "Le Roi est nu." Positif 46 (June):1-14.
A scathing put-down of the careerist Cahiers du Cinéma,
its opportunitistic politique des auteurs, and the amateur-
ish films of the nouvelle vague that it spawned and promoted.
Truffaut is especially criticized for making films like the
ones he used to attack. Reprinted in Graham, The New Wave:
Critical Landmarks (see entry 173).

69 BORDE, RAYMOND; BAUCHE, FREDDY; and CURTELIN, JEAN. Nouvelle
Vague. Lyons: Éditions Serdoc, 93+40 pp.
Reprints Borde's and Curtelin's 1960 articles from
Premier Plan, plus brief analyses of Truffaut's first three
films by Bauche; see entries 57, 41, and 46.

70 BILLARD, PIERRE. "Le 401eme Coup de François Truffaut." Le
Nouveau Candide--Spectateur (26 Apr.-3 May):21.
A history of Truffaut's relations with Cannes on the
occasion of his being a juror.

71 COLLET, JEAN. "L'Art de vivre." Cahiers du Cinéma 23, no.
135 (Sept.):44-48.
A review of Love at 20, almost entirely on Truffaut's

1962

segment. Collet focuses on the contrast between life and art and concludes that the beauty of the film lies in the "pulsation" of its almost abstract movement and in the faithfully etched tracing of the life that passes by.

72 _____. "De quelques mythes de cinéma." Signes du Temps, no. 7 (July):28-31.
Passing reference to Truffaut and Jules and Jim. Now films, vis-à-vis myths of sad love, for instance, mix genres and test the spectator's comprehension.

73 _____. "Portraits de femmes." Signes du Temps, no. 3 (Mar.): 30-32.
Catherine is special focus in this review of Jules and Jim. She is a queen without a king, a mother with two big children. Truffaut's humility and reserve noted.

74 DELAHAYE, MICHEL. "Les Tourbillons élémentaires." Cahiers du Cinéma 22, no. 129 (Mar.):39-44.
An influential analysis of Jules and Jim that deals with its use of black-and-white textures, its sense of film history, its organic structure, symmetries and inversions, and its "astonishingly lively" temps-morts.

75 DURGNAT, RAYMOND. "The Decade: France--A Mirror for Marianne." Films and Filming 9, no. 2 (Nov.):48-55.
Brief explanation of French politics and national character (contrasted with those of the British), followed by a survey of important films before New Wave and after. Truffaut mentioned but not singled out for extensive comment.

76 FARBER, MANNY. "White Elephant Art vs Termite Art." Film Culture, no. 27 (Winter):9-13.
Truffaut (along with Antonioni and Richardson) is an exemplar of white elephant art--"particularly the critic-devouring virtue of filling every pore of a work with glinting, darting Style and creative Vivacity." Reprinted in Negative Spaces (also called Movies), see entry 235.

77 FOX, JOAN. "The New Wave." Canadian Art 19, no. 80 (July-Aug.):303-5.
French films have evolved like the novel into "intellectualized experiments in form and technique." Truffaut, "by the way, is a genius." Shoot the Piano Player is singled out for comment and compared briefly to Hiroshima, mon amour as films involving the torment of memory. Reprinted in Sarris, ed., The Film (see entry 181).

78   GARRIGOU-LAGRANGE, MADALEINE.   "Jules et Jim."   Télé-Ciné,
         no. 105 (June-July):1-11.
              Full plot summary, analysis of characters and direction
         (construction, images, soundtrack), plus a final appraisal
         ("portee").

79   HOUSTON, PENELOPE.   "The Rewards of Quality."   Sight and Sound
         31, no. 2 (Spring):71-72.
              A look at the French cinema-aid system (which helped
         launch the New Wave) with an eye to adapting it to England.

80   JEAN, RAYMOND.   "Jules et Jim ou 'Tendre comme le souvenir.'"
         Cahiers du Sud, no. 366 (May-June).
              Brief appreciation. Reprinted in 1965; see entry 112.

81   KAEL, PAULINE.   "Shoot the Piano Player."   Film Culture, no.
         27 (Winter):14-16.
              In response to negative reviews, Kael contends that the
         film has style (anarchic and nihilistic) and that the sub-
         ject matter only seems small. Reprinted in I Lost It at
         the Movies, Great Film Directors, Movie Comedy, and Focus
         on "Shoot the Piano Player"; see entries 113, 392, 361, and
         239.

82   LEFEBVRE, JEAN-PIERRE.   "François Truffaut, un art ardente et
         triste."   Objectif 62 2, no. 4 (July):15-25.
              Full of insights into Jules and Jim and Truffaut's early
         career. On the themes (love and friendship), tones, mise-
         en-scène, "objective subjectivity," and use of actors.

83   MILNE, TOM.   "How Art Is True?"   Sight and Sound 31, no. 4
         (Autumn):166-71.
              An examination of improvisation to produce spontaneity
         and truth in film, which begins with a quote by Truffaut
         ("The film of tomorrow will be an act of love") and refers
         to his films in passing.

84   New York Film Bulletin 3, no. 3, issue 44 (Summer).
              Special Truffaut issue. It contains Truffaut's tribute
         to Bazin: "It Was Good to Be Alive" (pp. 3-5)--translated
         from Cahiers--see entries 1041 and 1104; Marshall Lewis'
         brief but packed essay on Shoot the Piano Player (pp. 7-8)
         in which he notes the similarity of Charlie and Henry Fonda
         in The Wrong Man, calls the film "Truffaut's first statement
         on commitment," which says "a great deal about loneliness,
         frustration, sacrifice, love and cinema." There is a script
         extract from Shoot the Piano Player on pp. 9-10. In "Inside
         the Piano Player" (p. 11), Andrew Sarris provides a list of
         seven private references in the film and denies two other

1962

alleged references. R. M. Franchi in an article on Jules
and Jim (pp. 12-14) calls it "the definitive third film,"
indebted to Renoir. Franchi notes Truffaut's eclecticism,
"over-self-consciousness," and concern for people. The issue is filled out with two valuable "conversations" with
Truffaut (pp. 15-22; see entry 1220) and a filmography.

85 RHODE, ERIC. "The Disordered Imagination." Listener 67, no.
1734 (21 June):1081.
"Good films are memorable not for the broad stretch of
their narrative but for their epiphanies . . . and the
cinema works best presenting images of the disordered imagination." Jules and Jim is used to validate this thesis.

86 SARRIS, ANDREW. "Notes on the Auteur Theory in 1962." Film
Culture, no. 27 (Winter):1-8.
The first in a series of exchanges on the auteur theory
in America. The major responses include: Pauline Kael,
"Circles and Squares," Film Quarterly 16, no. 3 (Spring
1963); Andrew Sarris, "The Auteur Theory," Film Quarterly
16, no. 4 (Summer 1963); the editors of Movie, "Movie vs.
Kael," Film Quarterly 17, no. 1 (Fall 1963); Marion Magid,
"Auteur Auteur," Commentary (Mar. 1964); and Sarris, "The
Auteur Theory Revisited," American Film 2, no. 9 (July-Aug.
1977). See also side-by-side ad hominem exchange between
Sarris and John Simon in New York Times (14 Feb. 1971):
sec. 2, pp. 1, 16-18. The Sarris and Kael articles have
been reprinted extensively (see entries 276 and 113).

87 Script, no. 5 (Apr.):2-44.
The entire issue is devoted to Truffaut, mainly to Jules
and Jim. There are nine sections, including an introduction,
an interview with Truffaut, a filmography, the song from
Jules and Jim, and a script extract: "histoire d'artilleur."
The essays are: "Poësie de l'instant" by René Salis (pp.
19-25) on style in Jules and Jim and Shoot the Piano Player;
"Une Leçon de réalisation" by Dan Cukier (pp. 26-31) and
"D'un viol fructeux" by Marcel Croës (pp. 33-36) on Jules
and Jim; and "Cinéma son amour" by Jo Gryn (pp. 37-42) on
the characters in Truffaut's second and third films.

88 "Truffaut Loses Libel Suit." New York Times (28 Mar.):36.
One-paragraph-long news article on Vadim case.

89 TYLER, PARKER. "The Lady Called 'A'; Or, If Jules and Jim
had Only Lived at Marienbad." Film Culture, no. 25
(Summer):21-24.
Briefly points out the resemblances between Truffaut's
film, Resnais' Last Year at Marienbad, and Rivette's Paris

Belongs to Us, and doubts that Catherine actually drives
Jim off bridge. Reprinted in The Three Faces of Film; see
entry 160.

1963

90   "The Best Directors and Twenty on Their Way." Cinema (U.S.A.)
     1, no. 4 (June–July):19–20.
          Truffaut is the youngest, and only New Wave, director
     mentioned.

91   BREEN, JAMES. "Twelve of the Best." Observer, no. 8989
     (13 Oct.):30.
          Thumbnail sketch of Truffaut, with eleven other great
     directors.

92   DURGNAT, RAYMOND. Nouvelle Vague: The First Decade. Loughton,
     Essex, England: Motion Publications, 90 pp.
          An alphabetical listing of thirty-five filmmakers, with
     a very brief introduction. Truffaut, Resnais, Franju, and
     Chabrol get the most space. Durgnat focused on Antoine's
     accidentproneness and the ellipses of 400 Blows, on
     Charlie's Hamlet-like qualities and the inversions of Shoot
     the Piano Player, and on the "female-active" Catherine and
     the "fraternity-in-solitude" of Jules and Jim.

93   FLAUS, JOHN. "Jules and Jim." Film Journal, no. 22 (Oct.):
     19–26.
          Praise for the film's freshness and lack of predictabil-
     ity. Flaus details Truffaut's methods of presenting his
     characters ("the events are not the primary source of in-
     terest"), the film's point of view ("the film is substan-
     tially a record of Jim's Catherine"), and its technical
     virtuosity (used for the "purpose of reinforcing subjective
     experience").

94   "François Truffaut." In International Film Guide 1964. Edited
     by Peter Cowie. London: Tantivy Press; New York: A. S.
     Barnes & Co., pp. 19–21.
          Introductory remarks covering first three feature-length
     films.

95   GRAHAM, PETER. "The Face of '63--France." Films and Filming,
     no. 8 (May):13–22.
          The decline of the New Wave with special attention to
     Truffaut, Godard, and Chabrol, to their defense of their
     films, their in-jokes and allusions.

1963

96   _____. "In the Picture: Report from Paris." Observer, no.
        8988 (6 Oct.):27.
            Truffaut's work since Jules and Jim reported on: his
        script for Soft Skin, the book on Hitchcock, the trouble
        raising money for Fahrenheit 451.

97   GREENSPUN, ROGER. "Elective Affinities: Aspects of Jules and
        Jim." Sight and Sound 32, no. 2 (Spring):78–82.
            A multifaceted analysis of the geometric patterns (cir-
        cles and triangles), the three central characters, the out-
        side world, and the artistic references of the film, con-
        cluding that "the burden of a work that is so at pains to
        distinguish the integrity of each of its several elements
        is exactly a love of multiple relations, tolerance, ele-
        mental order, gradualism, plentitude, the inclusion of all
        of 'les autres!'" Reprinted in Sarris, The Film; see entry
        181.

98   HOUSTON, PENELOPE. The Contemporary Cinema. London: Cox &
        Wyman, 222 pp.
            Truffaut mentioned in chapter 7, "The Free French." He
        is cited for making films (like Renoir) about friendship
        and having a "nostalgia for innocence."

99   ROUD, RICHARD. "The Left Bank." Sight and Sound 32, no. 1
        (Winter):24–27.
            An examination of Marker, Varda, and Resnais as members
        of the New Wave distinct from the "Godard-Truffaut group"
        (or Cahiers group).

100   SHATNOFF, JUDITH. "François Truffaut--The Anarchist
        Imagination." Film Quarterly 16, no. 3 (Spring):3–11.
            An examination of Truffaut's "dangerous talent" in his
        first three films, based on the observation that Truffaut
        is "an ex-j.d., a slum kid with a slum kid's energy and
        ability to thumb his nose and laugh and suffer simultane-
        ously. He's also a French intellectual." Reprinted in
        Braudy, Focus on "Shoot the Piano Player" (see entry 239).

101   STANBROOK, ALAN. "The Star They Couldn't Photograph." Films
        and Filming 9, no. 5 (Feb.):10–14.
            Profile of Jeanne Moreau that ends with her work with
        Truffaut.

                              1964

102   ALLOMBERT, GUY. "La peau douce de François Truffaut." La
        Cinématographie Française, no. 5 (May):1–19.

1964

Full plot summary, character descriptions, and extract from the script on "the rupture," followed by a biographical sketch: "François Truffaut--Le Gout de la tendresse et de l'humanité."

103 FIESCHI, JEAN-ANDRÉ. "Le Sourire de Reims." Cahiers du Cinéma 27, no. 157 (July):47-50.
Soft Skin is the first "direct" film by Truffaut, his first totally in the present; it is the work of a self-critical auteur looking for new roads to explore. In a sense it is a return to the salutary wickedness of his writings for Arts.

104 GARY, ROMAIN. "The Foamy Edge of the Wave." Show 4 (Apr.): 75-76.
A survey of the achievements of the New Wave--which do not include originality of thought or form: "They have not so much changed the movies themselves as the way we are looking at them."

105 GREENSPUN, ROGER. "Through the Looking Glass." Moviegoer, no. 1 (Winter):3-11.
Taking his cue from Delahaye's review of Jules and Jim, Greenspun fashions a commentary on Shoot the Piano Player --its "engrossing busyness," circles, its characters' drive toward completion and desire to tell their life stories, its reflecting surfaces, brilliant determinism, and especially its black and white imagery. Reprinted in Bellone, ed., Renaissance of the Film (see entry 204) and in Braudy, Focus on "Shoot the Piano Player" (see entry 239).

106 JACOB, GILLES. Le Cinéma moderne. Lyon: Serdoc, 232 pp.
Jacob's thesis is that today's films offer brilliant variations on the themes of isolation, violence, anxiety, and despair. A chapter entitled "Love and Friendship" (in the second section on "Man and Society") is devoted to Truffaut. Incidents and dialogue from films through Jules and Jim presented, plus brief, though accurate, analysis.

107 OXENHANDLER, NEAL. "Truffaut, Heir to Apollinaire." Shenandoah 15, no. 2 (Winter):8-13.
Basing his thesis on the story that Jim tells Jules and Albert--which, it is claimed, is the story of Apollinaire --Oxenhandler notes the Apollinairian atmosphere, "axes or themes," and poetic techniques in Jules and Jim.

108 STOLLER, JAMES. "After The 400 Blows." The Moviegoer, no. 1 (Winter):12-18.
Stoller dismisses other critics' negative appraisals of

1964

> Truffaut's section of Love at 20 and deals persuasively
> with the film's music, rhythms, and faces, and its rare
> combination of grace and spontaneity.

109 TAYLOR, JOHN RUSSELL. "The New Wave." In Cinema Eye, Cinema
Ear. New York: Hill & Wang, pp. 200-229.
The chapter is further subdivided into sections on
Truffaut, Godard, and Resnais. Truffaut is called the
"master of expressive metaphor." 400 Blows is "Wordsworth-
ian," technically conservative but with a revolutionary
message. Shoot the Piano Player and Jules and Jim are
lightly regarded by Taylor, who concludes that beneath the
"superficial eclecticism" of Truffaut's style there is a
"streak of Renoirian romantic warmth and tenderness," which
gives his films "definition and personality."

<u>1965</u>

110 GODARD, JEAN-LUC. "Apprenez le François." L'Avant-Scène du
Cinéma, no. 48 (May):5.
A fragmented series of impressions and recollections of
Truffaut's films and the two men's moviegoing days, which
ends by saying that Truffaut is "the only filmmaker increas-
ing in seriousness." Reprinted in Godard on Godard (see
entry 172).

111 JACOB, GILLES. "Nouvelle Vague or jeune cinéma." Sight and
Sound 34, no. 1 (Winter):4-8.
Beginning with a reference to the savage critical treatment of Soft Skin, Jacob comments (mostly through an interview with Alain Jessua) on the "collapse" of the New Wave.

112 JEAN, RAYMOND. "Jules et Jim ou 'Tendre comme le souvenir.'"
In La Littérature et le réel. De Diderot au 'Nouveau Roman.'
Paris: Edition Albin Michel, pp. 197-202.
Reprint of essay from Cahiers du Sud (see entry 80).

113 KAEL, PAULINE. I Lost It at the Movies. Boston: Little,
Brown, 368 pp.
Contains her reviews of Shoot the Piano Player and Jules
and Jim, and her "Circles and Squares" essay (see entries
80 and 86).

114 KLEIN, MICHAEL. "The Literary Sophistication of François
Truffaut." Film Comment 3, no. 3 (Summer):24-29.
Truffaut is working in a literary tradition by using
techniques of irony and dislocation "to exhaust the audience's conventional responses" and prevent it from

"responding in a conventional, sentimental way." Examples from Shoot the Piano Player and Jules and Jim.

115 MacDONALD, DWIGHT. "Films." Esquire 63, no. 5 (May):18, 20, 22, 28, 30.

A longish review of Soft Skin--"a curiously unambitious failure." MacDonald raises, but does not answer, many questions and points out Truffaut's two particular virtues: "He takes you right into the kitchen [of filmmaking]" and he "has a peculiar knack for presenting a mise-en-scene that is . . . exactly life-size."

116 MAGNAN, HENRY. "Beaucoup d'auteurs, peu de grands films: On demande des chef-d'oeuvres." Le Figaro Littéraire 20, no. 997 (27 May-2 June):10-11.

On the current state of the industry and the art of film in France and especially on government subsidies. Little on Truffaut specifically.

117 "Mata-Hari, Agent H-21." Cinema (U.S.A.) 2, no. 5 (Apr.): 14-15.

A pictorial with brief comment noting that Truffaut's ideas are apparent in the script.

118 NOWELL-SMITH, GEOFFREY. "François Truffaut." New Left Review 31 (May-June):86-90.

Truffaut's pose as a showman and his perceptions of the world as "a maelstrom of disorder and flux" provide insight into his career and his return "with a vengeance to the troubles of social existence" in Soft Skin.

119 PILARD, PHILIPPE. "Nouvelle Vague et politique." Revue du Cinéma/Image et Son, no. 188 (Nov.):90-102.

Three groups of New Wave directors are distinguished; Truffaut lumped with all other former Cahiers critics. Their protagonists are forever unable to adapt; confrontation with the world usually ends tragically. They look iconoclastic but accept world as it is.

120 PORCILE, FRANCOIS. Défense du court métrage français. Paris: Les Éditions du Cerf, 308 pp.

The Mischief Makers briefly examined and commended for its "justesse," accuracy.

121 TAYLOR, STEPHEN. "After the Nouvelle Vague." Film Quarterly 18, no. 3 (Spring):5-9.

Truffaut's "attention to detail is scrupulous, he exhausts his incontestably enormous technical virtuosity on a subject that stubbornly refuses to be enriched by the

1965

illumination he brings to it, and, most irritating of all,
he maintains that dubious objectivity known as scholarly
self-effacement." On Soft Skin.

1966

122   ARMES, ROY. French Cinema since 1946, vol. 2, The Personal
Style. Cranbury, N.J.: A. S. Barnes, 176 pp.
Chapter 3, "Critics Incorporated," deals with Truffaut,
Chabrol, Godard, and Rivette. A chronological review of
the films from The Mischief Makers to Fahrenheit 451, followed by a brief overview. Armes admits that "the surface
of his work is always lively, entertaining, and instantly
captivating," but believes Truffaut's interest in life's
"oddities and little incongruities" belies his "fatal un-
willingness to commit himself to use the camera to probe."
Expanded in 1970 (see entry 202).

123   B[ABY] Y[VONNE]. "Hommage à François Truffaut aux rencontres
cinématographiques d'Annecy." Le Monde, no. 6794 (16 Nov.):
16.
Report on the tribute paid to Truffaut.

124   BRODTKORB, PAUL. "Reims Revisited." Moviegoer 3 (Summer):
34-38.
An analysis of self-entrapment in Soft Skin. "Truffaut
has taken the cliché dialectic [of adultery], freshly rede-
fined its polarities, and arrived at a deeper analysis."

125   COLLET, JEAN. "L'Oeuvre de François Truffaut. Une Tragedie
de la connaissance." Études, no. 325 (Dec.):688-700.
Covers films from The Mischief Makers through Fahrenheit
451 succinctly and usefully. Sees Truffaut's film career
developing out of his criticism, proceeding like a series
of chain reactions. Reprinted in Le Cinéma en question
(see entry 244).

126   ____. "Fahreneit 451: Un Combat singulier." Signes du
Temps (Sept.-Oct.):29-31.
A measured yet positive analysis of the film that relates
it to other Truffaut films (the theme of fear and the father
figures) and notes its combination of dream and reality.

127   COMOLLI, JEAN-LOUIS. "L'Auteur, les masques, l'autre."
Cahiers du Cinéma, no. 184 (Nov.):64.
On Fahrenheit 451, which is seen to be built on the
"principle of privation" and thus makes a "clean sweep" of
"all that on which, specifically, films are grounded:

characters, fictions, language, dramatic laws." Reprinted in Cahiers in English (see entry 146).

128   DELAHAYE, MICHEL. "La Chute du plafond." Cahiers du Cinéma, no. 184 (Nov.):65-66.
      Like all of his other works, Fahrenheit 451 "implies or employs a reversal of norms," a series of "amusing inversions." Like Comolli's essay (entry 127), which Delahaye relies and expands upon, this is compelling, but one cannot help sensing, however slightly, that he is rationalizing. Reprinted in Cahiers in English (see entry 149).

129   FAURECASTEN, JACQUES. "Fahrenheit 451." Télé-Ciné, no. 131 (Dec.):19-30.
      Plot summary, brief overview, comments on the characters and themes and on the direction (point of view, color, editing, sound track, costumes, and decor), plus concluding remarks on "rigor, cold, and heat."

130   "French Film Directors Busy." Times (London), no. 56778 (2 Nov.):16.
      On Truffaut, Bresson, and Robbe-Grillet.

131   KAEL, PAULINE. "The Living Library." New Republic 155, no. 26 (24 Dec.):32-34.
      Kael's most negative review of a Truffaut film keeps coming back to questions: "Truffaut wanted to make Fahrenheit 451: why then . . . isn't it more imaginatively thought out, felt; why are the ideas dull, the characters bland, the situations . . . flat and clumsy? Why is the whole production so unformed?" Reprinted in Kiss Kiss Bang Bang (see entry 175).

132   LENNON, PETER. "The Star-Spangled Tricolour." Manchester Guardian, no. 37406 (13 Oct.):8.
      On American backing in the French film industry, with passing reference to Truffaut, Chabrol, Rivette, Demy.

133   MANVELL, ROGER. "The French Film." In New Cinema in Europe. London: Studio Vista, pp. 52-93.
      Contains very slight passing reference to Truffaut.

134   MARTIN, PAUL-LOUIS. "Le Paradoxe de la communication." Cahiers du Cinéma, no. 184 (Nov.):64-65.
      Fahrenheit 451 is a spectacle film and a deeply personal film; it is "cruelly beautiful," but it is a "film of defeat, of futility, and of dissatisfaction." Reprinted in Cahiers du Cinéma, in English (see entry 154).

1966

135 MELVILLE, JEAN-PIERRE. "Le Cas Truffaut." Arts-Loisirs, no.
     64 (14-20 Dec.):46-47.
          Recounts last meeting with Truffaut, almost four years
     earlier, when Truffaut had the blues. Melville says the
     perfect word to describe his former friend is "attentive"
     and claims that Truffaut's love or hate for a film is based
     more on his own theories than on his taste. Melville also
     thinks the secret to Truffaut's films is that he loves to
     expand material. Recent failures will turn him into an
     adult.

136 SARRIS, ANDREW. "Films." Village Voice 12, no. 5 (17 Nov.):
     27-28.
          Sarris chronicles his relationship with Truffaut since
     1961 and a recent interview concerning Fahrenheit 451.
     Little on that film, mostly on Truffaut himself. Ends on
     how he is similar to Fellini and different from Godard in
     nostalgia for past.

137 SICLIER, JACQUES, and GAUTEUR, CLAUDE. "Cinéma dans le
     cinéma." Revue du Cinéma/Image et Son, no. 200 (Dec.):
     50-94.
          An essay on films that contain films or present film-
     makers. Is more observation than analysis. The New Wave
     is covered on pages 67-91; Truffaut mentioned.

138 SOLOMON, STANLEY. "Modern Uses of the Moving Camera." Film
     Heritage 2, no. 2 (Winter):19-27.
          Of little value on Truffaut, whose use of the freely
     moving camera and especially the blur in Jules and Jim to
     induce in the spectator "a feeling of a disoriented or un-
     stable society" is rated above Demy's use of the same in
     The Umbrellas of Cherbourg, but below Frankenheimer's in
     The Train and Antonioni's in Red Desert.

139 T. R. "Fahrenheit 451, de François Truffaut." Positif, no.
     80 (Dec.):28-32.
          Unlike the novel on which it is based, the film has no
     sense of place, no America, therefore no analysis of a so-
     cial system. And Bradbury did not do away with all books.
     Uses the journal and Truffaut's own criticism of other
     (especially British) films to good advantage in attacking
     this one.

140 TAYLOR, JOHN RUSSELL. "Arts in Society: Ten Years of the
     New Wave." New Society 8, no. 198 (14 July):62-63.
          Comments on the fecundity of Godard. Prefers Truffaut
     over Resnais, though why, given his terse, negative remarks
     on Truffaut's work, is left unspecified.

141   "The Two Faces of Julie Christie." New York Times (24 Apr.):
      sec. 2, p. 9.
         Brief publicity piece for Fahrenheit 451.

1967

142   AJAME, PIERRE. "Les Batailles de François Truffaut." In
      Les Critiques de cinéma. Paris: Flammarion, pp. 65–83.
         This examination of Truffaut's work as a critic lists
      his loves and hates and then provides quotations for proof.
      Refers only to articles signed by Truffaut.

143   BLUESTONE, GEORGE. "The Fire and the Future." Film Quarterly
      20, no. 4 (Summer):3–10.
         Useful for the application of Bachelard's notions on the
      erotic nature of fire to Fahrenheit 451.

144   BONTEMPS, JACQUES. "Dictionnaire du nouveau cinéma français
      (mise à jour)." Cahiers du Cinéma, no. 187 (Feb.):53–64.
         Truffaut is mentioned on the last page of this alpha-
      betical, annotated list of filmmakers. Contradictions in
      his career noted.

145   Cinema (Zurich), no. 51 (Autumn):732 ff.
         Special issue on Truffaut in German, containing
      "Truffaut und die Versuchung des Stils" by Pierre Lachat
      (pp. 732–36), and "Truffaut, Hitchcock und die Reflexion
      des Kinos" by Walter Tecklenburg (pp. 740–43).

146   COMOLLI, JEAN-LOUIS. "The Auteur, the Masks, the Other."
      Cahiers du Cinema in English, no. 9 (Mar.):57–58.
         Reprinted from Cahiers du Cinéma (see entry 127).

147   _____. "Au coeur des paradoxes." Cahiers du Cinéma, no. 190
      (May):18.
         Using brief but suggestive incidents in Fahrenheit 451
      and Soft Skin, Comolli notes two contradictory tendencies
      in Truffaut's work that result in a little noticed quality
      in his films: uneasiness.

148   DADOUN, ROGER. "Une Vision du monde." La Nef 24, no. 29
      (Jan.-Mar.):95–106.
         Directors of the New Wave reexamined through their most
      recent films. Fahrenheit 451 and Soft Skin found wanting.

149   DELAHAYE, MICHEL. "The Fall to the Ceiling." Cahiers du
      Cinema in English, no. 9 (Mar.):58–59.
         Reprinted from Cahiers du Cinéma (see entry 128).

1967

150   FRENCH, PHILIP. "All the Better Books." <u>Sight and Sound</u> 36,
no. 1 (Winter):38-41.
An article on the use of books in movies with a terse
reference to <u>Fahrenheit 451</u>.

151   JACOB, GILLES. "Annecy an IV: Hommage à Truffaut." <u>Cinéma
67</u>, no. 112 (Jan.):30-37.
Respectful account of the Annecy tribute to Truffaut and
an overview of his themes and career. Truffaut is "a great
poet of the amorous encounter"; there is a distinct unity
to his career because of the similarities among the central
characters of each film--alone, shy, tormented, afraid, and
innocent--and themes of purification and purity.

152   JAMES, CLIVE. "Pour trouver du nouveau." <u>Cambridge Review</u>
89A, no. 2160 (2 Dec.):175-76.
Points out the weaknesses of Bradbury's book once it was
pumped up from the original short story "Fireman." Concludes
that "a good deal of [Truffaut's] huge creative energy [in
<u>Fahrenheit 451</u>] paradoxically goes into expressing [the
book's] weaknesses."

153   KAUFFMANN, STANLEY. <u>A World on Film: Criticism and Comment.</u>
New York: Harper & Row, 437 pp.
Contains his <u>New Republic</u> reviews of <u>Jules and Jim,
Shoot the Piano Player, The Soft Skin</u>, and <u>Breathless</u>, plus
an essay entitled "France," in which he discusses <u>The 400
Blows</u>.

154   MARTIN, PAUL-LOUIS. "The Paradox of Communication." <u>Cahiers
du Cinema in English</u>, no. 9 (Mar.):58.
Reprinted from <u>Cahiers du Cinéma</u> (see entry 134).

155   ROUD, RICHARD. <u>Jean-Luc Godard.</u> Collection Cinema World.
New York: Doubleday, 176 pp.
Updated in 1970. For comment, see entry 223.

156   SAWYER, PAUL. "<u>The 400 Blows</u>." <u>Cineaste</u> 1, no. 3 (Winter):
3-11.
Antoine is called "a kind of tragic hero," and the film,
compared in passing to <u>Catcher in the Rye</u> and Hardy's novels, is a masterpiece due to its techniques.

157   SIMON, JOHN. "The New Byzantinism." In <u>Private Screenings</u>.
New York: Macmillan, pp. 128-32.
<u>Soft Skin</u> dismissed as one of those "fiascos of retro-
gression into the commonplace," which can't be excused.
The entire New Wave is guilty of films that are "only eso-
teric, in-group-oriented and self-indulgent."

158   STAPLES, DONALD E. "The Auteur Theory Re-examined." In The
      Emergence of Film Art. Edited by Lewis Jacobs. New York:
      Hopkinson & Blake, pp. 392-99.
           Ably synopsizes Truffaut's "Une certaine tendance" and
      Bazin's "de la politique des Auteurs" and calls for a close
      examination of the theories. Reprinted from the Journal of
      the Society of Cinematologists (1967); reprinted in slightly
      expanded form in entry 226.

159   Travelling J., no. 18 (Oct.):3-32.
           Special issue on Truffaut, which contains an article by
      Truffaut on Bride Wore Black and short comments on each of
      his films plus the following essays: "Au début était le
      cinéma" by Gerard Hinault (pp. 3-4); "Décryptage à sens
      unique" by Robert Millie (pp. 5-7); "Truffaut et le temps"
      by François Albera (pp. 8-9); and "Plus qu'une touche" by
      Micha Sofer (pp. 9-10).

160   TYLER, PARKER. The Three Faces of Film. South Brunswick,
      N.J.: A. S. Barnes, 144 pp.
           Reprints his article on Jules and Jim (see entry 89).

                              1968

161   "A Cannes, un coup de téléphone marque l'ârret du Festival
      . . ." Paris-Match, no. 998 (15-22 June):160.
           Not much on Truffaut's role in closing Cannes Film
      Festival.

162   ADLER, RENATA. "Debate Rages over Centre du Cinéma" and
      "Fracas at Festival." New York Times (25 May):27 and
      (26 May):sec. 2, pp. 1, 22.
           Detailed accounts of strike-related events. Reprinted
      in entry 187.

163   BAGH, PETER von. "The Bride Wore Black." Movie, no. 16
      (Winter):34-36.
           One of the more positive and persuasive essays on the
      film, this claims that it is a "truly expert analysis--the
      most brilliant thing [done] on Hitchcock." Bagh also refers
      to the "unusually sympathetic quality" that is apparent in
      "the many beautiful, sensitively impressionistic variations
      which Truffaut produces from his recurring motif, the fra-
      gility of identity."

164   BRAUDY, LEO. "Hitchcock, Truffaut, and the Irresponsible
      Audience." Film Quarterly 21, no. 4 (Summer):21-27.
           An examination of voyeurism and audience manipulation

1968

in Psycho, which uses as its starting point a condemnation
of Truffaut's interviews with Hitchcock for being superficial and interested only in technique. Reprinted in Focus
on Hitchcock, edited by Albert T. Lavalley (Englewood
Cliffs, N.J.: Prentice-Hall, 1972), pp. 116-127.

165   "Cannes Officials Close Festival." New York Times (19 May):26.
News report mentions Truffaut's role.

166   COLLET, JEAN. "Baisers volés de François Truffaut." Études,
no. 329 (Nov.):587-90.
Truffaut briefly contrasted with Cournot, Lelouche, and
Godard. Stolen Kisses marked by beauty, fantasy, humor,
and pathos that arise from the playing on time. Reprinted
in Le Cinéma en question (see entry 244).

167   _____. "La Mariée était en noir, de François Truffaut."
Études, no. 328 (Apr.):550-54.
The film works a reversal on the theme of forbidden,
impossible love; it is the tragedy of the masculine world
pitted against the feminine, where the tragic fault is love.
Reprinted in Le Cinéma en question (see entry 244).

168   C[OMOLLI], J[EAN]-L[OUIS]. "Premiere semaine: L'Affair
Langlois." Cahiers du Cinéma, no. 199 (Mar.):33.
Beginning with Langlois' dismissal on 9 Feb., an account
of the day-by-day incidents that were part of the protest.

169   CRIST, JUDITH. The Private Eye, the Cowboy, and the Very
Naked Girl. New York: Holt, Rinehart, Winston, 292 pp.
Contains her review of Fahrenheit 451.

170   DELAHAYE, MICHEL. "Fin d'un festival: Cannes." Cahiers du
Cinéma, no. 203 (Aug.):26-27.
On the closing of the Cannes Festival. Truffaut's role
mentioned.

171   GENÊT. "Letter from Paris." New Yorker 44, no. 2 (2 Mar.):
98-100.
A brief account of l'affaire Langlois and Godard's and
Truffaut's roles.

172   Jean-Luc Godard par Jean-Luc Godard. Paris: Éditions Pierre
Belfond, 414 pp.
Two of the Cahiers du Cinéma articles anthologized here
are on Truffaut. Several others mention him. Translated
into English as Godard on Godard by Tom Milne. Edited by
Milne and Jean Narboni. (New York: Viking Press, 1972);
see entries 31 and 110.

173   GRAHAM, PETER, ed. <u>The New Wave: Critical Landmarks</u>. Cinema
         One Series. New York: Doubleday; London: Secker & Warburg,
         184 pp.
             Eight articles that provide background (pro and con) on
         the New Wave, including Astruc's famous "camera-stylo" essay,
         Bazin on film language (from <u>What Is Cinema</u>? vol. 1
         [Berkeley: University of California Press, 1967]) and on
         the "politique des auteurs" (from <u>Cahiers</u>, no. 70 [1957]),
         brief pieces by Chabrol and Godard, and negative views from
         <u>Positif</u>. Truffaut's <u>Cahiers</u> interview (no. 138 [1962]) is
         split in two and is used strategically at the start and in
         the middle. More journalistic than substantive; see entry
         68.

174   HOUSTON, PENELOPE. "The Show Must Come Off." <u>Spectator</u> 220,
         no. 7300 (24 May):713.
             Story of the closing of the Cannes Festival includes
         Truffaut's reading of the declaration of the committee.

175   KAEL, PAULINE. <u>Kiss Kiss Bang Bang</u>. New York: Little,
         Brown, 498 pp.
             Contains her review of <u>Fahrenheit 451</u> and a capsule com-
         ment on <u>The Mischief-Makers</u>; see entry 131.

176   KNIGHT, ARTHUR. "L'Affaire Langlois." <u>Saturday Review</u> 51,
         no. 17 (27 Apr.):51.
             No mention of Truffaut's role.

177   MacKILLOP, I. D. "The Child Able to Read: François Truffaut's
         Conte Philosophique." <u>Delta</u>, no. 44 (Oct.):25-35.
             A close reading of the final scene of <u>Fahrenheit 451</u> to
         show how integral it is and how artful Truffaut is in pre-
         senting his argument. The dominant characteristic of the
         "normal" world of the film is amnesia; the power that Montag
         discovers in books is the "power to remember."

178   PRÉDAL, RENÉ. "A Cannes, samedi 18 Mai." <u>Jeune Cinema</u>, no. 32
         (Sept.):17-18.
             On the closing of the film festival.

179   REISZ, KAREL, and MILLAR, GAVIN. "The Technique of <u>Shoot the
         Piano Player</u>." In <u>The Technique of Film Editing</u>. 2nd rev.
         ed. London: Focal Press, pp. 330-44.
             An examination of (1) the doorbell sequence and "the
         philosophy of discontinuity" and (2) Lena's description of
         meeting Charlie--a sequence that is "typical of Truffaut's
         work in its range of moods and technical dexterity." Re-
         printed in Braudy, <u>Focus on "Shoot the Piano Player"</u> (see
         entry 239).

1968

180   ROUD, RICHARD, and HOUSTON, PENELOPE. "Cannes '68." <u>Sight</u>
       <u>and Sound</u> 37, no. 3 (Summer):115-17.
          Truffaut's role in closing the festival is part of this
       report.

181   SARRIS, ANDREW, ed. <u>The Film</u>. New York: Bobbs-Merrill Co.,
       64 pp.
          Contains Roger Greenspun's <u>Sight and Sound</u> essay (1963)
       on <u>Jules and Jim</u> and Joan Fox's <u>Canadian Art</u> essay (1962)
       on the New Wave; see entries 76 and 97.

182   STERNBERG, JACQUES. "Revolution culturelle au Festival de
       Cannes." <u>Le Figaro Littéraire</u>, no. 1154 (14-23 June):40-41.
          An hour-by-hour diary of the closing of Cannes.

183   SWADOS, HARVEY. "How the Revolution Came to Cannes." <u>New</u>
       <u>York Times</u> (9 June):magazine sec., pp. 128-32.
          Complete account of the closing of Cannes. Includes not
       only Truffaut's role, but a short description of his past
       experiences there too.

*184   TANNER, CARLON LEE. "La Politique des Auteurs as a Critical
       Aesthetic." Master's thesis, University of California at
       Los Angeles.
          Listed in Michimoto, see entry 401a.

185   VEUILLOT, JEAN-LOUIS. "La Mariée était en noir." <u>Télé-Ciné</u>
       23, no. 142 (May-June):13-20.
          Plot summary, preliminary comment, analysis of the direc-
       tion ("une lique policière, une ligne pathétique"), examina-
       tion of the characters, and a final appraisal.

*186   ZAAGSMA, FRANK. "Maagden en Weduwen: Creativiteit en Verleden
       Bij Truffaut." <u>Critisch Filmforum</u> 4, nos. 7-8 (July-Aug.):
       127-35.
          Listed in the card files at the Centre de documentation
       cinematographique; see entry 1501.

<u>1969</u>

187   ADLER, RENATA. <u>A Year in the Dark: A Year in the Life of a</u>
       <u>Film Critic, 1968-69</u>. New York: Random House, 354 pp.
          Contains her review of <u>Bride Wore Black</u> and her reportage
       on Cannes strike; see entry 162.

188   ALLEN, DONALD. "Baisers volés." <u>Screen</u> 10, no. 3 (May-June):
       90-95.
          A full background piece rather than a review or analysis,

this essay provides production details and Truffaut's quotes and as terse and accurate an appraisal of the Truffaut touch, his originality, characters, and techniques as there is.

189   BOBKER, LEE. "François Truffaut." In Elements of Film. New York: Harcourt, Brace, & World, pp. 220-22.
      Four key elements listed: Truffaut's compassion and humanity; the revelation of human relationships through a richness of action and incident; lyrical, poetic images; the ability to elicit involvement from the audience. This description not changed in 1974 and 1979 revisions of the book.

190   CAMPBELL, DAVID. François Truffaut's Film Jules et Jim: A Study of Cinematic Technique in Relation to the Novel of Henri-Pierre Roche. Lund: Institute of Literary History Research Report, no. 4 (3 Nov.), 43 pp.
      An elementary but thorough analysis, which relies on much description of shots. Concludes that the first one-third of the film is faithful to the book; the remainder reduces the happiness of the novel by changing content and altering the visual style.

191   LANGLOIS, GÉRARD. "Visages non maquillés des comédiens français. I--Delphine Seyrig, une actrice magique." Les Letters Françaises, no. 1292 (16-22 July):17-18.
      An interview with comments on Truffaut.

192   _____. "Visages non maquillés des comédiens français. IV--Michel Lonsdale ou l'humour 'franglais.'" Les Lettres Françaises, no. 1295 (6-9 Aug.):19-20.
      An interview containing brief comments on this actor's ease in working twice with Truffaut.

193   LINDSAY, MICHAEL. "An Interview with Jeanne Moreau." Cinema (U.S.) 5, no. 3 (Winter):14-17.
      Some revealing remarks on Truffaut's shyness, his directorial advice, and their rapport ("as if twin brothers").

194   MacDONALD, DWIGHT. Dwight MacDonald on Movies. Englewood Cliffs, N.J.: Prentice-Hall, 492 pp.
      Contains his Esquire magazine reviews of 400 Blows (Mar. 1960), Jules and Jim (Sept. 1962), and Soft Skin (May 1965).

195   MILLAR, GAVIN. "Hitchcock vs. Truffaut." Sight and Sound 38, no. 2 (Spring):82-88.
      A two-part essay, which begins by emphasizing Hitchcock's weaknesses before turning to an enthusiastic analysis of The

1969

Bride Wore Black. Truffaut differs from Hitchcock because
he transforms Woolrich's (the novelist's) characters, that
is, character intrigues him more than situation.

196 OUDART, JEAN-PIERRE. "Rêverie bouclée." Cahiers du Cinéma,
no. 216 (Oct.):51-52.
    Opaque interpretation of the truth and the fiction of
Mississippi Mermaid.

197 PAUL, WILLIAM. "The Two Worlds of Stolen Kisses." Film
Heritage 5, no. 2 (Winter):11-16.
    The film contrasts people who act according to social
conventions and those who relate to others on a more personal basis. Antoine succeeds when he no longer sees women as
images, when he is no longer "a spectator viewing a per-
former."

198 RECASSENS, GÉRARD, and SALACHAS, GILBERT. "Baisers volés."
Télé-Ciné 24, no. 150 (Feb.):7-16.
    Plot summary, comments on the film in general and its
characters, an open letter to Truffaut complaining about
his abandoning past toughness, and a final appraisal.

199 "Truffaut, François." In Current Biography Yearbook 1969.
Edited by Charles Moritz. New York: H. W. Wilson Co.,
pp. 428-30.
    Biographical profile and career overview.

200 VEILLOT, CLAUDE. "Truffaut la tendresse apprivoise son enfant-
loup." L'Express, no. 944 (18-24 Aug.):42-43.
    Background article on The Wild Child, its source, actors,
its place in Truffaut's films about deficiencies, the way
it contrasts with his previous and upcoming films.

201 WOOD, ROBIN. "Chabrol and Truffaut." Movie, no. 17 (Winter):
16-24.
    Truffaut not only comes in second in this comparison
with Chabrol, but he is, Wood believes, a minor figure, not
in the same league as Godard or his mentors Hitchcock and
Renoir. Wood calculates Truffaut's affinities with
Hitchcock (passive, helpless, indecisive heroes) and Renoir
(tolerant and affectionate presentation of characters, and
a combination of farce and tragedy). He concludes that
Truffaut is too passively accepting of life's impurities
("passive" is repeated noticeably in the article) and that
the comedy of Stolen Kisses slightly trivializes life.

1970

202 ARMES, ROY. French Cinema since 1946. Vol. 2, The Personal
Style. New York: A. S. Barnes & Co.; London: A. Zwemmer,
228 pp.
Revised and expanded version. Two new paragraphs on
Bride Wore Black and Stolen Kisses (see entry 122).

203 _____. French Film. New York: Dutton, 160 pp.
A survey of forty major directors from the beginning of
French film history. Short critical/biographical sketches.
Truffaut included.

204 BELLONE, JULIUS, ed. Renaissance of the Film. New York:
Collier Books, 366 pp.
Contains reprint of Greenspun's review of Shoot the
Piano Player (see entry 105).

205 CANBY, VINCENT. "Movies? They Are No Joke, Mes Amis." New
York Times (31 May):sec. 2, pp. 1, 28.
Report from Paris on the French movie scene with brief
mention of Truffaut's current projects and the fact that
the financially troubled Cahiers du Cinéma "continues to
exist only because of the financial help of Truffaut, whose
films Cahiers now regards as mere bourgeois trifles."

206 _____. "This 'Child' Has to Be Truffaut's." New York Times
(13 Sept.):sec. 2, pp. 1, 13.
Longer article placing this "cool" film in the perspective of Truffaut's others, noting that in all there is a
"unifying severity of vision, relating to the rigors of
love," concluding that Victor is "the foetus of Stanley
Kubrick's 'Space Odyssey' on solid ground."

207 COLLET, JEAN. "L'Enfant sauvage de François Truffaut." Études,
no. 332 (Apr.):557-59.
The Wild Child is different from Truffaut's four preceding "Americanized" films; it is related to Fahrenheit 451
and is the inverse of The 400 Blows. It—and all of
Truffaut's films—pivots on the discovery Itard makes when
he unjustly punishes Victor. Reprinted in Le Cinéma en
question (see entry 244).

208 CHRISTOPHE, JEAN-BAPTISTE. "La Sirène du Mississipi." Télé-
Ciné 23, no. 160 (Mar.):11-16.
Plot summary, full commentary on the direction, examina-
tion of the characters, and final appraisal.

209 DANEY, SERGE. "L'Enfant sauvage." Cahiers du Cinéma, no. 222

117

1970

(July):31-32.
Back to back with a related article by Oudart (see entry 219). Daney discusses what The Wild Child has in common with other Truffaut films, especially the way in which one character must imitate another's model behavior.

210   ELSAESSER, THOMAS. "Truffaut." Brighton Film Review, no. 21 (June):17-19.
A reappraisal of Truffaut's solipsistic romantic characters and his "increasingly 'thematic' use of apparently formal elements, such as narrative technique, plot construction or—on a less important scale—the use of geometrical compositions (particularly verticals) as a correlative and comment on the action." Focuses on the less commonly discussed films such as Fahrenheit 451 and Soft Skin.

211   GESSNER, ROBERT. The Moving Image. New York: E. P. Dutton & Co., 444 pp.
Brief excerpt from the script of Fahrenheit 451 used to illustrate slow motion (pp. 338-40).

212   GILLIAT, PENELOPE. "Truffaut." New Yorker 46, no. 30 (2 Sept.):67-69.
Gilliat's response to The Wild Child is more impassioned than usual and focuses attention on the boy as a typical Truffaut hero, on Truffaut as Itard, and on the "staggeringly moving displaced metaphor for a family."

213   GREENSPUN, ROGER. "Stolen Kisses." On Film 1, no. 1:11-14.
Aware of the film's minor limitations as well as its multiple rewards, Greenspun weaves ideas about Truffaut's system of balances, his inclusion of the "real" world, time, and about how he differs from Godard into an essay that concludes that the subject of the film "is ultimately not so much young love as the conditions under which young love exists." Reprinted in Movie Comedy (see entry 361).

214   JORDAN, ISABELLE. "Pudique et prudent." Positif, no. 116 (May):68-71.
Jordan provides six reasons why society has seen fit to believe in the myth of the wild child and goes on to criticize Truffaut for not reflecting more on Itard's nineteenth-century document and on his subject.

215   KAEL, PAULINE. Going Steady. Boston: Little, Brown, 372 pp.
Contains her review of Stolen Kisses.

216   MAGNY, JOEL. "Domicile conjugal." Télé-Ciné 23, no. 166 (Oct.-Nov.):16-23.

Plot summary, preliminary overview, examination of the characters and the direction, plus a final appraisal.

217 MALSON, LUCIEN. "A propos du film de François Truffaut: Victor sous le regard des sciences humaines." Le Monde, no. 7819 (4 Mar.):19.
    A discussion of wolf-children and some of the conceptions and misconceptions on which The Wild Child is based.

218 MORGENSTERN, JOSEPH, and KANFER, STEFAN, eds. Film 69/70. New York: Simon & Schuster, 286 pp.
    Contains reviews of Stolen Kisses by Morgenstern, Hollis Alpert, and Robert Kotlowitz.

219 OUDART, JEAN-PIERRE. "L'Enfant sauvage." Cahiers du Cinéma, no. 222 (July):27-29.
    Rather convoluted but revealing discourse on the interrelationship between Truffaut as director and as actor/master, which relates the myths of lost childhood and the inaccessible mother to Truffaut's games of repetition and denial to show that the film is not ideological.

220 PETRIE, GRAHAM. The Cinema of François Truffaut. New York: A. S. Barnes & Co.; London: A. Zwemmer, 240 pp.
    A warm and sensitive examination of Truffaut's resourceful use of the camera and editing, objects and settings, dialogue and music to illustrate his "open" style, characters, and themes. Concludes with a close analysis of Mississippi Mermaid. Lack of index causes problems.

221 ROSS, WALTER S. "The Actor the French Dig the Most." New York Times (28 June):sec. 2, pp. 6, 14.
    Jean-Pierre Léaud interviewed on and off the set of Bed and Board. Léaud comments on Truffaut; Truffaut comments on Léaud.

222 ROUAULT, BEATRICE. "Lucien Malson: Les Enfants sauvages mythe et realité." Télé-Ciné 23, no. 160 (Mar.):46-47.
    Background piece on the characteristics and habits of children raised in the wild.

223 ROUD, RICHARD. Jean-Luc Godard. 2d ed. Collection Cinema One. London: Secker & Warburg; Bloomington: Indiana University Press, pp. 155-56.
    These two pages contain a long paragraph by Truffaut on the making of Une Histoire d'eau.

224 SARRIS, ANDREW. Confessions of a Cultist: On the Cinema 1955-1969. New York: Simon & Schuster, 480 pp.

1970

>Contains his Village Voice reviews of Jules and Jim, Shoot the Piano Player, The Bride Wore Black, and Stolen Kisses, plus a review of Truffaut's book on Hitchcock from Book World.

225 SERCEAU, MICHEL. "L'Enfant sauvage." Télé-Ciné 23, no. 160 (Mar.):21-27.
>Plot summary, preliminary comments on the themes and the director, more extensive comments on the characters and the realization, and a final overview.

226 STAPLES, DONALD E. "La Politique des auteurs--The Theory and Its Influence on the Cinema." Language and Style 3, no. 4 (Fall):303-11.
>Half of this is a virtual duplication of an article by Staples in The Journal of the Society of Cinematologists (reprinted in Lewis Jacobs' The Emergence of Film Art (see entry 158). The second, new section is a briefer examination of the influence of the theory. Convenient bibliography of major articles on auteur theory contained in the notes.

1971

227 A[RMES], R[OY]. "Truffaut." In A Concise History of the Cinema. vol. 2, Since 1940. Edited by Peter Cowie. New York: A. S. Barnes & Co.; London: A. Zwemmer, p. 116.
>Truffaut is prolific; his career blends a "purely personal tone" and "a concern with contrivance and effect in the manner of Hitchcock."

228 BABY, YVONNE. "Des Quatre Cents Coups aux Deux anglaises et le continent: Monsieur Léaud acteur." Le Monde, no. 8369 (10 Dec.):15.
>Very little, surprisingly, on Truffaut in this interview.

229 BORDWELL, DAVID. "A Man Can Serve Two Masters." Film Comment 7, no. 1 (Spring):18-23.
>On the characteristics of his films, especially the influence of Renoir and Hitchcock.

230 BOYUM, JOY GOULD, and SCOTT, ADRIENNE. "Jules and Jim." In Film as Film: Critical Responses to Film Art. Boston: Allyn & Bacon, pp. 209-18.
>Reprints of reviews by Stanley Kauffmann in The New Republic, R. M. Franchi in New York Film Bulletin, and James Breen in the Observer, with questions for discussion added (see entry 84).

231 BRODY, ALAN. "Jules and Catherine and Jim and Hedda."
     Journal of Aesthetic Education 5, no. 2 (Apr.):91-101.
          Jules and Jim compared to Hedda Gabler in characteriza-
     tion, theme, structure, and tone. The two are then con-
     trasted to suggest differences between drama and film.
     The issue of influence and the fact that Jules and Jim is
     an adaptation are entirely avoided.

232 CANBY, VINCENT. "Would I Pan a Truffaut Movie?" New York
     Times (7 Feb.):sec. 2, pp. 1, 36.
          Yes, "but I can't imagine ever dismissing it." On cri-
     tics' tastes, not on Truffaut.

233 CAST, DAVID. "Style without Style: Truffaut's La Peau douce."
     Film Heritage 7, no. 2 (Winter):10-14, 34.
          Argues that Truffaut uses his camera as "a documentary
     instrument" in this film and that the style is dispassion-
     ate and objective, keeping characters at arm's length from
     the audience and almost making objects into characters.

234 DENBY, DAVID, ed. Film 70/71. New York: Simon & Schuster,
     319 pp.
          Contains reviews by Denby and Robert Hatch on The Wild
     Child and Gary Arnold on Mississippi Mermaid ("a simpering,
     negligible little movie").

235 FARBER, MANNY. Negative Space. New York: Praeger, 288 pp.
          Contains his 1962 essay on "White Elephant Art" (see
     entry 76).

236 KAUFFMANN, STANLEY. Figures of Light: Film Comment and
     Criticism. New York: Harper & Row, 296 pp.
          Contains his New Republic reviews of Mississippi Mermaid
     and Stolen Kisses.

236a MARTIN, MARCEL. "Truffaut, François." In France. New York:
     A. S. Barnes & Co.; London: A. Zwemmer, pp. 129-31.
          Brief biographical sketch and career outline.

237 SIMON, JOHN. Movies into Film. New York: Dell, 446 pp.
          Contains his reviews of Stolen Kisses, Bride Wore Black,
     and Mississippi Mermaid.

1972

238 BELMANS, JACQUES. "Reflexions sur le cinéma d'anticipation."
     Revue Générale: Perspectives Européenes des Sciences
     Humaines 108, no. 10:96-102.

1972

On science fiction films. Fahrenheit 451 commented on
briefly.

239　BRAUDY, LEO, ed. Focus on "Shoot the Piano Player."
Englewood Cliffs, N.J.: Prentice-Hall, 182 pp.
Now unfortunately out of print, this anthology contains
two interviews with Truffaut; reviews from France and
America; essays by Kael, Torok, Shatnoff, Greenspun, Reisz,
and Millar; commentaries by Truffaut and others; and an extract from the script (the fight with Plyne), see entries
50, 60, 62, 66, 80, 100, 105, 179, 1203, 1213, 1219, 1271.

240　CIMENT, MICHEL. "Une Tendance certaine du cinéma français."
Positif, nos. 144-45 (Nov.-Dec.):103-9.
Chabrol and Truffaut lambasted for their latest films.
Ciment believes that Truffaut has become "profoundly con-
servative" because of the failure of his two most adult
films, Soft Skin and Shoot the Piano Player, and that
Gorgeous Kid was made to "refute the legend of the sweet
and tender Truffaut."

241　CLOUZOT, CLAIRE. Le Cinéma français depuis la Nouvelle Vague.
Paris: Fernand Nathan, 204 pp.
This overview of French films from 1958 to 1972 opens
with a chronological summary of important films and events
preceding the period and divides the filmmakers into seven
categories with an additional chapter on French film journals. Truffaut is dealt with in chapter one: "La Nouvelle
Vague: La Génération de 1960."

242　_____. "Il n'y a pas d'amour heureux." Écran 72, no. 1
(Jan.):10-14.
The most positive appraisal of Two English Girls. In
each of his previous films, whenever Truffaut got too close
to emotions that were too extreme or situations too explo-
sive, he distanced himself through irony and poetry. In
Two English Girls Truffaut matures. He is truer to Roché
than in Jules and Jim; his "resistance to emotion" finds
its perfect expression.

243　COLLET, JEAN. "Choix de films." Études, no. 336 (Jan.):
116-18.
Truffaut explores the relationship between language and
a make-believe world and how this becomes strained by wish
fulfillment in Two English Girls.

244　_____. Le cinéma en question: Rozier, Chabrol, Rivette,
Truffaut, Demy, Rohmer. Paris: Editions du Cerf, 192 pp.
The book is an anthology of Collet's critiques. The

Truffaut section (pages 75-123) includes an overview from Études (1966), and articles on The Bride Wore Black (Études [1968]), Stolen Kisses (Études [1968]), Wild Child (Études [1970]), and Bed and Board (Culture-Cinema [1970]); see entries 125, 166-67, 207.

245   CRISP, C. G. François Truffaut. New York: Praeger; London: November Books, 144 pp.
      Crisp's stated purpose is to approach the films in a meticulous, factual manner as the works of a craftsman, by sifting and consolidating what Truffaut has said about them in interviews and scenarios. He is especially good at providing background information and quick appraisals of the films and at seeing how Truffaut's Arts eulogy to Bazin is juxtaposed to a script extract of Charlie Kohler talking about his mentor. Opens with a discussion of Truffaut's work as a critic. Soft Skin, which Crisp feels is "most in need of rehabilitation," gets more space than is usual. The six stages in the development of Stolen Kisses are fully delineated. With bibliography.

246   DEGAND, CLAUDE. Le Cinéma . . . Cette Industrie. Paris: Editions Techniques et Economiques.
      The political and economic background of Western European --and especially French--filmmaking.

247   DELAIN, MICHEL. "Le Cinéma français est misogyne." L'Express, no. 1120 (25-31 Dec.):42, 44.
      Quick history of French cinema to show its misuse of women; refers to Truffaut's words about Hiroshima mon amour as a turning point.

248   FANNE, DOMINIQUE. "L'Amour fait mal." L'Avant-Scène du Cinéma, no. 121 (Jan.):9.
      Two English Girls affected Fanne as strongly as did 400 Blows and prompts a series of observations about the changes from the novel, about the film's beauty and tragedy, about the absence of a father, and about the great fear in all Truffaut's films: fear of meeting, of communicating.

249   _____. L'Univers de François Truffaut. Paris: Les Éditions du Cerf, 202 pp.
      A four-part book, which covers Truffaut's recognizable concerns in a thorough and readable manner. Part one is about his work as a critic; part two about the scenes, objects, dialogue, and actors that are repeated throughout his films; part three about barriers, mirrors, and reversals; part four is a film-by-film analysis through Bed and Board of the importance of the child and the couple in his work.

1972

Fanne's access to Truffaut's shooting scripts provides some useful insights. Excerpted in Braudy and Dickstein, Great Film Directors: A Critical Anthology (see entry 392).

250　GERLACH, JOHN. "Truffaut and Itard: The Wild Child." Film Heritage 7, no. 3 (Spring):1-9.
　　　In ending the story before puberty, in his selection of parts of Itard's journal to include in the narration, and in his choice of imagery and innuendo, Truffaut falsifies the "pathos and . . . sense of failure" of his source.

251　GILLING, TED. "The Colour of the Music--An Interview with Bernard Hermann." Sight and Sound 41, no. 1 (Winter):36-39.
　　　Hermann comments very briefly on Fahrenheit 451 and The Bride Wore Black; he observes that Truffaut keeps recutting his films.

252　JEANCOLAS, J. P. "Chabrol, Truffaut, après quinze ans." Jeune Cinéma 60 (Jan.):1-9.
　　　Two English Girls seen as the best and most personal Truffaut film since Shoot the Piano Player.

253　JEBB, JULIAN. "Truffaut: The Educated Heart." Sight and Sound 41, no. 3 (Summer):144-45.
　　　Extended comments on La Sirène du Mississipi ("not only a masterpiece but a turning point in Truffaut's career") and Two English Girls (a failure because of Truffaut's lack of understanding of Muriel).

253a　KATZ, JOHN STUART. "Fahrenheit 451." In A Curriculum in Film. Toronto: Ontario Institute for Studies in Education, pp. 59-63.
　　　Uses excerpts from reviews of the film to raise questions for discussion in high school classes.

254　KESTNER, JOSEPH. "Truffaut: Tale of Two Brontës?" Village Voice (14 Dec.):91.
　　　Notes how the actresses are made up to look like the paintings of the Brontës used in the film. Is Truffaut Branwell?

255　KINDER, MARSHA, and HOUSTON, BEVERLE. "François Truffaut." In Close-Up: A Critical Perspective on Film. New York: Harcourt Brace Jovanovich, pp. 183-97.
　　　Analyses of four films. On the "structural alternation between motion and stasis" in The 400 Blows, on the "pattern of incongruity" in Shoot the Piano Player, on freedom in Jules and Jim, and on The Wild Child as the embodiment of both freedom and restraint.

256 KLEIN, MICHAEL. "Two English Girls." Film Quarterly 26,
     no. 2 (Winter):24-28.
         Two English Girls contrasted to Jules and Jim, with which
     it is "obviously intended to be viewed." There is "sadness
     and [a] feeling of realism in" Two English Girls, with "few
     sudden shifts of mood" and a "hypotactic narrative" (spatial
     and causal connections are carefully delineated by Truffaut).

257 MOHRT, MICHAEL. "Le Temps comme il passe." La Nouvelle Revue
     Française 39, no. 230 (Feb.):108-11.
         On the problem of time in novels and film. Mohrt be-
     lieves that with Two English Girls Truffaut tried to make
     something that would be at the same time literary and cine-
     matic. This was doomed because the cinema can deal only
     with brief stretches of time and strong sentiments.

258 RENAUD, TRISTAN. "Une Rupture dans la continuité." Cinéma
     72, no. 163 (Feb.):67-74.
         Downbeat about the Nouvelle Vague, which "changed noth-
     ing." Breathless, for instance, is an "adroit treatment
     . . . of a perfectly insipid script." Truffaut has settled
     into "passé-ism . . . bittersweet, sentimental comedy."

259 SCHICKEL, RICHARD. Second Sight. New York: Simon & Schuster,
     352 pp.
         Reviews of Stolen Kisses and Wild Child reprinted.

260 SIMON, JOHN. Movies into Film: Film Criticism 1967-1970.
     New York: Dial Press, 601 pp.
         Truffaut's recent films are included in a section en-
     titled "Declines and Pratfalls of Major Directors" (rather
     than in "French Film in Eclipse"). The Bride Wore Black is
     neither thriller, nor love story, nor tribute to Hitchcock;
     it is "a piece of junk." Stolen Kisses is "aimless, casual,
     slight," perhaps because Truffaut's style is so accessible
     that his imitators have exhausted him before his time, per-
     haps because of the "lack of substance in his vision."
     Mississippi Mermaid is "rather less dislikable" than Bride
     Wore Black, but equally preposterous.

261 YOUNG, VERNON. On Film: Unpopular Essays on a Popular Art.
     Chicago: Quadrangle Books, 428 pp.
         Contains his reviews of Jules and Jim, Soft Skin,
     Fahrenheit 451, and The Bride Wore Black.

262 BAYER, WILLIAM. "Jules and Jim" and "The 400 Blows." In

1973

The Great Movies. New York: Grosset & Dunlap, pp. 159-60
and 217-18.
The former is "a great period film and more"; the latter
a "great film of concern."

263 BUSCOMBE, EDWARD. "Ideas of Authorship." Screen 14, no. 3
(Autumn):75-85.
Examines the background and usefulness of the auteur
theory, concluding that it must be displaced from its position of prominence because it produced new knowledge only
"of a very partial kind."

264 CANBY, VINCENT. "Night or Day, Truffaut's the One." New York
Times (6 Oct.):sec. 2, p. 1.
Truffaut emulates Balzac and Hawks, who were "fascinated
by the details of a profession"; but Day for Night is not
simply about how movies are made. "It's not the final dis-
position of things that is important, Truffaut's films keep
saying, but the adventures and risks enroute." Reprinted
in Film 73/74 (see entry 287).

265 CASTY, ALAN. "Truffaut." In Development of the Film: An
Interpretive History. New York: Harcourt Brace Jovanovich,
pp. 334-39.
Focuses on the "mixtures" at the core of Truffaut's work,
which are the result of his "sympathetic concern for many-
sided vulnerability, for the ambiguities of human emotion
and character," plus "a playful affection for the elements
of film-making itself." After Jules and Jim, Casty is increasingly terse and dismissive of Truffaut's work.

266 COLLET, JEAN. "Choix de films: La Nuit américaine de François
Truffaut." Études, no. 339 (Aug.-Sept.):239-43.
Points out the influence of Cocteau, outlines some themes
(waiting, narcissism), and comments on the importance of the
music.

267 DENBY, DAVID, ed. Film 72/73. New York: Bobbs-Merrill Co.,
266 pp.
Two English Girls reviewed by William Pechter and Roger
Ebert (who claims that it is more like Wild Child than
Jules and Jim).

268 HESS, JOHN. "Auteur Criticism: A Film Maker's Approach to
the Cinema." Journal of the University Film Association
24:50-53, 58.
Transcript of a UFA conference paper and therefore is an
accurate but not full-fledged account of the central issues
of and influences on the auteur critics. In presenting the

practical, aesthetic, and metaphysical levels of their attacks on existing French cinema, Hess is less critical
(political) here than in his 1974 Jump Cut versions (see
entry 293).

269   . "Auteurism and After." Film Quarterly 27, no. 2
(Winter):28-37.
A systematic response to Petrie's "Alternatives to
Auteurs," which refutes Petrie's six arguments against au-
teurism by comparing them with the original tenets of the
Cahiers' critics--especially citing Truffaut. Hess con-
cludes that Petrie is a self-defeating New Critic and that
this approach and the auteur theory have had their day,
having been replaced by structuralism, semiology, and
Marxism; see entry 274.

270   KAEL, PAULINE. Deeper into Movies. New York: Little, Brown,
528 pp.
Contains her review of Bed and Board.

271   KINDER, MARSHA, and HOUSTON, BEVERLE. "Truffaut's Gorgeous
Killers." Film Quarterly 27, no. 2 (Winter):2-10.
The basic polarities in Truffaut's films are "developed
along sexual lines: the men rely on will, civilization,
and reason; the women are the wild, natural creatures who
rely on chance." Prior to Day for Night (1973), with the
exception of Fahrenheit 451, all the women are characterized
by "a profound selfishness and irresponsibility, which makes
them a menace to everyone, especially men."

272   LYNDON, NEIL. "Fans." Listener 90, no. 2333 (13 Dec.):831-32.
Comment on BBC-TV program on Truffaut, who Lyndon feels
is overrated. On page 819 of the same issue, some parts of
the program are transcribed.

273   McBRIDE, JOSEPH. "The Private World of Fahrenheit 451." In
Favorite Movies: Critics' Choices. Edited by Philip Nobile.
New York: Macmillan, pp. 44-52.
A defensive appreciation that uses the scene in which
Montag reads David Copperfield by the light of the televi-
sion to comment on Truffaut's indirection as a story teller.

274   PETRIE, GRAHAM. "Alternatives to Auteurs." Film Quarterly
26, no. 3 (Spring):27-35.
This reappraisal of the auteur theory groups directors
into three categories: (1) creators; (2) misfits, rebels,
unfortunates, and professionals; and (3) scene-stealers and
harmonizers. No mention is made of Truffaut except to include him among the creators. For responses by John Hess

1973

and Andrew Sarris, see Winter 1973-74 and particularly Fall 1974 issues of Film Quarterly. Reprinted in Movies and Methods (see entry 1159).

275 ROSS, T. J. "Wild Lives." Literature/Film Quarterly 1, no. 3 (Summer):218-25.
Appreciative readings of Fahrenheit 451 and The Bride Wore Black, noting their brutal effects and the fact that "Truffaut's most memorable protagonists . . . are both barbarous and fascinating."

276 SARRIS, ANDREW. The Primal Screen: Essays on Film and Related Subjects. New York: Simon & Schuster, 337 pp.
Contains his two "Notes on the Auteur Theory" essays (of 1962 and 1970) and other essays on the topic (see entry 86).

277 SIMON, JOHN. "Films." Esquire 80, no. 5 (Nov.):56, 60, 62.
After recapping Truffaut's "inimitable" basic qualities and his floundering career, Simon reviews Day for Night: a "rather better film" with "an important, if somewhat trendy, subject," which "makes us regret the excellence that it could have attained."

278 TURIM, MAUREEN. "The Aesthetic Becomes Political." Velvet Light Trap, no. 9 (Summer):13-17.
Mostly on Cahiers' change to Marxist-Leninist politics and semiology and the way in which the journal differs from Positif and Cinéthique. But also describes the aesthetic approach of the 1950s in Cahiers, and Truffaut is quoted and referred to.

279 WALL, JAMES M. "François Truffaut." In Three European Directors. Grand Rapids, Mich.: William B. Eerdmans, pp. 11-63.
Half of this article deals with Bazin's influence on Truffaut. The other half, which divides Truffaut's career through The Wild Child into early, middle, and mature periods, highlights the autobiographical elements in the films and their ironic and ambiguous qualities.

280 _____. "Truffaut: 'Auteur' of Ambiguity." Christian Century (10 Oct.):995-996.
Compares Truffaut to John Updike; both "make the common things of life luminous."

281 WILMINGTON, MICHAEL. "Cahiers' Favorite Directors." Velvet Light Trap, no. 9 (Summer):18.
Based on the ten-best lists from 1954-58 in Cahiers du Cinéma, Wilmington compiles a list of their thirty-five top auteurs. Truffaut is seventeenth; Ophuls first.

1974

*282 WUNDERLICH, HANS-JÜRGEN, ed. <u>Ein Amerikaner in Paris/Das Kino</u>
   <u>des François Truffaut</u>. Nuremberg: Kino Meisengeige.
      A pamphlet listed in the Gregor et al. bibliography
   (see entry 291).

283 ZELENY, M., and SERCEAU, MICHEL. "<u>La Nuit américaine</u>."
   <u>Télé-Ciné</u>, no. 181 (Sept.):32-36.
      Plot transcription, character descriptions, analysis of
   the direction, concluding remarks.

<u>1974</u>

284 ALLEN, DON. <u>Truffaut</u>. Cinema One Series. New York: Viking,
   176 pp.
      In Allen's words, an "affectionate yet critical" elucida-
   tion of the unfolding of the plots of Truffaut's films and
   his recurring concerns (his films are "always about himself" and "always about love"). The two longest chapters
   (about ten pages each, not counting stills) are on
   <u>Fahrenheit 451</u> and <u>Two English Girls</u>; the last chapter, except for a hasty postscript, is on <u>Gorgeous Kid</u> and <u>Day for</u>
   <u>Night</u>; the films in the Doinel cycle are considered together.

285 BELMANS, JACQUES. <u>Le Cinéma et l'homme en état de guerre</u>.
   Collection "Mains et Chemins. Brussels: André De Roche,
   171 pp.
      Fleeting glances at <u>Fahrenheit 451</u> and <u>Jules and Jim</u>.

286 BROMWICH, DAVID. "Homage to François Truffaut." <u>Dissent</u> 21,
   no. 1 (Winter):97-98.
      Enthusiastically recalls <u>Shoot the Piano Player</u> and
   Truffaut's traits ("At the center of Truffaut's melancholy
   is a wish for delighted mayhem, yet in every comic interval
   he allows there is a secret gravity") before reviewing <u>Day</u>
   <u>for Night</u>.

287 COCKS, JAY, and DENBY, DAVID, eds. <u>Film 73/74</u>. New York:
   Bobbs-Merrill Co., 369 pp.
      <u>Day for Night</u> reviewed by Vincent Canby (see entry 264),
   Roger Greenspun (a film of "direct, dense lyricism"), and
   Gary Arnold (it has both the sentimental appeal and the ex-
   pressive limitations of a valentine). Penelope Gilliatt re-
   views <u>Such a Gorgeous Kid</u>.

288 COFFEY, BARBARA. "Art and Film in François Truffaut's <u>Jules</u>
   <u>and Jim</u> and <u>Two English Girls</u>." <u>Film Heritage</u> 9, no. 3
   (Spring):1-11.
      A look at how Truffaut uses Picasso paintings in <u>Jules</u>

1974

and Jim and Rodin sculpture in Two English Girls to express
the variety of human relationships and the never-ending
cycles of life.

289   DAWSON, JAN. "Truffaut's Starry Night" and "Getting Beyond
the Looking Glass." Sight and Sound 43, no. 1 (Winter):
44–48.
An enthusiastic review of Day for Night ("a spectacular
. . . synthesis of his earlier themes"), followed by an interview with Jean-Pierre Léaud (during which Léaud refers
to the differences between himself and Truffaut but little
more).

290   FULFORD, ROBERT. "Explorer of Love." In Marshall Delaney at
the Movies. Toronto: Peter Martin Associates, pp. 217–20.
"With Stolen Kisses, Truffaut has made another 'first
novel,' this time an even more traditional one--the young
hero finding himself in relation to woman.

291   GREGOR, ULRICH; LADIGES, PETER MICHEL; FISCHER, HANNS; and
PRINZLER, HANS HELMUT. François Truffaut. Munich: Carl
Hanser Verlag, 171 pp.
A four-part book containing an overview essay
("Wirklichkeit und Fantasie oder: die Entfaltung der
Widersprüche"), an interview with Truffaut, a filmography
with comments, and a bibliography. In German. Reissued in
1977 with an expanded bibliography (see entry 371).

292   HASKELL, MOLLY. From Reverence to Rape: The Treatment of
Women in the Movies. New York: Holt, Rinehart & Winston,
388 pp.
Truffaut's women are "sacrificial scapegoats" who die or
surrender so that his innocence and purity can live. On
Jules and Jim and Two English Girls, "his greatest film."

293   HESS, JOHN. "La Politique des auteurs; Part One: World View
as Aesthetic" and "Part Two: Truffaut's Manifesto." Jump
Cut, no. 1 (May-June):19–22 and no. 2 (July-Aug.):20–22.
"La politique des auteurs was a justification, couched
in aesthetic terms, of a culturally conservative, politically reactionary attempt to remove film from the realm of
social and political concern." Hess believes that it was
only when auteur critics "saw their own perception of the
world on screen: the individual . . . trapped in Solitude
Morale," recognizing it and escaping by "extend[ing] themselves to others and to God," that "they called its creator
an auteur." Part Two is an analysis of "Une Certaine
Tendance," which finds it characterized by "blandness and
overweening superficiality . . . [and] utter conventionality."

Hess thinks that for Truffaut art must be free from all
outside influences, that he objects to pessimism and nega-
tivity, and that he believes that only "special human beings,
not the common person, is to be the fit subject of art."
As with the first part, the second is based on unstated
(though fairly obvious) political disagreements with
Truffaut (see also entry 268).

294 JOHNSON, LINCOLN F. Film: Space, Time, Light, and Sound.
New York: Holt, Rinehart & Winston, 340 pp.
A full explication of The Mischief Makers is used to illustrate the "organic approach" to filmmaking, a "more flex-
ible" way than Eisenstein's "tectonic" approach or the theatrical approach revitalized by Welles (pp. 123-26). The
400 Blows is used to show "what may operate in deviation
from a strict realist canon" (pp. 220-22).

*295 KARKOSCH, K. "François Truffaut." Film und Ton, no. 20
(Feb.):32-35.
Listed in Film Literature Index.

296 KLEIN, MICHAEL. "Day for Night: A Truffaut Retrospective on
Women and the Rhetoric of Film." Film Heritage 9, no. 3
(Spring):21-26.
"Earlier Truffaut's way of rendering clichés put us in
touch with the human experience the clichés reflected or
obscured." But Day for Night is disappointing; "we only
admire Truffaut's capacity to create powerful illusion--to
render his own clichés. This finally is the limited message
of the film--life is a series of brief, yet sustaining, il-
lusions."

297 KOSTELANETZ, RICHARD. "Recent Film Reconsidered." Shenandoah
21, no. 4 (Summer):70-88.
Generalized overview of the new mood in filmmaking in
the 1960s, with sections on new European films. 400 Blows
mentioned as one of five pivotal films.

298 LeFANU, MARK. "The Cinema of Irony: Chabrol, Truffaut in the
1970s." Monogram, no. 5:3-7.
Not fully conclusive examination of how the tone of
Truffaut's Two English Girls, in contrast to that of Chabrol
in Le Boucher and other films, is puzzling but not ironic.
In Truffaut tragedy is undercut by farce; characters are
aware of the roles they are forced to play and of their
fatal consequences.

299 MARTIN, MARCEL. "Vingt ans après: Une Constante du cinéma
français." Écran, no. 21 (Jan.):33-36.

1974

> Twenty years later the arguments Truffaut advanced in
> 1954 in "A certain tendency" still apply, especially to his
> own work since Jules and Jim (1961).

300 MONACO, JAMES. The Films of François Truffaut. New York:
New School for Social Research Monograph. Zoetrope One.
> Program notes for a season of films held at the New
> School.

301 OXENHANDLER, NEAL. "The Dialectic of Emotion in New Wave
Cinema." Film Quarterly 27, no. 3 (Spring):10-19.
> Truffaut utilized the least, Resnais and Godard the
> most, in this analysis of emotion (a "polyvalent term")
> and attempt to "sketch a phenomenology of the emotions."

302 PRÉDAL, RENÉ. "Entretien avec Yves Montand." Cinéma 74, no.
185 (Mar.):30-42.
> Remarks on Truffaut, Godard, Costa-Gavras, et al.

1975

303 BOHN, THOMAS W., and STROMGREN, RICHARD L. "François Truffaut."
In Light and Shadows: A History of Motion Pictures. New
York: Alfred Publishing Co., pp. 347-50.
> Truffaut both articulated New Wave theory and is its
> most versatile and durable auteur.

304 BOLOGNA, BARBARA, and BLESCH, EDWIN, Jr. "Feature Films That
Work." Media and Methods 12, no. 4 (Dec.):14-20, 44-52.
> Fahrenheit 451 and Jules and Jim are two of the twenty-
> three films by various directors that are effective in a
> highschool classroom.

305 BRAUCOURT, GUY. ". . . . avec Isabel Adjani." Écran 75, no.
41 (15 Nov.):10-12.
> What Truffaut wanted to do, what lines were changed, how
> actor and director differed.

306 BRAUDY, LEO. "The Rise of the Auteur." Times Literary
Supplement, no. 3845 (21 Nov.):1374-76.
> A thorough and friendly review of Les Films de ma vie
> and Truffaut's career as critic. Analyzes Truffaut's criti-
> cal virtues; especially notable for contrasting them with
> Godard's.

307 CANBY, VINCENT. "Truffaut's Clear-Eyed Quest." New York
Times (14 Sept.):sec. 2, p. 13.
> Mississippi Mermaid and Soft Skin are variations on the

"war between those who demand and desperately need to believe in the permanence of all things, and those who have
had some fleeting glimpse of their impermanence, but who
move blithely on, living on outside chances."

308   Cinématographe, no. 15 (Oct.-Nov.):1-29.
        Special issue on Truffaut and especially on Adèle H. It
      contains interviews with Truffaut by Dominique Maillet (see
      entry 1400) and with Isabel Adjani, a report on the filming
      of Adèle H., and capsule reviews of it and Small Change.
      Also included are three more general articles: (1)
      "L'Enfance" by Jacques Fieschi (pp. 10-13)--mostly on 400
      Blows and Wild Child, but notes the presence of children in
      all Truffaut films, the different attitude toward boys and
      girls, and the importance of communication; (2) "Antoine
      Doinel" by Pierre Maraval (pp. 14-17)--on his development
      as a character; and (3) "Truffaut critique" by Fieschi
      (p. 20)--on his journalistic career. The issue ends with
      excerpts from Truffaut's introduction to Bazin's book on
      Welles; (see entry 1174).

309   COWIE, PETER. "François Truffaut." In Fifty Major Filmmakers.
      New York: A. S. Barnes & Company; London: A. Zwemmer,
      pp. 253-59.
        A rapid, sympathetic survey of Truffaut's career through
      Adèle H.

310   DANEY, SERGE et al. "Une Certaine Tendance du Cinéma
      Français." Cahiers du Cinéma, no. 257 (May-June):5-21.
        Appropriates Truffaut's title twenty years later, though
      he is never mentioned. Major problem in French filmmaking
      now is isolation into groups.

311   DeNITTO, DENNIS, and HERMAN, WILLIAM. "Jules and Jim:
      Truffaut" and "Shoot the Piano Player: Truffaut." In
      Film and the Critical Eye. New York: Macmillan, pp.
      458-86 and 491-95.
        Full credits for both films. Brief comments on Shoot
      the Piano Player. Extended analysis of five major sequences
      in Jules and Jim, plus brief background on the film's theme,
      style, and approach, as well as on the New Wave.

312   FELL, JOHN L. "Auteur Criticism." In Film: An Introduction.
      New York: Praeger, pp. 200-215.
        The usual historical overview of the auteur theory dat-
      ing it from Truffaut's Cahiers article and emphasizing the
      quirkiness of its choice of auteurs.

313   GUSSOW, MEL. "She Quit the Comédie Française for Truffaut."

1975

New York Times (26 Oct.):sec. 2, p. 15.
Profile of Isabel Adjani, how she sacrificed a twenty-year contract for Adèle H., and her work on the film.

314 HASKELL, MOLLY. "The Story of Adèle H. Is a Tribute to an Experience." Village Voice 20 (27 Oct.):144-45.
About how the film "becomes a meditation on the 'woman's film' rather than a direct experience, and skirts the depths and heights of the great tragedies of obsession [namely,] Vertigo and Madame de."

315 JONES, SHIRLEY, and RICHARDSON, JOANNA. "L'Histoire d'Adèle H." [Letters to the editor] Times Literary Supplement, no. 3850 (26 Dec.):1541.
Two letters that attempt to make clearer the story of the real Adele Hugo.

316 KAEL, PAULINE. "All for Love." New Yorker 51, no. 36 (27 Oct.):130-34.
One of Kael's most positive responses to a Truffaut film. She feels that Adèle "may be woman's inverse equiva-lent of the Don Juan"; that Isabel Adjani has "the downy opacity of a face in process, a character taking shape"; and that Adèle H is a great film--"Truffaut's most passion-ate work." Reprinted in When the Lights Go Down (see entry 417).

317 KAUFFMANN, STANLEY. Living Images: Film Comment and Criticism. New York: Harper & Row, 404 pp.
Contains his New Republic reviews of Bed and Board, Day for Night, Such a Gorgeous Kid like Me, Two English Girls, and The Wild Child.

318 LEONARD, JOHN. "Film: A Literary Sensibility at the Festival." New York Times (16 Oct.):48.
Anna Karenina, Madame Bovary, The Red and the Black, and Of Human Bondage kept coming to mind during a viewing of Adèle H.

319 MacKILLOP, I. D. "Two Films by François Truffaut." Delta, no. 53:31-38.
"Persistently Truffaut has been concerned with human beings' failure to live socially and cooperatively, as a result of a childhood dislocation which he calls 'deformity.' Une Belle Fille is a study of such deformity traceable back to girlhood; La Nuit americaine shows the opposite--success-ful human collaboration engaged in the making of a film."

320 NIGHTINGALE, PAUL. "Making the Transition: François Truffaut."

1975

Framework, no. 1 (May):25-28.
Inconclusive examination of Day for Night useful for its
delineation of two worlds in all of Truffaut's films.

*321   ROUDINESCO, ELISABETH. L'Inconscient et ses lettres. Paris:
Mame, 244 pp.
Contains essays on Truffaut, Chabrol, Breton, theater,
cinema, surrealism. Listed in French xx Bibliography.

322   TARANTINO, MICHAEL. "Truffaut: Antoine et Jean-Pierre Léaud."
Thousand Eyes Magazine 5 (Dec.):18-19.
An appraisal of Antoine's character and Léaud's work
through Bed and Board emphasizing the "circularity of
Doinel's development."

323   THOMAS, PAUL. "The Sorcerer's Apprentice: Bazin and Truffaut
on Renoir." Sight and Sound 44, no. 1 (Winter):16-18.
A negative review of Truffaut's edition of Bazin's writings on Renoir.

324   THOMPSON, DAVID. "François Truffaut." In A Biographical
Dictionary of the Cinema. London: Secker & Warburg, pp.
567-69.
A balanced appraisal of Truffaut's career through Day
for Night, distinguishing between successes, failures and
returns to form, and focusing on Truffaut's youthful enthusiasm for movies, his acute sense of the moment, the theme of
privacy, and the wistfulness.

325   VAN WERT, WILLIAM F. "The Theory and Practice of the Ciné-
Roman." Ph.D. dissertation, Indiana Univeristy.
Distinguishes between two New Waves: one involving
Cahiers du Cinéma critics who became directors (called the
"cinéma des critiques"); and one involving literary artists
(Resnais, Varda, Marker, Duras, Robbe-Grillet et al), who
attempted to approximate the novel form on film (called the
"cinéma des auteurs"). Examines the latter in depth.

326   WHEELOCK, ALAN S. "As Ever, 'Daddy's Girl': Incest Motifs
in Day for Night." Gypsy Scholar 2, no. 2:69-75.
A reading of the film as an "acknowledgement" of F.
Scott Fitzgerald's Tender Is the Night "in its preoccupation
with the incest theme."

327   WILLIAMS, A. "The 400 cuts vs. How to Shoot the Piano Player:
Montage and Mise-en-scene in Truffaut's Fahrenheit 451."
Movietone News, no. 41 (11 May):9-10, 25-27.
Montage (along with staccato music) is used to create
"the busy, fragmented, but meaningless world of the fireman"

1975

and is contrasted--except for "significant departures and
ambiguities"--to the mise-en-scène presentation of the book
people.

1976

328   ABITAN, GUY.   Jules, Jim, Penn, et Catherine: Un Choc à
      Hollywood."   In Hollywood aujourd'hui: Une Legende
      américaine.   Paris: La Table Ronde, pp. 95-113.
           Recounts the story of the making of Jules and Jim and
      Truffaut's rejection of Bonnie and Clyde.

329   AUMONT, JEAN-PIERRE.   Le Soleil et les ombres.   Paris:
      Éditions Robert Laffont, 405 pp.
           The actor's autobiography contains references to Truffaut
      and Day for Night.   Aumont is particularly illuminating on
      Truffaut's reserve.   Truffaut is quoted extensively.   Trans-
      lated by Bruce Benderson and released in 1977 by W. W.
      Norton as Sun and Shadow, with an introduction by Truffaut.

330   BARBERA, ALBERTO.   François Truffaut.   Firenze: La Nouva
      Italia, 157 pp.
           Film-by-film analysis through Adèle H.   In Italian.

331   BEAULIEU, JANICK.   "Les Enfants de Truffaut."   Sequences 22,
      no. 86 (Oct.):30-37.
           A review of Small Change, with a long introduction on
      Truffaut's career, at the center of which is the proposition
      that Truffaut's best films are about adults who have not
      outgrown childhood and his failures are about other things.

332   BLAKELY, RICHARD.   "Truffaut and Renoir."   Quarterly Review of
      Film Studies 1, no. 2:174-82.
           Not the much-needed article on Renoir's influence; rather
      this is a side-by-side review of the two filmmakers' books
      of movie criticism.   For response, see entry 376.

333   BOHNE, LUCIANA, and DUBBS, CHRIS.   "An Interview with Walter
      T. Secor: Completing the Diaries of Adèle Hugo."   Film
      Criticism 1, no. 1 (Spring):5-12.
           The husband of the recently-deceased decoder of Adèle's
      diaries reveals what Truffaut omitted from his film, exactly
      what he used for his source, and what themes he developed.

334   BRAUDY, LEO.   "Truffaut, Godard, and the Genre Film as Self-
      Conscious Art."   In The World in a Frame.   Garden City,
      N.Y.:   Anchor Press, pp. 163-69.
           Referring briefly to Shoot the Piano Player and

1976

Breathless, Braudy credits the New Wave with transforming genres by making them self-conscious and eliminating the distinctions between serious and popular films.

335   COLLET, JEAN. "L'Écriture et le feu." *L'Avant-Scène du Cinéma*, no. 165 (Jan.):6-7.
         Argues that Truffaut did not at thirty suddenly become the defender of books. The screen for Truffaut (unlike Bresson and Godard, who show words) is a place of passage from writing to the word, an exchange between them. His films reconcile books and cinema, past and future, the traditional and the modern.

335a   CUMBOW, ROBERT C. "Une Femme Sauvage." *Movietone News*, no. 49 (18 Apr.):27-32.
         Adèle H contrasted with *The Wild Child*. The former "depicts a progress from savagery to civilization in a classical age" and is about "the achievements (and perhaps, by implication, the limitations) of Classicism." The latter "portrays a plunge from civilization into madness in a Romantic age" and is about "the excesses of Romanticism."

336   EDER, RICHARD. "At the Movies." *New York Times* (11 June): sec. C, p. 7.
         Contains comments by Bob Balaban, an actor working with Truffaut on *Close Encounters*.

337   GOLDSHER, ART. "*The Story of Adèle H*.: Surnames and Siblings." *Film Criticism* 1, no. 3 (Winter):13-18.
         The film is not about romantic obsession but about the desire for recognition. "Adele was stifled by the Hugo reputation, driven mad by competition with her dead sister, and starved by the absence of artistic recognition."

338   GOODMAN, WALTER. "Movie Madness." *New York Times* (14 Mar.): sec. 2, p. 1.
         Adèle H. compared to two other films about obsession: *Taxi Driver* and *Confrontation*.

339   KAEL, PAULINE. "Charmed Lives." *New Yorker* 52, no. 33 (4 Oct.):129-33.
         Small Change is "a poetic comedy that's really funny," but when Truffaut takes the children's bouyancy and resilience too seriously, the film can be seen as an "adult's fantasy of normalcy" (reprinted in entry 419).

340   ____. *Reeling*. New York: Atlantic-Little, Brown, 663 pp.
         Contains her review of *Two English Girls* and the combined review of *Day for Night* and *Gorgeous Kid*.

137

1976

341   KAUFFMANN, STANLEY. "The Story of Adèle H." New Republic 174,
       no. 4 (24 Jan.):10-19.
          Truffaut's deftness and the film's distortions and falsi-
       fications are detailed. Reprinted in Great Film Directors
       (see entry 392).

342   KLEIN, GILLIAN PARKER. "L'Histoire d'Adèle H." Film Quarterly
       29, no. 3 (Spring):43-49.
          Quick, unforced analogies to Napoleon and Frankenstein
       and a Rossetti painting characterize this analysis. By al-
       ternately involving and distancing the viewer, the film both
       exposes and confirms Romantic conventions of the journey to
       a new world in an ill-fated pursuit of the ideal.

343   KLEIN, MICHAEL. "The Story of Adèle H.: The Twilight of
       Romanticism." Jump Cut, nos. 10-11 (June):13-15.
          "Adèle H's life is an archetypal heroic but self-
       destructive romantic quest for perfect love in which the
       role of the male Petrarchan suitor is played by a 'liberated
       woman.'" Points out the functions of the pre-World War I
       setting and the figures of Hugo and Balzac in the bourgeois
       revolution, a revolution whose contradictions are internal-
       ized by Adèle. Reprinted in Women in Cinema (see entry
       375).

344   KROLL, JACK. "Truffaut: Romantic Realist." Newsweek 87, no.
       1 (5 Jan.):74-75.
          A longer than usual Newsweek review, which indicates how
       Adele H's story is a "periodic replay of her father's [ro-
       mantic] sensibility" and is a synthesis of Truffaut's favor-
       ite themes: children, love, women, and identity.

345   LANE, HARLAN. The Wild Boy of Aveyron. Cambridge, Mass.:
       Harvard University Press, 351 pp.
          The Victor-Itard story that Truffaut used for The Wild
       Child is re-presented with new documentary evidence. See
       review by Roger Shattuck. "How Much Nature, How Much
       Nurture?" New York Times (16 May 1976):Book Review Sec.,
       pp. 27-32.

346   LAURANS, JACQUES. "L'Argent de poche." Études, no. 344 (Mar.):
       423-27.
          Laurans deals with the film's "dazzling narrative sure-
       ness," its poetry, and its contemporary application. The
       true hero of the film is youth itself. Like The Wild Child,
       it is about the apprenticeship of language and writing.

*347   LELLIS, GEORGE PATRICK. "From Formalism to Brecht: The
       Development of a Political and Aesthetic Sensibility in

'Cahiers du Cinéma.'" Ph.D. dissertation, University of
Texas at Austin.
   Truffaut would be in the first section, concerning the
"initial, formalist, pre-Brechtian period" at Cahiers, in
which the critics, "governed by both Platonist and phenom-
enological presuppositions," treated narrative film as an
art "based primarily on the physical presentation of actors." Listed in Dissertation Abstracts.

348   MONACO, JAMES. "Jean-Pierre Léaud: Coming of Age." Take One
      5, no. 4 (Sept.):17-20.
         Monaco contends that "more than any other actor of the
      1960s, Léaud has symbolized the generation who are, accord-
      ing to Godard, 'the children of Marx and Coca-Cola!'" Re-
      printed in his Celebrity (see entry 402).

349   _____. "Truffaut." In The New Wave. Oxford and New York:
      Oxford University Press, pp. 13-97.
         Monaco's study has a rather conventional framework (four
      chapters: on the Doinel cycle, "the statement of genres,"
      the explosion of genres, and "intimate politics") and fo-
      cuses primarily on the "strongly materialist cinema" that
      Truffaut has created out of "the poetry of everyday life."
      In the course of examining these he makes many incidental
      comments on Truffaut's work; on, for instance, Truffaut's
      "Bazinian moral courage," the fact that his films are best
      characterized by the French word "Sentiment," his use of a
      "technical metaphor"--the edited zoom.

350   POAGUE, LELAND A. "On Time and Truffaut." Film Criticism 1,
      no. 2 (Summer):15-20.
         Initially an examination of repetition in Truffaut's
      early films, then a comparison/contrast of Stolen Kisses
      and Bed and Board--which are different in tone from The 400
      Blows because of "the sort of time-cycle realistic picture
      of time."

351   PORCILE, FRANÇOIS. "Jaubert retrouvé." L'Avant-Scène du
      Cinéma, no. 165 (Jan.):7-9.
         The musical adviser for Adèle H. explains Truffaut's
      reasoning in choosing Jaubert's music for the film (the
      old-fashioned quality of the saxophone) and some of the
      problems and challenges of individual scenes.

352   PRÉDAL, RENÉ. "Images de l'adolescent dans le cinéma français."
      Cinéma 76, no. 214 (Oct.):19-28.
         One of the ways of depicting teenagers is "the Doinel
      syndrome": with his awkwardness and clumsiness "Doinel in-
      carnates the difficulty of integration in a society which
      inexorably rejects him."

1976

353 SEGUIN, LOUIS. Une Critique dispersée. Paris: Union
 Générale d'Édit., 445 pp.
 A collection of reviews of movies and books about the
 cinema. Day for Night (pp. 312-16) and Two English Girls
 (pp. 391-93) are commented upon.

354 SPIEGEL, ALAN. "The Mud on Napoleon's Boots: The Adventitious
 Detail in Film and Fiction." Virginia Quarterly Review 52,
 no. 2 (Spring):249-64.
 Ends with paragraph on the strewn clothes in Stolen
 Kisses.

355 THOMSON, DAVID. "Love and the Cinema." American Film 2, no.
 2 (Nov.):18-23.
 A chronicle of the "special affinity between an actress
 and someone behind the camera." Truffaut is briefly mentioned as one of the directors "who favor woman as a sort
 of human and artistic principle."

356 WESTERBECK, COLIN L., Jr. "Fearful Symmetries." Commonweal
 103, no. 5 (27 Feb.):143-47.
 Adele H. seen in the light of the rest of Truffaut's
 career. It has the same imagery and techniques and "revela-
 tions of human nature that have preoccupied him for years:
 the contrasts between private and public life, between romantic aspiration and daily reality, between indoors and
 outdoors."

1977

357 ADAIR, GILBERT. "From Paris." Film Comment 13, no. 6 (Nov.-
 Dec.):4, 63.
 An account of the Langlois affair.

358 BECHTOLD, CHARLES. "Valerie Bonnier." Cinématographe 27
 (May):45.
 The actress talks about The Man Who Loved Women, her
 role in it, and Truffaut as director.

359 BOLAND, BERNARD. "L'Image et le corps." Cahiers du Cinéma,
 nos. 278-280 (Aug.-Sept.):52-54.
 On the meta-cinematic dimensions of The Man Who Loved
 Women. Slightly convoluted, but interesting on the double
 narrative, Geneviève as "the other," and multiple fictions.

360 BRAUDY, LEO. "Truffaut, Godard, and the Genre Film as Self-
 Conscious Art." In The World in a Frame. Garden City,
 N.Y.: Anchor Books, pp. 163-69.

Shoot the Piano Player is used to show how New Wave refused to "make any absolute or even partial distinction between the methods and techniques of 'serious' films and the
methods and techniques of popular, genre films."

361   BYRON, STUART, and WEIS, ELISABETH, eds. Movie Comedy. New
York: Grossman, 308 pp.
Truffaut merits a section by himself (along with Renoir
and Tati) in the chapter on "European Comedy." Reprints
Kael's 1962 Film Culture essay on Shoot the Piano Player,
Westerbeck's 1973 Commonweal essay on Day for Night, in
addition to one by Roger Greenspun on Stolen Kisses from
On Film (1970); see entries 80 and 213.

362   CARCASSONNE, PHILIPPE. "Truffaut le narrateur." Cinématographe,
no. 32 (Nov.):15-17.
Truffaut "seems to have an insurmountable repugnance for
the brutality of the image, the immediacy of visual perception." An analysis of the importance of the word and of
naming things, as well as of the various levels of his films.

363   CHAMPAGNE, ROLAND A. "L'Argent de poche." Modern Language
Journal 41, no. 7 (Nov.):388-89.
A review of the ciné-roman.

364   "Charles Denner: 'Je continue a me poser des questions sur
L'Homme qui aimait les femmes.'" [Interviewed by Claude-
Marie Tremois]. L'Express (May):80-81.
The actor talks about his role.

365   COLLET, JEAN. Le Cinéma de François Truffaut. Paris: Pierre
L'Herminier, 335 pp.
Collet has consistently been the most sensitive and insightful critic of Truffaut's films, and this book, covering
the films one by one from The Mischief Makers (1957) to The
Man Who Loved Women (1977), demonstrates this once again.
Although the result of work for a doctoral thesis, it is
neither stuffy nor hidebound. He focuses on the need to
communicate. The final chapter on imagery ("l'écriture et
le feu") is particularly good. With bibliography.

366   CONLEY, TOM. "A Pan of Bricks: McDonald, Renoir, Truffaut."
Enclitic, no. 1 (Spring):27-33.
The fake brick facade of a McDonald's restaurant, Renoir's
panning shot of the brick courtyard in The Crime of M. Lange,
and the imagery of Small Change are linked in a dense and
polysyllabic exigesis.

367   COPELAND, ROGER. "When Films 'Quote' Films They Create a New

1977

Mythology." New York Times (25 Sept.):sec. 2, pp. 1, 24.
The tendency of Scorese, Lucas, and others to quote past
films and make films about films is seen as the "Americaniz-
ing of the New Wave sensibility" of Truffaut and Godard.

368   CROWTHER, BOSLEY. "The 400 Blows." In Vintage Films. New
York: G. P. Putnam's Sons, pp. 175-78.
Crowther sketches in the historical background of this
film as one of the New Wave films that had such a "purging"
effect on the industry, summarizes the story, and argues
that it is not a tragedy.

369   EYQUEM, OLIVIER. "La Romance du tricheur (L'Homme qui aimait
les femmes)." Positif, nos. 195-196 (July-Aug.):111-13.
Like almost all Truffaut films, The Man Who Loved Women
is "a film that lies, or rather a film on the necessity of
lying by omission (what has long been called the 'reserve'
of the director)." Similarities to other Truffaut films
noted.

370   FRENAIS, JACQUES. "Je revendique le statut d'interprete."
Cinéma 77, no. 226 (Oct.):26-32.
An interview with Brigitte Fossé during which she comments on Truffaut's love of the text and his precise direction in Man Who Loved Women.

371   GREGOR, ULRICH; LADIGES, PETER MICHEL; FISCHER, HANNS; and
PRINZLER, HANS HELMUT. François Truffaut. Munich: Carl
Hanser Verlag, 192 pp.
Reissue of 1974 book with bibliography inclusive through
The Man Who Loved Women (see entry 291).

372   HAUPTMAN, IRA. "Truffaut after Small Change." Western
Humanities Review 31, no. 4 (Autumn):331-38.
A study that focuses on Truffaut's romanticism, his belief in chance and accident, and his no-fault characters,
in order to illuminate the strengths and shortcomings of
his career.

373   HERRMANN, BERNARD. "The Contemporary Use of Music in Film:
Citizen Kane, Psycho, Fahrenheit 451." University Film
Study Center 7, no. 3:5-10.
Notes on the ways the three films utilized his talents.

374   KAUFFMANN, STANLEY. "Epiphany." New Republic 177, no. 24
(10 Dec.):20-22.
Truffaut's role in Close Encounters of the Third Kind
was mentioned in nearly every review of the film.
Kauffmann's comments (on the importance of Truffaut as a

1977

scientist who speaks French and on the impact of his "sensitive face and warm personality") are among the best.

375 KLEIN, MICHAEL. "The Twilight of Romanticism: Truffaut's
Adèle H." In Women and the Cinema. Edited by Karyn Kay
and Gerald Peary. New York: Dutton, pp. 50-55.
Shortened slightly from Jump Cut (1976); see entry 343.

376 KREIDL, JOHN FRANCIS. "Correspondence: re: 'Truffaut and
Renoir.'" Quarterly Review of Film Studies 2, no. 2:252-54.
Letter to the editor about article by Richard Blakely
(see entry 322), with response by Blakely. Kreidl accuses
Truffaut of not writing honest criticism: his negative
writing was mere hypocritical careerism, and his positive
writing was uncritical. Blakely calmly disagrees.

377 LAPORTE, CATHERINE. "Truffaut acteur." L'Express, no. 1346
(25 Apr.-1 May):18-19.
A report about Truffaut's activities on the sets of Close
Encounters.

378 LIPKIN, STEVEN N. "The Film Criticism of François Truffaut:
A Contextual Analysis." Ph.D. dissertation, University of
Iowa.
An analysis of Truffaut's critical ideas set in the
double context of the economics of the French film industry
in the 1950s and the ideology of Astruc and the existential-
ists. Lipkin pursues Truffaut's critical ideas to their
logical conclusion in his films. Pseudonymous articles not
referred to.

379 MAGNY, JOEL. "L'Homme qui aimait les femmes." Cinéma 77,
no. 223 (July):106-8.
Magny believes that Bertrand is "defined by the look [le
regard]" he gives women. This look is at the same time "desire for possession, for power, and at the same time a desire for distance, nonpossession, and nonpower." The film
is another "moral reflection on liberty" by Truffaut.

380 MARCHILLI, MASSIMO. François Truffaut. Milan: Moizzi
Editore/Contemporanea Edizioni, 93 pp.
In Italian.

381 MAST, GERALD. "From 400 Blows to Small Change: Truffaut's
Progress." New Republic 176, no. 14 (2 Apr.):23-25.
An overview of Truffaut's film career that sees The Wild
Child as "the autobiographical summation of the process" of
growth in the filmmaker, that points out the career comparisons with Renoir, and notes that "Small Change is a thor-
oughly sunny film--literally and figuratively."

1977

382   MORGAN, TED. "Victor Hugo's Wayward Daughter." Horizon 19,
         no. 1 (Jan.):35-40.
            Background information on the real Adèle Hugo built on
         quotations from her own diary and her father's diary and
         letters.

383   SAMUELS, CHARLES T. Mastering the Film and Other Essays.
         Knoxville: University of Tennessee Press, 228 pp.
            Contains his review of Two English Girls, in essay en-
         titled "Hyphens of the Self."

384   THIHER, ALLEN. "The Existential Play in Truffaut's Early
         Films." Literature/Film Quarterly 5, no. 3 (Summer):183-97.
            One of the few substantial articles on Truffaut in
         English with an overall validity and varied, cogent inci-
         dental insights. Thiher examines 400 Blows, Shoot the Piano
         Player, and Jules and Jim from the point of view of "the
         absurd," which "imposed three basic configurations that
         determined the limits of representation both in formal and
         thematic terms." Reprinted in The Cinematic Muse (see entry
         414).

385   THOMAS, PAUL. "Small Change." Film Quarterly 30, no. 3
         (Spring):42-45.
            "Small Change converts anger into acceptance, condemna-
         tion into complacency, potential for change into defeatism,
         conventionality, and the kind of supine resignation I would
         never have believed possible from the director of The 400
         Blows." Truffaut thoroughly attacked for not being heir to
         Renoir.

*386 WILLIAMS, LINDA PAGLIERANÍ. "Perceptual Ambiguity in Selected
         Modern Plays and Films." Ed.D. dissertation, Boston
         University.
            An analysis of ambiguity as perception (based on The
         Poetics of Space by Gaston Bachelard and the phenomenology
         of Maurice Merleau-Ponty). This kind of ambiguity is con-
         trasted to the seven types delineated by Empson and to
         textual, dramatic, syntactic, rhetorical, and structural
         ambiguity. Truffaut, Pirandello, Garcia-Lorca, Pinter,
         Albee provide examples. Listed in Dissertation Abstracts.

1978

387   ALION, EVES. "Entretien avec Catherine Deneuve." Écran 78,
         no. 73 (15 Oct.):13-25.
            Warm words for Truffaut, who knows acting and who is at
         the same time theoretical and practical.

388 ANDREW, DUDLEY. André Bazin. Oxford and New York: Oxford
     University Press, 253 pp.
         The fullest account of the friendship between Truffaut
     and his mentor. Truffaut first enters on page 150, leaves
     for the army on page 163, and returns on page 194 for about
     ten pages, which cover his work at Cahiers. With a forward
     by Truffaut (see entry 1175).

389 BALABAN, BOB. Close Encounters of the Third Kind: Diary.
     N.p.: Paradise Press, 177 pp.
         Truffaut was closer to Balaban than to anyone else on
     the film. Balaban includes information on Truffaut's be-
     havior, activities, plans, and opinions, ranging from act-
     ing to convertibles.

390 BONITZER, PASCAL. "La Chambre verte (François Truffaut)."
     Cahiers du Cinéma, no. 285 (May):40-42.
         Buñuel, The Man Who Loved Women, Hitchcock's Vertigo,
     and especially Bazin's theory on death and film used to ex-
     plicate The Green Room.

391 BOUJUT, MICHEL. "Truffaut trahi par Truffaut." Les Nouvelles
     Littéraires, no. 2630 (6-13 Apr.):10.
         Truffaut quoted at some length in this complaint about
     his inability to act.

392 BRAUDY, LEO, and DICKSTEIN, MORRIS. Great Film Directors:
     A Critical Anthology. Oxford and New York: Oxford
     University Press, pp. 713-48.
         Six essays--solid choices, though not entirely indicative
     of Truffaut's total career. Two excerpts from Fanne's book
     (on books and on Jules and Jim)--see entry 249; Arlene Croce
     on 400 Blows--see entry 45; an excerpt from Crisp's book on
     the same film--see entry 245; Kael on Shoot the Piano Player
     --see entry 81, and Jules and Jim, and Kauffmann on Adèle H
     --see entry 341.

393 COLLET, JEAN. "La Chambre verte." Études, no. 348 (May):
     643-47.
         One of Truffaut's most beautiful films; his very personal
     and original approach puts him back in the company of the
     greats: Dreyer, Bergman, Buñuel, Mizoguchi. Collet com-
     ments on the anticinematic material, the mute boy, the de-
     struction of the mannequin, the fire. He believes that the
     conflict in the film is between the force of dispersal and
     love with its desire for unity.

394 COURTADE, FRANCIS. "Les Mistons (1956-1964)." In Les
     Maledictions du cinéma français. Paris: Éditions Alain

1978

Moreau, pp. 256-95.
Frequent reference to Truffaut, Godard, and Chabrol in
this account of French cinema.

395 EIDSVIK, CHARLES. "Films from Fiction: Jules and Jim and
Blow-up: Two Ways toward the Future?" In Cineliteracy.
New York: Random House, pp. 189-229.
An examination of the "major ingredients" of the film--
actors, sound, cinematography, editing, and the novel--
which balance romance with irony and propel the story forward. Concludes that Truffaut uses nostalgic and old-
fashioned materials, but is a "genius of popular cinema"
because he is a master strategist. In Jules and Jim he
"treat[s] romantic love structurally as a sporting event,"
or he emphasizes "spectacle values" of the "passional ath-
letics" of the characters.

396 ESTRIN, BARBARA L. "Finding the Heroine of History: Adèle H.
as Lost Child Story." University of Windsor Review 14, no.
1 (Fall-Winter):5-13.
Comparing Adèle to Rosalind in As You Like It and
Webster's Duchess of Malfi, and using her diary and her
dream, Estrin proposes that Adele is "reborn in the act of
her own design [and] frees herself from the father who
shaped her world, having fostered, in the separation she
willed, her own destiny."

397 INSDORF, ANNETTE. François Truffaut. Boston: G. K. Hall,
Twayne Publishers, 250 pp.
This study is clear, aware of previous Truffaut scholar-
ship, and affectionate. Insdorf emphasizes the biography,
analyzes the influence of Renoir and Hitchcock and the importance of women and children, and concludes with
Truffaut's "First Person Singular" approach. Though it
seems somewhat limited (by the Twayne films series format?)
to the more obvious issues, does not fully consider
Truffaut's special cinematic qualities (acting, editing,
visual style), and is nonjudgmental, it is Truffaut's personal favorite. Especially interesting is the comparison
of Day for Night with Rules of the Game.

398 _____. "François Truffaut: Feminist Filmmaker?" Take One
6, no. 2 (Jan.):16-17.
An affectionate article on the occasion of the release
of The Man Who Loved Women, sprinkled freely with quotes
by Truffaut.

399 KINDER, MARSHA. "The Man Who Loved Women." Film Quarterly
31, no. 3 (Spring):48-52.

Using Giles Deleuze's Masochism, Kinder contrasts The
Man Who Loved Women (which "shares many characteristics of
a sadistic world") with Adèle H (which is "dominated by a
masochistic aesthetic").

400 MAGNY, JOEL. "François Truffaut: La Chambre verte." Cinéma
  78, no. 233 (May):70-73.
  Magny reads the film metaphorically, as a self-reflexive
  film. Julien's "creative activity is similar to a filmmaker's: the cult of the image." His obsession is obvious;
  his way of dealing with it--through writing, the mannequin,
  the candles illuminating the darkness--are the real focus
  of the film.

401 MARTIN, MARCEL. "La Chambre verte." Écran 78, no. 69
  (15 May):56-58.
  It is a "masterpiece of introspection," done with
  Truffaut's customary "pudeur" (modesty or reserve), discrete
  lyricism, and absence of pathos. Its true theme is "l'amour
  fou"; like Peter Ibbetson and other surrealist masterpieces,
  it is about a love that is stronger than death.

401a MICHIMOTO, LINDSAY RYOKO. "The History, Formation, and
  Criticism of the 'Nouvelle Vague.'" Ph.D. dissertation,
  University of Washington.
  Chapter five, pages 68-82, is on Truffaut -- "l'enfant
  terrible." Focuses on "Une Certaine Tendance" and uses
  material from interviews with Truffaut and Rohmer to emphasize his militancy and "missionary zeal" at Cahiers. No
  reference to pseudonymous articles.

402 MONACO, JAMES. "Coming of Age: Jean-Pierre Léaud." In
  Celebrity: The Media as Image Makers. New York: Dell
  Publishing Co., pp. 134-43.
  Reprint of article from Take One (1976); see entry 348.

403 MURRAY, EDWARD. "The 400 Blows 1959." In Ten Film Classics.
  New York: Frederick Ungar Publishing Co., pp. 121-33.
  Notes the "vertical" structure and episodic format with
  "no pattern of sustained conflict, no plot in the causal
  sense" because of Truffaut's concern for "character, mood,
  theme" within a "serio-comic form."

404 PORCILE, FRANÇOIS. "François Truffaut en compagnie de Maurice
  Jaubert." Image et Son--Revue du Cinéma, no. 327 (Apr.):
  37-41.
  The musical adviser for Adèle H comments on the differ-
  ent approaches to Jaubert's music in four Truffaut films:
  Adèle H, Small Change, The Man Who Loved Women, and The
  Green Room.

1978

405 SIMERAL, FRED. "The Child-Centred Films of Truffaut." French
Review 51, no. 5 (Apr.):761-62.
Discusses alienation and hostility in The Mischief Makers,
400 Blows, and Wild Child.

406 WESTERBECK, COLIN L., Jr. "Grateful Dead" and "Love and
Obsession: Death Be Not Proud." Commonweal 105, no. 23
(24 Nov.) and no. 24 (8 Dec.):759-60 and 782-84.
A two-part critical analysis of The Green Room. The
first part compares the film to Hawthorne's "The Birthmark"
and deals with the parodoxes in and beauty of the film. In
the second, Green Room is connected to Adèle H and The Man
Who Loved Women to emphasize Truffaut's circuitous approach
to a common subject: obsession. It ends by questioning
Truffaut's debt to Bresson.

407 YOST, ELWY. Magic Moments from the Movies. Garden City, N.Y.:
Doubleday & Co., pp. 206-07.
Incineration scene in Jules and Jim described.

1979

408 ADAIR, GILBERT. "The Cliché Expert's Guide to the Cinema."
Film Comment 15, no. 6 (Nov.-Dec.):56-57.
"Truffaut. Tender, chaste, sensitive. Good with child-
ren. Makes the kind of movies he once criticized."

409 BLANCHARD, ANNE-MARIE, and BLANCHARD, GERARD. "A propos: La
Chambre verte de François Truffaut?" Image et Son--Revue
du Cinéma, no. 337 (Mar.):44-50.
The Green Room is a self-reflexive film about the fixed
photographic image becoming animated; it is a ghost story.
Freud and Melanie Klein are brought to bear to indicate
Julien's "fear of having destroyed his mother."

410 BOUJUT, MICHEL. "A Cache-cache avec François Truffaut." Les
Nouvelles Littéraires, no. 2671 (25 Jan.-1 Feb.):12-13.
A collection of four brief articles and three even
briefer interviews on the occasion of the twentieth screen
anniversary of Antoine Doinel and the release of Love on
the Run. Jean Collet in "Le Mythe Antoine Doinel" observes
that Doinel is "only desire." Maurice Achard in "Le Mythe
Léaud" calls the actor "the living phantom of our age."
Suzanne Schiffman in "C'est un bon pere" comments on
Truffaut's working habits. Jean-Marc Roberts in "Des films
de chevet" writes about his influence on writers. And former assistants Claude Miller, Jean-François Adam, and Jean-
François Stevenin (who have all become directors) agree
about his influence on the young generation of directors.

1980

411 HENDERSON, BRIAN. "Bazin Defended against His Devotees."
Film Quarterly 32, no. 4 (Summer):26-37.
An article critical of Truffaut, Rohmer, and Dudley
Andrew. Henderson distinguishes between Truffaut "the
curator of the Bazin museum" (he is grateful that Truffaut
has so quickly made Bazin's work available) and "the pro-
prietor of the memory of André Bazin" (he faults Truffaut
for being general and idealizing--especially since 1971--
and for creating the myth of the "Good Man Bazin.")

412 HIRSH, ALLAN. "Truffaut's Subversive Siren: Intertextual
Narrative in Mississippi Mermaid." Film Criticism 4, no.
1 (Fall):81-88.
Alternately opaque and enlightening examination based on
Jonathan Culler's Structuralist Poetics, which concludes
that the film, through allusions, transcends classical film
melodrama to become an art film.

413 INSDORF, ANNETTE. François Truffaut. New York: William
Morrow, 250 pp.
Paperback edition of entry 397.

414 THIHER, ALLEN. The Cinematic Muse: Critical Studies in the
History of French Cinema. Columbia: University of
Missouri Press, 216 pp.
A book on the most significant moments in French film
history, with Truffaut listed as "the Existential Moment"
in a pairing with Bresson. The relevant chapter (pp.
143-64) is a reprint of Thiher's 1977 article (see entry
384).

1980

414a ALMENDROS, NESTOR. Un Homme à la caméra. Collection
Bibliotheque du Cinema; series Ma vie de . . . Paris:
Hattier/Cinq Continents, 192 pp.
The cinematographer who worked with Truffaut on eight
films from The Wild Child to The Last Metro provides reveal-
ing details about their collaborations. With a preface by
Truffaut; see entry 1183a.

415 "Dictionnaire du cinéma français des années soixante-dix."
Cinéma 80, no. 262 (Oct.):197.
Entry on Truffaut is shorter than one would expect.

416 DOUGLASS, WAYNE J. "Homage to Howard Hawks: François
Truffaut's Day for Night." Literature/Film Quarterly 8,
no. 2 (Apr.):71-77.

1980

> The film viewed as a trek to a realizable destination
> with "the archetypal Hawksian enclave of professionals dedi-
> cated to a common goal."

417   GILLAIN, ANNE. "Topologie de L'Amour en fuite." L'Avant-Scène
> du Cinéma, no. 254 (15 Oct.):5-7.
> Notes that there are two levels in Truffaut's films (the
> manifest and the latent), two poles (the dead child and
> writing), and two places (the print shop and the library).

418   HARCOURT, PETER. "Eros and Autobiography." Canadian Forum
> 60, no. 696 (Feb.):39-40.
> An examination of Love on the Run, Truffaut's most auto-
> biographical and self-reflexive film, in the light of the
> entire Doinel cycle and Denis de Rougement on romantic love.

418a INSDORF, ANNETTE. "Maurice Jaubert and François Truffaut:
> Musical Continuities from L'Atalante to L'Histoire d'Adèle
> H." Yale French Studies, no. 60 (special issue on cinema/
> sound):204-18.
> After a brief history of Jaubert's career writing music
> for movies in the thirties, Insdorf analyzes Truffaut's use
> of Jaubert's earlier music from La Vie d'un fleuve, Ile de
> Paques, and L'Atalante in specific scenes in Adèle H.

419   KAEL, PAULINE. When the Lights Go Down. New York: Holt,
> Rinehart & Winston, 592 pp.
> Contains her reviews of Adèle H., Small Change, and The
> Man Who Loved Women (see entries 316, 339).

419a KAUFFMANN, STANLEY. Before My Eyes: Film Criticism and
> Comment. New York: Harper & Row, 464 pp.
> Contains his reviews from Adèle H through Love on the
> Run, plus a book review of The Films of My Life.

420   KLEIN, MICHAEL. "Truffaut's Sanctuary: The Green Room."
> Film Quarterly 34, no. 1 (Fall):15-20.
> Emphasis on the film's restatement of frequent Truffald-
> ien concerns with characters who are isolated and romanti-
> cally obsessed, in order to clarify its moral and aesthetic
> dimensions.

421   MONACO, JAMES. "François Truffaut." In Cinema: A Critical
> Dictionary. vol. 2. Edited by Richard Roud. New York:
> Viking Press; London: Secker and Warburg, pp. 1009-19.
> A brief biographical sketch, plus a film-by-film analysis
> (an abbreviated and popularized version of the Truffaut sec-
> tion of Monaco's book on The New Wave--see entry 349), which
> covers his career up to Small Change. Roud adds five short
> paragraphs on The Man Who Loved Women and The Green Room.

422 PETRIE, GRAHAM. "Translation and Creation in the Film:
Truffaut's The Wild Child." Georgia Review 34, no. 1
(Spring):164-80.
A thorough (though not innovative) examination based on
George Steiner's four stages of translation: trust, pene-
tration, embodiment, and restitution.

423 ROUCHY, MARIE-ELISABETH. "François Truffaut, dix-huit ans
après . . ." Le Matin (18 June).
Remarks on Jules and Jim and on his latest film, The
Green Room, quoting Truffaut on both.

424 SOBCHACK, THOMAS, and SOBCHACK, VIVIAN C. "The French New
Wave." In An Introduction to Film. Boston: Little, Brown,
pp. 262-69.
Truffaut is said to possess "a wide-ranging talent marked
by a certain nostalgic lyricism often tinged with irony."
Although he lacks "overt political involvement," his films
are hardly "tame or complacent."

425 TINTER, ADELINE R. "Truffaut's La Chambre Verte: Homage to
Henry James." Literature/Film Quarterly 8, no. 2 (Apr.):
78-83.
Author's knowledge of James makes this a useful background article on the "similarities and sympathies between
the two creators" (especially their admiration for Balzac),
as well as the many stories by James that Truffaut used.

426 WESTERBECK, COLIN L., Jr. "Bottom of the Wave." Commonweal
107, no. 12 (June):372.
A look at the twenty-year decline of French cinema into
sentimentality. Truffaut mentioned in passing.

1981

426a CARLESIMO, CHERYL. "Painting with Light." American Film 6,
no. 6 (Apr.):30-34, 69-71.
An article on cinematographer Nestor Almendros, which
focuses on The Last Metro.

426b McDOUGAL, STUART Y. "Adaptation of an Auteur: Truffaut's
Jules et Jim." In Modern European Filmmakers and the Art
of Adaptation. Edited by Andrew S. Horton and Joan Magretta.
New York: Frederick Ungar, pp. 89-99.
Shows how Truffaut "adheres to the contours of Roche's
plot, . . . [and] displays an extraordinary fidelity to the
book's language," and honors Truffaut's relationship to
Roche by creating strong parallels between it and Jules's
relationship with Jim.

V. Writings by François Truffaut

SCRIPTS, BOOKS, EXCERPTS, AND EDITED WORKS

1958

427   "Les Quatre Cents Coups." [With Marcel Moussy]. Cahiers du
Cinéma 15, no. 90 (Dec.):75-76.
     This issue of Cahiers contains excerpts from nine New
Wave films. From 400 Blows: scene of father and son cook-
ing and talking (scene no. 30).

1959

428   Les 400 Coups. D'apres le film de François Truffaut, by Marcel
Moussy. Collection l'Air du Temps. Paris: Gallimard,
168 pp.
     Postproduction novelization.

1960

429   "Introduction à une methode de travail." Cinéma 60, no. 42
(Jan.):14-22.
     Descriptions of each of the four main characters in 400
Blows, plus an extract from the film--the psychologist's
interrogation.

1961

430   "Une Histoire d'Eau." L'Avant-Scène du Cinéma, no. 7 (Sept.):
60-63.
     Complete postproduction script.

431   "Les Mistons." L'Avant-Scène du Cinéma, no. 4 (May):41-45.
     Complete script.

1962

1962

432   "Jules et Jim." L'Avant-Scène du Cinéma, no. 16 (15 June):
       1-48.
          Complete postproduction script, plus an article on Roché,
       excerpts from eight letters from Roché to Truffaut, and ex-
       cerpts from reviews.

1963

433   "Conversation avec Alfred Hitchcock (au sujet des Oiseux)."
       Cahiers du Cinéma 25, no. 147 (Sept.):1-19.
          An extract from Le Cinéma selon Hitchcock on The Birds
       (see entry 435).

1965

434   "La Peau douce." L'Avant-Scène du Cinéma, no. 48 (May):5-52.
          Complete script and credits with an introductory essay
       by Godard and extracts from various French reviews. The
       issue also contains a "biofilmography" of Truffaut on page
       62.

1966

435   Le Cinéma selon Hitchcock. Paris: Robert Laffont, 256 pp.
          A dramatic dialogue between the auteur and the admirer.
       The result of fifty-five hours of interviews, the book is
       almost as interesting for what it does not reveal or reveals
       only indirectly as for what it covers. Neither man seems
       willing or able to push the discussion much beyond the fas-
       cinating production details and Hitchcock's clear-eyed de-
       cisions about technical and narrative matters. For all of
       Truffaut's adulation, the differences between the two final-
       ly seem to frustrate them. Discussions of theory ("pure
       cinema"), psychological preoccupations, and intellectual
       themes rarely move beyond the exchange of mild clichés.

          In the introduction Truffaut offers a lucid appraisal.
       He terms Hitchcock "the most complete filmmaker," says that
       he is a voyeur rather than a participant, and believes that
       his cynicism is a cover for a deeper pessimism. His films
       are distinctive because they are "at once commercial and
       experimental." Hitchcock is placed in the company of Poe,
       Dostoyevsky, and Kafka--"artists of anxiety." Translated
       in 1967 (see entry 442); reprinted in 1975 (see entry 463).

1966

Reviews (chronologically): Pierre Ajame, Les Nouvelles Littéraires, no. 2056 (26 Jan. 1967); Jean de Baroncelli, Le Monde, no. 6866 (8 Feb. 1967); Claude Pennell, Le Quinzaine Littéraire, no. 22 (15–22 Feb. 1967); Times Literary Supplement, no. 3398 (13 Apr. 1967); Raymond Bellour, Cahiers du Cinéma, no. 190 (May 1967); Claude Mauriac, Le Figaro Littéraire (29 May 1967); Elliott Fremont-Smith, New Times (11 Dec. 1967) and Arthur Knight (17 Dec. 1967); Oscar Handlin, Atlantic Monthly 221, no. 1 (Jan. 1968); Joseph Morgenstern, Newsweek 71, no. 1 (1 Jan. 1968); Andrew Sarris, Book World (14 Jan. 1968); Robert Sklar, Reporter 38, no. 3 (8 Feb. 1968); Jack Levitt, Nation 206, no. 10 (4 Mar. 1968); Frank Marchel, Film Society Review (May 1968); Penelope Gilliatt, New Yorker (6 July 1968); Kevin Gough-Yates, Screen 10, no. 1 (1969); Eric Rhode, Encounter 34, no. 1 (Jan. 1970); Robert Mazzocco, New York Review of Books 14, no. 4 (26 Feb. 1970); Susan Steinberg, Take One 2, no. 5 (10 May 1970); see also entries 164 and 195.

436   "Le Cinéma sélon Hitchcock." Cahiers du Cinéma, no. 184 (Nov.).
       Excerpt from the book of the same name, on Psycho (see entry 435).

437   "Fahrenheit 451." L'Avant-Scène du Cinéma, no. 64 (Nov.): 41–46.
       Synopsis, complete credits, excerpts from Truffaut's statements about the making of the film and from French reviews.

438   "Journal de Fahrenheit 451." Cahiers du Cinéma, no. 175 (Feb.):20–29; no. 176 (Mar.):18–30; no. 177 (Apr.):20–25; no. 178 (May):16–25; no. 179 (June):16–25; no. 180 (July): 14–19.
       A daily diary kept by Truffaut on the making of the movie, dealing with the people, problems, and situations encountered. Truffaut reveals where some incidents came from (newspapers) and how and why he altered the scenario (cutting scenes, adding ideas such as narcissism, doubling roles). He includes opinions on movies and people and veiled tips on moviemaking. All in all, a unique close-up look at the filmmaking process, which is somewhat hampered by an unwillingness to take a broader, more critically aware look at the project and some of its (and his own) contradictions.

439   "Journal of Fahrenheit 451." Cahiers du Cinéma in English, nos. 5–9 (1966–67).

1966

English translation of the above. German translation
is in Film (West Germany), nos. 4-8 (1966).

440 "Truffaut s'observe." Le Nouvel Observateur, no. 66 (16-22
Feb.):28-29.
Five brief extracts from Truffaut's journal on the direct-
ing of Fahrenheit 451.

1967

441 Dagbok med Fahrenheit 451. Translated into Swedish by Torsten
Manns. Stockholm: PAN/Norstedts, 86 pp.
Diary from Cahiers du Cinéma (see entry 438).

442 Hitchcock. Translated by Helen G. Scott. New York: Simon &
Schuster, 256 pp.
Translation of Le Cinéma selon Hitchcock (see entry 435).

1968

443 Hitchcock. Translated by Helen G. Scott. London: Secker &
Warburg, 256 pp.
Translation of Le Cinéma selon Hitchcock (1966); see
entry 435.

444 Jules and Jim. Translated by Nicholas Fry. New York: Simon
& Schuster; London: Lorrimer, 104 pp.
Postproduction script with frame blowups and credits.

445 "Le Scénario d'origine de François Truffaut." L'Avant-Scène
du Cinéma, no. 79 (Mar.):47-49.
Treatment of Breathless.

446 Schiessen Sie auf den Pianisten. Transcribed and translated
from the French by Dorle Fischer and Rudolf Thome.
Frankfurt/Main: Verlag Filmkritik. Cinemathek, vol. 22,
108 pp.
Script for Shoot the Piano Player in German.

1969

447 The 400 Blows. Edited and translated by David Denby. New
York: Grove Press, 256 pp.
Postproduction script with many frame enlargements from
the film. Includes comments from Cahiers du Cinéma, arti-
cles by Godard, Rivette, and Franju, two interviews with
Truffaut, and four critical appraisals.

1970

448 Les Aventures d'Antoine Doinel: Les Quatre Cents Coups,
     L'Amour à vingt ans, Baisers volés, Domicile conjugal.
     Paris: Mercure de France, 380 pp.
         Contains the first treatment, description of characters,
     and a comparison of Léaud's interview for the part and the
     psychologist's scene from 400 Blows; first treatment and
     final screenplay for Love at 20 and Stolen Kisses, plus
     work notes and final screenplay for Bed and Board. Trans-
     lated in 1971; see entry 452.

449 "L'Enfant sauvage." L'Avant-Scène du Cinéma, no. 107 (Oct.):
     7-44.
         Complete script and credits accompanied by an essay by
     Truffaut on the making of the film, (see entry 1108) ex-
     cerpts from French reviews, and a brief bibliography.

450 Pays, Jean-François. L'Enfant sauvage. Paris: Éditions G.
     P., 32 pp.
         Illustrated text based on Truffaut's film.

*451 [Script extracts] in L'Aesculape (a medical review), nos. 1-2.
      Reference provided by Truffaut.

1971

452 The Adventures of Antoine Doinel: Four Autobiographical
     Screenplays. Translated by Helen G. Scott. New York:
     Simon & Schuster, 320 pp.
         A translation of Les Aventures . . . with an added intro-
     ductory essay by Truffaut about the genesis of the films.
     Very revealing details about Doinel, Truffaut, and his
     ideas about film (see entry 448).

453 Jules et Jim. Paris: Éditions du Seuil/Avant-Scène, 128 pp.
         Script for Jules and Jim.

454 Jean Renoir, by André Bazin. Edited by François Truffaut.
     Paris: Éditions Champ Libre, 268 pp.
         Truffaut's editing has been criticized. Contains capsule
     comments from Cahiers (entry 907). For preface, see entry
     1122. Translated into English in 1973; see entry 458.

1972

455 "Commentaries." In Focus on "Shoot the Piano Player". Edited

1972

by Leo Braudy. Englewood Cliffs, N.J.: Prentice-Hall, pp. 161-71.
Contains a synopsis and outline, three scenes not included in the finished film, and an extract from the scenario (the fight between Charlie and Plyne).

456 "Les Deux Anglaises et le continent." L'Avant-Scène du Cinéma, no. 121 (Jan.):7-66.
Complete credits and script of Two English Girls, plus an introductory article, "L'Amour fait mal" by Dominique Fanne, Truffaut's comments on the making of the film, and excerpts from French reviews. Truffaut prefixes a note to the script indicating that he has cut fourteen minutes from the film because of poor critical reception in France.

457 "From 'The Journal of Fahrenheit 451.'" In Focus on the Science Fiction Film. Edited by William Johnson. Englewood Cliffs, N.J.: Prentice-Hall, pp. 121-25.
Nine entries of varying usefulness.

1973

458 Jean Renoir, by André Bazin. Edited by François Truffaut. New York: Simon & Schuster; London: W. H. Allen, 320 pp.
English edition translated by W. W. Haley III and W. H. Simon (see entry 454).

459 The Wild Child. Translated by Linda Lewin and Christine Lemery. New York: Washington Square Press, 189 pp.
The postproduction script includes a brief introduction by the translators and "How I Made The Wild Child" by Truffaut; see entries 449 and 1108.

1974

460 La Nuit américaine et le journal de tournage de Fahrenheit 451. Paris: Seghers (Cinéma 2000), 337 pp.
Illustrated script of Day for Night plus reprint of the daily diary of Fahrenheit 451 originally published in Cahiers du Cinéma (see entry 438).

1975

461 Le Cinéma de l'occupation et de la resistance, by André Bazin. Edited by François Truffaut. Paris: Union générale d'éditions, 194 pp.
Truffaut also provided a preface (see entry 1151).

1975

462   Le Cinéma de la cruauté: Eric von Stroheim, Carl Th. Dreyer,
       Preston Sturges, Luis Buñuel, Alfred Hitchcock, Akira
       Kurosawa, by André Bazin. Edited by François Truffaut.
       Paris: Flammarion, 224 pp.
            Truffaut also provided a preface (see entry 1156).

463   Le Cinéma selon Hitchcock. Paris: Éditions Seghers, 395 pp.
            Reissued with a new introduction (see entry 435).

464   Day for Night. Translated by Sam Flores. New York: Grove
       Press, 174 pp.
            Final script of the film with notes by the translator to
       signal differences in the final cut of the film. Foreward
       by Truffaut: "Cinema in Action," in which he comments on
       the genesis and development of the film and declares his
       hatred for the documentary. Includes frame enlargements.

465   Les Films de ma vie. Paris: Flammarion, 360 pp [hereafter
       referred to as FMV].
            A handpicked selection of his writing on films by auteur
       directors (plus articles on Bogart and James Dean). Almost
       entirely positive ("infinitely more difficult to write and
       more interesting after the passage of time") and mostly
       from 1954-1958 (except for pieces on the New Wave directors
       --more celebratory than critical--with whom Truffaut "wanted
       to affirm my position.") These are not exact reprints of
       his reviews. In some cases they are composites of several
       reviews; some have been modified, rearranged, added to.
       Translated into English in 1978--with additions; see entries
       473 and 477.

            Reviews (chronologically): Jean Collet, Études, no. 342
       (June 1975); Roland Duval, Écran 75, no. 37 (June-July 1975);
       Alexander Sesonske, Georgia Review 30, no. 1 (Spring 1976);
       James M. Purcell, Journal of Aesthetics and Art Criticism
       35, no. 1 (Fall 1976); Booklist 74 (15 May 1978); Publishers
       Weekly 213 (29 May 1978); Kirkus Reviews 46 (1 Apr. 1978);
       Library Journal 103 (1 June 1978); Roger Greenspun, American
       Film (July-Aug. 1978); David Bromwich, New York Times (23
       July 1978); Stanley Kauffmann, New Republic (29 July 1978);
       Peter Harcourt, Canadian Forum (Feb. 1979); New York Times
       Book Review (26 Aug. 1979); Walter Kerr, New York Times
       (23 Sept. 1979); Julian Jebb, Sight and Sound 49, no. 2
       (Spring 1980); Economist (31 May 1980); Observer (London)
       (17 Aug. 1980).

1976

1976

466   L'Argent de poche: ciné-roman. Paris: Flammarion, 137 pp.
         The script "novelized." Translated into English; see
      entry 468.

467   "L'Histoire d'Adèle H." L'Avant-Scène du Cinéma, no. 165
      (Jan.):3-47.
            Credits, script, and extracts from French reviews, plus
      a brief introductory essay by Truffaut, a condensation of
      Pauline Kael's New Yorker review, and essays by Jean Collet
      ("L'Écriture et le feu"--see entry 365) and François Porcile
      ("Jaubert retrouvé"--see entry 351).

468   Small Change: A Film Novel. Translated by Anselm Hollo. New
      York: Grove Press, 187 pp.
            A translation of the French ciné-roman (see entry 466).

469   The Story of Adèle H. Translated by Helen G. Scott. (English
      dialogue by Jan Dawson.) New York: Grove Press, 191 pp.
            Postproduction script plus frame enlargements and a
      foreword by Truffaut. He lists the eight factors that were
      most appealing in the story and states that "the emotion is
      father to the theme" in his creative processes and that he
      is "primarily concerned with the affective domain."

1977

470   L'Homme qui aimait les femmes. Paris: Flammarion, 126 pp.
            A "ciné-roman" (novelization) of the film without illus-
      trations.

471   Taschengeld. Translated by Eckhart Koch. Munich: Carl
      Hanser Verlag.
            German translation of the ciné-roman of Small Change.

1978

472   "La Chambre verte." L'Avant-Scène du Cinéma, no. 215 (Nov.):
      3-52.
            Full credits and script, plus an article on the film by
      Jean Mambrino; the credits for Small Change, The Man Who
      Loved Women, and Love on the Run; and a filmography on cine-
      matographer Nestor Almendros.

473   The Films in My Life. Translated by Leonard Mayhew. New York:
      Simon & Schuster, 358 pp.

1950

A translation of Truffaut's 1975 book with fourteen
added pieces, on films by LeRoy, Litvak, Tashlin, Wise,
Dassin, Melville, and four Japanese directors—Mizoguchi,
Ichikawa, Nakahira, and Kinoshita (see entry 465).

474 Hitchcock. New York: Paladin Books, 423 pp.
    Updated edition with a new introduction (see entries
    435 and 463).

1980

475 "L'Amour en fuite." L'Avant-Scène du Cinéma, no. 254 (15 Oct.):
    9-30, 47-50.
    Complete script for the film, plus samplings of the
    French reviews. Preceding the script is an essay by Anne
    Gillian.

476 "Le Dernier Metro." L'Avant-Scène du Cinéma, no. 254 (15 Oct.):
    61-63.
    Credits, an extract from an interview, photos, and ex-
    tracts from French reviews.

477 The Films in My Life. London: Allen Lane Publishers, 368 pp.
    British paperback edition (see entry 465).

REVIEWS, ESSAYS, AND INTERVIEWS BY TRUFFAUT

1950

*478 "Avenue de l'Opera: Trois Ladies de Panama." Elle, no. 237
     (12 June).
     This and the following five entries from 1950 were pro-
     vided by Truffaut.

*479 "Avis aux voyageurs." Elle, no. 250 (11 Sept.).
     How to say "I Love You" in twenty-eight languages.

*480 "Michelangelo Antonioni." [Truffaut and Jacques Rivette].
     Gazette du Cinema, no. 4 (Oct.).
     An interview.

481 "La Regle du jeu." Ciné-club du Quartier Latin 3, no. 5 (May).
    A comparison of the original and the commercially re-
    edited versions of Renoir's film. This is a film club
    bulletin.

*482 "René Clair au Ciné-club." [Truffaut and "Maurice Sherer"].

1950

    Ciné-Club du Quartier Latin 3, no. 4 (Feb.).
    Truffaut's first published article (?).

*483 "Vive Charlot, a bas Chaplin." Ciné-club du Quartier Latin
    3, no. 6 (May).

1953

484 "Affair in Trinidad (L'Affair de Trinidad)." Cahiers du
    Cinéma 4, no. 22 (Apr.):57-58.
       This Vincent Sherman film would like to be a reflection
    of Gilda, but is not negative enough; it is also indebted
    to Notorious and Key Largo.

485 "Annuaire biographique du cinéma." Cahiers du Cinéma 4, no.
    24 (June):61-62.
       Truffaut calls this the book of the year, partly because
    there are no adjectives in it and therefore "no false cri-
    ticism or presumptuous judgements, just facts and precise
    dates."

486 "Cette sacrée famille." Cahiers du Cinéma 5, no. 29 (Dec.):
    58-59.
       Brief and somewhat defensive review praising this tear-
    jerker as a work of art.

487 "Correspondance." [With J. Queval]. Cahiers du Cinéma 5, no.
    26 (Aug.-Sept.):64.
       An exchange of letters prompted by passing remarks in
    Cahiers (see entry 485) on Queval's book on Marcel Carné.

488 "Correspondance." [With Jean D'Yvoire]. Cahiers du Cinéma 5,
    no. 27 (Oct.):64.
       A protest on behalf of Télé-Ciné and a response occa-
    sioned by Truffaut's review in Cahiers (see entry 507).

489 "La Couronne noire." Cahiers du Cinéma 4, no. 22 (Apr.):58.
       Not the worst film of the year; it is sillier than it
    is evil.

490 "De A jusqu'à Z." Cahiers du Cinéma 4, no. 24 (June):53-55.
       Affectionate review of two American "films maudits" of
    1952, South Sea Sinner and Mystery on the Chicago Express,
    notable because Truffaut praises the one for using classical
    music and the other for allusions to other films, and be-
    cause he snipes at two other film critics for misrepresent-
    ing the films.

491   "Dead Line." Cahiers du Cinéma 4, no. 23 (May):63.
          Terse note that concludes that "the merit of Richard
      Brooks is to know that cinema is an art of small details."

492   "Les Dessous du Niagra." [Signed Robert Lachenay]. Cahiers
      du Cinéma 5, no. 28 (Nov.):60-61.
          This review of Henry Hathaway's Niagara concentrates al-
      most entirely on Marilyn Monroe.

493   "Dr. Cyclops." Cahiers du Cinéma 5, no. 25 (July):58.
          The film has the mental age of a ten-year-old, but it is
      better than films from the "tradition of quality." It also
      has a high regard for women. Reprinted in Focus on the
      Science Fiction Film (1972); see entry 1125.

494   "Du mépris considéré." Cahiers du Cinéma 5, no. 28 (Nov.):
      51-55.
          A lengthy review of Billy Wilder's Stalag 17, "a harsh
      and uncompromising film if ever there was one." Truffaut
      concentrates on the character of Sefton: "For the first
      time in films the philosophy of the solitary man is elabor-
      ated; this film is an apologia for individualism." In FMV.

495   "En avoir plein la vue." Cahiers du Cinéma 5, no. 25 (July):
      22-23.
          About cinemascope, which he favors because it breaks
      down the arbitrary limits of the screen.

496   "Les Extrêmes me touchent." Cahiers du Cinéma 4, no. 21
      (Mar.):61-65.
          Ostensibly a review of Sudden Fear by David Miller, this
      is more like a personal manifesto in which almost all of
      Truffaut's critical concerns are laid out.

497   "F comme femme." Cahiers du Cinéma 5, no. 30 (Christmas):
      29-41.
          A sometimes fanciful, alphabetical list of actresses,
      one for each letter, with comments for most and only photos
      for some. Truffaut is one of seven compilers.

498   "Un Index semestriel." Cahiers du Cinéma 5, no. 29 (Dec.):63.
          Two slight paragraphs praising this useful reference
      book.

499   "Ma vie à moi." Cahiers du Cinéma 5, no. 29 (Dec.):59.
          This is an admirable film because of the beauty of Lana
      Turner, the story, and Cukor's direction.

500   "Man in the Dark." Cahiers du Cinéma 5, no. 25 (July):59.

1953

      The only effective scene in this 3-D movie was done with an ordinary camera.

501   "The Mummy's Hand." Cahiers du Cinéma 5, no. 25 (July):59.
      It is "surrealist in spite of itself."

502   "La Neige n'est pas sale." Cahiers du Cinéma 4, no. 23 (May):57-59.
      A review of Snows of Kilimanjaro, which begins with the remark that some American films give a more exact sense of Paris than do French films, mentions his father's mountain climbing, and states that the American film industry is the greatest in the world not because of the superproductions it bankrolls but because of small films shown in cozy theaters.

503   "Notes sur d'autres films." [Signed "F. de M."--François de Monferrand]. Cahiers du Cinéma 5, no. 26 (Aug.-Sept.): 57-59.
      Three or four paragraphs each on five mostly forgettable films. The review of The Feathered Serpent (called Charlie Chan à Mexico) by William Beaudine is in FMV.

504   "Notes sur d'autres films." [Signed "R. L."]. Cahiers du Cinéma 5, no. 29 (Dec.):59-60.
      One paragraph each on films by Beaudine, Dieterle, Melville, Stevenson, and Pierre Louis.

505   "Le Quatrième Homme." Cahiers du Cinéma 5, no. 25 (July):58.
      Phil Karlson's film is reviewed in a condescending way.

506   "La Revue des revues." Cahiers du Cinéma 7, no. 27 (Oct.):63.
      A review of Bizarre, issue number 1.

507   "La Revue des revues." Cahiers du Cinéma 4, no. 24 (June):58.
      Truffaut attacks Télé-Ciné, a rival film journal, for its special issue on Renoir by listing all of Renoir's films and then quoting (out of context) the negative comments on each film that he has culled out of Télé-Ciné. Bazin tries to soft-pedal things in a prefatory paragraph.

508   "Terre année zéro." Cahiers du Cinéma 5, no. 25 (July):55-56.
      Arch Oboler's Five is an avant-garde film with great integrity, sincerity, and an authentic naiveté.

1954

509   "Abel Gance et la polyvision." [Signed Robert Lachenay].

France Observateur, no. 219 (22 July):26.
On the occasion of the release of July 14, 1953, Gance
is praised as an innovator and as the "V. Hugo of cinema."

510   "L'affaire Manderson." [Unsigned]. Arts, no. 461 (28 Apr.-
4 May):3.
Typical of what is wrong with the British cinema, which
is becoming the least lively cinema in Europe.

511   "Aimer Fritz Lang." Cahiers du Cinéma 6, no. 31 (Jan.):52–54.
Not much said about The Big Heat, the film that occasioned the essay. Emphasis on Lang as an auteur: his
themes ("moral solitude, a man struggling alone against a
half-hostile, half-indifferent universe"), techniques ("each
shot answers the question: how?), his use of genres, and
the overlap between his Hollywood and German films.

512   "Ali Baba." Arts, no. 495 (22–28 Dec.):5.
Although Ali Baba is not an ambitious film, it is a successful divertissement, in a genre (farcical comedy) not
yet tried by Becker. His direction and Fernandel's acting
compensate for problems.

513   "Les Amants de la Villa Borghese." [Signed R. L.]. Cahiers
du Cinéma 7, no. 38 (Aug.-Sept.):55.
Dismissed quickly as a lamentable film.

514   "L'Amour aux champs." [Signed Robert Lachenay]. Cahiers du
Cinéma 6, no. 32 (Feb.):45–48.
In this review of a Mexican film by Emilio Fernandez,
Truffaut distinguishes between eroticism and pornography
(erotic films are made by more sincere and more talented
filmmakers) and lists the ten films since 1945 worthy of
looking at with the eye and the ten moments in films in
which women captivated him.

515   "L'Amour d'une femme." [Unsigned]. Arts, no. 461 (28 Apr.-
4 May):3.
Gremillon's film tends toward melodrama and is not as
good as some of his previous work.

516   "Animal Crackers: Reprise d'un classique." [Unsigned].
Arts, no. 465 (26 May–1 June):3.
Several one-liners quoted from this, one of the Marx
Brothers' two best films.

517   "Autres films." [Signed F. T.]. Arts, no. 483 (29 Sept.–
5 Oct.):3.
One paragraph each on Naked Jungle by Byron Haskin and
Cause for Alarm by Tay Garnett.

1954

518   "Autres films." [Signed F. T.]. Arts, no. 484 (6-12 Oct.):3.
       Two or three sentences each on Le Grand Pavois, Robert
       Wise's Desert Rats, and George Seaton's Little Boy Lost.

519   "Autres films." [Signed F. T.]. Arts, no. 485 (13-19 Oct.):3.
       Ford's Mogambo and Henri Verneuil's Le Mouton a cinq
       pattes dismissed in a few sentences.

520   "Autres films." [Signed F. T.]. Arts, no. 486 (20-26 Oct.):3.
       Two to three brief paragraphs on Mann's Glenn Miller
       Story, a William Nigh film, and a Japanese film.

521   "Autres films." [Signed F. T.]. Arts, no. 487 (27 Oct.-
       2 Nov.):3.
       One paragraph each on two forgettable French films.

522   "Autres films." [Signed F. T.]. Arts, no. 489 (10-16 Nov.):5.
       One paragraph on Fregonese's Decameron Nights, two on
       Jerry Hopper's Naked Alibi.

523   "Autres films." Arts, no. 490 (17-23 Nov.):5.
       Brief reviews of three films, including Garden of Evil
       by Henry Hathaway and Houdini by George Marshall.

524   "Autres films." Arts, no. 491 (24-30 Nov.):5.
       La Belle Otero (a Franco-Italian film) and Nettoyage par
       le vide (a Mickey Spillane film) given about 200 words each.

525   "Autres films." [Unsigned]. Arts, no. 492 (1-7 Dec.):5.
       French films by Blistene and Dreville attacked.

526   "Autres films." [Signed F. T.]. Arts, no. 493 (8-14 Dec.):5.
       Short reviews of five films, including The Eternal Female
       and Richard the Lion-Hearted.

527   "Autres films." [Signed F. T.]. Arts, no. 494 (15-21 Dec.):5.
       Strongly deplores Bella Darvi's acting in Sam Fuller's
       first color and cinemascope film.

528   "Autres films." [Signed F. T.]. Arts, no. 495 (22-28 Dec.):5.
       Succinct reviews (150 words each) of five films, includ-
       ing Rhapsody, Plymouth Adventure (director Clarence Brown
       treated like an auteur), Hondo, and Hitchcock's Rebecca
       (better than the book and Hitchcock's English films, but
       not up to his masterpiece Under Capricorn).

529   "Avez-vous dans vos tiroirs des films impossibles à tourner?"
       [Signed "François de Monferrand"]. Radio-Cinéma-Télévision
       (2 May, 20 June, 4 July, 15 Aug., 5 Sept.).

1954

A series of interviews with Jacques Becker, Roger
Leenhardt, Max Ophuls, and Jean Renoir (2 May), Luis
Buñuel and Preston Sturges (20 June), Roberto Rossellini
(4 July), Jacques Tati (15 Aug.), and Abel Gance (5 Sept.).

530   "Une Certaine Tendance du cinéma français." Cahiers du Cinéma
        6, no. 31 (Jan.):15-29.
            This famous polemic against postwar French cinema hardly
        needs further comment (see Biographical Background above).
        Reprinted in Cahiers du Cinema in English, no. 1 (Jan. 1966)
        and in Movies and Methods, edited by Bill Nichols (1976);
        see entries 1084 and 1159.

531   "La Chasse au gang (City Is Dark). [Signed R. L.]. Cahiers
        du Cinéma 7, no. 38 (Aug.-Sept.)55.
            This one-eyed director (André de Toth) would be king if
        Hollywood were blind.

532   "Le Cinéma dans la rue." Arts, no. 485 (13-19 Oct.):5.
            It is neither the cinema nor the public that is failing,
        but the exploiters, the movie-house managers. An explana-
        tion of the procedures and results of the travelling ciné-
        clubs.

533   "La Comédie américaine." Arts, no. 480 (8-14 Sept.):3.
            On the golden age of comedy: 1934-1939. Of the great
        comic directors—Lubitsch, Capra, Sturges, and Cukor—only
        the latter remains (because of his scenarist Garson Kanin).
        Comic stories are all the same; they are "exercises in
        style."

534   "Comment épouser un millionaire." [Unsigned]. Arts, no. 462
        (5-11 May):3.
            Jean Negulesco's film, the first comedy in cinemascope,
        is used to talk about color and cinemascope.

535   "Drole de meurtre." [Signed R. L.]. Cahiers du Cinéma 7, no.
        37 (July):63.
            A charming film written by Sidney Sheldon, with attrac-
        tive acting from June Allyson.

536   "Écrit dans le ciel." [Signed F. T.]. Arts, no. 488 (3-9
        Nov.):3.
            The rudimentary psychology of American films can be cri-
        ticized only in films that pretend to be psychological.
        The High and the Mighty by William Wellman pretends.

537   "Les enfants d'Hiroshima." [Unsigned]. Arts, no. 453
        (3-9 Mar.):3.

1954

        Kaneto Shindo's film is the best Japanese film to reach
Paris in two years.

538   "Enquête sur la censure et l'erotisme." [With J. D.-V.--
Jacques Doniol-Valcroze]. Cahiers du Cinéma 7, no. 42
(11 Dec.):46-57.
        Special issue on love in the cinema. Truffaut and
Doniol-Valcroze compiled answers to questions on censorship
asked of a dozen directors--among them Renoir, Gance,
Becker, Preminger.

539   "Entretien avec Jacques Becker." [With Jacques Rivette].
Cahiers du Cinéma 6, no. 32 (Feb.):3-19.
        The interviewers prefer Casque d'or and note two themes
in Becker's work: "la comedie 'à l'américaine'" and
"l'histoire policière." Becker comments on his films, his
preference for characters over story and milieu, his feelings about Bresson and Hitchcock.

540   "Entretien avec Jean Renoir." [With Jacques Rivette].
Cahiers du Cinéma 6, no. 34 (Apr.):3-22.
        Renoir begins by discussing Rules of the Game and improv-
isation and commercial filmmaking. He comments at length
on his American films from Swamp Water to Woman on the Beach
and his complete responsibility for these films--with only
minimal questioning, observing, complimenting by the interviewers. Translated and shortened in Sight and Sound (July-
Sept. 1954); see entry 597.

541   "Entretien avec Jean Renoir." [With Jacques Rivette].
Cahiers du Cinéma 6, no. 35 (May):14-30.
        Renoir talks about The River and The Golden Coach and
about his work with actors. He ends by noting that human-
kind is now more intellectual than sensual and that an artist must recreate the direct contact between people and
nature.

542   "Entretien avec Roberto Rossellini." [With "Maurice Sherer"].
Cahiers du Cinéma 7, no. 37 (July):1-13.
        Rossellini comments on the "moral standpoint" of his
filmmaking, on dispensing with the "hypocrisy of the script"
and shooting more spontaneously, and on his current lack of
fashion among critics. He asks the interviewers about this;
their reply: "You don't give special emphasis to important
moments, you always remain not only objective but impassive."
Reprinted in Film Culture, in Politique des auteurs, and in
Sarris' Interviews with Film Directors (see entries 700,
1129, and 1089).

543 "L'Equippée sauvage." [Unsigned]. Arts, no. 460 (21-27 Apr.):
3.
Very little on Brando in this review of The Wild One.
It is mostly on Stanley Kramer's development of an independent cinema.

544 "Eros' Time." [Signed Robert Lachenay]. Cahiers du Cinéma
7, no. 42 (11 Dec.):32-42.
A categorization of films according to varieties of sex
(paradoxical, sadistic, fetishistic, homosexual, zoophilic,
etc.), which mentions Truffaut.

545 "Une Femme qui s'affiche." [Unsigned]. Arts, no. 458
(7-13 Apr.):3.
The contrast between this review of It Should Happen to
You and the one in Cahiers (see entry 616) illuminates
Truffaut's approaches to both journals.

546 "Femmes interdites." [Signed "R. L."]. Cahiers du Cinéma 6,
no. 32 (Feb.):51.
This Alberto Gout film from Mexico is passed over
quickly.

547 "Fille d'amour." [Unsigned]. Arts, no. 461 (28 Apr.-4 May):
3.
Subtitled Traviata 53, this is one of the best Italian
films in Paris this year.

548 "Fille d'amour." [Signed R. L.]. Cahiers du Cinéma 7, no. 37
(July):60.
Cottafavi's film is a surprise to Truffaut since he has
refused to believe in the existence of Italian cinema except
for Rossellini and Antonioni.

549 No entry.

550 "Le Film de Castellani." Arts, no. 492 (1-7 Dec.):5.
Why Romeo and Juliet is a neorealist film, whose use of
technicolor rivals Renoir's in Golden Coach.

551 "Les Frontières de la vie." [Signed R. L.]. Cahiers du
Cinéma 7, no. 38 (Aug.-Sept.):54.
The Glass Wall is so bad it could almost make Cahiers
hate Gloria Grahame.

552 "Georges Sadoul et la vérité historique." La Parisienne, no.
21 (Oct.):1114-18.
Sadoul's books briefly recommended and lengthily cor-
rected for inaccuracies and leftist leanings.

1954

553 "Girls in the Night." [Signed "R. L."]. Cahiers du Cinéma 6,
      no. 32 (Feb.):51-52.
        This Jack Arnold film leaves Truffaut halfway between
      "surprise and rapture."

554 "Le Grand Jeu." [Unsigned]. Arts, no. 463 (12-18 May):5.
        A "laborious remake" of Feyder's film.

555 "Une Grande Oeuvre: El, de Buñuel." [Unsigned]. Arts, no.
      467 (9-15 June):2.
        From Un Chien andalou to this, his best film, Buñuel has
      made in Bazin's words the trip to "la revolution au moral-
      isme."

556 "La Guerre de dieu." [Signed R. L.]. Cahiers du Cinéma 6,
      no. 35 (May):57-58.
        Rafael Gil is trying to be a Spanish Bresson.

557 "Le Guerisseur." [Unsigned]. Arts, no. 454 (10-16 Mar):3.
        Even films with a thesis must tell a story.

558 "La Guerra de Dios." [Unsigned]. Arts, no. 452 (24 Feb.-
      2 Mar.):3.
        This highly regarded Spanish film is closer to Delannoy
      than to Bresson.

559 "Le Heritiers de Bizet contre Carmen (Jones)." [Signed Robert
      Lachenay]. Arts, no. 490 (17-23 Nov.).
        On Otto Preminger's film.

560 "Les Hommes ne regardent pas le ciel." [Signed R. L.].
      Cahiers du Cinéma 7, no. 38 (Aug.-Sept.):55.
        A deplorable film.

561 "Howard Hawks intellectual." Arts, no. 477 (18-24 Aug.):5.
        A review of Gentlemen Prefer Blondes, during which
      Truffaut distinguishes between Hawks's comedies and adven-
      tures and points out his "explosion of genres." Slightly
      altered in FMV.

*562 "Il faut savoir faire confiance au cinémascope." [Signed
      "François de Monferrand"]. Radio-Cinéma-Télévision, no.
      227 (23 May).
        Reference provided by Truffaut.

*563 "Il y a dix ans, avec Jean Giraudaux, le cinéma perdait un
      admirable auteur." [Signed "François de Monferrand"].
      Radio-Cinéma-Télévision, no. 211 (31 Jan.).
        Reference provided by Truffaut.

1954

564   "Il y a dix ans Robert Bresson . . ." <u>Arts</u>, no. 482 (22-28
      Sept.):5.
      On Bresson's and Cocteau's astonishing adaptation, <u>Les</u>
      <u>Dames du bois de Boulogne</u>, which is "at the same time faith-
      ful and unfaithful." Bresson's direction is abstract: he
      seduces us by his "intentions rather than his execution."
      In <u>FMV</u>.

565   "<u>Les Indifeles</u>." [<u>sic</u>]. [Signed Robert Lachenay]. <u>Cahiers</u>
      <u>du Cinéma</u> 7, no. 38 (Aug.-Sept.):54.
      A film on a grand subject with nice women.

566   "Les Inutiles." [Unsigned]. <u>Arts</u>, no. 461 (28 Apr.-4 May):3.
      Fellini's <u>I Vitelloni</u> is agreeable because the actors
      are spontaneous enough to overcome nonexistent directing,
      the countryside photogenic enough to compensate for poor
      cinematography, etc.

567   "Jean Renoir, qui rêva d'etre . . ." [Unsigned]. <u>Arts</u>, no.
      463 (12-18 May):2.
      Portrait of Renoir, for whom "the cinema is an act of
      love," which chronicles his career from prefilm days to the
      present.

568   "Le Jeu des boites." <u>Arts</u>, no. 496 (29 Dec.-4 Jan.):5.
      Renoir's <u>Golden Coach</u> is the subject of one of Truffaut's
      longest <u>Arts</u> reviews. The film is compared to the game of
      boxes within boxes and to <u>Rules of the Game</u>. "It's the only
      film to treat from the inside the perilous subject of the
      theater, . . . art and the metier of spectacle."

569   "Jules Dassin et le <u>Rififi</u>." <u>Arts</u>, no. 494 (15-21 Dec.):5.
      A promotional piece that describes previous Dassin
      films, Dassin's exile, and a visit to the set of <u>Rififi</u>.

570   "Livre: <u>Le Cinéma</u> d'Henri Agel." [Signed F. T.]. <u>Arts</u>, no.
      496 (29 Dec.-4 Jan.):5.
      Favorable review of this book because of its balance.
      The only quibble: Agel does not see enough films.

571   "Livres de cinéma." <u>Cahiers du Cinéma</u> 6, no. 32 (Feb.):59-60.
      A calmly dismissive review of Bardeche and Brassilach's
      <u>Histoire du cinéma</u> because of its many errors. The editors
      preface the review with a note against the book's "unaccept-
      able neofascist aspect and puerile and odious anti-semitism."

572   No entry.

573   "Maison de plaisir." [Unsigned]. <u>Arts</u>, no. 453 (3-9 Mar):3.

1954

>   Dancer Ninon Seville is the only thing of interest in
> this Mexican film by Alberto Gout.

574 "Mam'zelle Nitouche." [Unsigned]. Arts, no. 460 (21-27 Apr.):
>   3.
>   The first Fernandel film without a laugh. How Allegret
> took over for Ophuls is recounted.

575 "The Manderson Affair." [Signed R. L.]. Cahiers du Cinéma 6,
>   no. 35 (May):59.
>   English cinema has been at a loss since Hitchcock's
> departure.

576 "Le Manteau." [Unsigned]. Arts, no. 455 (17-23 Mar.):3.
>   Lattuada's film is the third adaptation of Gogol's story;
> it shows how close Gogol is to Pirandello.

577 "Marlon Brando à Paris." Arts, no. 485 (13-19 Oct.):3.
>   Short biographical sketch amplified by comments about
> him by coworkers and friends.

578 "Meurte à bord." [Signed R. L.]. Cahiers du Cinéma 7, no.
>   37 (July):62.
>   Joseph Newman's film was made on a shoestring.

579 "Mon grand." [Unsigned]. Arts, no. 464 (19-25 May.):3.
>   Robert Wise has by sheer force of talent made a kind of
> masterpiece of this long melodrama.

580 "Monsieur Ripois et la nemesis." [Unsigned]. Arts, no. 465
>   (26 May-1 June):3.
>   Faithful to neither the spirit nor the letter of the
> brilliant novel, but it is an agreeable film.

581 "Monsieur Ripois sans la nemesis." La Parisienne, no. 19
>   (July):862-64.
>   René Clement betrayed Hémon by adapting only half of his
> book and Queneau by not using his dialogues. Slightly ex-
> panded in FMV.

582 "Les Nègres de la rue Blanche." Cahiers du Cinéma 7, no. 38
>   (Aug.-Sept.):48-51.
>   Combined review of River of No Return, Prince Valiant,
> and King of the Khyber Rifles, three cinemascope pictures,
> which dismisses the latter two ("Son of audacity and clair-
> voyance, cinemascope has sired flabbiness and folly").
> River of No Return is not the best Preminger, but it is
> the best cinemascope.

1954

583   "Ne me quitte jamais (Never Let Me Go)." [Signed R. L.].
      Cahiers du Cinéma 6, no. 35 (May):56-57.
         Briefly on Delmer Davies' film with Clarck [sic] Gable.

584   "Nettoyage par le vide." [Unsigned]. Arts, no. 491 (24-30
      Nov.):5.
         On The Long Wait.

585   "Nous, les femmes." [Unsigned]. Arts, no. 457 (31 Mar.-
      6 Apr.):3.
         A film composed of sketches by four stars who talk about
      their lives. Visconti directs Anna Magnani, Rossellini di-
      rects Ingrid Bergmann. They get the most space in Truffaut's
      account.

586   "Opera des gueux." [Unsigned]. Arts, no. 456 (24 Mar.):3.
         Peter Brook and Lawrence Olivier's Beggar's Opera is
      closer to Fanfan la tulipe than to Brecht.

587   "Ouragan sur le Caine." Arts, no. 484 (6-12 Oct.):3.
         Dmitryk's Caine Mutiny, another American attempt at in-
      tellectual cinema by using best-sellers, is better than
      Zinneman's because the script is more original.

588   "Petit journal intime du cinéma." Cahiers du Cinéma 7, no. 37
      (July):34-38.
         A chronological account from 1 June to 11 July (not every
      day) of Truffaut's many movie-related activities: movies
      seen, books read or to read, musings, statistics, but espe-
      cially personalities met--Buñuel, Rossellini, Renoir,
      Hitchcock et al.

589   "Petit journal intime du cinéma." [Signed Robert Lachenay].
      Cahiers du Cinéma 7, no. 41 (Dec.):10-15.
         Movie diary from 22 Sept. to 20 Oct. with a photo of the
      real Robert Lachenay at the start (as a ruse) and mention
      made of Truffaut in 24 Sept. entry. Includes aphorisms on
      filmmakers and snippets from conversation.

590   "Petit lexique des formats nouveaux." [Signed F. T.]. Arts,
      no. 487 (27 Oct.-2 Nov.):3.
         Brief explanations of cinemascope, cinepanoramic, cine-
      rama, and superscope.

591   "Portrait de Jacques Becker." [Signed Robert Lachenay]. Arts,
      no. 496 (29 Dec.-4 Jan.):5.
         Background information on Becker's career, amplified by
      generous quotations.

1954

592 "Premier bilan du cinémascope." Arts, no. 474 (28 July-
     3 Aug.):3.
          An essay on the newly invented cinemascope system, com-
     plete with a chart of important dates, which notes the ad-
     vantages and disadvantages, and ends by predicting that
     Hawks's Land of the Pharoahs will be the first cinemascope
     masterpiece.

593 "Prisonniers du Marais." [Signed R. L.]. Cahiers du Cinéma
     6, no. 35 (May):57.
          Lure of the Wildernen [sic] by Jean Negulesco is boring.

594 "La Public n'a jamais tort by Adolphe Zukor." [Signed Robert
     Lachenay]. Cahiers du Cinéma 7, no. 38 (Aug.-Sept.):57.
          Lists seven things that make it best book on film and
     seven that make it the worst.

595 "Quai des blondes." [Unsigned]. Arts, no. 459 (14-20 Apr.):3.
          It is instructive to watch first-time directors; they are
     either interesting or they are not. Paul Cadeac is not.

596 "Quai des blondes." [Signed R. L.]. Cahiers du Cinéma 7, no.
     37 (June):65.
          A mediocre first film by Paul Cadeac that is reviewed as
     if the director were talking to us in film language.
     Truffaut translates what the film is really saying about
     the director's ambitions.

597 "Renoir in America." [With Jacques Rivette]. Sight and Sound
     24, no. 1 (July-Sept.):12-17.
          Translated and abridged version of interview from Cahiers
     (see entry 540).

598 "Retour au paradis." [Signed R. L.]. Cahiers du Cinéma 6,
     no. 35 (May):57.
          Truffaut would like to like this Mark Robson film more.

*599 "Rivière sans retour." [Signed Robert Lachenay]. France-
     Observateur (2 Sept.).
          On Preminger's River of No Return. Reference provided
     by Truffaut.

600 "Roberto Rossellini: Je ne suis pas . . . ." [Unsigned].
     Arts, no. 468 (16-22 June):3.
          A rambling discourse on himself and his filmmaking, fol-
     lowed by an announcement and comment by Truffaut on a bal-
     let Rossellini and Bergman are to give.

601 "Robinson Crusoe." [F. T. and J. A.--Jean Aurel]. Arts, no.

479 (1-9 Sept.):3.
Not an important work in Buñuel's career, but an interesting study of solitude.

602   "Le Roi de la Pagaille." [Signed R. L.]. Cahiers du Cinéma
       6, no. 35 (May):59.
       On Trouble in the Store by J. P. Carstairs.

603   "Le Rose et le gris." Arts, no. 488 (3-9 Nov.):3.
       On adaptations and the diluted adaptation of The Red and
       the Black by Autant-Lara, Aurenche, and Bost.

604   "Le Rouge et le noir." [Signed "Stendhal"]. Arts, no. 488
       (3-9 Nov.):3.
       How Stendhal would criticize the film made from his
       book.

605   "Le Rouge et le noir (suite)." Arts, no. 489 (10-16 Nov.):5.
       The anticlericalism of Stendhal is "rigorously incompati-
       ble with that of Claude Autant-Lara, Aurenche, and Bost."
       This is a film without soul.

606   "Sang et lumières." [Unsigned]. Arts, no. 464 (19-25 May):3.
       Georges Rouquier is a documentarist; his work with pro-
       fessional actors remains the film's weak point.

607   "Le Secret d'Hélène Marimon." [Unsigned]. Arts, no. 464
       (19-25 May):3.
       Henri Calef's film reviews the possibilities and limits
       of the French, as opposed to the American, cinema.

608   "Le Secret d'Hélène Marimon." [Signed R. L.]. Cahiers du
       Cinéma 7, no. 37 (July):63.
       An exercise in style limited by the melodramatic narrow-
       ness of the subject.

609   "Silence! Jean Renoir tourne French Can Can." Arts, no. 487
       (27 Oct.-2 Nov.):3.
       Four days on the set of Renoir's film. Activities de-
       scribed; director quoted.

610   "Sir Abel Gance." Arts, no. 479 (1-7 Sept.):3.
       A defense of Gance's sound films, during which Truffaut
       distinguishes between the art of silent and of sound films
       and calls Gance "the Victor Hugo of the cinema" and "our
       grand lyric filmmaker."

611   "Si Versailles m'était conte." [Signed "R. L."]. Cahiers du
       Cinéma 6, no. 34 (Apr.):64.

1954

        Guitry is preferable to René Clair; despite what critics say, this film pleases.

612   "Tant qu'il y aura des hommes." [Unsigned]. <u>Arts</u>, no. 457 (31 Mar.-6 Apr.):3.
        Despite all the hoopla and awards, Truffaut is cool to <u>From Here to Eternity</u>, pointing out its shortcomings and willing to wait and see if it will stand the test of time.

613   "<u>Tempête sous la mer</u>." [Unsigned]. <u>Arts</u>, no. 459 (14-20 Apr.): 3.
        The double story of Romeo and Juliet and the Cid. It is pleasurable.

614   "<u>Touchez pas au Grisbi</u>." [Unsigned]. <u>Arts</u>, no. 455 (17-23 Mar.):3.
        Although advertised as a gangster film, this is the most "interior" French film of the year.

615   "<u>Le Tour des ambitieux</u>." <u>Arts</u>, no. 482 (22-28 Sept.):3.
        <u>Executive Suite</u> is one of those films in which the producer counts as much as the director.

616   "Le Train de la Ciotat." [Signed Robert Lachenay]. <u>Cahiers du Cinéma</u> 6, no. 35 (May):50-52.
        Cukor's "masterpiece" <u>It Should Happen to You</u> prompts Truffaut to detail what kinds of films he likes: those with recountable stories, those with good pictures to use at entrances to theaters, and genre films. In <u>FMV</u>.

617   "<u>La Tresor du Guatemala</u>." [Signed R. L.]. <u>Cahiers du Cinéma</u> 7, no. 36 (June):62.
        Delmer Davies' film will be pleasing to those who will not realize that it was shot in Peru.

618   "Un Trousseau de fausses clés." <u>Cahiers du Cinéma</u> 7, no. 39 (Oct.):45-52.
        Truffaut sets out to prove to Bazin that Hitchcock is aware of his themes, more aware than Renoir and Rossellini, though less great because his films lack "the share of God" (Gide's term). He examines Hitchcock's American films, especially <u>Shadow of a Doubt</u> and <u>Under Capricorn</u>, and concludes with three reasons for Hitchcock's lies, his genius, and French cinema's mediocrity. Reprinted as "Skeleton Keys" in <u>Film Culture</u> and <u>Cahiers du Cinema in English</u> (see entries 1077 and 1086).

619   "Les Truands sont fatigués." <u>Cahiers du Cinéma</u> 6, no. 34 (Apr.):54-57.

A review of Becker's <u>Touchez pas au Grisbi</u> that avoids
specifics about the film in favor of general points about
Becker: his participation in scripting and his treatment
of the subject (not the subject itself) as a distinguishing
characteristic. Becker breaks the rules of French film;
his are the most elegant films with the most dignified characters. He is compared to Renoir; his obvious love for cinema is noted.

620 "<u>Vacances romaines.</u>" [Unsigned]. <u>Arts</u>, no. 458 (7-13 Apr.):3.
     <u>Roman Holidays</u> is full of contradictions because William
     Wyler's talent resides "more in minutia, in precision, than
     in verve."

621 "<u>Vedettes sans maquillage</u> de Georges Baume." [Signed Robert
     Lachenay]. <u>Cahiers du Cinéma</u> 7, no. 38 (Aug.-Sept.):55-57.
     A book review that quotes one sentence each from many of
     the insignificant conversations that accompany photos of
     stars included in this portrait book.

622 "<u>Vol sur Tanger.</u>" [Signed Robert Lachenay]. <u>Cahiers du
     Cinéma</u> 7, no. 37 (July):53.
     Can recommend this C. H. Warren film only to his worst
     enemies.

623 "Western et comedie." <u>Arts</u>, no. 481 (15-21 Sept.):3.
     More about comedies than Westerns, which are as differ-
     ent as "a wild animal and a domestic animal." American
     comedy is an exercise in style in which "the genius of di-
     rectors and actors better asserts itself."

<u>1955</u>

624 "<u>A l'est d'Eden.</u>" <u>Arts</u>, no. 539 (26 Oct.-1 Nov.):5.
     The best film of a bad director (Elia Kazan). A good
     story, but the actors suffer from "theatrical" direction.

625 "A Propos de <u>Chiens perdus sans collier.</u>" [Unsigned]. <u>Arts</u>,
     no. 543 (23-29 Nov.):5.
     Defensive preamble by Truffaut to a letter from Jean
     Delannoy.

626 "Abel Gance, désordre et génie." [Signed Robert Lachenay].
     <u>Cahiers du Cinéma</u> 8, no. 47 (May):44-46.
     Though <u>La Tour de Nesle</u>, the subject of the review, is
     the "least good" Gance film, he is a genius. Like Renoir
     he sacrifices things. Article includes a list of fourteen
     great films that were failures. In <u>FMV</u>.

1955

627   "L'Admirable Certitude." [Signed Robert Lachenay]. Cahiers
       du Cinéma 8, no. 46 (Apr.):38-40.
            Nick Ray is not a great technician and Johnny Guitar is
       far from his best film, but he is an auteur, since all his
       films tell the same story. "The mark of his great talent
       resides in his absolute sincerity." Combined with Arts re-
       view in FMV.

628   "Ali Baba et la 'Politique des auteurs.'" Cahiers du Cinéma
       8, no. 44 (Feb.):45-47.
            Becker is an auteur. Much huffing and puffing to defend
       Ali Baba, including recourse to Giraudoux's "there are no
       works; there are only auteurs."

629   "L'Amant de Lady Chatterly." Arts, no. 546 (14-20 Dec.):5.
            Marc Allegret's best film in a while, whose only grave
       fault is lack of direction. Adaptation of sex to screen
       suffers because some of the book's best parts must be omit-
       ted.

630   "Angine, orage et polemique au Festival de Venise." Arts, no.
       533 (14-20 Sept.):5.
            Gossip about what is happening. The critics are divided,
       old versus young, over Astruc's film. Grouping films by
       country, Truffaut comments on their chances for a prize.
       Antonioni's Les Amies and Ulmer's Naked Dawn are best.
       British entries reinforce the notion already proven that
       there is no more British cinema.

631   "Antoine et l'orpheline." La Parisienne, no. 28 (May):515-21.
            The first public Antoine tale, this short story by
       Truffaut is a parody of Jean Cocteau about a twenty-year-
       old youth named Antoine and the woman who jilts him--
       Henriette.

632   "Les Aristocrates." Arts, no. 539 (26 Oct.-1 Nov.):5.
            Although commercially successful, this film is nothing
       but nonsense and vulgarity, characterized by a bad script
       and terrible direction. Critics are unable to stop the
       success of these films, released as "quality" French pro-
       ductions; their weak, facile maxims and aphorisms, passed
       off as intelligence and wit, merely pander to an audience.
       The review provoked a response in Arts, no. 591 (see entry
       671).

633   "Autres films." [Unsigned]. Arts, no. 498 (12-18 Jan.):5.
            Ring of Fear and Saskatchewan reviewed.

634   "Autres films." [Signed F. T.]. Arts, no. 499 (19-25 Jan.):5.

Lucky Me by Jack Donohue is "a poor film"--made without enough money.

635   "Autres films." [Signed "R. L."--Robert Lachenay]. Arts, no. 503 (16-22 Feb.):5.
      Ten negative adjectives to describe what Michael Curtiz' The Egyptian is not; but it is a "prodigious bore."

636   "Autres films." Arts, no. 505 (2-8 Mar.):5.
      Two paragraphs each on Richard Quine's Pushover, Lesley Selander's I Was an American Spy, and Berthomieu's Les Deux font la paire.

637   "Autres films." Arts, no. 506 (9-15 Mar.):5.
      The Black Shield of Falworth by Rudy Maté is an agreeable film in its genre; Les Fruits de l'eté by Raymond Bernard has very little to like.

638   "Autres films." Arts, no. 510 (6-12 Apr.):5.
      Titanic betrays all of the faults of Negulesco's style.

639   "Autres films." [Signed Robert Lachenay]. Arts, no. 514 (4-10 May):5.
      Cukor's A Star Is Born is "a great film failed, but passionate." Night People by Nunnally Johnson is "ingenious and intelligent enough." Ça va barder, a French film by John Berry, is "no worse than other films noirs."

640   "Autres films." [Unsigned]. Arts, no. 526 (27 July-2 Aug.):5.
      Two short paragraphs each on Allan Dwan's Passion, Henry King's Untamed, and Victor Saville's The Silver Chalice.

641   "Autres films." [Signed F. T.]. Arts, no. 528 (10-16 Aug.):3.
      A Mexican, a British, and two American films curtly dismissed.

642   "Battle Cry de Raoul Walsh et 08/15 de Paul May." Arts, no. 520 (15-21 June):6.
      Opens with generalities about Walsh, Hathaway, and Hollywood directors of their ilk. Battle Cry is perfect; the director is "conscientious and adroit" and has a sense of humor. 08/15 has a good script; with it Walsh could have made a masterpiece, but May has not.

643   "La Biennale de Venise." Arts, no. 532 (7-13 Sept.):3.
      The ambiance and activities of the Venice Film Festival described. Three films reviewed: Ordet, To Catch a Thief, and Les Mauvaises Rencontres.

1955

644   "Cannes: Palmarès anticipé selon les regles du jeu." [Signed
      Robert Lachenay]. <u>Arts</u>, no. 513 (27 Apr.-3 May):5.
        Big countries do not send best films. Gripes and predic-
      tions about the annual film festival.

645   "Ce n'est qu'un au revoir." <u>Arts</u>, no. 527 (3-9 Aug.):3.
        A devastatingly negative review of John Ford's <u>The Long
      Gray Line</u>. Truffaut outlines the plot at length to show
      how foolish it is and points out its manifest technical in-
      competence, especially in the use of cinemascope. He lists
      Ford's films and claims not to like any. He concludes by
      stating that Ford is overrated, less important than Walsh,
      Mann, and Vidor.

646   "Ce que vous verrez en 1955." [Signed R. Lachenay]. <u>Arts</u>,
      no. 497 (5-11 Jan.):5.
        The coming year will be an exceptional one for films in
      France and Italy because of Dassin's <u>Rififi</u> and Sturges'
      <u>Major Thomson</u>.

647   "<u>Le Cercle infernal</u> de Henry Hathaway." <u>Arts</u>, no. 525
      (20-26 July):5.
        The Racers is Hathaway's best film since <u>Niagara</u>. The
      director's "virtuosity" is noted as well as his cinematog-
      rapher's extraordinary talent with technicolor. "The sole
      refuge of the Hollywood filmmaker is technique."

648   "<u>Chéri Bibi</u>." <u>Arts</u>, no. 521 (22-28 June):5.
        Especially critical of director Marcel Pagliero, whom
      Truffaut accuses of intellectual laziness. Final sentence:
      "To <u>not</u> see <u>Chéri Bibi</u> is to pass an enjoyable evening."

649   "<u>Chiens perdus sans collier</u>." <u>Arts</u>, no. 541 (9-15 Nov.):5.
        The film is being passed off as a quality film, but it
      is the "basest demagoguery" and its director, Jean Delannoy,
      is "so certain of his genius that he . . . would think a
      [negative] critic was after him personally."

650   "Le Cinéma a soixante ans: l'Arroseur arrosé." <u>Arts</u>, no. 547
      (21-27 Dec.):5.
        Amusing series of plot summaries describing how de Mille,
      Autant-Lara, Hitchcock, de Sica, and others would film the
      famous "sprinkler sprinkled" scene from early film history.

651   "<u>Le Cinéma</u> d'Henri Agel." [Signed F. T.]. <u>Cahiers du Cinéma</u>
      8, no. 45 (Mar.):56-57.
        Agel's virtue is his total impartiality; his book is
      without errors and is a good introductory text.

652　"La Cinématheque sur la rue." Arts, no. 501 (2-8 Feb.):7.
　　　　Truffaut provides a long list of films that can be seen
at the cinémathèque and then laments its closing; he hopes
Langlois can find a new home for his important collection.
For reopening, see entry 739.

653　"La Colline 24 ne répond pas." Arts, no. 523 (6-12 July):5.
　　　　Although officially an Israeli film, aesthetically it is
an English film and thus suffers from the usual afflictions
of that type:　insipidity, decency and dullness, awkwardness, etc., etc.

654　"Comicos." Arts, no. 539 (26 Oct.-1 Nov.):5.
　　　　An "abominable film." Film critics should not let Bardem
get away with uninventive plagiarisms like this copy of All
about Eve.

655　"Comment fut tourné Napoléon." [Signed Robert Lachenay].
Arts, no. 505 (2-8 Mar.):5.
　　　　Production details on Gance's filming of Napoléon. It
forms the basis of article in Films of My Life; one paragraph at beginning and two at end used from article that
appeared next to it in Arts (see entry 715).

656　"Le Comte de Monté-Cristo." Arts, no. 500 (26 Jan.-1 Feb.):5.
　　　　Truffaut likes this adaptation, especially the fact that
two films were made so as not to distort the time frame of
the novel.

657　"Le Comte de Monté-Cristo." [Signed by F. T.]. Arts, no. 502
(9-15 Feb.):5.
　　　　Truffaut hopes that Vernay will not make a third episode
to follow this two-part film (see entry 656). He says that
films are "not only for those who know how to watch and who
miss no details, but also for those who return."

658　"La Comtesse aux pieds nus." Arts, no. 522 (29 June-5 July):5.
　　　　Barefoot Contessa, the portrait of a woman placed in four
different situations, is the kind of film that is either accepted or rejected in toto. Truffaut accepts it for its
novelty, intelligence, and beauty.

659　"La Comtesse était Beyle." Cahiers du Cinéma 9, no. 49
(July):41-44.
　　　　Barefoot Contessa is perplexing, unquestionably. But
there is no doubt about its "sincerity, novelty, audacity,
and ability to fascinate." Truffaut disagrees with Bazin
here and calls him the Sainte-Beuve of cinema. In FMV.

1955

660   "Le Courrier des lecteurs (ouvert et répondu par F. T.)."
      Cahiers du Cinéma 9, no. 52 (Nov.):57-60.
          Truffaut responds briefly and pointedly to five letters
      to the editor.

661   "Le Court Métrage manque d'auteurs." Arts, no. 536 (5-11
      Oct.):5.
          Reviews of four films at festival of short films at
      Tours. Review of Norman McLaren's Blinkity-Blank is in
      FMV.

662   "Le Crime était presque parfait." Arts, no. 502 (9-15 Feb.):5.
          Disappointed that this film, Dial M for Murder, is being
      shown flat and not in 3-D. Notes Hitchcock's remarkable use
      of color and his recent scorn for his characters, a tendency
      he shares with Balzac.

663   "La Crise d'ambition du cinéma français." Arts, no. 509
      (30 Mar.-5 Apr.):5.
          At the center of this article is a list of eighty-nine
      French directors described according to four categories:
      (1) ambitious, (2) semiambitious, (3) commercially honest,
      (4) deliberately commercial. Thirty directors are in cate-
      gory four, and they, on the average, have made more films
      than the others. In addition, critics have been too easy
      on films, actors are not selective, producers are afraid of
      quality films, and movie houses will show anything.

664   "Le Derby des psaumes." Cahiers du Cinéma 8, no. 48 (June):
      42-45.
          Vera Cruz is a "dazzling lesson in the construction of
      a story." The main features of the plot are presented in
      twenty-three scenes. Script is better than execution. In
      FMV.

665   "Désirs humains." Arts, no. 524 (13-19 July):5.
          This Fritz Lang film is compared to Renoir's La Bête
      humaine, of which it is a remake.

666   "Dessous d'espoir." La Parisienne, no. 32 (Oct.):1111-13.
          "Ours will be the age of transparency." Truffaut com-
      ments not on movies but on feminine fashion.

667   "Destination Gobi." Arts, no. 506 (9-15 Mar.):5.
          A great script helps this film transcend the limitations
      of its genre. Director Robert Wise's work is "unusually
      serious, intelligent, tasteful, direct, and precise." In
      FMV.

668   "Dictionnaire des réalisateurs américains contemporains."
      Cahiers du Cinéma 9, no. 54 (Christmas):47-63.
          Truffaut was one of five writers contributing critical
      commentaries for these biographies and filmographies.

669   "Les Dix Meilleurs Films de l'année." Cahiers du Cinéma 8,
      no. 43 (Jan.):5.
          Includes Truffaut's and Lachenay's top ten films of
      1954. Only three films in common.

670   "Dommage que tu sois une canaille." [Unsigned]. Arts, no.
      523 (6-12 July):5.
          A swift kill for this Alessandro Blasetti film. Notable
      is the counterreview, critical of Truffaut's negative posi-
      tion on the film, by the managing editor of Arts, Claude
      Martine, in issue 527 (3-9 Aug.).

671   "Dont acte." Arts, no. 541 (9-15 Nov.):5.
          A letter from René Cloerec, musical composer for Les
      Aristocrats, correcting an error in Truffaut's review
      (Arts no. 539; see entry 632). Truffaut apologizes.

672   "Dossier noir." Arts, no. 517 (25-31 May):5.
          Each film by André Cayatte is worse than the last, and
      this one is no different. Most of review is given over to
      list of eight changes that should be made, ranging from
      sacking cowriter Charles Spaak to putting a stop to court-
      ing just youthful audiences.

673   "Double destin." Arts, no. 500 (26 Jan.-1 Feb.):5.
          The direction and dialogue in this adaptation are deplor-
      able. In fact, everything about the film is stupid and vul-
      gar. Although taken from one of his novels, there is noth-
      ing of Giraudoux in this film.

674   "Drôles de bobines." Arts, no. 500 (26 Jan.-1 Feb.):5.
          Noncomittal paragraph except for the remark that the
      film has such a strong resemblance to Singin' in the Rain
      and Renoir's Golden Coach in some scenes that it almost
      amounts to plagiarism.

675   "Du Rififi à la compétence." Arts, no. 516 (18-24 May):5.
          A second look at Dassin's film, which singles out the
      director's ability to make us believe in the characters,
      their value and importance despite their crime. Truffaut
      goes on to compare the competence and indispensability of
      each thief to the success of the robbery with the same qual-
      ities in a director and technicians in making a film; ex-
      cerpted in entry 1050.

1955

676   "Du Rififi chez les hommes." <u>Arts</u>, no. 512 (20-26 Apr.):5.
        Dassin's film shows that success depends more on a good
        director than on a big budget, inflated production, and big-
        name stars. In <u>FMV</u>.

677   "L'Emprisonné de Peter Grenville." [Signed Robert Lachenay].
        <u>Arts</u>, no. 545 (7-13 Dec.):5.
        Surprisingly, Truffaut praises an English film. In this
        first film by Grenville, "everything is very honestly said
        and done."

678   "En quatrième vitesse." <u>Arts</u>, no. 534 (21-27 Sept.):5.
        <u>Kiss Me Deadly</u> lavishly praised for its richness and in-
        tensity. Robert Aldrich is a director to be reckoned with.
        In <u>FMV</u>.

679   "Entretien avec Abel Gance." [With Jacques Rivette]. <u>Cahiers
        du Cinéma</u> 8, no. 43 (Jan.):6-17.
        A rather sad interview on Gance's lost films and abortive
        projects. Notable primarily for its prefatory remarks,
        which outline the rules of all <u>Cahiers</u> interviews: (1)
        choose only directors we love and (2) let them express
        themselves in their own way without ever asking embarrass-
        ing questions.

680   "Entretien avec Alfred Hitchcock." [With Claude Chabrol].
        <u>Cahiers du Cinéma</u> 8, no. 44 (Feb.):19-31.
        Hitchcock talks about his recent films (primarily <u>Rope</u>,
        <u>Under Capricorn</u>, and <u>I Confess</u>), his projects, and his pref-
        erences (his American films more than his British; serious
        films like <u>I Confess</u> more than humorous ones). Reprinted
        in <u>Politique des auteurs</u> (see entry 1129).

681   "Entretien avec Jules Dassin." [With Claude Chabrol].
        <u>Cahiers du Cinéma</u> 8, no. 46 (Apr.):3-13.
        Dassin talks about his early Hollywood career, <u>Brute
        Force</u>, <u>Naked City</u>, and <u>Night and the City</u> (the interviewer's
        favorite), and about Nick Ray.

682   "Entretien avec Jules Dassin." [With Claude Chabrol].
        <u>Cahiers du Cinéma</u> 8, no. 47 (May):11-16.
        Dassin on unfinished projects, Joseph Losey and John
        Berry, and cinema as the art of the masses. A filmography
        is appended.

683   "Les Evadés." <u>Arts</u>, no. 524 (13-19 July):5.
        Truffaut points out the startling similarities between
        Lechanois' film and Renoir's <u>Grand Illusion</u>. But "every-
        thing that is beautiful and noble in Renoir's film is

ridiculous and shabby in comparison in Les Evadés." The
jury that voted this the "Grand Prize of French Cinema" is
incompetent.

684 "Un Événement cinématographique: Reprise de Hallelujah."
[Signed Robert Lachenay]. Arts, no. 542 (16–22 Nov.):5.
Tribute to "the forgotten" King Vidor, who is like Abel
Gance.

685 "Faiblesses et qualités des films soviétiques." Arts, no. 546
(14–20 Dec.):5.
Description of the characteristics and especially the
shortcomings of Russian films, particularly the surface
reality and childish psychology. They are like Capra's
films, only insincere. One exception: La Cigale.

686 "Fenêtre sur cour." Arts, no. 510 (6–12 Apr.):5.
Hitchcock's Rear Window is one of his most important
films, one of those "rare films without any imperfection,
any weakness, any concessions." It is "about indiscretion,
about the impossibility of happiness . . . about moral solitude." Two introductory paragraphs added (from the Arts,
no. 588 review of The Man Who Knew Too Much; see entry 807)
in FMV.

687 "Le Festival de Venise 1955." Cahiers du Cinéma 9, no. 51
(Oct.):10–22.
Brief reviews of five films, among them Il Bidone (which
he likes because of Broderick Crawford and despite Fellini's
faults), The Naked Dawn, and The Big Knife.

688 "La Fin d'Hitler." Arts, no. 539 (26 Oct.–11 Nov.):5.
Quick review of the G. W. Pabst film.

689 "French Can-Can." Arts, no. 514 (4–10 May):5.
The film, an homage to the music hall, is not as important as The Golden Coach or Rules of the Game; yet it is a
brilliant film attesting to Renoir's strength, wholesome-
ness, and youthfulness.

690 "Future vedette." Arts, no. 521 (22–28 June):5.
Marc Allegret has lost his faith and enthusiasm. His
films before the war were better (even better than those of
his brother, Yves); this one is a complete waste of time
and money.

691 "Le Grand Couteau." Arts, no. 544 (30 Nov.–6 Dec.):5.
Director Robert Aldrich compared to Welles and Cocteau.
This refined and intelligent film progresses not by a play

1955

of sentiments or by the unfolding of the action, but by the
moral development of the characters, a rare technique, but
one that is more effective and demands better actors. In
FMV.

692   "Les Héros sont fatigués." Arts, no. 541 (9-15 Nov.):5.
      This could have been a masterpiece if the director,
      Yves Ciampi, had written it too.

693   "Hitchcock aime l'invraisemblance." Arts, no. 548 (28 Dec.-
      3 Jan.):5.
      Overview dealing mainly with Hitchcock's precision and
      exacting realism within scenes and a kind of imprecision
      in the film as a whole.

694   "Hollywood, petite île . . . par Max Ophuls." [By Truffaut
      and Jacques Rivette]. Cahiers du Cinéma 9, no. 54
      (Christmas):4-9.
      Because the questions were eliminated in the transcription
      of this interview (on producers, writers, actors, editing,
      and B-films in Hollywood), it appears that Ophuls simply
      talked nonstop about his career.

695   "L'Homme de la plaine." Arts, no. 545 (7-13 Dec.):5.
      Director Anthony Mann seems to have set as a goal the
      perfection of the traditional Western. The Man from Laramie
      succeeds because of its natural poetry and strong, calm,
      and effective direction.

696   "Huis clos de Jacqueline Audry." Arts, no. 497 (5-11 Jan.):5.
      This adaptation of Sartre's play is a total failure.
      His heroes are "condemned anew and this time to the hell of
      the adaptation."

697   "Hulot parmi nous." Arts, no. 515 (11-17 May):5.
      Using a new book on Tati as a starting point, Truffaut
      analyses Tati's comic sense, comparing him to Keaton and
      noting that his is "exclusively a comedy of observation."
      Also contains an odd breakdown of audience responses to
      Tati: 15 percent do not laugh and are angry.

698   "Les Hussards." Arts, no. 547 (21-27 Dec.):5.
      Outside of Jacques Becker, Alex Joffé is the only good
      maker of film comedies. This film is like a page out of a
      picaresque novel. The construction is ingenious, the pace
      never slows, and the acting is excellent.

699   "Ingrid Bergman: J'ai échappé à Hollywood . . . et à Sacha
      Guitry." Arts, no. 510 (6-12 Apr.):1, 5.

An exclusive interview: Bergman talks about the cruelty of journalists, her first meeting with Rossellini, her projects.

700 "Interview with Roberto Rossellini." [With "Maurice Sherer."]. Film Culture 1, no. 2 (Mar.-Apr.):12-14.
Translation of Cahiers du Cinéma interview (see entry 542).

701 "Jeanne au butcher." Arts, no. 518 (1-7 June):5.
Rossellini's simple neorealist style perfectly suits its source, Claudel's play. Though almost experimental in style, audience liked it.

702 "Je suis un adventurier." [Signed R. L.]. Arts, no. 511 (13-19 Apr.):5.
Anthony Mann's film The Far Country is "a spectacle of rare quality."

703 "John Ford de Jean Mitry." [Signed F. T.]. Cahiers du Cinéma 8, no. 45 (Mar.):57-58.
Truffaut lists all the chapter titles. He disagrees with Mitry's preferences, but likes the idea of the book.

704 "John Ford par Jean Mitry." Arts, no. 506 (9-15 Mar.):5.
The book is "indispensable." One long passage quoted.

*705 "John Huston--Le Cinéma de la chasse à l'impossible." Plaisir de Paris (Dec.).
Reference provided by Truffaut.

706 "Johny Guitare." Arts, no. 504 (23 Feb.-1 Mar.):5.
Of the two kinds of directors, cerebral and instinctual, Nick Ray is the second; he belongs to "the school of sincerity and sensitivity." Johnny Guitar is "dreamed, a fairy tale, a hallucinatory Western." It is actually two films, one on Ray's recurring theme of the relationships of men and women and a second "extravagant catchall done in Joseph von Sternberg style." Excerpted in L'Avant-Scène du Cinéma (1974); see entry 1142. Modified in FMV.

707 "Les Journées internationales de Court Métrage." Arts, no. 534 (21-27 Sept.):5.
Simply an announcement about the Tours festival for short films, which Truffaut feels will provide an opportunity for studying the possibility of short films as entertainment, as culture, and as a teaching tool.

708 "La Lance brisée." Arts, no. 509 (30 Mar.-5 Apr.):5.

1955

<blockquote>
<u>Broken Lance</u>: good script, poor casting, unimaginative director. Review focuses mainly on beauties of the new cinemascope technique.
</blockquote>

709 "<u>Lola Montès</u>." <u>Arts</u>, no. 548 (28 Dec.-3 Jan.):5.
Ophuls is a nineteenth-century filmmaker; his film is not so much a story as "the full, rich portrait of a woman." Everything about the film is admirable, from its use of cinemascope and color to its audacious structure and ultilitarian, intelligent dialogue. Combined with <u>Cahiers</u> review in <u>FMV</u> (see entry 819).

710 "La Long Misère du court métrage (II)." <u>Arts</u>, no. 501 (2-8 Feb.):7.
The position of Louis Cluny, president of the Association of Independent Producers and Directors of Short Films, is presented. Cluny is against the proposed law providing financial aid to "quality" short films. Truffaut feels the controversy is out of proportion with the issue and hopes it is resolved soon.

711 "<u>La Main au collet</u>." <u>Arts</u>, no. 548 (28 Dec.-3 Jan.):5.
On Hitchcock's favorite themes (role reversal and the moral and physical identification of two people) and his techniques (effectiveness of special effects, rhythm of scenes, ingenuity of each detail, and poetic use of color). In <u>FMV</u>.

712 "<u>Les Mauvaises Rencontres</u>." <u>Arts</u>, no. 538 (19-25 Oct.):5.
Praises Astruc for qualities that could later be applied to himself (Truffaut): innovative use of flashbacks, nonjudgmental examination of characters (he looks at them with "lucidity, tenderness, and frankness"), use of recognizable characters who are weak and vulnerable. In <u>FMV</u>.

713 "Max Ophuls tourne <u>Lola Montès</u>." [Unsigned]. <u>Arts</u>, no. 508 (23-29 Mar.):5.
Brief anecdote about the details of production, comparing it to the creation of the world.

714 "<u>La Mulatresse</u>." <u>Arts</u>, no. 543 (23-29 Nov.):5.
A quickie Mexican film made for export that has no artistic ambition, but does have an indefinable charm.

715 "<u>Napoléon</u>." <u>Arts</u>, no. 505 (2-8 Mar.):5.
Gance's film is "an unassailable monument," which must be "spoken of with humility." Not a review but a report on the twenty-eight-year-old movie. Parts of this article are combined with a longer article from the same issue (see entry 655), in <u>FMV</u>.

1955

716 "Oasis." Arts, no. 513 (27 Apr.-3 May):5.
        The worst film of an esteemed, but not a gifted, direc-
     tor, Yves Allegret. The special problems of cinemascope
     make clear which directors are talented.

717 "L'Or de Naples." Arts, no. 516 (18-24 May):5
        Focuses on characters and attitude of a director. "One
     must be able to relate to poverty and misery to be able to
     film it effectively; one must be humble; one must truly love
     one's characters and not just protect and pity them; DeSica
     does none of these things."

718 "Orvet, mon amour." Cahiers du Cinéma 8, no. 47 (May):57.
        Truffaut complains that there have been only three fa-
     vorable reviews of Renoir's play. He describes how the play
     began and what it has in common with Renoir's films, noting
     especially Renoir's love of actors. Truffaut, a very infre-
     quent theatergoer, marvels at the fact that the play has
     been different at each of the five performances he has at-
     tended.

719 "Le Pain vivant." Arts, no. 501 (2-8 Feb.):7.
        This film, from a script by Mauriac, is characterized by
     the kind of "quality" that Truffaut so despised, "quality"
     that he claims is inversely proportional to the loftiness
     of ambition. At the end Truffaut questions whether the
     role of the critic truly is to advise the public to go to
     a film or not. No answer given.

720 "Palmarès du Festival de Cannes." [Unsigned]. Arts, no. 516
     (18-24 May):5.
        Marty won big, but "it is not a great film." Truffaut
     comments on and makes his own recommendations about the
     awards. Renoir's French Can-Can and Preminger's Carmen
     Jones praised.

721 "Petit journal du cinema." Cahiers du Cinéma 8, no. 45 (Mar.):
     39-41.
        Truffaut's contribution to this collective movie diary
     is a brief note about a private screening of Rossellini's
     The Fear.

722 "Petit journal du cinéma." [Truffaut and "R. Lachenay"].
     Cahiers du Cinéma 8, no. 46 (Apr.):53-55.
        Truffaut contributes notes on seeing Renoir in a theatri-
     cal production, beginning with an explanation of why he goes
     so rarely to the theater. "Lachenay" reprints a letter from
     Raymond Borde to Bresson and provides Bresson with a possi-
     ble response.

1955

723   "Petit journal du cinéma." [Truffaut and "Robert Lachenay"].
Cahiers du Cinéma 8, no. 47 (May):31-34.
      Truffaut contributes a brief opinion about Lang's remake
of Renoir's La Bete humaine. "Lachenay" points out errors
he found in an article in Positif.

724   "Petit journal du cinéma." [Signed Robert Lachenay]. Cahiers
du Cinéma 8, no. 48 (June):36-39.
      "Lachenay" fills entire diary, in the course of which he
contrasts himself, an "antistradiste," with the "indecisive"
Truffaut.

725   "Petit journal du cinéma." [Robert Lachenay]. Cahiers du
Cinéma 9, no. 49 (July):35.
      Although "Lachenay" is credited in the headline, nothing
in the journal is specifically attributed to him.

726   "Petit journal du cinéma." [Truffaut and "Robert Lachenay"].
Cahiers du Cinéma 9, no. 50 (Aug.-Sept.):32-39.
      Truffaut's contribution is a two-paragraph quotation
from a review of John Ford's The Long Gray Line in Le Figaro.
Truffaut calls it the best review of the film and congratu-
lates the reviewer for becoming a follower of the "politique
des auteurs." He also tells of going to interview Joseph
Mankiewicz and finding Wolf Mankovitz there instead.

727   "Petit journal du cinéma." [Signed Robert Lachenay]. Cahiers
du Cinéma 9, no. 51 (Oct.):34.
      Quotations from two journals with brief, one-sentence
put-downs.

728   "Petit journal du cinéma." Cahiers du Cinéma 9, no. 52
(Nov.):38-50.
      Truffaut is one of ten Cahiers critics who rate seven-
teen films on a scale of one to five stars. He gives Marty
the lowest rating. This feature, "Le Conseil des dix," appears in Cahiers regularly, and Truffaut usually is more
extreme in his opinions than the others.

729   "Petit journal du cinéma." [Truffaut and "R. Lachenay"].
Cahiers du Cinéma 9, no. 53 (Dec.):34-38.
      "Lachenay" merely quotes from a letter in Sight and Sound.
Truffaut in "Photo du mois" gives a brief profile of Robert
Aldrich and lists several American directors' current ac-
tivities.

730   "Phfft." Arts, no. 500 (26 Jan.-1 Feb.):5.
      A pleasing comedy that would have been better had George
Cukor directed and Garson Kanin scripted it. Debut of Kim
Novak noted enthusiastically.

731   "Portrait d'Humphrey Bogart." [Signed Robert Lachenay].
        Cahiers du Cinéma 9, no. 52 (Nov.):30-35.
                Brief career overview and character analysis shortened
        and re-arranged for Arts (see entry 929). Translated in
        Saturday Review of the Arts (3 Mar. 1973); see entry 1141.
        In FMV.

732   "La Prime à la qualité va-t-elle reformer le cinéma français."
        Arts, no. 519 (8-14 June):5.
                About the new law to aid the film industry by helping
        "quality" films. Since it is impossible to define "quali-
        ty," films with the exterior "appearance of quality" will
        be rewarded. Thus popular directors will get preference,
        and the others will turn to supposed "quality material":
        adapting best-sellers.

733   "Le Printemps, l'automne et l'amour." Arts, no. 520 (15-21
        June):6.
                Criticizes the "implicit obscenity" of this Fernandel
        vehicle. Director Grangier is inept with actors.

734   "La Rançon de plaisir." Arts, no. 500 (26 Jan.-1 Feb.):5.
                Claims editors did not want to review this erotic film,
        but simply wanted to quote from its promotional material.
        Truffaut quotes it, agrees that actors and actresses are
        beautiful.

735   "Rencontre avec Alexandre Astruc." Arts, no. 520 (15-21 June):
        5.
                Short article and conversation about Astruc's Les
        Mauvaises Rencontres.

736   "Rencontre avec Hitchcock." [With Claude Chabrol]. Arts,
        no. 502 (9-15 Feb.):5.
                Interview on his recent films, preceded by a biographical
        sketch, filmography, and a comment on his American films'
        similarity of theme.

737   "Rencontre avec Luis Buñuel." Arts, no. 525 (27 July-2 Aug.):
        5.
                Conversation on the occasion of Buñuel's return from
        nine years in Mexico to make his first French film in
        twenty-five years.

738   "Rencontre avec Max Ophuls." Arts, no. 517 (25-31 May):5.
                Truffaut's introduction and concluding notes are longer
        than the interview. He feels that Ophuls is underestimated
        and describes his attributes.

1955

739   "Réouverture de la cinémathèque au Musée d'Art Moderne."
       Arts, no. 524 (13-19 July):5.
            After three months and much indignation from press and
       public, the cinémathèque is reopening in a better location
       with an exposition on "Sixty Years of Cinema" (see Arts,
       no. 501, entry 652).

740   "Repris de Justice." Arts, no. 524 (13-19 July):5.
            Although Vittorio Cottafavi is a good director and has
       good taste in film music, the three stories that are strung
       together here are too stupid to make the film worth recom-
       mending.

741   "Reprises." Arts, no. 515 (11-17 May):5.
            Since he can recommend no film he saw last week, Truffaut
       looks at several older films: Modern Times, Le Jour se lève,
       Rope, Notorious, Tobacco Road, and those shown at the Renoir
       festival.

742   "Reprises." Arts, no. 529 (17-23 Aug.):3.
            Brief looks at five films returning to Paris, by Van
       Dyke, Leo MacCarey, Hitchcock, and especially Hawks's
       Scarface and Bresson's Diary of a Country Priest.

743   "Rossellini 55." Arts, no. 499 (19-25 Jan.):5.
            The Italian director stops in Paris on his way from Rome
       to Spain to talk very hurriedly about La Peur and a bull-
       fighting movie.

744   "Saadia." Arts, no. 528 (10-16 Aug.):3.
            Albert Lewin is a "self-made" director, a big boss at
       Metro-Goldwyn-Mayer, who votes himself a budget every five
       years and makes a movie for his own enjoyment. The result
       is detestable, boring, and incompetent.

745   "Les Sept Femmes de Barberousse." Arts, no. 525 (20-26 July):
       5.
            Seven Brides for Seven Brothers is the occasion for a
       heated complaint about the irreparable damage done to films
       when distributors make the cuts.

746   "Les Sept Péchés capitaux de la critique." Arts, no. 523
       (6-12 July):5.
            A long and amusing article on the sins of film critics.
       Truffaut gives examples of films that critics helped or
       hurt, and he points out specific errors made by some cri-
       tics. Advice: do not attach too much importance to critics.

747   "La Télévision démagogique." Arts, no. 519 (8-14 June):5.

The audience for television is the social unit of the
family. TV actors are like visitors, invited to one's home.
The difference between them and stage and film actors amounts
to one extra quality: moral value. Thus Hitler would not
have worked on TV, but anyone who can enter a home via TV
like a guest has the potential of becoming a demagogue.

748 "La Terre des pharoahs." Arts, no. 542 (16-22 Nov.):5.
Not Hawks's best film, but it is intelligent and uses
cinemascope very effectively; it is the first film about
ancient Egypt that is not ridiculous.

749 "Théatre et cinéma: Bilan d'un mois." [Signed Robert
Lachenay]. Arts, no. 523 (6-12 July):3.
An article about an upcoming series on the rapport between film and theater, in the course of which Truffaut
proposes other areas for study in film.

750 "Théatre et cinéma: 'Les Films qui resistent au temps.'"
[Signed Robert Lachenay]. Arts, no. 521 (22-28 June):3.
Recommends that people attend a retrospective of films
with commentators.

751 "Toujours le cirque: Lettre de Rome." [Signed Robert
Lachenay]. Arts, no. 534 (21-27 Sept.):5.
Report on Roman movie houses and on L'Amour en ville, a
compilation film with parts by Antonioni, Fellini, Lattuada,
and others, which is restricted from export.

752 "La Tour de Nesle." Arts, no. 508 (23-29 Mar.):5.
This is "the least good of Abel Gance's films. But,
since Gance is a genius, it is also a film of genius."
Truffaut complains about censorship regarding the film because "Surely cinema is also eroticism." In FMV.

753 "Triomphes des jeunes cinéastes." Arts, no. 534 (21-27 Sept.):
5.
Truffaut is happy with the awards to young filmmakers at
the Venice festival except for the fact that Il Bidone received hostile notices in the press and the ten to twelve
excellent films were outweighed by thirty bad ones.

754 "Trois comédiens de genie." Arts, no. 503 (16-22 Feb.):5.
Truffaut affirms the importance of actors, overlooked
lately in the elevation of producers and directors, and
discusses three very good "amateur" actors--writers André
Gide, Alain Bombard, and François Mauriac, each of whom
appeared in a film portrait of himself.

1955

755   "Trois meurtres." Arts, no. 504 (23 Feb.-1 Mar.):5.
       The film in question is mentioned only briefly at the
       end of this article; it serves as the occasion for a general
       attack on all British films. They are all based on dream,
       fantasy, and the extraordinary, and they lack invention and
       poetry. Even the best filmmakers in the world are ruined
       by working in England.

756   "Vacances à Venise." Arts, no. 542 (16-22 Nov.):5.
       Like his Brief Encounter, this David Lean film is a tear-
       jerker; it is vain and useless with a pleasing, but back-
       ward, aesthetic.

757   "Versailles en couleurs." [Signed Robert Lachenay]. Arts,
       no. 500 (26 Jan.-1 Feb.):5.
       Praise for Lagrave's film made of 300 stills.

758   "Le Vieillissement de films." Arts, no. 535 (28 Sept.-4 Oct.):
       5.
       Films do not age; our criteria change, as well as the
       way we see and judge films. A director who is not "audaci-
       ous" will not create lasting masterpieces. Based on his
       own experience, Truffaut lists films that have aged, films
       that have not, and films that were successful only the sec-
       ond time around.

759   "Le Village magique." [Signed Robert Lachenay]. Arts, no.
       511 (13-19 Apr.):5.
       Three short paragraphs on this Lechanois film, which is
       audacious only in dialogue.

760   "Voyage en Italie." Arts, no. 512 (20-26 Apr.):5.
       Rossellini's film is "a spiritual itinerary, a diary of
       a couple, a suite with variations on marriage, a poem to
       the glory of Italy."

                              1956

761   "A Berlin: Les américains raflent tout." Arts, no. 577
       (18-24 July):5.
       On the exciting and deceiving events of the festival,
       and the "audacity" of the awards given, but mostly a posi-
       tive review of Aldrich's Autumn Leaves.

762   "Amis pour la vie." Arts, no. 592 (7-13 Nov.):3.
       A drama of adolescence and friendship, filmed with tact
       and good taste.

763 "Amore." <u>Arts</u>, no. 562 (4-10 Apr.):5.
  A look at three Rossellini films from 1948-49 to demonstrate his youthful virtuosity.

764 "Arsene Lupin." <u>Arts</u>, no. 564 (18-24 Apr.):5.
  Not a review, but an announcement of Becker's new film.

765 "Les Assassins du dimanche." <u>Arts</u>, no. 574 (27 June-3 July):5.
  Joffé is a realistic director interested in characters.
When he goes beyond realism, exaggerates it, poeticizes it,
he surpasses himself and overwhelms the audience.

766 "Attaque." <u>Arts</u>, no. 588 (10-16 Oct.):3.
  Some time spent justifying the violence in this "strong,
audacious" antiwar film by Robert Aldrich--"one of the three
or four great filmmakers of the present."

767 "Les Aventures de Till l'Espiegle." <u>Arts</u>, no. 593 (14-20
Nov.):3.
  Gérard Philipe's debut as a director results in the
year's worst and most boring French film.

768 "B. B. est victime d'une cabale." <u>Arts</u>, no. 597 (12-18 Dec.):
3.
  An attack on film critics for being hypocritical and
prejudiced with regard to Bardot and the film <u>And God
Created Woman</u>--which many critics did not like. Truffaut
claims that critics consider only scripts and directors;
thus the strange situation arises of films made and seen
by people who love actors, judged by people who do not like
actors, and especially do not like beautiful actresses.

769 "Le Ballon rouge." <u>Arts</u>, no. 589 (17-23 Oct.):3.
  The Red Balloon is a carefully made film, admirably directed and photographed; but it is formulaic and decorative.
There is no real poetry, fantasy, sensitivity, and truth in
it. In <u>FMV</u>.

770 "Le Bandit." <u>Arts</u>, no. 559 (14-20 Mar.):5.
  Noteworthy chiefly because Truffaut mentions here that
this film, by Ulmer, gave him the impression that <u>Jules and
Jim</u> could be filmed. Ulmer, who is compared to Renoir and
Ophuls, obviously made his film with love.

771 "Bresson tourne." <u>Arts</u>, no. 574 (27 June-3 July):5.
  General piece on Bresson, not on individual films, at
the center of which is this statement: "Bresson seeks to
create a harmony by a combination of many elements--acting,
sound, looks, noises, lighting, commentary, music--that

1956

defies analysis, but when successful evokes pure emotion in
the audience." Ends with note on interview with Bresson
that turned out to be an exact duplicate of another.

772   "C'est arrivé à Aden . . . ." <u>Arts</u>, no. 582 (29 Aug.–4 Sept.):
      3.
          Besides this Michel Boisrond film, five other films are
      reviewed: <u>Brigadoon</u> with Gene Kelly, <u>Le Bigame</u> by L. Emmer,
      <u>Le Cheval et l'enfant</u> by Koji Shima, <u>Jubal</u> by Delmer Davies,
      and <u>Le Sang à la tete</u> by G. Granger. Only the first is
      recommended.

773   "<u>La Charge des tuniques bleues.</u>" <u>Arts</u>, no. 581 (22–28 Aug.):3.
          Anthony Mann makes "frank, pure Westerns" and he is "more
      intelligent" than John Ford. <u>The Last Frontier</u> is perhaps
      Mann's best Western.

774   "<u>Chéri, ne fais pas le zouave et Artistes et modèles.</u>" <u>Arts</u>,
      no. 575 (4–10 July):5.
          Neither film a standout; the first is a Hawks remake,
      the second featured Dean Martin and Jerry Lewis, whom
      Truffaut does not much like.

775   "<u>La Cinquième Victime.</u>" <u>Arts</u>, no. 581 (22–28 Aug.):3.
          An essay on Fritz Lang, "the most underrated filmmaker,"
      his style, characteristics, and evolution. "To not like
      Lang is to not understand him, and to not understand him
      is to not understand the cinema."

776   "<u>Club de femmes.</u>" <u>Arts</u>, no. 599 (26 Dec.–1 Jan.):3.
          A comedy made by Ralph Habib, a man with no sense of
      humor.

777   "<u>Commando dans la Gironde.</u>" <u>Arts</u>, no. 588 (10–16 Oct.):3.
          A British film directed by Jose Ferrer. Truffaut espe-
      cially dislikes the stoic response to pain.

778   "<u>Un Condamné à mort s'est échappé.</u>" <u>Arts</u>, no. 593 (14–20
      Nov.):3.
          This is "not only Bresson's most beautiful film, but
      also the most important French film of the past ten years."
      This review concentrates on the acting. Follow-up review:
      see entry 781. In <u>FMV</u>.

779   "<u>Condamné au silence.</u>" <u>Arts</u>, no. 579 (1–7 Aug.):3.
          Truffaut wonders why Preminger made this historic film,
      then provides the answer: it is a political film.
      Preminger is compared to the film's hero, Billy Mitchell.

780 "Le Congrès s'ennuie." Arts, no. 569 (23-29 May):1.
Report on a meeting of scenarists and directors that
proposed that only the French be allowed to film French subjects like Joan of Arc. Truffaut dismisses meeting because
best French filmmakers were not there: Becker, Bresson,
Ophuls, Renoir, Astruc, Cluzot, Tati, Leenhardt, Resnais,
and Cocteau.

781 "Depuis Bresson nous savons qu'il y a quelque chose de neuf
dans l'art du film." Arts, no. 596 (5-11 Dec.):3.
Follow-up to Truffaut's first review of the film in
Arts no. 593 (see entry 778). "Bresson's film is pure
music; its essential richness is in its rhythm . . . he has
pulverized classic cutting . . . and exerts all his effort
toward filming the face, or, more accurately, the seriousness of the human face." A review that not only indicates
Truffaut's great sensitivity to Bresson, but also provides
insight into some of his own films.

782 "La Dernière Fois que j'ai vu Paris." Arts, no. 573 (20-26
June):5.
Director Richard Brooks previously showed an honest talent, but here direction, color, acting, and sets are all
bad.

783 "Des gens sans importance." Arts, no. 556 (22-28 Feb.):5.
"What is new about this film and makes it superior to
many recent films is the construction of the subject. The
tempo is romanesque rather than theatrical."

784 "Les Dix Meilleurs Films de l'année." Cahiers du Cinéma 10,
no. 55 (Jan.):6-7.
Truffaut and sixteen others list top ten films of 1955.

785 "La Double Crise du cinéma." [Signed Robert Lachenay]. Arts,
no. 592 (7-13 Nov.):4.
On the high cost of production and the poor quality of
films.

786 "Le Double Jeu." Cahiers du Cinéma 11, no. 66 (Christmas):
45-55.
An alphabetical list of actors who are "metteurs en
scène," with brief profile of each and an introductory
statement. Truffaut is one of six compilers.

787 "L'Enigmatique Monsieur D." Arts, no. 578 (25-31 July):5.
Sheldon Reynolds' sense of humor and easygoing style
save many weak moments, but this first film suffers from
imitation of Orson Welles's surface elements without the
underlying ones.

1956

788　"En 1956, cinq grands films, sept bons films." Arts, no. 598
　　　(19-25 Dec.):3.
　　　　　　Resnais' Night and Fog dominated the year. Autant-Lara's
　　　Traversée de Paris is the exception that proves the rule of
　　　the politique des auteurs. Films by Renoir, Vadim, Bresson
　　　among the year's best.

789　"Entrée des artistes." Arts, nos. 553, 556, 562 (1-7 and
　　　22-28 Feb.; 4-10 Apr.):5.
　　　　　　Thumbnail sketches of three actresses: Anne Doat,
　　　Joelle Robin, and Mistigri.

790　"Entretien avec Howard Hawks." [With Jacques Becker and
　　　Jacques Rivette]. Cahiers du Cinéma 10, no. 56 (Feb.):4-17.
　　　　　　Hawks discusses recently completed The Land of the
　　　Pharaohs, which he made just because of cinemascope, and
　　　several of his other films, most notably Scarface. Ideas
　　　that surely impressed Truffaut include making films on in-
　　　teresting subjects, not following script literally, trying
　　　to anticipate audience response (trying something new and
　　　not just for your own pleasure), and distinguishing between
　　　comedy and drama. In Politique des auteurs; see entry 1129.
　　　Translated in Sarris' Interviews with Film Directors (see
　　　entry 1089).

791　"Et Dieu créa la femme." Arts, no. 596 (5-11 Dec.):3.
　　　　　　Truffaut talks about the problems of eroticism in film
　　　here. He calls Vadim's film simultaneously amoral and puri-
　　　tanical; it is not perfect, but what is good is very good.
　　　In FMV.

792　"Une Fée pas comme les autres." Arts, no. 592 (7-13 Nov.):3.
　　　　　　Opens with an attack on Walt Disney and his animated
　　　animals; continues with an attack on this film and director
　　　Jean Tourane, the Walt Disney of live animals.

793　"Fellini derrière sa caméra." Arts, no. 587 (3-9 Oct.):3.
　　　　　　A letter from Rome that includes witty remarks on Italian
　　　movie houses and an account of a visit to the set of Nights
　　　of Cabiria. Truffaut notes the serenity of "the exquisite
　　　Fellini" and the fact that he lets actors improvise.

794　"Une Femme diabolique." Arts, no. 577 (18-24 July):5.
　　　　　　After seeing this first film by Ronald MacDougall,
　　　Truffaut does not want to see any more.

795　"Feu James Dean." Arts, no. 586 (26 Sept.-2 Oct.):3.
　　　　　　Uses biographical details to try to explain Dean's pop-
　　　ularity. Says he was more real than other actors; "he has

and shows all the human ambiguities and weaknesses." Successful because allowed to improvise.

796 "Feuilles d'automne." Arts, no. 594 (21-27 Nov.):3.
     An important subject (the solitude of woman, the anguish of adolescence), but Aldrich did this Joan Crawford melodrama just to regain the confidence of his backers after failure of The Big Knife.

797 "La Fille de l'ambassadeur." Arts, no. 581 (22-28 Aug.):3.
     Norman Krasna's film is a minor work. "It's tiring when you guess the ending ten minutes into the film."

798 "Les Films que l'on verra en 1956." Arts, no. 550 (11-17 Jan.):5.
     Preview of films to be released. France will have a weak year with only films by Buñuel, Renoir, Clement, and Cluzot showing any promise. Italy will maintain its excellence because of films by Rossellini, Fellini, Visconti, and Zavattini. England will save face. America, which gets the most space, will produce cinema for adults. Films by Hitchcock, Ray, Mann, Fleisher, Ulmer, Mankiewicz, Welles, and Huston noted, as well as battle over censorship of Man with the Golden Arm.

799 "La Fureur de vivre." Arts, no. 562 (4-10 Apr.):5.
     Everything in Rebel without a Cause--direction, color, cinemascope, and acting--merits the highest praise. Nicholas Ray is "a bitter and pessimistic poet."

800 "François Mauriac et le cinéma." La Parisienne, no. 33 (May): 92-94.
     On the basis of Roger Leenhardt's forty-minute documentary, Mauriac is a great actor. Because of his blessed voice and distinctive manner, he can take his place next to Chaplin, Gish, Fernandel, and James Dean, and "all those who make the history of cinema a fabulous song of gestures."

801 "Le Général du diable." Arts, no. 555 (15-21 Feb.):5.
     Interesting for its fusion of fiction and history.

802 "Guerre et paix." [Signed Robert Lachenay]. Arts, no. 598 (19-25 Dec.):3.
     Making a film out of this novel is an impossible task, which perhaps only George Cukor could have accomplished as well as King Vidor did.

803 "Les Haricots du mal." Cahiers du Cinéma 10, no. 56 (Feb.): 40-42.

1956

James Dean, a "freshly cut fleur de mal . . . makes commercial a film [East of Eden] that hardly is, vivifies an
abstraction." Kazan, the film director, classed with
Ophuls, Nick Ray, Rossellini, and Hawks and not with
Hitchcock, Lang, and Renoir.

804   "Une Histoire de fous." Arts, no. 567 (9-15 May):1, 5.
Of the films shown at the Cannes Festival, Truffaut likes
Night and Fog, The Man Who Knew Too Much, and Mr. Arkadin
and dislikes, among others, The Red Balloon and Smiles of a
Summer's Night, and is appalled that Marie-Antoinette was
chosen as the winner. The choice proves the incompetence
of the Cannes selection committee.

805   "Hitchcock à la cinémathèque." Arts, no. 571 (6-12 June):5.
Truffaut talks about The Lodger and Hitchcock's technique
as part of announcement of fifteen-day retrospective on
Hitchcock's British films.

806   "Hitchcock Anglais." [By "Robert Lachenay" et al.]. Cahiers
du Cinéma 11, no. 62 (Aug.-Sept.):8-16.
Truffaut is one of six writers contributing to these
notes on Hitchcock's British films.

807   "L'Homme qui en savait trop." Arts, no. 588 (10-16 Oct.):3.
There are two kinds of directors: those who do not care
what the public thinks and for whom film is an individual
adventure; and those who keep the audience in mind while
making a film. And for Hitchcock, there are two kinds of
films: serious, important ones and films for entertainment.
This is the latter. A bit too long, but perfectly directed.
Opening paragraphs of this review appended to Rear Window
article in FMV.

808   "Un Homme traqué." Arts, no. 576 (11-17 July):5.
Ray Milland is no better as a director than as an actor.

809   "Il y a dix ans . . . Citizen Kane." Cahiers du Cinéma 11,
no. 61 (July):36.
Brief tribute on the tenth anniversary of the film's release in Paris.

810   "L'Impossible Rendez-vous." Cahiers du Cinéma 10, no. 57
(Mar.):52-53.
Prior to his review, the editors note that Truffaut is
the only defender of the film, Sacha Guitry's Si Paris nous
était conte. Truffaut says it is impossible to analyze,
tries anyway, and contrasts Guitry to Astruc.

811   "L'Insommise." Arts, no. 592 (7-13 Nov.):3.
        This Wyler film has gone out of date terribly. Truffaut
        dislikes Wyler for his false seriousness and false classic-
        ism.

812   "James Dean est mort." Arts, no. 563 (11-17 Apr.):1, 5.
        Glowing eulogy, which dissects Dean's genius. His acting
        is "a slap at the psychological tradition." It is "more
        animal than human, and that makes him unpredictable."
        Truffaut compares Dean to Chaplin, talks about his seduc-
        tiveness and how he represents his generation. In FMV.

813   "Joe Macbeth." Arts, no. 571 (6-12 June):5.
        The film has none of Shakespeare's lyricism of poetic
        violence. Truffaut has already denounced the director for
        his bad imitation of Hitchcock (see Arts, entry 850).

814   "John Huston ne sera-t-il toujours qu'un amateur?" [Signed
        Robert Lachenay]. Arts, no. 593 (14-20 Nov.):3.
        An article that begins with comments on Moby Dick, deals
        with the theme of failure in Huston's films, and ends with
        comments on his life and his belief that "work [itself] is
        more important than its result."

815   "Joshua Logan en Picnic à Paris." Arts, no. 589 (17-23 Oct.):
        3.
        Interview about Picnic and Bus-Stop, his favorite film-
        makers, projects.

816   "Journal du Festival de Cannes, 1956." Arts, no. 566 (2-8
        May):1, 5.
        Every film mentioned is dismissed. The grand event of
        the festival is the presence of Kim Novak, upon whom
        Truffaut spends four paragraphs. Everyone is waiting for
        a good American film.

817   "Les Journées du cinéma de Bourges ont réveillé les
        spectateurs." Arts, no. 587 (3-9 Oct.):3.
        Favorable review of this traveling festival, with films
        from around the world used to try to counteract the drop in
        movie attendance.

818   "Lifeboat." Arts, no. 571 (6-12 June):5.
        Not vintage Hitchcock. A banal psychological drama.

819   "Lola au bûcher." Cahiers du Cinéma 10, no. 55 (Jan.):28-31.
        All film specialists "whose taste, intuition, and sensi-
        bility I appreciate" admire Lola Montès. Ophuls is a film-
        maker of the nineteenth century, best at costume drama, who

1956

    like Balzac "pushes sentiments to their extreme physical consequences." In commenting on Ophuls, Truffaut throws considerable light on his own films. Combined with <u>Arts</u> review in <u>FMV</u> (see entry 709).

820   "<u>La Lumière d'en face</u>." <u>Arts</u>, no. 560 (21-27 Mar.):5.
    The eroticism of this film is more ridiculous than scandalous.

821   "<u>La Main de Marilyn</u>." [Signed Robert Lachenay]. <u>Cahiers du Cinéma</u> 10, no. 57 (Mar.):45-46.
    <u>The Seven-Year Itch</u> is a daring film, "filmed cinematographic criticism."

822   "<u>La Maison de bambou</u>." <u>Arts</u>, no. 554 (8-14 Feb.):5.
    An overdone subject rejuvenated by shooting on location in Japan and by Sam Fuller's incisive, terse, dry, brutal, very inventive and effective direction.

823   "<u>Marguerite de la nuit</u>." <u>Arts</u>, no. 552 (25-31 Jan.):5.
    The blame for this picture's being so bad can be placed squarely on Claude Autant-Lara, whose direction is banal, without audacity or invention.

824   "<u>La Mariée est trop belle</u>." <u>Arts</u>, no. 596 (5-11 Dec.):3.
    Director Gaspard-Huit is so tight-fisted that even his fellow directors attack him, claiming a Western done in fourteen days is better directed.

825   "<u>La Mauvaise Graine</u>." <u>Arts</u>, no. 595 (28 Nov.-4 Dec.):3.
    <u>The Bad Seed</u> is "indecent and vulgar . . . overblown and empty"; it might even justify censorship. Mervyn LeRoy has "no preferences, no themes, no obsessions, no style, and very little temperament." He will make anything. In <u>FMV</u>.

826   "Max Ophuls: Il faut tuer la publicité." <u>Arts</u>, no. 549 (4-10 Jan.):1, 5.
    An interview (questions omitted) on the ideas and procedures behind the making of <u>Lola Montès</u>.

827   "<u>La Meilleur Part</u>." <u>Arts</u>, no. 563 (11-17 Apr.):5.
    Principally an attack on "undirectable" actor Gérard Philipe, who changes scripts for the worse and terrorizes good directors.

828   "1956." <u>Arts</u>, no. 598 (19-25 Dec.):3.
    The year was better than 1955, with five great films and seven good ones. The improvement is due mainly to "B" films and scripts for films that are "more intelligent,

more sincere, and more personal." Bad, good, and great films listed.

829   "Mr. Arkadin." Arts, no. 572 (13-19 June):5.
      An unsettling film, but also exciting, stimulating, en-
riching. Every Welles film is influenced by Shakespeare,
and this one is so filled with poetry, lyricism, and invention that one wants to talk of it for hours. In FMV.

*830 "Le Mystère Picasso." [Signed Robert Lachenay]. Bulletin de
      Paris, no. 134 (3 May).
      Truffaut also reviewed this Clouzot film for Le Temps de
Paris about a month later. Reference provided by Truffaut.

831   "La Nuit du chasseur." Arts, no. 569 (23-29 May):5.
      "Despite failures of style, The Night of the Hunter is
immensely inventive." Here is experimental cinema that
truly experiments. In FMV.

832   "Ordet." Arts, no. 549 (4-10 Jan.):5.
      A "drama of faith and a metaphysical fable" by one of
the most demanding directors, Carl Dreyer. This review
forms the center of the essay on Dreyer in FMV.

833   "Un Palmarès ridicules." Arts, no. 568 (16-22 May):1, 5.
      According to Truffaut, "The jury denied the films that
were well thought-out, well written, well acted, well directed, and ignored too many well-known directors and actors." At the end of the article, he awards his own prizes.

834   "Papa, maman, ma femme, et moi." Arts, no. 551 (18-24 Jan.):5.
      Director Le Chanois has given up his sincerity and in-
tellectual honesty and acquired a solid trade. Though the
direction is careful, the film's moral and intellectual
levels are not high.

835   "Pardonnez nos offenses." Arts, no. 580 (8-14 Aug.):3.
      In the process of criticizing director Robert Hossien
for lacking lucidity, sensitivity, and sincerity, Truffaut
confesses that he is by nature not a "generous" critic as
is Bazin, the best critic.

836   "Paris--Canaille." Arts, no. 562 (4-10 Apr.):5.
      French cinema could use more comedies "à l'américaine"
such as this, though the direction by Pierre Gaspard-Huit
could be livelier.

837   "Paris--Palace Hotel." Arts, no. 591 (31 Oct.-6 Nov.):3.
      An unpleasant avant-garde subject and bad script rescued
by director Henry Verneuil.

1956

838 "Le Pays d'où je viens." Arts, no. 591 (31 Oct.-6 Nov.):3.
       Marcel Carné is a technician, a careful director. If
       the script/subject is intelligent or idiotic, the film is
       too. This one is the latter.

839 "La Peau d'un autre." Arts, no. 576 (11-17 July):5.
       Jack Webb's film, Pete Kelly's Blues, is called a
       "Wellesian biography." Webb is "a shrewd director who,
       knowing that half the young public likes jazz, the other
       half brawls and fights, gives them both in this film."

840 "Petit bloc-notes du cinématographe." [Signed Robert Lachenay].
       Arts, no. 578 (25-31 July):4.
       One or two paragraphs each on a variety of film topics.

841 "Le Petit Carrousel de fête." Arts, no. 588 (10-16 Oct.):3.
       Hungarian film is Zoltan Fabri. This film, though seen
       by few at Cannes, caused a sensation. Qualities that
       Truffaut admires: naiveté, sincerity, generosity, spon-
       taneity.

842 "Petit journal intime du cinéma." Cahiers du Cinéma 10, no.
       58 (Apr.):28-33.
       Truffaut acknowledges the dedication to himself in Borde
       and Chaumeton's Panorama du film noire americain. Under the
       subheading "La Photo du mois," he comments on Renoir and the
       making of Elena.

843 "Petit journal du cinéma." [Truffaut and "R. Lachenay"].
       Cahiers du Cinéma 10, no. 56 (Feb.):28-36.
       Truffaut tells of meeting Nick Ray and calls Rebel
       without a Cause his best film.

844 "Petit journal du cinéma." [Truffaut and "R. Lachenay"].
       Cahiers du Cinéma 10, no. 56 (Feb.):28-36.
       Includes four brief paragraphs by Truffaut extolling
       Resnais' Night and Fog, the "most noble and most necessary"
       film ever made; six longer paragraphs on Hitchcock in Paris;
       and three brief paragraphs on a new Canadian movie journal,
       Images.

845 "Petit journal du cinéma." [Signed Robert Lachenay]. Cahiers
       du Cinéma 11, no. 64 (Nov.):35.
       One paragraph on L'Ombre by Jerzy Kawalerowicz.

846 "Petit journal du cinéma." [Truffaut and "R. Lachenay"].
       Cahiers du Cinéma 11, no. 61 (July):33-34.
       Aldrich's The Way We Are is good but not his best.

846a   "Petit journal du cinéma." [Signed Robert Lachenay]. <u>Cahiers du Cinéma</u> 11, no. 65 (Dec.):37–39.
       On <u>Blonde Venus</u> by Joseph von Sternberg, plus a list of 120 Hollywood personalities and whether they supported Ike or Stevenson.

847   "<u>La Peur</u>." <u>Arts</u>, no. 576 (11–17 July):5.
       This, the third film in Rossellini's trilogy on couples with marital troubles, is a beautiful and great film—and his most commercial. Rossellini's films "don't tell stories. They paint characters who change on contact with certain geographic, social, spiritual, and political realities."

848   "La Photo du Mois." [By F. T.]. <u>Cahiers du Cinéma</u> 10, no. 60 (June):33.
       Four paragraphs of high praise for Bresson and his <u>Un Condamné à mort s'est échappé</u>.

849   "Picnic." <u>Arts</u>, no. 587 (3–9 Oct.):3.
       The script is close to being a work of genius; the film is "always inventive; every image is fulled with energy." Director Joshua Logan is compared favorably to Renoir. In <u>FMV</u>.

850   "<u>Piège pour une canaille</u>." <u>Arts</u>, no. 565 (25 Apr.–1 May):4.
       <u>Confession</u> is a pastiche of Hitchcock's American films and shows only more clearly the genius of Hitchcock and the decadence of the British cinema.

851   "Les Pièges de la passion." <u>Arts</u>, no. 565 (25 Apr.–1 May):4.
       "Searing flashes of truth, nuances whose sincerity is beyond doubt, creative and sublime mimicry of all sorts" are often found in conventional Hollywood films. Thus this musical, <u>Love Me or Leave Me</u>, is "a story of rare finesse and authority." Doris Day and James Cagney are especially good. In <u>FMV</u>.

852   "<u>La Pointe courte</u>." <u>Arts</u>, no. 550 (11–17 Jan.):5.
       Kindly but tentative review of Agnes Varda's first film. "It is difficult to form a judgment of a film in which the true and the false, the true-false and the false-true, are intermingled according to barely perceived rules." In <u>FMV</u>.

*853   "<u>La pointe courte</u>." <u>Plaisir de France</u> (Feb.).
       Reference provided by Truffaut.

854   "Presence de Marilyn Monroe." [Signed "R. L."]. <u>Arts</u>, no. 582 (29 Aug.–4 Sept.):3.
       On her life and career.

1956

855   "Prisonniere du desert." Arts, no. 581 (22-28 Aug.):3.
        The Searchers dismissed. In Hollywood "sincerity" has
    replaced Ford's "trickery and cunning," and "poetry has
    triumphed over diversion."

856   "La Prix de la peur." Arts, no. 577 (18-24 July):5.
        This wins the prize as the week's most boring film.

857   "Que deviendront les films staliniens?" [Signed Robert
    Lachenay]. Arts, no. 562 (4-10 Apr.):5.
        Resorts often to Bazin in this article on films about
    Stalin.

858   "Quelques films recents." La Parisienne, no. 33 (May):113-14.
        One paragraph each on Lola Montès, Rebel without a Cause,
    The Trouble with Harry, Il Bidone, and two other minor films.

859   "Qui a tué Harry." Arts, no. 560 (21-27 Mar.):5.
        Since Hitchcock has mastered the arts of direction and
    storytelling, he invents difficulties so as not to get
    bored. The Trouble with Harry is a fable whose moral is
    perhaps Pascal's "misery of a world without God."

860   "Le Règlement de comptes." La Parisienne, no. 35 (July-Aug.):
    358-61.
        Reappraisal of Chaplin's "noxious" qualities to point
    out his genius.

861   "La Règne de L'à-peu-près." Arts, no. 560 (21-27 Mar.):5.
        Extended remarks on film books. Most are too general,
    not specialized enough. A book devoted to just one film,
    La Strada, is one noteworthy exception.

862   "Renaissance du court métrage." Arts, no. 594 (21-27 Nov.):3.
        The second festival of short films at Tours covered.
    Truffaut lists the best shorts, including the winner
    Dimanche à Pekin by Chris Marker, and provides a brief com-
    ment on them.

863   "Rencontre avec Alain Resnais." Arts, no. 556 (22-28 Feb.):5.
        Biographical information on Resnais and conversation
    with him about his short films.

864   "Rencontre avec Alfred Hitchcock." [With C. Bitsch]. Cahiers
    du Cinéma 11, no. 62 (Aug.-Sept.):1-5.
        Hitchcock talks at length about The Wrong Man, briefly
    on the color in Trouble with Harry, and on his preference
    for Shadow of a Doubt.

865 "Rencontre avec Otto Preminger." Arts, no. 576 (11-17 July):5.
     Conversation with the producer-director about his recent
     films. They caused scandals because he believes films must
     keep up with the times and deal with new subjects.

866 "Rencontre avec Robert Aldrich." Cahiers du Cinéma 11, no.
     64 (Nov.):2-11.
     An interview characterized by quick questions and answers.
     Aldrich talks about his career, especially Kiss Me Deadly,
     about directors who influenced him (including Renoir), and
     gives his opinion briefly of several Hollywood directors.

867 "Responsabilité limitée." Cahiers du Cinéma 11, no. 61
     (July):43-44.
     Alex Joffé's Les Assassins du dimanche praised for its
     "inexhaustible verve." The review is noteworthy for
     Truffaut's admission that he praises or damns without re-
     serve and for his use of Picasso's words: "It is not what
     an artist makes that counts, but what he is."

868 "La Revue des films." La Parisienne, no. 34 (June):232-33.
     One paragraph each on new films by Delannoy, Preminger,
     Clouzot, and Buñuel.

869 "La Revue des films." La Parisienne, no. 35 (July-Aug.).
     Briefly on The Last Time I Saw Paris, Lifeboat, Joe
     Macbeth, Toni, and Artists and Models.

870 "Robert Aldrich va-t-il acheter Hollywood?" [Signed F. T.].
     Arts, no. 555 (15-21 Feb.):5.
     Background piece on Aldrich's many talents, energy, and
     independence. Included is a letter published by Bogart
     criticizing Aldrich's irresponsible judgments of actors.

871 "La Rose Tatouée." Arts, no. 563 (11-17 Apr.):5.
     This film was "produced by deafmen, financed by blind
     men." The direction is sad, the camera work of the same
     inexplicable ugliness as that in Marty and Come Back, Little
     Sheba.

872 "Les Salauds vont en enfer." Arts, no. 557 (29 Feb.-6 Mar.):5.
     Robert Hossein's film is so bad it is not even commer-
     cial. Truffaut spends some time talking about problems of
     succeeding with a film on both artistic and commercial
     levels.

873 "Le Scandale des Oscars à Hollywood." Arts, no. 561 (28 Mar.-
     3 Apr.):5.
     Critical of the Hollywood Academy Awards, based on box

1956

office success rather than merit. Ends with story of
Joseph Mankiewicz writing a part just to win Edmund O'Brien
an Oscar.

874   "Le Secret de Soeur Angele." Arts, no. 561 (28 Mar.-3 Apr.):5.
        The film is demagoguery that lacks verisimilitude. The
director, Leo Joannon, is awkward, naive, and malicious.

875   "Le Secret professionnel: Debat sur Duvivier." Arts, no. 564
        (18-24 Apr.):5.
        Truffaut intervenes only once in this discussion between
the filmmaker Duvivier and two other critics, Alexandre
Astruc and "M. Arlaud."

876   "Sept ans de reflexion." Arts, no. 558 (7-13 Mar.):5.
        Focuses first on Marilyn Monroe, then on Wilder.
Truffaut admires the "verve and inventiveness" in The Seven
Year Itch, its sincerity, and the fact that it is "a filmed
critique of films." He notes some of the "deliberate cita-
tions" of other directors. In FMV.

877   "Si Paris nous était conte." Arts, no. 554 (8-14 Feb.):5.
        This Sacha Guitry film has two qualities missing from
current French films: firm, true-to-life direction of actors and spontaneity. It seems to be the victim of the un-
written rule of critics: to condemn a director in every
other film.

878   "Tati." Arts, no. 580 (8-14 Aug.):1, 3.
        A conversation about Mon oncle.

879   "Temps des assassins." Arts, no. 564 (19-25 Apr.):5.
        Of Duvivier's fifty-seven films, Truffaut has seen twenty-
three and liked eight; this is his best. Quality and commercialism come together in a lovingly made film.

880   "Le Toit." Arts, no. 595 (28 Nov.-4 Dec.):3.
        De Sica is the "pope of miserableness"; he sacrifices
scripts to sentimentality and triviality. There is an excellent film to be made on this subject; this is not it.

881   "Toni." Arts, no. 572 (13-19 June):5.
        This Renoir film is pivotal in his career. Neorealist
ten years before the Italians; great acting yields truth in
gestures and in emotion. Incorporated into Renoir overview
in FMV.

882   "Toute la ville accuse." Arts, no. 570 (30 May-5 June):5.
        Director Boissol is one of those giving French films new

style, new themes: middle-budget quality films. Truffaut talks about reconciling art and commercialism.

883 "La Traversée de Paris." Arts, no. 591 (31 Oct.-6 Nov.):3.
     Autant-Lara praised. The best dialogue in French cinema and the portrait of the average Frenchman is thought-provoking. Director, storywriter, and screenwriters meshed to modify their individual weaknesses.

884 "La Traversée de Paris: Adaptation idéale." Arts, no. 592 (7-15 Nov.):3.
     Truffaut's second positive review of this film in two weeks, this time emphasizing the changes from story to film.

885 "Une Tueur s'est évadé." Arts, no. 579 (1-7 Aug.):3.
     Boetticher is an agreeable filmmaker; this is an original, "different" story, which deteriorates at the end. In FMV.

886 "Tu seras un homme non fils." Arts, no. 573 (20-26 June):5.
     Only Kim Novak makes this poorly directed tearjerker worthwhile.

887 "Venise après la bataille." Arts, no. 585 (19-25 Sept.):3.
     Truffaut is happy with films chosen for showing at the Venice Festival, but not with prizes given, and especially angry that Robert Aldrich's Attack did not win. Bus Stop recommended.

888 "Venise Festival courageux donne un exemple d'austérité." Arts, no. 584 (12-18 Sept.):1, 3.
     In lauding this festival, Truffaut attacks Cannes again. Singles out Mizoguchi's Street of Shame, Aldrich's Attack and, surprisingly, Autant-Lara's La Traversée de Paris and Clement's Gervaise for commendations.

889 "Venise: Journal du Festival." Arts, no. 583 (5-11 Sept.):1, 3.
     Quick film reviews plus added information. The festival has been reformed as Truffaut suggested. No British films accepted because the British cinema is dead. Nick Ray's Bigger Than Life rated the best, a "strong incisive, terse film."

890 "Vêtir ceux qui sont nus." Arts, no. 555 (15-21 Feb.):5.
     There is confusion in this film, typical of present-day filmmaking, as to what parts the producer, director, et al. should play. Thus many contradictions.

*891 "Voici le temps des assassins . . ." [Signed "François de

1956

Monferrand"]. Le Temps de Paris, no. 1 (18 Apr.).
Reference for this Julian Duvivier film review provided
by Truffaut.

1957

892 "A 23 pas du mystère." Arts, no. 605 (6-12 Feb.):3.
A minor detective film, but admirably made by Henry
Hathaway and accomplishing what it wants to.

893 "Alexandre Astruc; On m'attend, on me guette je risque ma
carrière avec mon nouveau film 'Une Vie.'" [Signed Robert
Lachenay]. Arts, no. 644 (13-19 Nov.):5.
An interview about Astruc's adaptation of Maupassant and
the film's differences from Astruc's earlier Les Mauvaises
Rencontres.

894 "Alex Joffé, éléphant bafouilleur, sauve Les Fanatiques en
tuant les suspense." Arts, no. 645 (20-26 Nov.):6.
Joffé is very talented, but does scripts that are beneath him. He excels in directing actors, and he is unable
to create an unsympathetic character.

895 "L'Ami de la famille." Arts, no. 627 (10-16 July):5.
The play was mediocre, but the film is pleasant and re-
freshing, thanks to the director, Jack Pinoteau, and the
main actor, Darry Cowl.

896 "L'Amour à la ville." Arts, no. 607 (20-26 Feb.):3.
This is a series of six supposedly real episodes, only
three of which are at all worth watching.

897 "Anastasia." [Signed Robert Lachenay]. Arts, no. 610
(13-19 Mar.):3.
Anatole Litvak has directed this film "with laziness,
poverty of imagination, and bad taste." In FMV.

898 "L'Ardente Gitane." Arts, no. 602 (16-22 Jan.):3.
Less brilliant than Johnny Guitar, this is the only Nick
Ray film in which gaiety wins over bitterness. It contains
Jane Russell's best performance.

899 "Arsene Lupin." Arts, no. 611 (27 Mar.-2 Apr.):3.
Actor Robert Lamoureux saves this film. Otherwise it is
"soft, lacking vigor and strength; the important things are
too light; and what should be light is too heavy." In FMV
(slightly modified).

900   "Assassins et voleurs." Arts, no. 606 (13-19 Feb.):3.
        This essential Guitry film proves that the art of film
        has no set laws, that a film made in a few days by a devil-
        may-care group can be an important work.

901   "L'Attraction des sexes." Cahiers du Cinéma 12, no. 67
        (Jan.):37-39.
        After a longish introduction about Kazan's problems with
        Tennessee Williams as producer, and difficulties in the do-
        main of thought and political action, Truffaut describes
        Kazan's achievement in Baby Doll: he has done what all
        great filmmakers dream of, namely, being free of the con-
        straints of drama, making a film without progression or
        psychology. Altered in FMV (see entry 958).

902   "Au Festival de Cannes." Arts, no. 618 (8-14 May):3.
        Around The World in 80 Days is a witty, carefree, cyni-
        cal, and engaging film, full of the unexpected and the im-
        provised. Jules Dassin in Celui qui doit mourir tries to
        do too much and ends up with nothing but confusion. Sec-
        tion on Dassin is reprinted in FMV.

903   "Autant pour Lara." Arts, no. 626 (3-9 July):5.
        Autant-Lara sent a letter to Arts picking a quarrel with
        Truffaut, assuming he wanted to get paid for a clipping he
        sent to Autant-Lara on a good idea for a film. This is
        Truffaut's response. Although he admires La Traversée de
        Paris, he still can only use words like "grossness, peevish-
        ness, wickedness, meanness, caddishness, petty baseness,
        delirium, and exaggeration" to describe the man personally.
        Truffaut admits that he will probably abandon criticism for
        more creative work. The letter is published as "La Lettre
        perdue."

904   "Avec le Faux Coupable Hitchcock nous offre le plus grand film
        de sa carrière." Arts, no. 617 (1-7 May):3.
        The "purest and best Hitchcock," The Wrong Man is com-
        pared to Bresson's Un Condamné à mort s'est échappé, which
        is especially interesting given Fonda's impassive, unsympa-
        thetic acting. In FMV.

905   "Avec Max Ophuls nous perdons un de nos meilleurs cinéastes."
        Arts, no. 613 (3-9 Apr.):3.
        Eulogy on the death of Ophuls is divided into two parts:
        (1) biography and career overview, and (2) analysis of his
        contributions and qualities. Put on a par with Renoir. In
        FMV.

906   "Avec 'Oeil pour Oeil' Cayatte et Curd Jergens font reculer

1957

les bornes du grotesque à l'écran." [Signed Louis Chabert]. *Arts*, no. 636 (18-24 Sept.):5.
  Lengthy attack on the film, the director, and the star using quotes from Renoir, Vigo, and Bazin to formulate points.

907   "Bio-filmographie de Jean Renoir." *Cahiers du Cinéma* 13, no. 78 (Christmas):59-86.
  Truffaut provides the capsule comments on the following: *Nana*, *Charleston*, *Marquitta*, *Tiré au flanc*, *Toni*, *Le Crime de M. Lange*, *La Vie est à nous*, *La Grande Illusion*, *La Marseillaise*, *La Regle du jeu*, *This Land Is Mine*; reprinted in André Bazin's *Jean Renoir* (see entry 454), where Truffaut also comments on *Carrosse d'or*. Rohmer's comments on *La Marseillaise* replace his here.

908   "La Blonde et moi." *Arts*, no. 614 (10-16 Apr.):3.
  On parody and Pygmalion in Frank Tashlin's *The Girl Can't Help It*, a movie "put together out of 347 gags, which is funny and beautiful all the way through." In *FMV*.

909   "Le Brave et le téméraire." *Arts*, no. 604 (30 Jan.-5 Feb.):3.
  Very engaging, naïve, clever, and sincere at the same time. A surprise on first viewing, but it probably will not stand up to a second one.

910   "C. Bernard-Aubert: Si j'étais censeur . . . ." *Arts*, no. 628 (17-23 July):5.
  An interview about Bernard-Aubert's film of the Indochina war, *Patrouille sans espoir*.

911   "Calabuig." *Arts*, no. 613 (3-9 Apr.):3.
  The atomic bomb is an audacious, violent invention and should be treated by audacious, violent filmmakers such as the team of Autant-Lara, Aymé, Aurenche, and Bost.

912   "Cannes 1957." *Cahiers du Cinéma* 12, no. 72 (June):26-34.
  Truffaut reviews, briefly, Bergman's *The Seventh Seal* ("a beautiful and great film"), *The Bachelor Party* ("a pleasant surprise" by "the gang from *Marty*"--Chayevsky, Hecht, Lancaster, and Delbert Mann), *La Maison de l'ange* (an Argentinian film), and Lattuada's *Guenudalina*.

913   "Cannes: Un Échec, dominé par les compromis, les combines et les faux pas." *Arts*, no. 620 (22-28 May):1, 3.
  Virulent indictment of the festival organizers and jury. Prizes awarded not on merit but on the basis of politics, friendships, etc. The festival is a gimmick used to fill hotels during the off-season by people who know nothing

about film. Further deterioration predicted unless quality of films and manner of judging are improved. For letters of protest, see Arts, no. 623 (entry 926).

914 "Le Cas du Dr. Laurent." Arts, no. 614 (10-16 Apr.):3.
This is a useful film with a modern, even audacious subject, but the camera techniques used by La Chanois are from 1935.

915 "Le Cinéma est-il un art ou une industrie?" Arts, no. 605 (6-12 Feb.):3.
Response to accusation that Truffaut is prejudiced against French films. Truffaut claims French must compete with the best, that is, Hollywood. He makes his usual distinction between filmmakers who keep audience in mind and those who do not. He ends by contending that each artist is an individual and each film a different case.

916 "Le Cinéma crève sous les fausses légendes." Arts, no. 619 (15-21 May):1, 3-4.
An attack on expensive, mediocre French films and a call for new, audacious, inexpensive personal films. Hollywood, Bardot, Vadim, and Astruc seen as agents for change. Contains the famous line, "there are no good or bad films, only good or bad directors." Excerpted in entry 1050.

917 "Cinérama Holiday." Arts, no. 603 (23-29 Jan.):3.
Totally negative review.

918 "Claude Autant-Lara, faux martyr, n'est qu' un cinéaste bourgeois." Arts, no. 624 (19-25 June):5.
Autant-Lara is an "applied" director, an illustrator of texts, not an auteur. He blames censors and producers, but he changes things himself to accord with his own bourgeois morality. He criticizes others for not being audacious, yet he will not risk his own money on his films.

919 "Clouzot au travail--ou le règne de la terreur." Cahiers du Cinéma 13, no. 77 (Dec.):18-22.
A devastating attack on Clouzot, one of the "untouchables" (the others are Clair and Clément) of French cinema, occasioned by the publication of a book about him (Le Premier Spectateur by Michel Cournot) and the making of Les Espions. Truffaut first sets down the rules of Cahiers criticism and then quotes freely from the book, using Clouzot's own words and practices to criticize him.

920 "Clouzot: Les Espions voudrait evoquer le monde 'antilogique' de Franz Kafka." [With André Parinaud]. Arts, no. 602

1957

(16-22 Jan.):1, 3.
Fairly lengthy interview covering Clouzot's career, his
style, the films he has made that he prefers, and a preview
of this, his latest film.

921 "Collines brulantes." Arts, no. 603 (23-29 Jan.):3.
Stuart Heisler is a modest filmmaker--kindly, benevolent;
his film, which is pleasant enough, reflects this.

922 "Côte 465." Arts, no. 623 (12-18 June):5.
Anthony Mann's antiwar film is like Aldrich's Attack,
but "purer and less theatrical: firm, solid, rigorous."

923 "Courte tête." Arts, no. 609 (6-12 Mar.):3.
Not a masterpiece, but a good comedy because there is an
elegance to the film, the result of the richness of detail,
lack of vulgarity or awkwardness, and the joy and easygoing
style of director Charbonneau.

924 "Derrière le miroir." Arts, no. 607 (20-26 Feb.):3.
Truffaut's third review of the film, this time dealing
with the film's major idea, portrayal of character, and
techniques.

925 "Les Dix Meilleurs Films de l'année." Cahiers du Cinéma 12,
no. 67 (Jan.):2-3.
Contains Truffaut's list of top ten films of 1956.

926 "Le Droit de reponse." Arts, no. 623 (12-18 June):5.
Truffaut's attack on the Cannes Film Festival in issue
no. 620 provoked several angry letters, which are arranged
here like a "superproduction script," with Truffaut responding to each (including one from Cocteau); see entry 913.

927 "Du cinéma pur." Cahiers du Cinéma 12, no. 70 (Apr.):46-47.
In contrast to all the other films that Cahiers defends,
Guitry's Assassins et voleurs is "devoid of any aesthetic
ambitions." But it has "verve, fantasy, a swift pace, and
a richness of invention." Slightly altered in FMV.

928 "La Dynamique de l'érotisme." [Signed Robert Lachenay]. Arts,
no. 601 (9-15 Jan.):3.
Lo Duca's book L'Érotisme au cinéma provides the occasion
for speculation and excerpting.

929 "L'Écran fit de Bogart le meilleur en tout." [Signed Robert
Lachenay]. Arts, no. 603 (23-29 Jan.):3.
A look at Bogart's life and career plus an analysis of
his success as a modern hero. Much of this is simply a

digested and rearranged version of an article in <u>Cahiers</u>; see entry 731.

930 "<u>Écrit sur du vent</u>." <u>Arts</u>, no. 607 (20–26 Feb.):3.
   "This is moviemaking unashamed of what it is, with no complexes, no hesitations, simply good workmanship." Color is especially good. In <u>FMV</u>.

931 "Entretien avec Max Ophuls." [With Jacques Rivette]. <u>Cahiers du Cinéma</u> 12, no. 72 (June):7–25.
   A brief, affectionate character sketch of Ophuls precedes this interview covering his entire career. The interviewers ask fewer questions than usual as Ophuls talks uninterruptedly at length.

932 "Les <u>Étoiles ne meurent jamais</u>." <u>Arts</u>, no. 621 (29 May–4 June): 5.
   A compilation film about great actors, which contradicts its title at every point. Those who are poetic actors do not go out of style, while psychological actors do, because psychology is in constant evolution.

933 "<u>Le Faiseur de pluie</u>." <u>Arts</u>, no. 624 (19–25 June):5.
   Everything about <u>The Rainmaker</u> leaves a great deal to be desired--camera work, directing, acting.

934 "<u>Folies Bergères</u>." <u>Arts</u>, no. 602 (16–22 Jan.):3.
   If you are not a fan of musical comedies and are not expecting a film on a par with the great Hollywood successes of this genre, then this first French musical comedy will please you.

935 "Gangsters, 'filles,' cinéastes, censeurs dans le même panier." <u>Arts</u>, no. 627 (10–16 July):1, 3.
   An insincere gangster film by Yves Allegret threatened with banning, but cuts cannot hurt a bad film with no ideas. Allegret could have used his film to make some important and bold points.

936 "<u>Géant</u>." <u>Arts</u>, no. 611 (20–26 Mar.):3.
   <u>Giant</u> is everything bad about Hollywood--stupid, paternalistic, demagogical, without boldness, full of concessions and baseness. A dead film made to get Oscars.

937 "<u>Le Grand Bluff</u>." <u>Arts</u>, no. 624 (19–25 June):5.
   Actor Eddie Constantine has total control over script, actors, and directors, and he has never made a good film.

938 "<u>La Harpe Birmane</u>." <u>Arts</u>, no. 617 (1–7 May):3.

1957

In Kon Ichikawa's film, "the extraordinary dignity of the personalities and the great nobility of the subject capture our interest, as long as a bit of literature and a touch of sentimentality don't frighten us off." Slightly modified in FMV.

939 "L'Homme à l'imperméable." Arts, no. 610 (13–19 Mar.):3.
Everyone laughed but Truffaut. To him Fernandel is not funny and director Duvivier, though possessed of more than the usual professional conscientiousness, is without taste or intuition.

940 "Un Homme dans la foule." Arts, no. 641 (23–29 Oct.):7.
Unlike On the Waterfront, Kazan's A Face in the Crowd is an antidemagogical film. It lacks consistency, but it is "passionate, exalted, fierce, . . . inexorable." In FMV.

941 "L'Homme qui n'a jamais existé." [Signed R. L.]. Arts, no. 606 (13–19 Feb.):3.
Truffaut hopes Gloria Grahame survives this "triumph of incompetence."

942 "L'Inspecteur aime la bagarre." Arts, no. 625 (26 June–2 July):5.
Whether good or bad, a film by Jean Devaivré always possesses, if not a certain style, then a pleasing tone, playful and attractive. But the tone cannot save this one.

943 "Je reviendrai à Kandara." Arts, no. 604 (30 Jan.–5 Feb.):3.
The film is dismissed. Difficulties of creating suspense are discussed.

944 "La Jungle en folie." Arts, no. 600 (2–8 Jan.):3.
Claude Lalande's 1952 comedy is awkward yet charming.

945 "Livres de cinéma." Arts, no. 616 (24–30 Apr.):3.
Truffaut dismisses a book on James Dean by Yves Salgues and one on eroticism in movies by Lo Duca, recommends Kyrou's book on love and eroticism, Mitry's book on Chaplin, and Leprohon's book on French filmmakers.

946 "Lola Montès." Arts, no. 608 (27 Feb.–5 Mar.):3.
A new version has been released for commercial reasons—recut and put in chronological order, or "mutilated" in Truffaut's words. The original is a masterpiece of taste and sensitivity.

947 "Malgré Darry Cowl." [Signed Robert Lachenay]. Arts, no. 648 (11–17 Dec.):5.
Pinoteau's Le Triporteur is without intensity or poetry.

216

948   "Une manche et la belle." [Signed Robert Lachenay]. Arts,
        no. 647 (4-10 Dec.):7.
           Henri Verneuil's adaptation of a James Hadley Chase nov-
        el fails because these ventures need "more science than
        care, more virtuosity than application, more talent than
        labor, more ease than mania." The article is more signifi-
        cant for the fact that it ends by mentioning Marcel Moussy,
        Truffaut's collaborator on The 400 Blows, and his television
        series.

949   "Max Ophuls." [By F. T.]. Cahiers du Cinéma 12, no. 70
        (1 Apr.).
           Death notice with brief account of circumstances sur-
        rounding an interview with Ophuls to appear later in Cahiers.

950   "Le monstre." Arts, no. 615 (17-23 Apr.):3.
           A fantasy film that lacks fantasy and imagination; but
        the entire British film industry lacks fantasy, enthusiasm,
        warmth.

951   "Nick Ray dans Derriere le miroir." Arts, no. 606 (13-19
        Feb.):3.
           Truffaut elaborates on ideas first expressed in Arts,
        no. 583 (see entry 889), with a full description, inside
        information on the making of the film (Bigger Than Life)
        and a well-rounded, positive appraisal. In FMV.

952   "Nous sommes tous des condamnés." Arts, no. 621 (29 May-
        4 June):5.
           His major statement about the profession of criticism.
        See Biographical Background (above) for synopsis.

953   "Nouvel entretien avec Jean Renoir." [With Jacques Rivette].
        Cahiers du Cinéma 13, no. 78 (Christmas):11-54.
           A lengthy interview covering Renoir's entire career, dur-
        ing which he reveals his optimism and concludes with a dis-
        cussion of the genesis of his drama Orvet. Translated into
        Danish in 1970: Samtale med Jean Renoir (see entry 1112).
        Reprinted in Politique des auteurs (see entry 1129).

954   "Parlons-en!" Cahiers du Cinéma 13, no. 77 (Dec.):57-58.
           Praise for the script and direction of Lumet's Twelve
        Angry Men.

955   "Une Parodie de Gervaise." Cahiers du Cinéma 13, no. 77
        (Dec.):58.
           A condescending review of Pot-Bouille by Julien Duvivier,
        a filmmaker with an "obstinate sweetness," who is not an
        auteur, but at least is always more amusing than Autant-Lara,
        Jeanson, Aurenche, and Bost.

1957

956   "Patrouille de choc." Arts, no. 628 (17-23 July):5.
              A fictional film with sections of a documentary nature
       on the absurdity of the war in Indochina. Courageous ef-
       fort but naive, without force or intelligence.

957   "Un Pitre au pensionnat." Arts, no. 601 (9-15 Jan.):3.
              Truffaut is not crazy about Jerry Lewis. His films are
       based on the misadventures of a character dumber than the
       audience and are invariably misogynistic; however, this
       one's script is ingenious and the direction clever.

958   "La Poupée de Chair." Arts, no. 600 (2-8 Jan.):3.
              "What is new [in Baby Doll], and fairly daring, is that
       sex is the only focus of attention." Kazan has no more to
       say than what screenwriters give him, but he is good at re-
       vealing actors to themselves. Parts of this review are
       combined with Cahiers du Cinéma review of the film (see
       entry 901) in FMV.

959   "La Première Balle tue." Arts, no. 625 (26 June-2 July):5.
              The Western is a lyrical, moral genre. This one has
       problems. The premise is boring, and the audience laughs
       during dramatic scenes.

960   "Que sera le festival de Cannes 57." [Signed Robert Lachenay].
              Arts, no. 611 (20-26 Mar.):3.
              Background piece on how films are chosen, who will be on
       the juries, what the prizes are, and generally what will
       happen.

961   "Qui est Elia Kazan?" [Signed Robert Lachenay]. Arts, no. 600
              (2-8 Jan.):3.
              Background piece on Kazan's life and his careers in thea-
       ter and film.

962   "La Rançon." Arts, no. 603 (23-29 Jan.):3.
              Alex Segal has brought the worst from his television
       directing experience to this quickie MGM vehicle for Glenn
       Ford.

963   "Réalisateur de 45 films en 34 ans, Hitchcock est le plus
              grand 'inventeur de formes' de l'epoque." Arts, no. 647
              (4-10 Dec.):7.
              Rohmer and Chabrol's book (Hitchcock) is praised.
       Truffaut outlines some of Hitchcock's themes and theories,
       using lengthy quotes from the book.

964   "Le Règne du cochon de payant est terminé." Arts, no. 643
              (6-12 Nov.):1, 5.

1957

Another attack on filmmakers (Delannoy, Clement, Cluzot) who underestimate their audiences. Important for Truffaut's opinion that "aesthetic criteria are linked to moral criteria; there are successful films and failures, but there are also noble films and abject ones. There is an artistic morality, which has nothing to do with current morality, but which exists."

965   "Renoir fait répéter Le Grand Couteau." Arts, no. 636
      (18–24 Sept.):1.
         An interview consisting of five questions and answers on Renoir's adaptation of Odets' play, his book and film projects.

966   "Robert Aldrich: Nous subissons la dictature des vedettes.
      Il devient impossible de faire de bons films." [Signed Robert Lachenay]. Arts, no. 614 (10–16 Apr.):3.
         An interview about the problems of distribution, the filming of Attack!, and the best recent films seen.

967   "Un Roi à New York est un film génial." Arts, no. 642
      (29 Sept.–5 Oct.):7.
         The biblical parallels, "awful gentleness," and documentary-like qualities of Chaplin's film. In FMV.

968   "Le Rouge est mis." Arts, no. 616 (24–30 Apr.):3.
         Touchez pas au Grisbi had a disastrous effect, creating a new genre, "the thriller for concierges," which is an awkward synthesis of violence, sentimentality, humanism, melodrama, eroticism, and psychological realism. This film is an involuntary caricature of it.

969   "Sacha Guitry fut un grand cinéaste réaliste." Arts, no. 630
      (31 July–5 Aug.):5.
         Praise for the filmmaker who refused to follow the public taste and, like Renoir, paints clearly life as it really is, even if it involves cruelty and cynicism.

970   "Sait-on jamais . . ." Arts, no. 622 (5–11 June):5.
         Vadim's talent cannot be doubted. In this film he shows Venice in winter, typical of his way of filming unusual things not done or seen before.

971   "Le Salaire du péché." Arts, no. 600 (2–8 Jan.):3.
         This film is a failure both commercially (it is boring) and artistically (it is a pretentious copy of American film noir).

972   "Sénéchal le magnifique." Arts, no. 623 (12–18 June):5.

219

1957

           An amusing film with a good script and excellent dia-
logue, but directed mechanically.

973   "7 Hommes à abattre." Arts, no. 629 (24-30 July):5.
           Truffaut disagrees with Bazin, who says it is one of
three best Westerns in the last ten years. The script is
excellent, but the direction is timid, gauche.

974   "Les Sorcières de Salem." Arts, no. 617 (1-7 May):3.
           A vague, overloaded parable that proves nothing while
giving the impression it has something to say.

975   "S.O.S. Norohna." Arts, no. 625 (26 June-2 July):5.
           A serious and honest movie, but boring. Director
Rouquier does not dominate his work, does not translate any
of his own sense pleasure or personal participation in the
film to the public.

976   "Soupe à la citrouille." Arts, no. 614 (10-16 Apr.):3.
           This short film has little in common with The Private
Life of Uncle Sam, the other film covered in this review,
except that both are so different from all other films.

977   "Tout le monde peut devenir un grand acteur de cinéma." Arts,
      no. 608 (27 Feb.-5 Mar.):3.
           A personal list of the great actors of tomorrow, with an
introduction comparing actors to children in their vulnerability and sensitivity, and stating that good directors make
good actors.

978   "Les Trois font la paire." Arts, no. 621 (29 May-4 June):5.
           Admits he is one of the few who like this Sacha Guitry
film full of surprises, inventions, and contrasts.

979   "Typhon sur Nagasaki." [Signed Robert Lachenay]. Arts, no.
      606 (13-19 Feb.):3.
           The story of Yves Ciampi's best film is recounted in
full because this "honestly realized film, courageous in
its manner [and] adroitly spectacular" does not encourage
"filmic exegesis."

980   "Vadim: Je n'aime pas les histoires, je ne m'interesse qu'à
      la verité des personnages." Arts, no. 622 (5-11 June):5.
           Conversation with Vadim on And God Created Woman, eroti-
cism, Bardot, and projects he is undertaking.

981   "Vous etes tous temoins . . ." Arts, no. 619 (15-21 May):3.
           On La Parisienne by Michel Boisrond.

982   "Un Vrai cinglé de cinéma." Arts, no. 616 (24–30 Apr.):3.
      Hollywood or Bust is a good satire on the film industry.
      Tashlin is intelligent and refined and may become the best
      director of American comedies. Jerry Lewis more likable
      in every film. In FMV.

1958

983   "L'Adaptation littéraire au cinéma." La Revue des Lettres
      Modernes (Cinéma et Roman) 5, nos. 36–38 (Summer):243–48.
      Less a theoretical piece than a polemical one. Truffaut
      attacks Aurenche and Bost, providing several examples of
      how they went wrong. He concludes by citing Preminger's
      Bonjour tristesse and stating that there are no good or bad
      adaptations, only good or bad films.

984   "Adieu à André Bazin." Arts, no. 697 (19–25 Nov.):7.
      A moving eulogy on the occasion of the death of this
      extraordinary good man, friend, and mentor.

985   "Astruc a manqué Une Vie." Arts, no. 686 (3–9 Sept.):1, 7.
      Astruc should do only films he wants to, films that move
      him. This film is a failure, a skeleton of the film Astruc
      would like to have made.

986   "Bonjour tristesse est un poème d'amour." Arts, no. 661
      (12–18 Mar.):1, 7.
      Truffaut begins with comments on "the inherent sterility
      of [the critics'] function" and the fact that "cinema is an
      art of the woman, that is, of the actress." His long review
      is concerned with showing how well Preminger succeeds in his
      "exhibition" of Jean Seberg. In FMV.

987   "Cannes: Le Cinéma passe son conseil de révision." Arts,
      no. 668 (30 Apr.–6 May):1, 7.
      Truffaut is the only critic not invited to Cannes. This
      year the festival is important because there is a crisis in
      European cinema. He discusses the problem.

988   "Cannes 1958." Cahiers du Cinéma 14, no. 84 (June):22–28.
      Goha by Jacques Baratier is hard to evaluate and defend
      because the story is so personal and the style so new to
      the screen. Truffaut is one of six reviewers whose reviews
      are included here.

989   "Cannes: Onze ans d'intriques politiques et de scandales
      publicitaires." [Unsigned]. Arts, no. 670 (14–20 May):9.
      One full page devoted to a year-by-year history of the

1958

Cannes Film Festival from 1939, when it was first proposed, but especially from 1946 to 1957.

990 "Cannes s'endort malgré Jacques Tati." Arts, no. 670 (14-20 May):1, 9.
Tati's Mon oncle termed good but uneven. Festival attendance is down, no faith or enthusiasm left despite some good films. Truffaut takes a look back at the years of the festival, the scandals and intrigues.

991 "Charlotte et Véronique." Cahiers du Cinéma 14, no. 83 (May):41.
Brief review of Godard's short film (which was later to be retitled All Boys Are Called Patrick), praised as an easy, graceful avant-garde film influenced by Lumiere. Renais and Franju are the best makers of short films.

992 "Le Cinéma trahi pour les beaux yeux de Sophia Loren." Arts, no. 669 (7-13 May):1, 7.
A report on the first three days of the Cannes Festival, again critical of its choices. With Desire under the Elms, the selection committee has again sacrificed quality to the cult of the star, this time Sophia Loren.

993 "Claude Chabrol, cinéaste de 28 ans." Arts, no. 658 (19-25 Feb.):8.
An interview with Chabrol about his first film, his theories, who influenced him, what his future projects are.

994 "Demain ce seront des hommes." Arts, no. 653 (15-21 Jan.):8.
A confused, independent production by Jack Garfein--a disciple of Welles--which is totally unworthy of him.

995 "Le Désir mène les hommes." [Signed Robert Lachenay]. Arts, no. 670 (14-20 May):5.
Poor direction of actors undermines Mick Roussel's otherwise good film.

996 "La Dictateur va envoyer Charlot sur la lune." Arts, no. 680 (23-29 July):1, 6.
The Great Dictator is still an admirable document--a useful object that has become an art object. Truffaut compares the film to A King in New York and provides historical background. Substantially modified in FMV.

997 "Les Dix Meilleurs Films de l'année." Cahiers du Cinéma 14, no. 79 (Jan.):3-4.
Includes Truffaut's and Lachenay's lists of top ten films for 1957. No films in common.

998   "Les Dix Plus Grand Cinéastes du monde ont plus de 50 ans."
       Arts, no. 653 (15-21 Jan.):1, 8.
       Except for Welles, who is forty-three, there are no
       geniuses under fifty. Ten greatest are listed. Truffaut
       laments France not taking the young seriously.

999   "Entretien avec Jacques Tati." [With André Bazin]. Cahiers
       du Cinéma 14, no. 83 (May):2-20.
       At the center of this interview is a contrast of Tati's
       character and techniques with those of Chaplin.

1000   "L'Escroquerie de Quitte ou double réhabilite un art: La Mise
       en scène." Arts, no. 686 (3-9 Sept.):6.
       Analysis of the success of a television quiz show.

1001   "Les Espions qui s'amusent; L'Homme qui tua la peur." Arts,
       no. 678 (9-15 July):6.
       Joseph von Sternberg's Jet Pilot is reviewed with Martin
       Ritt's first film, the former a right-wing and the latter a
       left-wing film. Truffaut suggests that if you think the
       message in itself is enough, see the latter; if you think
       beauty is itself a message, see the former. In FMV.

1002   "Les Festivals: Un Bluff." Arts, no. 688 (17-23 Sept.):7.
       Too many festivals, too many boring, mediocre films, and
       not enough good ones. The presumed rigor of the Venice Film
       Festival turned out to be a bluff; half of the fourteen films
       were not worthy of competition.

1003   "Un Film miracle est actuellement tourné à Paris." Arts, no.
       682 (2-8 Aug.):1, 6.
       Jacques Rivette's Paris nous appartient, "this pure,
       proud, modest but hopeful enterprise," is offered as a
       model of what French cinema needs. The rules of the indus-
       try actually hold back creativity and new blood. The qual-
       ity of films is lower now because fewer risks taken.

1004   "Georges Franju trouve sa chance dans un asile, entournant La
       Tête contre les murs." Arts, no. 677 (2-8 July):6.
       An interview with Franju concerning his first full-
       length film, with a short review as introduction.

1005   "Les Girls." Arts, no. 665 (9-15 Apr.):7.
       A successful musical creates a euphoric atmosphere in
       which audience and film are joined by love. This happens
       in Cukor's film.

1006   "Le Grand Chantage." Arts, no. 652 (8-14 Jan.):9.
       Tony Curtis is good; the camerawork is bold; the film is
       not at all boring.

1958

1007 "La Grande Illusion de Jean Renoir est d'une brûlante
      actualité." Arts, no. 691 (8-14 Oct.):7.
          Renoir is a scorned filmmaker, ahead of his time. This
      film was perhaps successful because it depended on psycholo-
      gy more than on poetry. Truffaut deals at some length with
      the film's antichauvinist theme.

1008 "Les Grandes Familles." [Signed Louis Chabert]. Arts, no.
      698 (26 Nov.-2 Dec.):7.
          Defects outweigh the good points in this careful adapta-
      tion by Denys de la Patelliere of Maurice Druon's award-
      winning novel.

1009 "Hold Up." [Signed Robert Lachenay]. Arts, no. 681 (30 July-
      5 Aug.):6.
          Review of this Hubert Cornfield movie notable only be-
      cause of Truffaut's reference to the "poetic metamorphosis
      of character" in the novels of David Goodis, a novelist
      whose thriller he himself would later adapt as Shoot the
      Piano Player.

1010 "L'Homme qui tua la peur." Arts, no. 678 (9-15 July):6.
          Sincere, sympathetic film, on the same theme as On the
      Waterfront, that is sabotaged by amateurish techniques.

1011 "J'ai vu tourner Robert Aldrich dans les ruines de Berlin."
      Arts, no. 660 (5-11 Mar.):7.
          Positive appraisal of Aldrich and a preview of his new
      film through a conversation with him.

1012 "Jacques Tati raconte Mon oncle." [Unsigned]. Arts, no. 663
      (26 Mar.-1 Apr.):6.
          Tati recounts the story of his film at great length.

1013 "Louis Malle a filmé la première nuit d'amour du cinéma."
      Arts, no. 687 (9-16 Sept.):1, 7.
          Praise for Malle's Les Amants and for jury of Venice
      Film Festival for giving it a prize; qualified praise for
      Autant-Lara's En cas de malheur. Both reviews are reprinted
      separately in FMV.

1014 "Louis Malle: Je ne me prends pas pour un phénix." Arts, no.
      682 (13-19 Aug.):1, 6.
          An interview with Malle about Les Amants.

1015 "La Marque." Arts, no. 666 (16-22 Apr.):7.
          An attack on the film, an ugly and silly British science
      fiction film, that expands into an attack on the entire
      genre and its fans (who are "blasé about fiction, too lazy

to devote [themselves] to science, incapable of dreams and
fantasy").

1016   "Mon bilan: Une Mauvaise Année pour le cinéma français."
        [Unsigned]. Arts, no. 651 (1-7 Jan.):9.
            A month-by-month recapitulation of the previous year's
        film events.

1017   "Le Nouveau 'Grand' du cinéma mondial: Ingmar Bergman a dédié
        son oeuvre aux femmes." Arts, no. 674 (11-17 June):7.
            Career overview that emphasizes the things Bergman has
        in common with other directors, his treatment of women, the
        three stages in his career. Two paragraphs added to the
        end of this discussion (on Seventh Seal and So Close to
        Life) in FMV.

1018   "Orson Welles donne la recette d'un bon film . . ." Arts,
        no. 673 (4-10 June):1, 7.
            Two-part article on Touch of Evil: the first presents
        Welles's theory on how to make a good film, the second a
        positive appraisal of this "magical film that makes us
        think of fairy tales," one of the films "that call cinema
        to order." Second part in FMV.

1019   "Petit journal du cinéma." [by F. T.]. Cahiers du Cinéma 14,
        no. 80 (Feb.):42-47.
            Anecdote about a general asking Disney to do cartoons to
        convince ordinary people about extraterrestrial life.
        "Photo du mois," a feature which commented briefly on a
        still photograph from a movie set, is by Truffaut; it is
        a short review of Jet Pilot.

1020   "Petit journal du cinéma." Cahiers du Cinéma 14, no. 81
        (Mar.):47-49.
            Truffaut quotes a good-night wish from Ophuls to Hitler
        that forced Ophuls to flee France and that was echoed in
        Lola Montès.

1020a   "Petit journal du cinéma." [Signed Robert Lachenay]. Cahiers
        du Cinéma 14, no. 82 (Apr.):49.
            An appraisal of Paths of Glory by Stanley Kubrick.

1020b   "Petit journal du cinéma." Cahiers du Cinéma 14, no. 84
        (June):42-43.
            On Vertigo by Hitchcock and Varda's O Saisons! O Chateux.

1021   "Petit journal du cinéma." Cahiers du Cinéma 15, no. 85
        (July):41-44.
            A brief amusing tribute to Claude de Givray, who is now
        in the army.

1958

1022 "Petit journal du cinéma." Cahiers du Cinéma 15, no. 88
      (Oct.):48-49.
           Truffaut quotes three lengthy paragraphs from a televi-
      sion program on Bresson; he uses a quote by Autant-Lara on
      Simenon ironically; he compliments Rivette on his steadfast-
      ness in making Paris nous appartient.

1023 "Positif: copie zero." Cahiers du Cinéma 14, no. 79 (Jan.):
      60-62.
           A full-scale attack on the journal Positif, which changes
      the colors of its cover while inside all is "solidarity of
      thought and taste." Truffaut uses his favorite tactic,
      short quotations turned against the writers, and singles
      out for special criticism Kyrou and Raymond Borde. Ends
      with Truffaut indirectly accusing Kyrou of being a hypocrite
      and a fascist.

1023a "Prisonnier de la peur." Arts, no. 651 (1-7 Jan.):9.
           Robert Mulligan, a member of the anti-Hollywood, "New
      York School," whose first film this is, is recommended as
      model for French filmmakers. In FMV.

1024 "Le Prochain Festival est condomné." Arts, no. 671 (21-27
      May):1, 5.
           Only three or four of thirty films shown at Cannes were
      worthy of competing. Cannes is being passed up by profes-
      sionals and scorned by critics in favor of Venice, Berlin,
      and Brussels festivals. Films that should have been in-
      vited are listed. Good films shown are described, the best
      of which was Chabrol's Le Beau Serge.

1025 "Rédecouvrons Max Ophuls (mort il y a un an), cinéaste des
      sentiments éternels." Arts, no. 663 (26 Mar.-1 Apr.):7.
           Ophuls is an admirable artist concerned with human truth.
      His films were always well acted. His three favorite themes:
      love with reciprocity, desire without love, pleasure with
      love.

1026 "Rencontre avec Robert Aldrich." Cahiers du Cinéma 14, no. 82
      (Apr.):4-10.
           Another seemingly forced interview with Aldrich. The
      questions are mechanical and superficial--at least half re-
      fer to Aldrich's opinions of others.

1027 "Retrospective Max Ophuls." Cahiers du Cinéma 14, no. 81
      (Mar.):13-20.
           Truffaut's article, on Divine, is the briefest contribu-
      tion to this special issue on Ophuls.

1028   "Les Sentiers de la gloire." Arts, no. 661 (12-18 Mar.):7.
        Paths of Glory is an admirable film in many ways--direct-
        ing, camerawork, acting; its major weaknesses are theatri-
        cality and lack of psychological verisimilitude. In FMV.

1029   "Seule la crise sauvera le cinéma français." Arts, no. 652
        (8-14 Jan.):1.
        The crisis in filmmaking is allowing young new directors
        to work because they are cheaper. Truffaut offers advice:
        do not imitate old directors; use authentic locations and
        dialogue; be sincere, ambitious, without restraint. For ex-
        cerpts, see entry 1050.

1030   "Si jeunes et les Japonais." Cahiers du Cinéma 14, no. 83
        (May):53-56.
        On Nakahira's Juvenile Passion and the lessons it pro-
        vides about full, rich shots, and on the two ways of making
        films, fast and slow. In FMV.

1031   "'Si votre techniramage . . .'" Cahiers du Cinéma 14, no. 84
        (June):52-55.
        A spirited criticism of René Clement, who "stands for
        films against which we at Cahiers fight." Clement is a
        good technician with the intellectual means and energy to
        make movies. He is not an artist, just an imitator inter-
        ested only in bigger and bigger budgets.

1032   "Tamango." Arts, no. 655 (29 Jan.-4 Feb.):7.
        Merimée's story has all the elements for an excellent
        film, but this version is empty, boring, and stupid. The
        actors are terrible and cost too much. The sets are obvi-
        ously fake; it should have been filmed on location in Africa.

1033   "Venise 1958." Cahiers du Cinéma 15, no. 88 (Oct.):38-42.
        Le Defi is indefensible; Mariage et bébé is "not ordi-
        nary."

1034   "20 ans après sa sortie, J'ai le droit de vivre reste un film
        jeune." Arts, no. 567 (12-18 Feb.):7.
        An analysis of Fritz Lang's themes, techniques, and char-
        acters, based on You Only Live Once, a film which has not
        aged at all. In FMV.

1035   "Les Violents." [Signed Robert Lachenay]. Arts, no. 654
        (22-28 Jan.):7.
        Henri Calef has a love of cinema and a professional con-
        science, but his film is all out of proportion.

1036   "Voici les trente nouveau noms du cinéma français." [Signed

1958

Robert Lachenay]. <u>Arts</u>, no. 652 (8-14 Jan.):9.
Comments on people to watch among assistants, makers of
shorts, scriptwriters, and critics.

<u>1959</u>

*1037   "<u>A bout de souffle</u>." <u>Radio-Cinéma-Télévision</u> (1 Oct.).
A review of the film, cited in the bibliography of Jean
Collet's <u>Jean-Luc Godard</u> (see entry 1068). Hereafter listed
simply as Collet.

1038   "Claude-Bernard Aubert: Il faut codifier la censure."
[Signed Louis Chabert]. <u>Arts</u>, no. 712 (4-10 Mar.):5.
Aubert's statement on censorship, introduced by Truffaut/
Chabert.

1039   "Les Dix Meilleurs Films de l'année." <u>Cahiers du Cinéma</u> 16,
no. 91 (Jan.):2-3.
Truffaut's (and others') top ten films of 1958.

1040   "Entretien avec Georges Franju." <u>Cahiers du Cinéma</u> 17, no.
101 (Nov.):1-15.
Franju had seen <u>400 Blows</u>, and he opens the interview
with an enthusiastic monologue about it, at the heart of
which is the question: "one can't make a film about correction correctly, can one?" Excerpted in <u>The 400 Blows</u>
book (see entry 447).

1041   "Il faisait bon vivre." <u>Cahiers du Cinéma</u> 16, no. 91 (Jan.):
25-27.
An emotional salute to Bazin in a special issue published
just after his death. Truffaut describes how Bazin rescued
him from jail, focuses on his generosity and fatherliness.
Translated in <u>New York Film Bulletin</u> (1962); see entry 1060;
and in <u>The 400 Blows</u> book, see entry 1105.

1042   "Je n'ai pas écrit ma biographie en <u>400 Coups</u>." <u>Arts</u>, no. 715
(2-8 Apr.):1-5.
Emphasizes dialogue-writer Marcel Moussy's contribution
in order to deny claim that the film is autobiographical.
Although Antoine resembles Truffaut, the latter's parents
are not at all like those in the film. Personal memories
and brief explanations of the theme and main character fill
out this defensive article.

1043   "Les Jeunes Metteurs en scène. . . ." [Signed Louis Chabert].
<u>Arts</u>, no. 712 (4-10 Mar.):5.
Two amendments proposed for Association of Independent
Creators of the French Cinema.

1044   "Les Jeunes Réalisateurs français ont-ils quelque chose a
        dire?" Radio-Cinéma-Télévision, no. 470 (18 Jan.).
              Truffaut is one of several young directors to reply to
        this questionnaire.

1045   "Ma tante." [Signed "L. C."--Louis Chabert]. Arts, no. 719
        (22-28 Apr.):5.
              A one-paragraph review of Auntie Mame; in a word, it is
        "penible."

1046   "Orson Welles." L'Express, no. 441 (26 Nov.):36-37.
              Although he now prefers other Welles films, Citizen Kane
        remains a "total film," the film of a radio man, journalist,
        and man of the theater. Welles is not a sedentary film-
        maker, but one of those "cinéastes voyageurs" whose films
        reveal a world view "at once very personal, generous, and
        noble." Reprinted in Focus on Citizen Kane (see entry
        1116).

1046a   "Petit journal du cinéma." [Signed Robert Lachenay]. Cahiers
        du Cinéma 17, no. 99 (Sept.):51.
              On Rossellini's General della Rovere.

*1047   "Les Trois Generations." Le Film Français-Cinémonde (4 May).
              Reference provided by Truffaut.

1960

*1048   "L'Affaire Vadim." France-Observateur, no. 555 (22 Dec.).
              Listed in bibliography in L'Avant-Scène du Cinéma, no.
        107; see entry 449.

1049   "Aznavour donne le 'la.'" Cinémonde, no. 1343 (5 May):36-37.
              Intimate portrait of Aznavour and explanation of why
        Truffaut chose him for Shoot the Piano Player--which is
        most revealing of Truffaut's approach to casting and di-
        recting. Reprinted in Braudy's Focus on "Shoot the Piano
        Player" (see entry 1124).

1050   "Le Cinéma à la première personne." In L'Art du cinéma.
        Edited by Pierre Lherminier. Paris: Éditions Seghers,
        pp. 529-31.
               Excerpts from Arts (18 May 1955), see entry 675; from
        Arts (15 May 1957), see entry 916; and from Arts (8 Jan.
        1958), see entry 1029.

1051   "Les Dix Meilleurs Films de l'année." Cahiers du Cinéma 18,
        no. 104 (Feb.):2.
               Includes Truffaut's list.

1960

*1052   [Essay] in <u>Cinéma univers de l'abscence?</u>: <u>Le Sort de la</u>
       <u>personne dous l'oeuvre filmique</u>. Paris: Presses
       Universitaires de France, 149 pp.
          Listed in the card files at the Centre de documentation
       cinematographique; see entry 1501.

1053   "François Truffaut: Une Leçon de cinéma." <u>France-Observateur</u>,
       no. 521 (28 Apr.):27.
          Short but very revealing reaction to Jacques Doniol-
       Valcroze's comments on Sam Fuller's <u>Verboten</u>. The scathing-
       ly negative adjectives used on <u>Verboten</u>, Truffaut applies
       to Doniol-Valcroze's first film. He also delineates briefly
       a standard of criticism based on a kind of theory of compen-
       sation.

1054   "Mon imagination fonctionne avec le réel." In <u>L'Art du cinéma</u>.
       Edited by Pierre Lherminier. Paris: Editions Seghers,
       p. 384.
          Excerpts from <u>Les Lettres françaises</u> (see entry 1198).

1055   "Reflexions sur Jacques Becker." <u>France-Observateur</u>, no. 516
       (24 Mar.):23.
          Becker is the most reflective, scrupulous, controlled
       director of his generation. <u>Le Trou</u> "seems to be as much
       above criticism in its details as it is in its overall con-
       ception." In <u>FMV</u>. Reprinted in <u>L'Avant-Scène</u> (see entry
       1062).

<u>1961</u>

1056   "L'Agonie de la nouvelle vague n'est pas pour demain." <u>Arts</u>,
       no. 848 (20-26 Dec.):1, 13.
          Sincere tribute to Rivette and his fierce determination
       to make movies. He inspired the rest of the <u>Cahiers</u> group
       to make films. <u>Paris nous appartient</u> finally finished, co-
       produced by Truffaut.

1057   "Audiberti, poète du divin mystère de la femme." <u>Arts</u>, no.
       862 (28 Mar.-3 Apr.):5.
          A brief tribute. "I think of him when I film a man, of
       his work when I film a woman. I also think of him when I
       see a good pair of legs on the street."

1058   "Cent-soixante-deux nouveaux cinéastes français." <u>Cahiers du</u>
       <u>Cinéma</u> 21, no. 138 (Dec.):60-84.
          Some of the entries are by Truffaut.

1059   "Les Dix Meilleurs Films de l'année." <u>Cahiers du Cinéma</u> 20,

no. 116 (Feb.):2.
Contains Truffaut's list.

1060   "It Was Good to Be Alive." New York Film Bulletin 3, no. 3,
        issue 44 (Summer):3-5.
            On Bazin and his role in Truffaut's life. Translated
        from Cahiers du Cinéma (see entry 1041). (This special
        issue of NYFB on Truffaut also contains reviews, interviews,
        and a transcript of the improvised cabaret scene from Shoot
        the Piano Player).

1061   "Que chacun vive sa vie." L'Avant-Scène du Cinéma, no. 19
        (15 Oct.):7.
            Introduction to Godard's Vivre sa vie.

1062   "Le Testament de Jacques Becker." L'Avant-Scène du Cinéma,
        no. 13 (15 Mar.).
            Reprinted from France-Observateur (see entry 1055).

1063   "Trois points d'economie." Cahiers du Cinéma, no. 138 (Dec.):
        85-100.
            French film production is discussed by Truffaut and
        others.

                                1962

1063a   "La Photo du mois." Cahiers du Cinéma 23, no. 137 (Nov.):33.
            On Hitchcock's The Birds, its incremental development
        and virtuosity.

                                1963

1064   "Adieu Philippine." Lui, no. 1 (Nov.).
            Jacques Rozier's film is praised for its authenticity,
        its spontaneity; it is "an uninterrupted poem." In FMV.

1065   "Les Dix Meilleurs Films de l'année." Cahiers du Cinéma, nos.
        150-151 (Dec.-Jan.):1-2.
            Truffaut's last ten-best list.

*1066   "Dragées au poivre." Lui, no. 1 (Nov.).
            Comments on this Jacques Baratier film. Reference pro-
        vided by Truffaut.

1067   "Huit et Demi: La Pointure du genie." Lui, no. 1 (Nov.).
            Fellini's film is "simple, beautiful, honest"; it "is to
        the preparation of a film what Rififi is to the planning of
        a robbery." In FMV.

1963

1068   "Notes sur Godard." In Jean-Luc Godard. Edited by Jean
        Collet. Series Cinéma d'aujourdhui, no. 18. Paris:
        Éditions Seghers.
            Truffaut is one of several friends or associates who
        provide biographical information. He talks at length about
        Histoire d'eau and Breathless. The book was revised in 1968
        and 1974 (see entry 1099) and translated in 1970 (see entry
        1114).

1069   "Les Oiseaux." Lui, no. 1 (Nov.).
            "Cinema was invented so that [The Birds] could be made."
        Hitchcock is "the ultimate athlete of cinema." In FMV.

*1069a Preface to Jules and Jim, by Henri-Pierre Roché. Translated
        by Patrick Evans. New York: Avon; London: Calder and
        Boyars.
            Listed in the bibliography in Monaco, see entry 349.
        The reissue of this book by Avon/Bard in 1980 does not have
        a preface.

*1070   "Roberto Rossellini." In Rossellini. Edited by Mario Verdone.
        Paris: Éditions Seghers, pp. 199-205.
            Listed in L'Avant-Scène du Cinéma, no. 107; see entry
        449.

1071   "Sept hommes a debattre." Cahiers du Cinéma 25, nos. 150-151
        (Dec.-Jan.):12-23.
            A round table discussion on the plight of the American
        cinema involving Truffaut, Godard, Chabrol, and others.
        Truffaut believes decline began when location shooting ar-
        rived and because films no longer look like each other.

                            1964

1072   "Les Collaborateurs de l'ombre." La Cinématographie Française
        12, no. 9 (7 May):1-2.
            Truffaut writes about the making of Soft Skin from its
        inception, through Mata-Hari to the conclusion, focusing on
        his work with his scenarist, cinematographer, and music di-
        rector.

1073   "De vrais moustaches." L'Avant-Scène du Cinéma, no. 43
        (Dec.):6.
            Glowing tribute to Casque d'or--a character film, but
        also a great "plastic" success.

1074   "Le Feu follet." Lui, no. 2 (Jan.).
            Malle's film is "simple, personal, sincere." Truffaut

claims that "criticizing a film amounts to criticizing its maker." In FMV.

1075   "Muriel." Lui, no. 2 (Jan.).
        Recounts an anecdote told by Hitchcock, calls Muriel a
        tribute to Hitchcock, and talks about beginning his own
        film and the way filming affects him. In FMV.

1076   "Parlez-vous d'amours." Candide (13 May).
        An essay on the diversity of love.

1077   "Skeleton Keys." Film Culture 32 (Spring):63–67.
        Translation from Cahiers du Cinéma (see entry 618).

1078   "Le Testament d'Orphée." Cahiers du Cinéma 26, no. 152
        (Feb.):14–18.
        Truffaut describes Cocteau's generosity and cynicism and
        singles out three short scenes at the end of The Testament
        of Orpheus to show that Cocteau "practiced his art totally
        and worked to satisfy himself."

1079   "Vacances portugaises." Lui, no. 2 (Jan.).
        A film about intellectuals that is praised highly. In
        FMV.

1965

1080   "Du systeme." Cahiers du Cinéma 28, no. 161–62 (Jan.):72–76.
        An analysis with graphs and personal comments by
        Truffaut, Doniol-Valcroze, Godard, Kast, and Moullet of the
        problems and conditions of making feature films in France.

1081   "Modification." Cahiers du Cinéma, no. 172 (Nov.):6.
        In a terse paragraph, Truffaut denies having said what
        he was quoted as saying about Pierrot le Fou in the previ-
        ous issue.

1082   "Presentation de François Truffaut." Cahiers du Cinéma, no.
        170 (Sept.):52.
        In a prefatory paragraph, Truffaut acknowledges that he
        was to have filmed Audiberti's film L'Orgueil.

1083   "Le Scénariste F. Truffaut: 'Montrer peu de chose.'" Le
        Nouvel Observateur, n.s. no. 11 (28 Jan.):28.
        On the writing of Mata-Hari.

1966

1966

1084   "A Certain Tendency of the French Cinema." Cahiers du Cinema
        in English 1 (Jan.):31-41.
            Translation from Cahiers du Cinéma (see entry 530).

1085   "Julie Christie, un garçon en mini-jupe." Arts-Loisirs, no.
        53 (28 Sept.-4 Oct.):10-13.
            How and why Truffaut chose her for Fahrenheit 451. In-
        cludes passages from his journal on the making of the film,
        plus observations about her insecurities and talents.

1086   "Skeleton Keys." Cahiers du Cinema in English, no. 2:67-71.
            Translated from Cahiers du Cinéma (see entry 618).

1967

1087   "Georges Sadoul sera pleuré." Les Lettres Françaises, no. 1204
        (18-24 Oct.):14.
            Sadoul memorial issue. Truffaut praises him as the only
        critic who reconsidered his judgments and amended them. He
        claims to have challenged Sadoul once on Hollywood films,
        and Sadoul accepted it. Truffaut's way of honoring Sadoul
        was to go to October, which Sadoul knew by heart, and to
        think of Sadoul while watching the film.

1088   "Howard Hawks" and "Roberto Rossellini." In Interviews with
        Film Directors. Edited by Andrew Sarris. New York: Bobbs-
        Merrill, pp. 228-40 and 474-78.
            Translations of Cahiers du Cinéma interviews (see entries
        790 and 542).

1089   "La Mariée était en noir." Travelling J, no. 18 (Oct.):29-31.
            Truffaut discusses the decision-making involved in creat-
        ing this film, admits he is not "modern," and claims that
        for him "cinema is an art of prose."

*1089a "La Marseillaise." L'Express (30 Oct.-5 Nov.).
            Reference provided by Truffaut.

1090   "Le Savate et la finance ou deux ou trois choses que je sais
        de lui." Les Lettres Françaises, no. 1174 (16-22 Mar.):21.
            High praise for Godard, partly through comparisons to
        many other directors. Breathless marked a turning point in
        cinema similar to that provided by Citizen Kane. Truffaut
        says he has decided to coproduce Two or Three Things because
        Godard's previous producers are all rich. Reprinted in
        L'Avant-Scène du Cinéma no. 70 (May 1967), p. 45 and in the

reprint of it in 1971: <u>Deux ou trois choses que je sais</u>
<u>d'elle</u>. Collection Point-Films. (Paris: Éditions de
Seuil, Avant-Scène).

1091 "La Savate et le finance ou deux ou trois choses que je sais
de lui." <u>L'Avant-Scène du Cinéma</u>, no. 70 (May):45.
Reprint of article from <u>Les Lettres Françaises</u> (see
entry 1090).

1092 "<u>Le Viel Homme et l'enfant</u>." <u>Le Nouvel Observateur</u>, no. 121
(8-15 Mar.):50-51.
An unrestrainedly positive review of Claude Berri's
"comic and daring film." Berri is classed with Vigo,
Guitry, and Renoir. Truffaut distinguishes between "films
that present only dishonest circumstances--exceptional people in exceptional situations" and "films that seek to con-
quer truth--real people in real situations." Reprinted in
Claude Berri, <u>Le Vieil Homme et l'enfant</u> (Paris: Jerome
Martineau, 1967) and in <u>FMV</u>.

1968

1093 "L'Affaire Langlois (suite)." <u>Le Nouvel Observateur</u>, no. 175
(20-26 Mar.):51.
Truffaut clarifies some matters including his confrontation with Pierre Moinot and the objectives of the Langlois
Defense Committee.

*1094 "L'Antimemoire courte." <u>Combat</u>, no. 7334 (12 Feb.).
On the Langlois Affair. Listed in the bibliography in
Crisp (see entry 245).

*1095 "Comme il vous plaira. . . ." <u>France-Culture</u> (2 Apr.).
On autistic children. Reference provided by Truffaut.

1096 "Elle s'appelait Françoise. . . ." <u>Cahiers du Cinéma</u>, nos.
200-201 (Apr.-May):20-21.
Moving eulogy to the woman he called "Framboise" (rasp-
berry) Dorléac, an incomparable, dedicated actress because
of her "charm, femininity, intelligence, grace, and incredi-
ble moral force."

1097 "Jean Renoir, le patron." <u>Le Monde</u>, no. 7158 (18 Jan.):13.
General comments on Renoir and his infallibility, plus
one paragraph each on his five best films (which are being
screened at a retrospective).

1098 "Lubitsch était un prince." <u>Cahiers du Cinéma</u>, no. 198

1968

(Feb.):13.
The Lubitsch "touch" is compared briefly to Hitchcock's
because they both used fairy tales and tried not to tell
the story. Lubitsch has a "sly mischievous charm"; his
films are games between director, film, and audience; from
beginning to end we are "immersed in the essential." Translated in Annette Insdorf, American Film (see entry 1178).

1099   "Notes sur Godard." In Jean-Luc Godard. Edited by Jean
Collet. Paris: Éditions Seghers.
Updated version of Collet's 1963 book (see entry 1068).
Truffaut's reminiscences slightly revised. Translated in
1970 (see entry 1114).

*1100 "La Résistible Ascension de Pierre Barbin." Combat, no. 7338
(16 Feb.).
On the Langlois Affair. Listed in the bibliography in
Crisp (see entry 245).

*1101 "Toujour la cinématheque." Combat, no. 7362 (15 Mar.).
On the Langlois Affair. Listed in the bibliography in
Crisp (see entry 245).

1969

1102   "A propos de Catherine Deneuve." Unifrance Film, no. 370
(15 Feb.):1821.
Three very brief paragraphs.

1103   "A propos de Jean-Paul Belmondo." Unifrance Film, no. 369
(1 Feb.):1793.
Four very brief paragraphs of admiration.

1104   "François Truffaut parle de La Sirène du Mississipi. . . ."
Télérama, no. 996 (16-22 Feb.):51-53.
Brief announcements written by Truffaut on the film, on
Catherine Deneuve, and on Jean-Paul Belmondo.

1105   "It Was Good to Be Alive." In The 400 Blows. Edited by David
Denby. New York: Grove Press, pp. 190-93.
Translated from Cahiers du Cinéma (see entry 1041).

1106   "Vive Glenariff!" Le Monde, no. 7701 (17 Oct.):12.
Four paragraphs of praise for a play by Henri Garçin
and Danièle Lord.

1970

1107   "Comment j'ai tourné L'Enfant sauvage." Télé-Ciné 23, no.
160 (Mar.):17-19.
Truffaut reveals where he got the idea for the film and
talks at some length about the real story. He mentions the
books of Maria Montessori and the medical films about autistic children that he studied as preparation. And he dis-
closes why he played Itard, how he chose the boy actor and
worked with him. Reprinted in L'Avant-Scène du Cinéma (see
entry 1108), and translated in Meanjin Quarterly (see entry
1121).

1108   "Comment j'ai tourné L'Enfant sauvage." L'Avant-Scène du
Cinéma, no. 107 (Oct.):8-10.
Reprint of article in Télé-Ciné (see entry 1107).

1109   "Is Truffaut the Happiest Man on Earth?" Esquire 74, no. 2
(Aug.):67, 135-36.
Yes, because he makes his daydreams come true on film
and gets paid for it. A pastiche of Truffaut's responses
to specific questions ingeniously disguised as an article.
Comments on professional jealousy, the family of filmmakers,
critics, and pessimism about the future of film.

1110   "Le Moral des civils." L'Express, no. 979 (13-19 Apr.):46.
Truffaut laments the overuse of the terms auteur and
extracinematographic polemics. He does not know whether
Claude Berri's Le Pistonne is a "film d'auteur," but it is
a "simple, beautiful, intelligent, and droll" film, which
he loves.

*1111   Preface to Le Testament d'un cancre, by Bernard Gheur. Paris:
Albin Michel.
Reference provided by Truffaut.

*1112   Samtale med Jean Renoir. Translated by Mette Knudsen.
Copenhagen: Danske Filmmuseum, 40 pp.
Translation of interview in Cahiers (see entry 953).

1113   "Une Situation dramatique sans égale." Le Figaro (20 Feb.):30.
Four short paragraphs announcing Wild Child, a film that
is faithful to the true story and made Truffaut happier than
any other.

1114   "Witnesses: Notes on Godard." In Jean-Luc Godard. Edited by
Jean Collet. Translated by Ciba Vaughan. New York: Crown,
pp. 167-73.
Truffaut's reminiscences were "reviewed and completed"
for this updating of the 1963 book (see entry 1068).

1970

*1115   "Zum erstenmal ein Film über ein Paar." <u>Filmkritik</u>, no. 2.
       On <u>Mississippi Mermaid</u>. Listed in the International
    Index.

1971

1116   "Citizen Kane." In <u>Focus on Citizen Kane</u>. Edited by Ronald
    Gottesman. Englewood Cliffs, N.J.: Prentice-Hall, pp.
    129-33.
       Translated by Mark Bernheim and Ronald Gottesman. Re-
    printed from <u>L'Express</u> (see entry 1046).

1117   "<u>Les Deux Anglaises</u>. Truffaut: 'A Physical Film about Love.'"
    <u>Le Monde/Weekly English Edition</u>, no. 138 (11 Dec.):16.
       Translation of article in <u>Le Monde</u> (25 Nov. 1971).

1118   "Forword," In <u>What Is Cinema</u>? by André Bazin. Essays selected
    and translated by Hugh Gray. Berkeley: University of
    California Press, v-vii.
       On Bazin's generosity, intelligence, and intellectual
    honesty.

1119   "François Truffaut." In <u>Carl Dreyer's Jesus</u>. Edited by Ib
    Monty. New York: Dell Publishing Co., a Delta Book, pp.
    309-10.
       On the "whiteness," the formal perfection, the static
    attitude of the actors in Dreyer's films. Truffaut says
    he works from a chair once owned by Dreyer. In <u>FMV</u>.

*1120   "François Truffaut über <u>Les Deux Anglaises et le continent</u>."
    <u>Filmkritik</u>, no. 77.
       On <u>Two English Girls</u>. Listed in the International
    Index.

1121   "How I Filmed <u>L'Enfant sauvage</u>." <u>Meanjin Quarterly</u> 30, no. 2
    (June):234-38.
       Article from <u>Télé-Ciné</u>, translated and introduced by
    Inge Pruks (see entry 1107).

1122   Preface to <u>Jean Renoir</u>, by André Bazin. Edited by François
    Truffaut. Paris: Éditions Champ Libre, 268 pp.
       An exercise in superlatives. Truffaut claims this is
    "the <u>best</u> book on the cinema, written by the <u>best</u> critic,
    about the <u>best</u> director," though later he explains that
    Bazin is not a critic but "a writer of the cinema." Renoir's
    films are good because they are guided by sympathy. Trans-
    lated into English in 1973 (see entry 1134; for books, see
    entries 454 and 458).

1972

1123   "Why I Have Made Les Deux Anglaises et le continent."
        Cinémonde, no. 1853 (July-Aug.):32-33.
        A publicity-oriented background piece.

                            1972

1124   "Aznavour Gives the Tone." In Focus on "Shoot the Piano
        Player". Edited by Leo Braudy. Englewood Cliffs, N.J.:
        Prentice-Hall, pp. 95-97.
        Translated from Cinémonde (see entry 1049).

1125   "Dr. Cyclops." In Focus on the Science Fiction Film. Edited
        by William Johnson. Englewood Cliffs, N.J.: Prentice-Hall,
        pp. 48-49.
        Translated from Cahiers du Cinéma (see entry 493).

1126   "'Les dossiers de l'ecran': sans François Truffaut: Lettre
        ouverte a Armand Jammot et Guy Darbois." Le Nouvel
        Observateur, no. 399 (3-9 July):27.
        An open letter of complaint about censorship.

1127   "Un gateau Hitchcock fait à la maison." Paris-Match, no. 1205
        (10 June):83.
        Frenzy is a combination of two kinds of Hitchcock films:
        those which follow the itinerary of an assassin or the per-
        petrator of a perfect crime and those which describe the
        torments of an innocent victim. He uses "everyday women"
        here; his triumph is one of style "in recitative." In FMV.

1128   "Mes Deux Anglaises, mon onzieme film." L'Avant-Scène du
        Cinéma, no. 121 (Jan.):10-11.
        Truffaut states that his films based on books are not
        adaptations but "filmed homages." He explains what he had
        hoped to do: squeeze love like a lemon and make "not only
        a film about physical love but a physical film about love."
        Ends with comments on his actors and technicians.

1129   La politique des auteurs. [Truffaut et al.]. Paris: Éditions
        Champ Libre, 331 pp.
        A collection of interviews by Truffaut and others from
        Cahiers du Cinéma. Included are interviews by Truffaut
        with Jean Renoir (1957), see entry 953; Rossellini (1954),
        see entry 542; Hawks (1956), see entry 790; and Hitchcock
        (1955), see entry 680.

1130   "'Tous mes personages sont fous. . . .'" Unifrance Film, no.
        437.
        Such a Gorgeous Kid is a film of "comic pretentions."
        Truffaut describes its preparation.

1972

*1131   "Zwei Filme von Truffaut. Une Belle Fille comme moi."
        Filmkritik 16, no. 7 (July):355-57.
           Listed in International Index.

                              1973

1132   "About John Ford." Action 8, no. 6 (Nov.-Dec.):11.
           One of thirteen eulogies in this issue of Action. Ford
        is praised for "invisible direction." Trimmed slightly for
        FMV.

1133   "Charlot a frôlé l'alienation." Une Semaine de Paris--
        Pariscop, no. 260 (19 Apr.):4.
           A shortened version of the preface to Bazin and Rohmer's
        book on Chaplin (see entry 1139).

1134   Introduction to Jean Renoir, by André Bazin. Edited by
        François Truffaut. Translated by W. W. Haley III and W. H.
        Simon. New York: Simon & Schuster; London: W. H. Allen,
        320 pp.
           For comment see French edition (entry 1122).

1135   "Je suis un type formidable!" Une Semaine de Paris--Pariscop,
        no. 263 (10 May):4.
           The cinema is competitive; that is why he gives inter-
        views--to make people want to see his films. He does not
        really like this competitiveness, however; thus he entered
        Day for Night out-of-competition at Cannes.

1136   "La Leçon d'Ingmar Bergman." L'Express (28 May-3 June).
           Bergman is "more feminine than feminist"; he works with
        short story themes. His lesson "hinges on three points:
        liberation of dialogue, a radical cleansing of image, and
        absolute primacy granted to the human face." Reprinted in
        Take One (see entry 1137). Slightly expanded in FMV.

1137   "The Lesson of Ingmar Bergman." Take One 3, no. 10 (Mar.-Apr.
        1972, published 30 July 1973):40.
           Translated from L'Express by Peter Lebensoll. See above,
        entry 1136.

1138   "Mes six jours au festival de Cannes." Paris-Match (May).
           Written for the release of Day for Night.

1139   Preface to Charlie Chaplin, by André Bazin and Eric Rohmer.
        Paris: Éditions du Cerf, pp. 5-10.
           Charlot, "the most marginal of all marginal" characters,
        is what Bazin saw and makes us see, according to Truffaut
        (see entry 1133).

1974

1140   "Six jours de François Truffaut." <u>Paris-Match</u>, no. 1256
         (2 June):6.
             Mostly trivia about variety of day-to-day film activities.

1141   "Truffaut on Bogart." <u>Saturday Review of the Arts</u> 1, no. 3
         (3 Mar.):31-32.
             Translation of essay from <u>Cahiers</u> (see entry 731).

1974

1142   "La Belle et la bête du western." <u>L'Avant-Scène du Cinéma</u> 145
         (Mar.):48.
             Reprint of review in <u>Arts</u> (see entry 706).

1143   "Les 'Cinémomoires' de Jean Renoir." <u>Le Monde</u>, no. 9147
         (13 June):1, 22.
             A review of Renoir's autobiography, which "combines
         harmoniously the well-written style of the nineteenth-
         century memoir writers and the liberty of tone of Henry
         Miller."

1144   "Claude Sautet, c'est la vitalité." <u>L'Avant-Scène du Cinéma</u>,
         no. 153 (Dec.):5-6.
             Anecdotal introduction to Claude Sautet's film <u>Vincent,</u>
         <u>François, Paul et les autres</u>, during which Truffaut states
         that it is good to study American films (as Renoir did).
         Reprinted from <u>Une Semaine de Paris--Pariscop</u> (see entry
         1189). In <u>FMV</u>.

1145   "Un Film simple comme bonjour." <u>Une Semaine de Paris--</u>
         <u>Pariscop</u> (Dec.).
             An introduction to Jacques Doillon's comedy <u>Les Doigts</u>
         <u>dans la tete</u>, which is compared to Renoir's <u>Toni</u>. Doillon's
         film is not like recent pseudodocumentaries, which make one
         yearn for old studio films. Reprinted in <u>L'Avant-Scène du</u>
         <u>Cinéma</u> (see entry 1153) and in <u>FMV</u>.

*1146   "<u>Ma vie et mes films</u> par Jean Renoir." <u>Une Semaine de Paris--</u>
         <u>Pariscop</u> (19 June).
             Reference provided by Truffaut.

*1147   "Naissance de l'Olympic: André Bazin." <u>Une Semaine de Paris--</u>
         <u>Pariscop</u> (6 July).
             Reference provided by Truffaut.

*1148   "<u>La Nuit du chasseur</u>." <u>Midi Minuit Fantastique</u> (18 Jan.).
             Reference provided by Truffaut.

1974

1149   Preface to <u>La Grande Illusion</u>, by Jean Renoir. Paris:
         Balland, pp. 7-13.
             Background information on the making and the suppression
         of the film, plus comments on its artistry.

1150   "Truffaut presente Renoir." <u>Le Film Français</u>, no. 1537
         (14 June):7.
             Extracts from Renoir's book chosen by Truffaut.

1975

1151   "André Bazin, l'occupation, et moi." In <u>Le Cinéma de</u>
         <u>l'occupation et de la résistance</u>. Paris: Union générale
         d'éditions, pp. 11-31.
             With personal recollections and quotations from others,
         Truffaut attempts to evoke the cinematic ambience of war-
         time France so that he might better situate the writings
         of Bazin he has assembled and edited (see entry 461).

1152   "En avant-première du Festival de Cannes: La critique des
         critiques." <u>Le Figaro Littéraire</u>, no. 1506 (28 Mar.):13.
             Sixteen paragraphs on critics and criticism excerpted
         from the middle of the preface to <u>FMV</u>.

1153   "Un Film simple comme bonjour." <u>L'Avant-Scène du Cinéma</u>, no.
         157 (Apr.):4.
             Reprinted from <u>Une Semaine de Paris--Pariscope</u> (see
         entry 1145).

1154   "James Dean est mort." <u>L'Avant-Scène du Cinéma</u>, no. 163
         (Nov.):64-66.
             Extracted from <u>FMV</u>.

1155   "Je ne connais pas Isabelle Adjani." <u>L'Express</u>, no. 1234
         (3-9 Mar.):10.
             Truffaut will understand her only when the shooting is
         done, when their work, not together but side-by-side, is
         over. Then his disatisfaction will make him impatient to
         make another film. An odd kind of poetic reverie on film-
         making, not on Isabelle A.

1156   Preface to <u>Le Cinéma de la cruauté: Eric von Stroheim, Carl</u>
         <u>Th. Dreyer, Preston Sturges, Luis Buñuel, Alfred Hitchcock,</u>
         <u>Akira Kurosawa</u>, by André Bazin. Paris: Flammarion, pp.
         9-18.
             Biographical sketch of and tribute to Bazin followed by
         three paragraphs or so on each of the directors included in
         the book (see entry 462).

1977

*1157   "Trenet: Oui, nous nous reverrons." <u>Le Point</u>, no. 135
      (21 Apr.).
        Reference provided by Truffaut.

*1158   "Warum diesen Film?" <u>Film Bulletin</u> (Zurich), no. 94 (Dec.):2.
        Explanation of why he made <u>Adèle H.</u> Listed in the
      International Index.

<u>1976</u>

1159   "A certain Tendency of the French Cinema." In <u>Movies and</u>
      <u>Methods</u>. Edited by Bill Nichols. Berkeley: University of
      California Press, pp. 224-37.
        Translation of <u>Cahiers</u> article (see entry 530).

1160   "De l'abstrait au concret." <u>L'Avant-Scène du Cinéma</u>, no. 168
      (Apr.):5-6.
        An introduction to Claude Miller's film <u>La Meilleure</u>
      <u>Façon de marcher</u>. (Miller was production manager on seven
      of Truffaut's films.)

1161   "Foreword: Between Action and Cut." In <u>Hollywood Directors:</u>
      <u>1914-1940</u>. Edited by Richard Koszarski. London and New
      York: Oxford University Press, pp. vii-x.
        A breezy piece promoting mise-en-scène by using Polti's
      notion of thirty-six basic story situations and his own
      notion of a "cinematic crisis" every fifteen years.

1162   "Hitchcock in 1976." <u>Take One</u> 5, no. 2 (May):43-44.
        The preface to the new edition of Truffaut's book on
      Hitchcock.

1163   "Pourquoi ce film? Pourquoi pas?" <u>L'Avant-Scène du Cinéma</u>,
      no. 165 (Jan.):4.
        Brief introduction to <u>Adèle H.</u>

1164   "Le Soleil de Jean-Pierre Aumont." <u>Une Semaine de Paris--</u>
      <u>Pariscop</u>, no. 405 (25 Feb.-2 Mar.):6-7.
        Appraisal of Aumont's book, with most of the points in-
      corporated into the introduction to the American edition
      (see entry 1166).

<u>1977</u>

1165   "Citizen Kane, An Appreciation." In <u>The Greatest American</u>
      <u>Films</u> [commemorative book by The American Film Institute on
      its tenth anniversary]. Washington, D.C., no page numbers.

1977

> A "total" film: "psychological, sociological, poetic, political, dramatic, comic, baroque." It is also "a great 'radiophonic' film. Each scene is founded upon a conception of sound and has a distinct tonality."

1166　Foreword to Sun and Shadow, by Jean-Pierre Aumont. New York: W. W. Norton & Co., pp. 13-14.
> Aumont is promoted as a witty, mischievous writer of the "antisolemn school" of Guitry, Lubitsch, Renoir, and David Niven. Taken from Une Semaine de Paris--Pariscop (see entry 1164).

1167　"François Truffaut." In The Films of Frank Capra, by Victor Scherle and William Turner Levy. Secaucus, N.J.: Citadel Press.
> Mentions the filmmakers Capra influenced and "the secrets of the commedia dell'arte that he brought to Hollywood." In FMV.

1168　"Un Homme comme les autres, Charlie Chaplin." Le Monde, no. 10235 (27 Dec.):15.
> Makes extensive use of Chaplin's autobiography to eulogize him.

1169　"A Kind Word for Critics." Harper's 255, no. 1529 (Oct.):95-96.
> Adapted from FMV. Truffaut believes American film critics are better than French ones and notes that they have been more positive about his films. He then provides reason why films are better understood outside their own countries.

*1170　"Pour Bresson: Haute fidélité sur longue durée ou Le Diable probablement . . . est un film voluptueux." Une Semaine de Paris--Pariscope (6 July).
> Reference provided by Truffaut.

*1171　"Roberto Rossellini est mort." Le Matin de Paris (4 June).
> Reference provided by Truffaut.

1172　"Sacha Guitry, cinéaste." In Le Cinéma et moi, by Sacha Guitry. Edited by André Bernard and Claude Gauteur. Paris: Éditions Ramsay, pp. 13-22.
> Truffaut here provides the preface to a collection of essays by Guitry. In it he comments on Guitry's transition from stage to screen. He compares Guitry to Welles in his use of sound and to Chaplin in his stories of survival and individualism. Most of article is given over to Roman d'un tricheur, his masterpiece.

1978

1978

*1173   "Woody Allen: 'Le Pessimiste gai.'" Une Semaine de Paris--
         Pariscop (7 Sept.).
              Reference provided by Truffaut.

1174   Foreword to Orson Welles: A Critical View, by André Bazin.
         Translated by Jonathan Rosenbaum. New York: Harper & Row,
         pp. 1-27.
              A rambling discourse on Welles, who is compared to
         Chaplin (both make films that are "subterranean autobiogra-
         ph[ies]"), called a film poet in spite of himself. His con-
         ception of film is musical; in his "right-handed films"
         there is always snow, and in his "left-handed" ones always
         gunshots. There is no forward in the 1972 French edition
         of this book.

1175   "Foreword: 'Yes, We Miss André Bazin.'" In André Bazin, by
         Dudley Andrew. London and New York: Oxford University
         Press, pp. vii-xi.
              Brief tribute to Bazin as "écrivain de cinéma," teacher,
         foster father, almost a brother, and altruist. Dated Dec.
         1977.

*1176   "La Genie de Sacha Guitry." Program for Mon pere avait raison.
         Theatre Hebertot (May).
              Reference provided by Truffaut.

1177   "Jean Renoir, quatre-vingts ans d'étounements." Le Nouvel
         Observateur, no. 695 (4-10 Mar.):74-76.
              A review of Renoir's novel, Le Coeur à l'aise, which be-
         gins and ends with description of Renoir's life in Hollywood
         and pivots on the idea that "those who know his work, know
         him."

1178   "Lubitsch Was a Prince." Translated by Annette Insdorf.
         American Film 3, no. 7 (May):55-57.
              Reprint of Cahiers du Cinéma article (see entry 1098).

1179   "What's the Score? The Best of the Decade." Compiled by
         James Monaco. Take One 6, no. 8 (July):26-29, 45.
              Truffaut, as one of "20 leading film critics," picks
         the ten best American and European films of the 1970s.
         His list is sometimes idiosyncratic and sometimes conven-
         tional.

1979

1979

*1180   "Children Are Born Actors." UNESCO Courier 32 (May):13-14.
         Reference provided by Truffaut.

1181   "Hitchcock--His True Power Is Emotion." New York Times
         (4 Mar.):sec. 2, pp. 1, 19.
              Extended remarks on the occasion of the American Film
         Institute's presentation of its Life Achievement Award to
         Hitchcock. What distinguishes Hitchcock is his "rigorously
         masterful 'mise-en-scène,'" which is "less a question of
         technique [which his imitators can master] than of écriture,
         a personal means of expression." Little that is new.

1182   "My Friend Hitchcock." Translated by Annette Insdorf.
         American Film 4, no. 5 (Mar.):24-25.
              Shortened version of the preface to the new English edi-
         tion of Truffaut's Hitchcock (see entry 474), the central
         part of which is a recounting of the Lincoln Center tribute
         to Hitchcock.

*1183   Preface to The Book of the Cinema, by Mitchell Beazley.
         London: Artists House, 456 pp.
              Reference provided by Truffaut.

*1183a   Preface to Un Homme à la caméra by Nestor Almendros. Collection
         Bibliotheque du Cinéma; serie "Ma vie de . . . . " Paris:
         Hatier/Cinq Continents, 192 pp.
              Reference provided by Truffaut.

*1183b   "Preface: Les espadrilles de William Irish" to La Toile de
         l'araignée, by William Irish. Edited by Marc A. Michaud.
         Paris: Les Éditions Pierre Belfond. Collection: Les
         Portes de la nuit.
              Reference provided by Truffaut.

UNDATED REVIEWS AND ESSAYS

(Reprinted in FMV; specific dates unknown.)

*1184   "Jacques Becker." Cinéma 61 (1961).

*1185   "Les Vierges." Lui (1965).
              A film by Jean-Pierre Mocky.

*1186   "Le Cinéma de papa." Une Semaine de Paris--Pariscop (1971).
              A film by Claude Berri.

*1187   "Cette tête de lard de Gérard Blain." <u>Une Semaine de Paris--</u>
       <u>Pariscop</u> (1972).
          On <u>Les Amis</u>.

*1188   "Les Gants blancs du diable." <u>Une Semaine du Paris--Pariscop</u>
       (1973).
          A film by Laszlo Szabo.

*1189   "<u>Vincent, François, Paul, et les autres</u>." <u>Une Semaine du</u>
       <u>Paris--Pariscop</u> (1974).
          A film by Claude Sautet. Reprinted in <u>L'Avant-Scène</u>
       (see entry 1144).

PROGRAMS AND BULLETINS TO WHICH TRUFFAUT CONTRIBUTED

*1189a   Jean Renoir and Sacha Guitry. Annecy Homage (Feb. 1965).
       Marie Dubois. Programme du Theatre Antoine ("Jessica") (1966).
       Georges Sadoul. Pamphlet by L'Association française des
         critiques (Oct. 1967).
       Jean Renoir. Festival, Maison de la culture de Vidauban (1967).
       Michel Simon. Retrospective, Museum of Modern Art, New York
         (Feb. 1968).
       Luis Buñuel. Festival, Ciné-club de la Victorine (1971).
       Jacques Audiberti. Programme de Theatre de la Cothurne in
         Lyon ("Marechal") (1973).
       Jean-Pierre Melville. New York Film Festival (Sept. 1974).
       Jean-Claude Brialy. Programme du Theatre Marigny ("La Puce a
       l'oreille") (undated).
         Reference provided by Truffaut.

VI. Interviews with François Truffaut

1959

1190 BABY, YVONNE. "Les Quatre Cents Coups: Une Chronique de
      l'adolescence nous dit François Truffaut." Le Monde
      (21 Apr.):12.
          How the film originated and was developed, plus the auto-
      biographical and cinematic influences.

1191 BILLARD, PIERRE. "Les 400 Coups du pere François." Cinéma 59,
      no. 37 (June):24-29, 136-37.
          About children in films, Moussy's contribution, other
      influential films.

1192 "François Truffaut." Radio-Cinéma-Télévision, no. 470
      (18 Jan.):4-5.
          Four brief answers to questions on filmmaking.

*1193 [Interview]. Ciné-Revue 39, no. 20 (May).
          On 400 Blows. Listed in Collet (see entry 365).

1194 LEGER, GUY. "Entretien sur le cinéma. Avec François Truffaut
      et Jacques Rivette." Signes du Temps, no. 12 (Dec.):33-38.
          Rivette answers the more theoretical and abstract ques-
      tions (on the relationship of ethics and film), while
      Truffaut handles the more concrete ones (how the term New
      Wave originated, what young filmmakers have in common, the
      unique problems he faces on his second film).

1195 MANCEAUX, MICHÈLE. "François Truffaut." L'Express (23 Apr.).
          An excellent source of information on Truffaut's youth,
      his rescue by Bazin, and his first films. Translated in
      Denby's edition of the script of The 400 Blows (see entries
      447 and 1195).

1196 PARINAUD, ANDRÉ. "Truffaut: 'Le Jeune Cinéma n'existe pas.'"
      Arts, no. 720 (29 Apr.-5 May):1, 9.
          What unites young French filmmakers? Pinball machines,

1959

freedom in making films, the importance of characters and subjects over techniques. Truffaut also comments on location shooting, cinemascope, nontheatrical dialogue, and the three stages of film history. He ends by talking about the making of 400 Blows. An essential interview. Reprinted in The 400 Blows (see entry 1308).

1197 REY, PIERRE. "Avec Les 400 Coups François Truffaut a toujours les dents longues." Paris-Journal (5 May):6.
Truffaut to pursue filmmaking with the same passion he had as a critic.

1198 S[ADOUL], G[EORGES]. "'Je crois à l'improvisation.'" Les Lettres Françaises, no. 775 (28 May-3 June):1, 6.
Truffaut is just one of several young directors asked to comment under the heading "Les Jeunes Turcs crèvent l'écran." He talks about the differences among young filmmakers, his debt to de Broca and Decae in The 400 Blows, as well as Hitchcock's and Renoir's influence on specific scenes in the film, and on his reading material. Excerpted in Lherminier's L'Art du cinéma (see entry 1054).

1199 TREMOIS, CLAUDE-MARIE. "François Truffaut . . ." Radio-Cinéma-Télévision, no. 507 (4 Oct.):2-3, 54.
Interview about Breathless: Godard's techniques, what the film is about, Truffaut's part (admittedly "minimum").

1200 WILDENSTEIN, PIERRE. "Conversation avec François Truffaut." Télé-Ciné, no. 83 (June-July):2-8.
On The 400 Blows, previous work (especially The Mischief Makers), and other directors (Chabrol, Resnais, Tati, Bergman, Cocteau).

1960

1201 ANON. "The Talk of the Town." New Yorker 36, no. 1 (20 Feb.): 36-37.
Amiable conversation, the first of five over the years, about childhood, The 400 Blows, and a proposed film on conflict among teachers.

1202 ARCHER, EUGENE. "'Enfant Terrible': Delinquent to Director." New York Times (31 Jan.):sec. 2, p. 7.
Biographical material plus mention of Truffaut's antagonism to montage in favor of packing contrasting images into each shot; his belief that "cinema is an intellectual medium"; Shoot the Piano Player will be about "involvement"; a director's career is a lifetime diary.

1961

1203   BABY, YVONNE. "J'ai voulu traiter <u>Tirez sur le pianiste</u> à la
manière d'un conte de Perrault." <u>Le Monde</u> (24 Nov.).
     The film is a reaction against certain detective films
and an homage to others, unified by theme of love. Two
kinds of filmmkers: those who think about public and those
who do not. Translated in <u>Focus on "Shoot the Piano Player"</u>
(see entries 239 and 1348).

*1204   [Interview]. <u>Definition</u>, no. 1 (Feb.):27-29.
     Listed in the BFI card files.

1205   MARCORELLES, LOUIS. "Crest of the Wave." <u>London Observer</u>
(13 Mar.).
     On critics in United States and France, on <u>Shoot the
Piano Player</u>, low budgets, and improvisation.

1206   MORGENSTERN, JOE. "'Adolsecence Is Only a Bad Moment to Get
Through'--François Truffaut." <u>New York Herald Tribune</u>
(31 Jan).
     On <u>The 400 Blows</u>.

1207   "Tomorrow--The Artists." <u>Films and Filming</u> 7, no. 1 (Oct.):17.
     Responses to four questions: on qualities needed by a
director ("sensitivity, intuition, good taste, and intelligence"), on nonprofessional actors, on possibilities for
the New Wave, and on needs of the French film industry.

1208   WINSTEN, ARCHER. "Rages and Outrages." <u>New York Post</u>
(25 Jan.).
     Revealing remarks on the opening and closing sequences
of <u>The 400 Blows</u>. Best film ever: <u>St. Francis</u> by
Rossellini. Best American director: Edgar Ulmer.

1961

1209   "François Truffaut réalisateur." <u>Télé-Ciné</u>, no. 94 (Mar.).
     A long (ten-page) interview that is short on specifics
and long on generalities about the New Wave, on changing
from a critic to a director, on being an auteur.

*1210   GRAHAM, PETER. "Conversations with François Truffaut."
<u>Granta</u> 65, no. 1211 (Oct.):9-13.
     Listed in <u>French xx Bibliography</u>.

*1211   [Interview]. <u>France-Film Cinéma Nouveau</u>, no. 9 (Feb.).
     On general matters. Listed in Collet (see entry 365).

1212   MARCORELLES, LOUIS. "Cinéma-spectacle ou cinéma-langage."

1961

> France Observateur, no. 598 (19 Oct.):26-27.
> Hardly a wasted word here. Truffaut talks about the
> New Wave, but emphasizes its flaws. He divides filmmakers
> into two groups, namely, followers of Lumiere and Delluc;
> he also delineates three "tendencies": à la Sagan, Queneau,
> and "le cinéma Éditions de Minuit." This interview also
> contains his famous remark that cinema is a circus, with
> the distinction made between the cinema of compromise and
> that of concession. There are comments on why he does not
> film current events or workers. Translated in Sight and
> Sound (see entry 1227).

1213   "Questions à l'auteur." Cinéma 61, no. 52 (Jan.):7-11.
> How Shoot the Piano Player is different from The 400
> Blows; it is an "explosion of a genre" and a "respectful
> pastiche of the Hollywood B-films." Truffaut heatedly ex-
> presses his contempt for great subjects, in the process
> putting down Stanley Kramer and Autant-Lara. Reprinted in
> Braudy's Focus on "Shoot the Piano Player" (see entries 239
> and 1361).

*1214   RODE, HENRI. [Interview]. Cinémonde, no. 1421 (31 Oct.):8.
> Listed in L'Avant-Scène du Cinéma (see entry 449).

1962

1215   AJAME, PIERRE. "François Truffaut: Du terrorisme à
> l'autodafé." Les Nouvelles Littéraires, no. 1837 (15 Nov.):
> 12.
> Title irrelevant to interview, which is a conversation
> that begins with Truffaut's youthful film experiences,
> moves through his years as a critic, and deals with some of
> the things that went into the making of A Visit, The Mischief
> Makers, his first three feature films, and plans to make
> Fahrenheit 431 [sic].

1216   BABY, YVONNE. "Un entretien avec François Truffaut. . . ."
> Le Monde, no. 5294 (24 Jan.):12.
> What attracted him to the novel Jules and Jim, ideas
> about adapting it into a "filmed book," the theme, this
> film as a synthesis of past work.

1217   B[ILLARD], P[IERRE]. "En attendant Jules et Jim." Cinéma 62,
> no. 62 (Jan.):4-13.
> Truffaut describes his steps from reading Roché's book
> to making the film, its good points, its dominant feature
> (characters rather than story or setting), and how and why
> the actors were chosen. More generally, he turns against

the auteur theory and reveals why (he lists the helpers he
has relied upon in each of his films).

1218   COLLET, JEAN and four others. "Entretien avec François
        Truffaut." Cahiers du Cinéma 23, no. 138 (Dec.):40–59.
            A famous interview in which Truffaut expounds on the New
        Wave, its accomplishments, current problems, and hetero-
        geneity; on American films and on his own work as a director
        and critic. Reprinted in Graham's The New Wave (1968),
        Braudy's Focus on "Shoot the Piano Player" (1972), and in
        Film Quarterly (Fall 1963); see entries 239, 1235, 1290,
        and 1355.

1219   CUKIER, DAN A., and GRYN, JO. "Entretien avec François
        Truffaut." Script, no. 5 (Apr.):5–15.
            On Shoot the Piano Player and Jules and Jim, on feeling
        the life in a book or script, on Jeanne Moreau, Hitchcock,
        and Renoir and their strengths. Translated in Focus on
        "Shoot the Piano Player" (see entries 239 and 1354).

1220   FRANCHI, R. M., and LEWIS, MARSHALL. "Conversations with
        François Truffaut." New York Film Bulletin 3, no. 3,
        issue 44 (Summer):16–25.
            A valuable two-part interview contrasting "the French
        tradition of quality" with the politique des auteurs.
        Renoir is used to demonstrate the politique. The stages
        in a director's career are sketched. Part two begins with
        a contrast of popular and nonpopular directors and focuses
        on Shoot the Piano Player and Jules and Jim. Part one re-
        printed in Film Journal (see entry 1221) and in Sarris'
        Interviews with Film Directors (see entry 1278).

1221   FRANCHI, R. M., and LEWIS, MARSHALL. "Conversation with
        Truffaut." Film Journal (Apr.):37–39.
            Reprint of the first conversation from New York Film
        Bulletin (Summer 1962), see entry 1220.

1222   "François Truffaut." In Film Book 2: Films of Peace and War.
        Edited by Robert Hughes. New York: Grove Press, pp. 189–91.
            Truffaut is one of many filmmakers who respond to ques-
        tions on the most effective war/peace films (he terms Night
        and Fog "the greatest film ever made") and on what films
        need to be made (he proposes one on a deserter).

*1223   [Interview]. Film Ideal, no. 92 (15 Mar.):167–69.
            Listed in the BFI card files.

*1224   [Interview]. Télécinéma, no. 94.
            On general matters. Listed in Collet (see entry 365).

1962

*1225   [Interview]. <u>Télé-Sept Jours</u> (27 Jan.-2 Feb.).
        On general matters. Listed in Collet (see entry 365).

1226   "<u>Jules and Jim</u>: Sex and Life." <u>Films and Filming</u> 8, no. 10
       (July):19.
        About the accomplishments of the New Wave, how he himself
       makes a film, why he dislikes "social cinema," how he is
       concerned about audience reaction--especially in dealing
       with sex.

1227   MARCORELLES, LOUIS. "Interview with Truffaut." <u>Sight and</u>
       <u>Sound</u> 31, no. 1 (Winter):35-37, 48.
        Reprinted from <u>France Observateur</u> (see entry 1212).

1228   MARDORE, MICHEL. "Les Aveux de Jekyll Truffaut." <u>Les Lettres</u>
       <u>Françaises</u>, no. 911 (25-31 Jan.):1, 6.
        Interesting (negative) reappraisals of <u>The Mischief</u>
       <u>Makers</u> and <u>The 400 Blows</u>--what is wrong with them and how
       he would do them now. Valuable also for revelation that
       style for him is "empirical," that is, dependent on econom-
       ics.

1229   "Rendez-vous avec François Truffaut." <u>Unifrance Film</u>, no.
       208:157.
        Answers to two questions: on what made him choose <u>Jules</u>
       <u>and Jim</u> as a film project and what it has in common with his
       previous work.

*1230   RODE, HENRI. [Interview]. <u>Cinémonde</u>, no. 1450 (22 May).
        Listed in <u>L'Avant-Scène du Cinéma</u> (see entry 449).

1231   "Trois points d'economie." <u>Cahiers du Cinéma</u> 23, no. 138
       (Dec.):85-100.
        Truffaut is one of several people who comment on the cur-
       rent state of the French film industry. Most notable for
       his opinion that "a critic should not so much judge as de-
       scribe, not so much praise and blame as explain."

<u>1963</u>

1232   BELLOUR, RAYMOND, and MICHAUD, JEAN. "François Truffaut: <u>La</u>
       <u>Peau douce</u> donnera de l'amour une image anti-poétique."
       <u>Les Lettres Françaises</u>, no. 1000 (24-30 Oct.):25.
        On general matters, though <u>Soft Skin</u> (which Truffaut sees
       as "a polemical response" to <u>Jules and Jim</u>) does get some
       space. Truffaut admits he is not as doctrinaire as he was
       and prefers "contrary" directors. He contrasts French and
       American films and situates himself as a director.

1964

*1233   COLLET, JEAN. [Entretien]. Télérama, no. 630:6-7, 29-30.
        Listed in Collet (see entry 365).

1234   MANCEAU, MICHÈLE. "L'Homme de nulle part." L'Express
        (24 Jan.).
            Truffaut talks about Aznavour and Shoot the Piano Player.

1235   RONDER, PAUL. "François Truffaut--An Interview." Film
        Quarterly 17, no. 1 (Fall):3-13.
            Translated and condensed reprint of interview from
        Cahiers du Cinéma (see entry 1218).

                        1964

1236   ANON. "The Talk of the Town." New Yorker 40, no. 37
        (31 Oct.):45-46.
            An interview in which Truffaut talks about the Hitchcock
        book, about Soft Skin, and about the fact that he prefers
        Love at Twenty to his other feature films.

1237   BABY, YVONNE. "Entretien avec François Truffaut, réalisateur
        de La Peau douce." Le Monde, no. 6018 (22 May):14.
            On the factual aspects of the film (the characters are
        based on Pierre Jaccoud and Linda Baud; the ending of the
        film is modelled on their story). Soft Skin contrasted to
        Jules and Jim.

1238   BILLARD, PIERRE. "François Truffaut: Voix Off." Cinéma 64,
        no. 86 (May):36-45; no. 87 (June):64-73; no. 89 (Sept.):
        40-49.
            The first systematic and comprehensive questioning of
        Truffaut on the various stages in filmmaking from inspira-
        tion and influences to distribution of films. The first
        part deals with the starting points of his films, the adap-
        tation process (in writing, it is easier to invent than
        adapt; in directing, it is exactly the opposite), collabora-
        tion, the guiding principle in each film, and matching wits
        with the audience. Number 87 covers practical matters:
        location shooting, editing, and music. In number 89,
        Truffaut acknowledges his specific debts to Renoir,
        Rossellini, Buñuel, and especially Hitchcock. He concludes
        by spelling out how his films are reactions to other films
        (including his own) and what is important about settings
        in his films. Translated into German in Wie sie filmen
        (see entry 1254). Excerpted and translated into English
        in entry 1250.

1239   CADIEU, MARTINE. "François Truffaut: 'Je commence ma

1964

carrière.'" Les Nouvelles Littéraires, no. 1916 (21 May): 12.

Soft Skin is not about adultery but about a very weak man and about love—as with all Truffaut's films. The film's ending is also explained.

1240 GELMIS, JOSEPH. "New Wave Is Not Old Hat: Truffaut." Newsday (11 Nov.).

Truffaut's comments here are already "old hat."

1241 HALE, WANDA. "Accent on Realism." New York Daily News (19 Oct.).

On Soft Skin and other projects.

*1242 [Interview]. Cinématographie Française, no. 2062 (25 Apr.).

On Soft Skin. Listed in Collet (see entry 365).

*1243 [Interview]. Télérama, no. 733.

Listed in Collet (see entry 365).

*1244 LABRO, PHILIPPE. [Interview]. Lui, no. 9 (Sept.).

Listed in L'Avant-Scène du Cinéma (see entry 449).

1245 MANCEAUX, MICHÈLE. "Les Entre-Deux de l'adultère." L'Express (14 May):29-30.

Truffaut explains why Soft Skin is good. He talks about the characters, especially Pierre, and the attacks on the film by critics (because the film has little dialogue).

1246 MITHOIS, MARCEL. "François Truffaut." Réalités, no. 220 (May):68-70.

One of the better sources of information on Truffaut's youth. Also covered: what he was attempting to do in his first four films.

1247 RODE, HENRI. "Qui êtes-vous François Truffaut?" Cinémonde, no. 1554 (19 May).

Short, almost curt answers to about two dozen questions. Interesting only for his comments that he wishes to make a big budget film and to do nothing but discuss, watch, and make films.

1248 TILLIER, MAURICE. "François Truffaut veut rehabiliter Hitchcock." Le Figaro Littéraire, no. 948 (18-24 June):9.

Predictable interview on Soft Skin, plans for Fahrenheit 451, and publication of Hitchcock book.

1249 WARREN, JEAN-PAUL, and LEFÈVRE, RAYMOND. "A bout de souffle." Image et Son: Revue du Cinéma, nos. 176-177 (Sept.-Oct.): 3-8.

1966

Truffaut is quoted from a <u>Radio-Cinéma-Télévision</u> broadcast of 4 Oct. 1959 on his script for <u>Breathless</u> and on Godard's new style of filmmaking, its spontaneity, rapid shooting, and elliptical editing. (Also contains credits, plot summary of the film, and a brief analysis, plus biography of Godard.)

1965

1250   BILLARD, PIERRE. "From Critic to Director." <u>Atlas</u> 10, no. 3 (Sept.):178-83.
       Excerpted and translated by Heather Gordon-Horwood from interviews in <u>Cinéma 64</u> (see entry 1238).

1251   "Sept questions aux cinéastes." <u>Cahiers du Cinéma</u>, nos. 161-162 (Jan.):59-60.
       Sixty-six filmmakers questioned about production conditions in France. Truffaut criticizes Malraux's ignorance of the problems of filmmakers.

1966

1252   ARBOIS, JANICK. "François Truffaut ou l'amour du cinéma." <u>Télérama</u>, no. 865 (14-20 Aug.):59-61.
       Excerpts from a television program, "François Truffaut ou l'esprit critique," on his viewing, criticizing, and making films.

1253   BABY, YVONNE. "Entretien avec François Truffaut à propos de <u>Fahrenheit 451</u>; Un Problème de dosage entre le quotidien et l'extraordinaire." <u>Le Monde</u>, no. 6744 (18-19 Sept.):18.
       On the lengthy trials and tribulations of making the film, the primacy of its visual impact, and how it compares to others.

1254   BILLARD, PIERRE. "François Truffaut." In <u>Wie sie filmen</u>. Edited by Ulrich Gregor. Gütersloh: Siegbert Mohn Verlag, pp. 138-87.
       Reprint of interviews from <u>Cinéma 64</u>, nos. 86, 87, and 89 (see entry 1238).

1255   CAPELLE, ANNE. "François Truffaut: Dans les prix, il y a toujours des injustices ou des malchances. . . ." <u>Arts-Loisirs</u>, no. 51 (14-20 Sept.):18-19.
       On the making of <u>Fahrenheit 451</u> from wish, to commitment, to delays and problems with Oscar Werner. New wrinkle: Truffaut's answers amplified by description of his behavior during the interview.

1966

1256   CEZAN, CLAUDE. "'La Musique au cinéma n'est pas un bouche-
        trou!' nous dit François Truffaut." Journal Musical
        Français, no. 150 (Sept.-Oct.):42-43.
            Truffaut does talk fleetingly about his first two films
        and offers Vigo's Atalante as the best film with music.
        Mostly a theoretical discussion.

1257   "Un Cinéaste: François Truffaut." Télé-Ciné, no. 128
        (May-June):13-15.
            Transcript of a television broadcast with the director
        during which Truffaut comments on directing, adapting, act-
        ing, and realism. Ends with this formula for his films:
        20 percent autobiography, 20 percent taken from newspapers,
        20 percent taken from the lives of acquaintances, 20 percent
        pure fiction [which equals only 80 percent].

1258   "Fahrenheit 451." Amis du Film et de la Télévision, no. 126
        (Nov.):4-6.
            Some production details. Science fiction elements played
        down.

1259   GILSON, RENÉ. "Truffaut: Comment j'ai pu faire le film
        impossible." Paris-Match, no. 912 (1 Oct.):100-101.
            Truffaut talks about Ray Bradbury, about meeting him,
        and about some of the ideas he had in making Bradbury's
        book (Fahrenheit 451) a film.

*1260   de GIVRAY, CLAUDE. "Une Choix de textes de Truffaut." Cinéma
        et Télé-Cinéma, no. 341 (Oct.).
            Listed in Collet (see entry 365).

*1261   [Interview]. Art et Essai, no. 7 (Feb.):56-58; no. 8 (Mar.):
        55-58; no. 9 (Apr.):57-58.
            A three-part interview listed in the BFI card files.

*1262   [Interview]. Jeunesse Cinéma, no. 13
            On Fahrenheit 451. Listed in Collet (see entry 365).

1263   JAMET, DOMINIQUE. "Un Bradbury signé Truffaut." Le Figaro
        Littéraire, no. 1063 (1 Sept.):13.
            Truffaut denies that Fahrenheit 451, his "toughest" film,
        is didactic, but draws a moral: "the books are the princi-
        pal characters; the film will be successful if audiences
        don't want to see the books die."

1264   LANGLEY, LEE. "François Truffaut: Filmstruck Truant."
        Manchester Guardian, no. 37229 (19 Mar.):7.
            On the set of Fahrenheit 451, Truffaut talks about his
        debt to Rossellini, his faults, and films about love.

1265 MARTIN, MARCEL. "De Venise à Paris François Truffaut: 'Il
suffit de montrer un livre qui brûle pour le faire aimer.'"
Les Lettres Françaises, no. 1148 (15-21 Sept.):18.
Brief points about the making of Fahrenheit 451--suppress-
ing the science fiction and polemical speeches, acknowledg-
ing 60 percent is Bradbury's.

1266 PHILIPPE, CLAUDE-JEAN. "François Truffaut: 'J'ai voulu faire
un film qui n'ait l'air de rien.'" Télérama, no. 872
(2-8 Oct.):72-73.
Opinions on pretentious science fiction and the various
stages in creating a film, related to Fahrenheit 451.

1267 STAKERLEE, NEAL. "Truffaut et les pompiers incendiares."
Arts-Loisirs, no. 23 (2-8 Mar.):7.
Truffaut talks about two kinds of science fiction, about
Fahrenheit 451, and the French Resistance, about three kinds
of attitudes toward books, and the difference between real-
ity and actuality.

1268 "Une Cinéaste: François Truffaut." Télé-Ciné, no. 128
(May-June):13-15.
Lengthy quotes taken from television program, in which
Truffaut talks about the film industry and about directing.

1269 WADDY, STACY. "Visite à François Truffaut." Midi-Minuit
Fantastique, nos. 15-16 (Dec.-Jan 1967):36-38.
On the making of Fahrenheit 451.

1967

1270 CAPDENAC, MICHEL. "Tour d'horizon avec François Truffaut:
Des 400 coups à La mariée était en noir." Les Lettres
Françaises, no. 1179 (20-26 Apr.):18.
On the changes just made in The Mischief Makers and The
400 Blows and on the three elements that attracted him to
Bride Wore Black: a splendid novel, Jeanne Moreau, and
other good actors.

1271 "Ce qu'a dit François Truffaut." Cinéma 67, no. 112 (Jan.):
38-51.
Truffaut talks about each of his films through Soft Skin
and a few of the other films included in the Annecy homage
to him. Of particular interest are his remarks on Shoot
the Piano Player (the importance of casting Aznavour, the
influence of Audiberti and Johnny Guitar, and the idea of
mixing things), on the detached tone of Jules and Jim, and
on Soft Skin (the anachronistic protagonist, the fact that

1967

this film contradicts the exalted romanticism of Jules and Jim). Partially reprinted in Braudy's Focus on "Shoot the Piano Player" (see entries 239 and 1347).

1272 [COMOLLI, JEAN-LOUIS, and NARBONI, JEAN]. "Entretien avec François Truffaut." Cahiers du Cinéma, no. 190 (May):20-31, 69-70.
Much of this is given over to directors Truffaut likes (Berri, Resnais, Buñuel, Welles, Godard, Hawks, Wilder, Bergman, Rohmer, Hitchcock, and Renoir) and dislikes (Huston especially, plus Stevens, Wyler, and Zinneman) and why. Truffaut defends the New Wave, provides examples of some of the controlling ideas in his films, talks about working in England on Fahrenheit 451, and gives many insights into his films. One of his richest interviews.

1273 JACOB, GILLES. "François Truffaut et la mariée." Cinéma 67, no. 121 (Dec.):32-39.
Hardly a wasted word in this interview on The Bride Wore Black, which is compared to The 400 Blows; Truffaut explains why and how he chose and changed the novel, and why it is not as Hitchcockian as Fahrenheit 451 and Soft Skin.

1274 _____. "Truffaut's Bride Wore Black." Sight and Sound 36, no. 4 (Autumn):164-66.
The film is not psychological, not a portrait of woman. Comparisons made to earlier films.

*1275 KUMMER, ELKE, and ENGEL, ANDI. "Entretien avec François Truffaut." Kino (West Berlin), no. 4.
Listed in Gregor et al. bibliography (see entry 291).

1276 LENNON, PETER. "The Cinema according to Truffaut." Manchester Guardian (27 June):5.
Quick sketch of Truffaut's career and life on the set of Bride Wore Black, followed by a short interview on his own failures and those of others, on actors, rehearsing, and being an asocial filmmaker.

*1277 RODE, HENRI. [Interview]. Cinémonde, no. 1712 (26 Sept.).
Listed in L'Avant-Scène du Cinéma (see entry 449).

1278 SARRIS, ANDREW. Interviews with Film Directors. New York: Avon Books, 557 pp.
Reprints interview with Truffaut by R. M. Franchi and Marshall Lewis from the New York Film Bulletin (see entry 1220) and Truffaut's interview with Howard Hawks from Cahiers du Cinéma (see entry 790).

1279   "Truffaut: 'J'ai hésité huit ans avant de livrer au public les 8 minutes secrètes des 400 coups.'" France-Soir (7 Apr.).

        The interview, on the release of the re-edited version of The 400 Blows, is not much longer than the title.

1968

*1280   AJAME, PIERRE. [Interview]. Le Nouvel Adam, no. 19 (Feb.).

        Listed in bibliography in L'Avant-Scène du Cinéma (see entry 449).

1281   BABY, YVONNE. "Entretien avec François Truffaut: Le Mariée était en noir est un film de pur sentiment." Le Monde, no. 7236 (18 Apr.):15.

        On the differences between book and film, his deliberate avoidance of the enigma of a Hitchcock film, and his equally deliberate use of simple and straightforward plot to give it a fairy-tale quality. Also on the moral of the film and the similarities between his "tenacious and purposeful" heroines.

1282   BILLARD, PIERRE; COLLANGE, CHRISTIANE; and VEILLOT, CLAUDE. "François Truffaut." L'Express, no. 883 (20–26 May):148–49, 151, 153, 155–58, 160, 162, 164, 169–70, 175–76, 178, 183–84, 186.

        A long and revealing interview during which Truffaut discusses American B movies, his critical approaches to films, his attraction to love stories (can make same story over again with different actors), his aversion to theories and systems, and his preference for women.

1283   "Le Cinéma et l'état." Cahiers du Cinéma, nos. 200–201 (Apr.–May):73–93.

        Several filmmakers questioned. Truffaut is surprisingly harsh about oppressive government.

*1284   "Le Cinéma: François Truffaut raconte." In Mai 68: Ce n'est qu'un debut, by Philippe Labro. Édition Speciale, Éditions et Publications Premières, no. 2. Paris: Denoel, pp. 148–51.

        Listed in L'Avant-Scène du Cinéma (see entry 449).

1285   COLLET, JEAN. "François Truffaut: La Mariée était en noir. C'est presque Blanche-Neige et les sept nains." Télérama, no. 954 (28 Apr.–4 May):57–59.

        On strong women and weak men, relative and absolute love, Truffaut's dream of "clandestine persuasion," and his attraction to Hitchcock.

1968

1286   HOVALD, PATRICE. "Le Beau Visage de François Truffaut."
          Séquences, no. 54 (Oct.):50-56.
              Covers the period between Fahrenheit 451 and The Bride
          Wore Black, but without any significant revelations.

*1287   [Interview]. Cinéma et Télé-cinéma, no. 422 (Oct.).
              On Stolen Kisses. Listed in Collet (see entry 365).

*1288   [Interview]. Journal du Dimanche (15-16 Sept.).
              On Stolen Kisses. Listed in Collet (see entry 365).

*1289   [Interview]. Photo, no. 11 (July-Aug.).
              Listed in Collet (see entry 365).

1290   "Interview with François Truffaut." In The New Wave: Critical
          Landmarks. Edited by Peter Graham. London: Secker &
          Warburg, pp. 9-15, 85-113.
              Reprinted from Cahiers du Cinéma (see entry 1218).

1291   JACOB, GILLES. "The 400 Blows of François Truffaut." Sight
          and Sound 37, no. 4 (Autumn):190-91.
              About his role in the shutdown of the Cannes Film
          Festival and other political events of the year. Truffaut
          confirms that he considers a filmmaker's concern with making
          money valid and necessary.

*1292   KLIEB, WERNER. "François Truffauts Rache für (Fahrenheit)."
          Film (West Germany), no. 5 (May):22-25.
              Interview and photo essay on Fahrenheit 451. Listed in
          International Index.

1293   LANGLOIS, GÉRARD. "La Vie en 24 images-seconds." Les Lettres
          Françaises, no. 1229 (10-16 Apr.):25, 28.
              Mostly on Bride Wore Black, though Truffaut does mention
          the changes he refused to make in Fahrenheit 451 and the
          hectic filming of Stolen Kisses. Best on what attracted
          him to the project and what it has in common with his other
          films (including The Mischief Makers).

1294   NUSSER, RICHARD. "An Interview with François Truffaut."
          After Dark (Aug.):25-27.
              On Bride Wore Black--especially the changes made from
          the book (the ending and the prudery).

*1295   "Reportage sur le tournage de La Sirène du Mississipi." Elle
          (Dec.):35-39.
              Listed in the bibliography in Collet (see entry 365).

1296   ROMI, YVETTE. "Portrait: Truffaut par Truffaut." Le Nouvel

Observateur, no. 200 (9-15 Sept.):52-54.
A rambling and multifaceted interview about filming
Stolen Kisses during "events of May," about summer camp and
the past, about choosing actors and working indirectly, and
about Welles and Godard.

1297   R[OULET], S[EBASTIAN]. "Baisers volés." Cahiers du Cinéma,
nos. 200-201 (Apr.-May):95-96.
A hurried interview about his busy days--politics in the
morning, filming afternoons. The improvisation and concrete-
ness of Stolen Kisses contrasted to abstractness of the rig-
orously prepared Fahrenheit 451. Also on the script, Léaud,
and Delphine Seyrig.

*1298   SAND, LUCE. [Interview]. Jeune Cinéma, no. 31 (May):9-15.
Mainly on Bride Wore Black. Listed in Fanne (see entry
248).

*1299   SOBIESKI, MONIQUE. [Interview]. Le Journal du Show-Business,
no. 2 (11 Oct.).
Listed in bibliography in L'Avant-Scène du Cinéma (see
entry 449).

1300   WINSTEN, ARCHER. "Rages and Outrages." New York Post
(22 July):30.
Mostly on Bride Wore Black and on not directing in
Hollywood.

1969

1301   BABY, YVONNE. "Le Recit d'une degradation par amour, d'une
passion." Le Monde, no. 7600 (21 June):15.
On Mississippi Mermaid as an adaptation (or, better, "a
choice of scenes"). Why he chose the book and the stars
and alluded to Johnny Guitar.

1302   "Ex-Critic Truffaut Analysis Crix . . ." Variety (30 July):2,
78.
Rationalizing the failure of Mississippi Mermaid.

1303   de GRAMONT, SANCHE. "Life Style of Homo Cinematicus." New
York Times (15 June):12-13, 34-44.
The longest and arguably the best profile of Truffaut in
English. Truffaut's own views (in an extended "monologue"
that comprises two-thirds of the piece) on his life as re-
flected in his films, on each of his films up to Stolen
Kisses, and on actors good and bad, contain little that is
new.

1969

*1304 [Interview]. Club-Inter (Dec.).
          On The Wild Child. Listed in Collet (see entry 365).

*1305 [Interview]. Film Ideal, nos. 220-222:23-72.
          Listed in BFI card files.

*1306 [Interview]. La Vie Catholique (Summer).
          On The Wild Child. Listed in Collet (see entry 365).

1307   MANCEAUX, MICHÈLE. "People: François Truffaut." In The 400
          Blows. Edited by David Denby. New York: Grove Press,
          pp. 215-23.
             Translated from L'Express (see entry 1195).

1308   PARINAUD, ANDRÉ. "Truffaut: 'The Young Cinema Doesn't Exist.'"
          In The 400 Blows. Edited by David Denby. New York: Grove
          Press, pp. 224-35.
             Translated from Arts (see entry 1196).

*1309 SOBIESKI, MONIQUE. [Interview]. Le Journal du Show-Business,
          no. 36 (27 June).
             Listed in bibliography in L'Avant-Scène du Cinéma (see
          entry 449).

1310   TALLENAY, JEAN-LOUIS. "Truffaut tourne L'Enfant sauvage."
          Télérama, no. 1028 (27 Sept.-4 Oct.):51-53.
             Less an interview than an article, with quotes inter-
          spersed, on why he made the film and played Itard.

*1311 THOMAS, PAUL. [Interview]. Elle (Aug.):42-47.
          On The Wild Child. Listed in Fanne (see entry 248).

1312   TILLIER, MAURICE. "Cette semaine . . . Viens voir le comédien."
          Le Figaro Littéraire, no. 1220 (6-12 Oct.):42.
             Brief interview on the making of and acting in Wild Child.

1313   _____. "Le Plus Sévère Critique de François Truffaut:
          François Truffaut." Le Figaro Littéraire, no. 1194
          (24-30 Mar.):32.
             On the relative failure of Bride Wore Black and Oscar
          possibilities for Stolen Kisses.

1314   TREMOIS, CLAUDE-MARIE. "François Truffaut parle de La Sirène
          du Mississipi." Télérama, no. 1013 (14-21 June):55-57.
             What attracted him to the project, why Belmondo character
          is not entirely a victim, and the fact that this is his
          first film truly to treat a couple.

1315   VEILLOT, CLAUDE. "Truffaut la tendresse apprivoise son

enfant-loup." L'Express, no. 945 (18-24 Aug.):42-43.
An interview on the set of The Wild Child.

1970

1316 ANON. "The Talk of the Town." New Yorker 46, no. 35
(17 Oct.):35-37.
Remarks on deaths of friends, tense social relationships
in France, and his preference for America because eating is
"less solemn here" and because Americans are "bigger" and
still believe in fair play.

1317 BENICHOU, PIERRE. "Truffaut chez les hommes." Le Nouvel
Observateur, no. 277 (2-8 Mar.):48-50, 52, 54, 56, 58.
Occasioned by the completion of The Wild Child, this interview deals only briefly with that film (why he filmed it
and played Itard). It is more about general career questions
and especially about Truffaut's politics. (Truffaut protests that he is apolitical, that he is a man of sensations,
not ideas.) Central section recounts some childhood feelings and incidents.

1318 BRAUCOURT, GUY. "Entretien avec François Truffaut." Cinéma
70, no. 150 (Nov.):134-38.
Primarily on Bed and Board and the many filmmakers who
have influenced him. Hitchcock (Dial M for Murder),
Lubitsch, Leo McCarey, Tati. Guitry is not a conscious influence here.

1319 _____. "François Truffaut: Moi et mon double." Les
Nouvelles Littéraires 48, no. 2242 (10 Sept.):1, 12.
On Stolen Kisses and Bed and Board: shooting them,
Lubitsch's influence, his scriptwriters' research, and his
antagonism to documentary.

1320 "Cinéastes de notre temps: François Truffaut." Télé-Ciné 23,
no. 160 (Mar.):34-42.
Transcription of a television program on Truffaut during
which he talks about approaches to filmmaking as illustrated
by his films from Fahrenheit 451 to Bed and Board.

1321 FLATLEY, GUY. "So Truffaut Decided to Work His Own Miracle."
New York Times (27 Sept.):13, 32.
An interview/article covering a wide variety of topics,
ranging from comments on the just-released The Wild Child
and The Miracle Worker; on his disdain for politics; on his
youth in Pigalle; on Godard; on Hollywood's lack of good
directors (Truffaut dislikes M*A*S*H, The Graduate, Bonnie

1970

and Clyde, and 2001); on hating Joseph Strick and being
bored by Vadim; and, finally and surprisingly, Truffaut
admits to liaison with Catherine Deneuve.

1322   "François Truffaut: Je crois comprendre 'Les enfants
        sauvages.'" Unifrance Film, no. 382:2090-91.
             Brief comments on the making of The Wild Child.

*1323   "François Truffaut ou le temps retrouvé." Cinémonde, no. 1844
        (Sept.):14-16.
             Listed in BFI card files.

1324   HASKELL, MOLLY. "A Declaration of Love." Village Voice 15,
        no. 16 (16 Apr.):57, 61, 63.
             A career overview based on a Paris interview about
        sources, themes, actors and actresses in his films, on the
        occasion of release of Mississippi Mermaid to unanimously
        negative French reviews.

1325   HOVALD, PATRICE. "François Truffaut m'a dit. . . ." Séquences
        12, no. 60 (Feb.):30-35.
             Covers activities of past two years on and off screen.

*1326   [Interview]. La Croix (4-5 Jan.).
             On The Wild Child. Listed in Collet (see entry 365).

*1327   [Interview]. Les Echoes (16 Mar.).
             On The Wild Child. Listed in Collet (see entry 365).

*1328   [Interview]. Photo, no. 33.
             On Bed and Board. Listed in Collet (see entry 365).

*1329   [Interview]. Pomme d'Api, no. 53.
             On The Wild Child. Listed in Collet (see entry 365).

*1330   [Interview]. Sandorama, no. 16.
             On The Wild Child. Listed in Collet (see entry 365).

*1331   [Interview]. Spirou, no. 1661 (12 Feb.).
             Cited by Isabelle Jordan in Positif (see entry 214).

*1332   [Interview]. La Vie Lyonnaise (Nov.).
             An excerpt from this appears in Cahiers du Cinéma (see
        entry 1343).

1333   LANGLOIS, GÉRARD. "Entretien. François Truffaut: Domicile
        conjugal ou les debuts de l'age adulte." Les Lettres
        Françaises, no. 1350 (9-15 Sept.):13.
             The most important part of this interview is Truffaut's

acknowledgment of the many similarities among his films, especially of the protagonists. He also explains the differences between this film and Stolen Kisses, the influence of Lubitsch and MacCarey, the asocial nature of Doinel.

1334   LOUBIERE, PIERRE; and SALACHAS, GILBERT. "François Truffaut: Libre cours." Télé-Ciné 23, no. 160 (Mar.):2-9.
         Not much that is specific, new, or useful here, except perhaps for ideas on interviews and choosing actors. Other ideas on politics, improvisation, adaptation, etc., expressed better elsewhere.

1335   MALCOLM, DEREK. "A Wild Boy Civilised." Manchester Guardian (19 Nov.):10.
         On The Wild Child.

1336   SIMSOLO, NOEL. "Entretien avec François Truffaut." Image et Son--Revue du Cinéma, no. 245 (Dec.):88-98.
         Truffaut talks about his reputation as a "bourgeois filmmaker," about the strong influence of Lubitsch and Cocteau, and about editing and rehearsing. Though specifically about Bed and Board, the interview ends with remarks on The Visit and Mississippi Mermaid. It also contains two of Truffaut's more revealing quotations--about life ("a trial which one comes to accept") and about creativity ("an artist has nothing to say; he must find something to say").

*1337   SOBIESKI, MONIQUE. [Interview]. Le Journal du Show-Business, no. 68 (20 Mar.).
         Listed in bibliography in L'Avant-Scène du Cinéma (see entry 449).

1338   SWEENEY, LOUISE. "Truffaut: 'Making Films Look Easy.'" Christian Science Monitor (16 Oct.):9.
         Career overview with emphasis on The Wild Child.

1339   TREMOIS, CLAUDE-MARIE. "Chez Truffaut tout part du coeur . . ." Télérama, no. 1045 (24-31 Jan.):58-59.
         Excerpts from a television program (transcripts of voice-over comments and quotations) on Truffaut and The Wild Child.

1971

1340   BABY, YVONNE. "'Si on n'aime pas entendre parler d'amour.'" Le Monde, no. 8356 (25 Nov.):17.
         About his adaptations in general (his model is Bresson's Diary of a Country Priest) and how Two English Girls contrasts with Jules and Jim in regard to love, characters,

1971

      and the things that influenced him (especially <u>Magnificent Ambersons</u>). Reprinted in <u>Atlas</u> (see entry 1349).

1341   BRAUCOURT, GUY. "François Truffaut: 'Roché était un Cocteau paysan.'" <u>Les Nouvelles Littéraires</u> 49, no. 2306 (3-9 Dec.):24-25.
      About Roché, his books and journal, and how Roché and Truffaut are similar and different.

1342   CHANCEL, JACQUES. "Truffaut: 'La Mauvaise Télé aide le bon cinéma.'" <u>Paris-Jour</u> (22-23 May):6.
      An article on the Cannes festival, which is mainly a conversation with Truffaut on the state of the industry.

1343   "Le Départ de F. Truffaut." <u>Cahiers du Cinéma</u>, nos. 226-227 (Jan.-Feb.):121.
      An explanation of his split with <u>Cahiers</u> excerpted from a longer interview in <u>La Vie Lyonnaise</u> (see entry 1332). Truffaut was listed as a member of the Editorial Committee from Nov. 1964 (issue no. 160) to July 1970 (issue no. 222).

1344   "François Truffaut tourne <u>Deux Anglaises et le continent</u>." <u>Télérama</u>, no. 1126 (14-21 Aug.):42-44.
      Truffaut responds in writing to seven questions on the contrasts to <u>Jules and Jim</u>, the use of Léaud, directing, auteur theory, and favorite recent films.

1345   SAMUELS, CHARLES THOMAS. "Talking with Truffaut." <u>American Scholar</u> 40, no. 3 (Summer):482-86.
      Excerpted from his book, <u>Encountering Directors</u> (see entry 1360).

1346   SOBIESKI, MONIQUE. "Cannes Seen by Truffaut." <u>Le Journal du Show-Business</u>, no. 10 (21 May):1.
      Semifavorable comments on the festival.

<u>1972</u>

1347   "Adapting <u>Shoot the Piano Player</u>." In <u>Focus on "Shoot the Piano Player</u>." Edited by Leo Braudy. Englewood Cliffs, N.J.: Prentice-Hall, pp. 123-26.
      Translated and excerpted from <u>Cinéma 67</u> (see entry 1271).

1348   BABY, YVONNE. "I Wanted to Treat <u>Shoot the Piano Player</u> like a Tale by Perrault: An Interview with François Truffaut." In <u>Focus on "Shoot the Piano Player"</u>. Edited by Leo Braudy. Englewood Cliffs, N.J.: Prentice-Hall, pp. 22-24.
      Translated from <u>Le Monde</u> (see entry 1203).

1349 ____. "A Physical Film about Love." Atlas 21, no. 2
    (Feb.):59-60.
        Translated from Le Monde (see entry 1340).

1350 BAIGNÈRES, CLAUDE. "Les Écrivains au secours des cinéastes
    français? Sept 'sages' de l'écran répondent." Le Figaro
    Littéraire, no. 1363 (1 July):13, 18.
        Seven people asked to comment on collaboration with
    great writers and dramatists as a possible solution to the
    crisis in filmmaking. Truffaut disagrees.

1351 BERNARD, LUC. "François Truffaut à Beziers." Technicien du
    Film, no. 191 (15 Mar.):29-31.
        An interview from the set of Gorgeous Kid.

1352 BEYLIE, CLAUDE. "Entretien avec le réalisateur: '. . . ma
    petite version des Hauts de Hurlevent.'" Écran 72 1
    (Jan.):6-10.
        About the changes he made, because of Roché's journals,
    in adapting Two English Girls, about Anne's death and Emily
    Brontë, about working against sentimentality, about Claude's
    neutral, aesthetic look, and about avoiding modern film de-
    vices in favor of imitating The Magnificent Ambersons.

1353 BOURLA, ALAIN. "Qu'attendez-vous des livres?" Les Lettres
    Françaises, no. 1443 (5 July):8.
        Truffaut is one of six celebrities asked about books.
    He talks about Roché and lists the eight writers he rereads.

1354 CUKIER, DAN A., and GRYN, JO. "A Conversation with François
    Truffaut." In Focus on "Shoot the Piano Player". Edited
    by Leo Braudy. Englewood Cliffs, N.J.: Prentice-Hall,
    pp. 12-21.
        Translated from Script (see entry 1219).

1355 "From an Interview with François Truffaut." In Focus on
    "Shoot the Piano Player". Edited by Leo Braudy. Englewood
    Cliffs, N.J.: Prentice-Hall, pp. 145-47.
        Translated and excerpted from Cahiers (see entry 1218).

1356 GOW, GORDON. "Intensification: François Truffaut in an
    Interview with Gordon Gow." Films and Filming 18, no. 10
    (July):18-22.
        An overview on Truffaut's "diverse" career and a specific
    look at Mississippi Mermaid, but valuable mainly for
    Truffaut's own words on his career, on Bazin, and on
    Hitchcock.

1357 HAYMAN, RONALD. "François Truffaut and Henri-Pierre Roché."

1972

Times Saturday Review (London) (12 Aug.):9.
    On Two English Girls as book and film.

*1358   PERRET, JACQUES. "Entretien avec François Truffaut."
        Télé-Médicine (8 Apr.).
            On Fahrenheit 451. Citation provided by Truffaut.

*1359   RAYNS, TONY. "Interview: François Truffaut." Cinema Rising
        2 (May).
            Listed in the bibliography in Monaco's The New-Wave
        (see entry 349).

1360   SAMUELS, CHARLES THOMAS. "François Truffaut." In
        Encountering Directors. New York: Putnam, pp. 33-55.
            Wide-ranging and complete; questions sometimes testy.
        Covers films individually through Bed and Board, with more
        general issues such as adaptation, music, acting, directing
        by contradiction, and focusing on "units of emotion." Ex-
        cerpted in American Scholar (see entry 1345).

1361   "Should Films Be Politically Committed?" In Focus on "Shoot
        the Piano Player". Edited by Leo Braudy. Englewood Cliffs,
        N.J.: Prentice-Hall, pp. 133-37.
            Translated from Cinéma 61 (see entry 1213).

1362   THOMAS, PASCAL. "François Truffaut, propos." Cinéma 72, no.
        162 (Jan.):135.
            A condensed interview about Truffaut's five central
        ideas in Two English Girls.

1363   TREMOIS, CLAUDE-MARIE. "En regardant tourner François
        Truffaut." Télérama, no. 1160 (8-15 Apr.):56-61 and no.
        1161 (5-22 Apr.):54-56.
            A two-part article on the shooting of Such a Gorgeous
        Kid, describing what happens on the set, and containing an
        interview with Truffaut (especially in the second part) on
        what he is doing and why.

*1364   "Truffaut Talks about a Gorgeous Girl." Continental Film
        Review (June):14-15, 24.
            Listed in the card files of the British Film Institute
        (see entry 1509).

1973

1365   ANON. "The Talk of the Town." New Yorker 49, no. 34
        (15 Oct.):34-35.
            Casual conversations with Truffaut about English lessons
        and Watergate-watching on television.

1366   BABY, YVONNE. "Le Cinéma est'il plus important que la vie?"
        Le Monde, no. 8815 (18 May):25.
                Six reasons for making Day for Night, plus ways in which
        Truffaut resembles Ferrand, the fact that he likes films
        like "Meet Pamela," and was bucking auteur fashion.

1367   BEYLIE, CLAUDE. "Entretien avec François Truffaut." Écran 73,
        no. 17 (July-Aug.):69-71.
                Starts with remarks on Two English Girls and Such a
        Gorgeous Kid, which Day for Night synthesizes. Continues
        on the themes, the starting point, and the film-within-a-
        film in Day for Night.

1368   CARROLL, KATHLEEN. "The Cinema World of François Truffaut."
        New York Daily News (21 Oct.):7.
                On his development from critic to maker of Day for Night.
        Especially interesting for remarks on Jules and Jim: like
        "a very old-fashioned Greer Garson and Walter Pidgeon film,"
        an MGM film.

1369   "Un Cobaye comme les autres: François Truffaut." Cinéma
        Quebec 2, no. 10 (July-Aug.):26-28.
                Transcription of press conference with Truffaut and Léaud
        at Cannes after screening Day for Night. Terse responses to
        specific questions about why he played the director, why the
        propman had the last words in the film, whether butter scene
        was a reference to Last Tango, etc.

1370   DESJARDINES, ALINE. Aline Desjardines s'entretient avec
        François Truffaut. Ottawa: Les Éditions Leméac, 76 pp.
                Good source of information on Truffaut's life up to The
        400 Blows and his feelings about May 1968. Also contains
        his opinions on women, death, and politics and mention of
        his preoccupation with film to the exclusion of all else.
        Only films discussed, briefly, are The 400 Blows, The Wild
        Child, and Two English Girls.

*1371   "Entrevista Las dos inglesas" and "Entrevista La noche
        americana." Cinestudio (Madrid), no. 126 (Nov.):33 ff.
                In Spanish. Listed in the card files at the Centre de
        documentation cinématographique (see entry 1501).

1372   GIRARD, PIERRE. "Truffaut: aux USA . . ." Le Film Français,
        no. 1507-2525 (16 Nov.):10.
                On recent American films and the growing awareness about
        film in academe.

*1373   GODARD, AGATHE. "Entretien avec François Truffaut." 20 Ans
        (3 Jan.).
                Reference provided by Truffaut.

1973

1374   GUSSOW, MEL. "Truffaut Describes Adventure of Film." New
        York Times (9 Oct.):42.
            Comments (on the eve of the New York opening of Day for
        Night) especially on where certain bits of dialogue and ac-
        tion came from (his own life and, oddly enough, Two for the
        Road). Truffaut admits to being an autodidact ("One who
        is self-taught always wants to convince other people") and
        is worrying only about whether his filming would be disrupted
        during the Algerian crisis (moviemaking is "solipsistic.")

1375   KISSEL, HOWARD. "François Truffaut . . . On Directing His Own
        Madness." Women's Wear Daily (2 Oct.):36.
            Career overview with focus on Day for Night.

1376   MAILLET, DOMINIQUE. "Entretien: François Truffaut--La Nuit
        américaine." Cinématographe, no. 3 (Summer):14-18.
            It is a film of recapitulation, closer to Singin' in
        the Rain than 8 1/2; Truffaut contrasts it to The Wild
        Child, compares it to Soft Skin. He ends by talking about
        Léaud.

1377   MALINA, MARTIN. "Truffaut Is a Gentle, But Almost Frightening
        Man." Montreal Star (12 Oct.).
            Composed of quotes from Cannes and Montreal Press confer-
        ences. Good on Day for Night as farewell.

1378   MALLOW, SUNI. "A Portrait of François Truffaut." Filmmakers
        Newsletter 7, no. 2 (Dec.):22-27.
            Begins with Truffaut rephrasing the first question but
        goes on to be more informative than the usual. Comments
        on preproduction, the financial and technical aspects of
        filmmaking, and specifically about Day for Night: his
        choice of Bisset, the function of the dream and hearing
        aid, etc.

1379   PETIT, CHRIS, and GLAESSNER, VERINA. "Truffaut in London."
        Time Out, no. 197 (30 Nov.-6 Dec.):24-25.
            Comments on Day for Night include remarks about "hiding
        behind" Léaud and Aumont and imitating Hawks and Singin' in
        the Rain. Also remarks about "Meet Pamela" being like Soft
        Skin and about the failure of Gorgeous Kid.

1380   ROSENTHAL, STUART. "Truffaut Interview." Focus on Film, no.
        16 (Autumn):6-7.
            Truffaut contrasts Day for Night with 8 1/2, contrasts
        Two English Girls with Jules and Jim, and Godard with him-
        self. He also mentions his role in dubbing.

1381   SWEENEY, LOUISE. "François Truffaut: The Filmmaker Who Films

1974

Films about Filmmakers." <u>Christian Science Monitor</u>
(18 June):7.
  <u>Two English Girls</u> and <u>Gorgeous Kid</u> reflect an unhappy
period in his life and mark the end of his romanticism.

1382   TEISSEIRE, GUY. "François Truffaut: 'La télévision? Une
faillité mais qui cause un tort immense au cinéma. . . ."
<u>Ciné Revue</u> 53, no. 27 (5 July):32-35.
  An article-interview on Truffaut's opinions about
television.

1383   TOPOR, TOM. "François Truffaut and Jean-Pierre Léaud: Now
There's Just the Two of Them." <u>New York Post</u> (6 Oct.):15.
  The director and the actor comment on <u>Day for Night</u>.

1384   TREMOIS, CLAUDE-MARIE. "François Truffaut: 'Quand on
crie. . . .'" <u>Télérama</u>, no. 1217 (12-18 May):62-63.
  What caused him to make <u>Day for Night</u> and what he hoped
to do.

<u>1974</u>

1385   BALLERINI, ÉTIENNE et al. "François Truffaut: Le Metier et
le jeu." <u>Jeune Cinéma</u>, no. 77 (Mar.):20-30.
  On the occasion of a Cannes retrospective, Truffaut defends himself smartly as a popular filmmaker who believes
in the importance of story. He also has some new things to
say here about music, editing, and preplanning.

1386   BARRON, FRED, and MICHAUD, PAUL. "François Truffaut: An
Exclusive Interview." <u>Real Paper</u> (2 Jan.):7-11.
  A revealing interview featuring unusual appraisals of
<u>Two English Girls</u>, <u>Gorgeous Kid</u>, and <u>Day for Night</u>. Each
film was made "in response to" something.

1387   BOCKRIS, VICTOR, and WYLIE, ANDREW. "Conversation with
François Truffaut." <u>Oui</u> 3, no. 9 (Sept.):72-74, 136-37.
  On a variety of general topics: the need for movies to
acknowledge both the exalting and the disgraceful; on being
nonviolent in middle age; on fiction as opposed to ideas;
on Léaud versus James Dean; on Godard, Murnau, and Andy
Warhol; on the use of color; on using improvisation and
children to "deny the masterpiece."

1388   "Le Cinéma est un jeu." <u>Cinéma Quebec</u> 3, no. 4 (Dec.-Jan.):
35-40.
  A wide-ranging interview covering specific incidents in
<u>Day for Night</u>, improvisation, adaptation, mixing tones and
genres, and Truffaut's preferences in films.

1974

1389   DUDINSKY, DONNA. "I Wish." Translated by Peter Lebensold.
       Take One 4, no. 2 (issues of Nov.-Dec. 1972, published
       Mar. 1974):8-10.
           Brief comments on his work habits during the making of
       Day for Night and Stolen Kisses, on Two English Girls, and
       on the fact that the non-Doinel films are more revealing
       personally.

1390   DUPONT, CLAUDE. "François Truffaut et l'enfance." Ciné
       Jeunes, no. 78 (n.d.):1-7.
           Almost entirely on The 400 Blows, its origins, problems,
       apparent mistakes; also on directing children. Conducted
       at Cannes retrospective of Truffaut.

1391   FIELDS, SIDNEY. "Films like a Confession." New York Daily
       News (29 Jan.):51.
           Career overview. Good quote on army life.

1392   GAUTEUR, CLAUDE. "Truffaut: 5 Films, 3 Livres." Film
       Français (8 Nov.):8.
           On current and future projects as director, as coproducer,
       writer, and editor of Bazin's works.

1392a GRENIER, RICHARD. "François Truffaut: Cinéphile Extraordin-
       aire." Gallery (precise month unknown):135-37, 157.
           As is to be expected, this article/interview emphasizes
       Truffaut's personal relationships and "love life." It is
       especially good on his youth. Unfortunately, Gallery does
       not keep all back issues; it appears in either the February,
       August, November, or December issue. A xerox copy of this
       is in the clipping files at the Museum of Modern Art (see
       entry 1514).

1393   HIGHAM, CHARLES. "François Truffaut." Action 9, no. 1
       (Jan.-Feb.):20-25.
           Truffaut discusses his favorite American films and di-
       rectors--from Rage in Heaven by the first American director
       to stimulate his imagination (W. S. VanDyke) to Adam Had
       Four Sons by Gregory Ratoff and Mr. Skeffington by Vincent
       Sherman. Perceptive capsule comments on Welles, Hitchcock,
       and Hawks and one-sentence remarks on several others. Re-
       printed in Celebrity Circus (see entry 1456a).

1394   McBRIDE, JOE. "Truffaut: Plans and Precepts." Variety
       (28 Aug.).
           On recent work, plans, pressures, favorite recent di-
       rectors.

1395   NEY, JOANNA. "Night and Day, Truffaut Is the One." Village

Voice, no. 19 (24 Jan.):87.
  An interview-article that reveals much of the minutia of
Day for Night, the real life experiences that found their
way into the script.

1396 [OAKES, PHILIP]. "Coming On: Truffaut in Aspic." _Sunday
     Times_ (London), no. 7865 (10 Mar.):36.
        What he is planning to do on his sabbatical from film-
     making. Also on financing and on using actors a second
     time.

1975

1397 ADAIR, GILBERT. "Adèle H." _Sight and Sound_ 44, no. 3
     (Summer):156.
        Briefly on the film; reveals his sensitivity to criticism.

1398 "François Truffaut Talks about His Film L'Histoire d'Adèle H."
     Unifrance Film News (Paris), no. 218 (June):7-9.
        Promotional piece.

1399 JOLIVET, NICOLE. "Truffaut a engagé une infirmière pour
     soigner les bobos des 250 enfants de _L'Argent de poche_."
     France-Soir (16 Aug.).
        A report on the shooting of _Small Change_, full of the
     director's opinions on the production.

1400 MAILLET, DOMINIQUE. "François Truffaut." _Cinématographe_,
     no. 15 (Oct.-Nov.):2-9.
        The main focus here is _Adèle H._, the title, Isabel Adjani,
     the music, the film's combination of the emotional climate
     of _Two English Girls_ with the rigor of _The Wild Child_.
     Gorgeous Kid and _Small Change_ are also discussed. More
     substantially, Truffaut proposes the final scene in _Stolen
     Kisses_ as the key to all his films and distinguishes between
     two basic kinds of Truffaut films: dramatic comedies and
     liturgical films.

1401 THEVENON, PATRICK. "Isabelle A. joue Adèle H." _L'Express_,
     no. 1234 (3-9 Mar.):10-12.
        On the "urgent" filming of _Adèle H._ Truffaut refuses to
     talk about Adjani and her conduct.

1402 TREMOIS, CLAUDE-MARIE. "François Truffaut: Parlez-moi
     d'amour." _Télérama_, no. 1319 (26 Apr.-2 May):60-62.
        On _Adèle H._, Isabel Adjani, and his next project: _Small
     Change_.

1976

1403 ADLER, MELANIE. "François Truffaut: The Romantic Bachelor."
Andy Warhol's Interview 6, no. 3 (Mar.):8-10.
    On the just-released Adèle H., women, Howard Hawks,
Henry Miller, Al Pacino and Jack Nicholson--two of his
favorite actors.

1404 ANON. "The Talk of the Town." New Yorker 52, no. 35
(18 Oct.):32-34.
    Truffaut's appearance, English, family, and career up-
dated. His reclusive habits, compulsive file-keeping, and
a book-buying spree (film acquisitions listed). Opinions
on television, film financing, acting in Close Encounters,
and himself: he has many ideas and little time. "One works
with what happens to one in the first twelve years of life."

1405 BEYLIE, CLAUDE. "Entretien avec François Truffaut." Écran 76,
no. 45 (15 Mar.):48-50.
    Covers technical and intellectual points in Small Change,
how it started and developed, the facts that it is organized
according to Lubitsch and seems to be a combination of Day
for Night and Stolen Kisses. Also on the desire for autonomy
and adaptability and on the tough skin of kids.

1406 CLARISSE, PATRICK, and de BONGNIE, JEAN. "Dites-moi, Mr.
François Truffaut." Amis du Film et le la Télévision, nos.
240-241 (May-June):4-6.
    On general questions, initially with reference to Belgium,
then about financing, writing, the New Wave, his latest projects.

1407 CLARITY, JAMES F. "François Truffaut: A Man for All
Festivals." New York Times (26 Sept.):sec. 2, pp. 15, 35.
    On Small Change and Close Encounters of the Third Kind.
Notable for his outspoken criticism of CE3K as being badly
organized because Julie Phillips, the producer, is "incompetent" and "unprofessional."

1408 DELMAS, JEAN. "Entretien avec François Truffaut." Jeune
Cinéma, no. 95 (May-June):8-14.
    On the making of Small Change, how it differs from his
other films on children.

1409 "Dialogue on Film: François Truffaut and Jeanne Moreau."
American Film 1, no. 7 (May):33-48.
    Truffaut responds to student questions at AFI seminar,
mostly on Adèle H. (the ending, the cinematography, the
ideas), but also on general filmmaking practices (on

originality versus adaptation, on directing actors, on all films as experimental).

1410 FALK, QUENTIN. "I Make the Films I Would Like to Have Seen as a Young Man." Screen International, no. 22 (7 Feb.): 12-13.
Interview on Adèle H. and on financing films.

1411 GASPERI, ANNE de. "François Truffaut et les enfants: Avec eux, pas de cinéma!" Les Nouvelles Littéraires 54, no. 2524 (18 Mar.):3.
On childhood: briefly, his own, and in general. Truffaut claims he is no theoretician and that he "works mostly with his memories." The worst memory for a child is treason, a promise unfulfilled.

1412 GOLD, SYLVIANE. "Truffaut's Small Charges." New York Post (1 Oct.):17, 25.
A career overview composed of quotations, especially about children.

*1413 [Interview]. Ciné Revue, no. 44 (28 Oct.):26-27.
On the French film industry and his own films. Listed in the BFI card files.

1414 McBRIDE, JOSEPH. "Say Directors Fear Screams." Variety (14 Jan.):7, 38.
On women and antagonism to politics.

1415 McBRIDE, JOSEPH, and McCARTHY, TODD. "Kid Stuff: François Truffaut Interviewed." Film Comment 12, no. 5 (Sept.-Oct.): 42-45.
Small Change contrasted variously with The 400 Blows; Truffaut talks about the children as collaborators, his scripting methods, and initial ideas.

1416 PANTEL, MONIQUE. "Il tourne son seizième film: Truffaut-- 'J'aime mieux mon travail que moi.'" France-Soir (24 Nov.):20.
Interview on the set of The Man Who Loved Women.

1417 STERRITT, DAVID. "Filmmaker to the World." Christian Science Monitor 69, no. 4 (1 Dec.):38.
Contrasting his work in Close Encounters and Small Change, Truffaut comments: "I think I am not a showman . . . I'm interested in characters." Comments about children on screen (for example, "with a child nothing is documentary--everything is vibrant"), the theme of survival (which he sees at the root of his work), and his responsibility as an artist to show his love of life.

1976

1418   _____. "France's Truffaut--Filmmaker to the World." <u>Christian Science Monitor</u> 68, no. 54 (12 Feb.):26.
        Starts and ends with <u>Adèle H.</u> (which Truffaut "just couldn't <u>prevent</u> myself <u>from</u> doing"), but covers a wide variety of topics very briefly, from love of books to film criticism, from the state of the film industry to some of his other films.

<u>1977</u>

1419   ANON. "A Bout Portant . . . François Truffaut." <u>Paris-Match</u> (20 Apr.).
        Truffaut questioned about his celebrity status, the pleasures of directing, aging, and <u>The Man Who Loved Women.</u>

1420   CUIF, FRANÇOIS. "Rencontre avec François Truffaut." <u>La Voix du Sourd</u> (Mar.):10-11.
        This journal on deafness interviews Truffaut on his own deafness (exacerbated by artillery practice during his military training) in connection with <u>Day for Night</u> and <u>The Man Who Loved Women.</u>

1421   FIESCHI, JACQUES. "Entretiens: François Truffaut." <u>Cinématographe</u>, no. 27 (May):20-24.
        Not much happens in this interview occasioned by the premiere of <u>The Man Who Loved Women.</u> Promising questions on Truffaut's <u>pudeur</u> ("modesty, reserve") and groups and dreams in his <u>films</u> do not go anywhere. Some incidental revelations.

1421a   "François Truffaut." In <u>Voices of Film Experience.</u> Edited by Jay Leyda. New York: Macmillan Publishing Co., pp. 468-71.
        Excerpts from the introduction to <u>The Adventures of Antoine Doinel</u> and from five interviews mostly on Truffaut's general concerns as a filmmaker or on his reasons for doing specific things in certain films (see entries 452, 1218, 1226-1227, 1356, and 1378).

1422   GASPERI, ANNE de. "François Truffaut: L'Amour du cinéma ou l'amour des femmes." <u>Le Quotidien de Paris</u> (26 Apr.).
        <u>The Man Who Loved Women</u> is less autobiographical than people think. Truffaut was interested in the character's anxiety and secretiveness more than his womanizing; the screenwriting process and the rhythm established through shots of women's legs were also important.

1423   KISSELL, HOWARD. "Film Is Not the Only Art." <u>Women's Wear Daily</u> (14 Oct.):22.

1978

Opinions (mostly negative) on contemporary films--
especially antagonistic to American parody.

1424   MAILLET, DOMINIQUE. "L'Homme qui aimait les femmes: Interview
        de François Truffaut." Lumière du Cinéma, no. 4 (May):
        18-25, 78.
            A good deal of new material here. On voice-overs,
        scripting, color; on Suzanne Schiffman's contributions, and
        his various coscenarists; on The Man Who Loved Women, Adèle
        H, and Fahrenheit 451; on Fellini's genius and the decline
        in American films.

1425   MANNONI, OLIVIER. "Histoires de tournages: Un Dialogue entre
        François Truffaut et Wim Wenders." Les Nouvelles Littéraires,
        no. 2605 (6-13 Oct.):13.
            Brief exchange on dialogue writing, preparation and shoot-
        ing of a film. Little in common between the two filmmakers.

1426   PANTEL, MONIQUE. "François Truffaut aime bien faire tourner
        les femmes." France-Soir (22 Apr.):23.
            On acting, his main characters, and writing script for
        The Man Who Loved Women.

*1427   SPOTO, DONALD. "Visiting François Truffaut." Print 31
        (May-June):81-85.

                                1978

1428   ANDREWS, COLMAN. "Tracking Truffaut." Radio Times 220, no.
        2860 (2-8 Sept.):10-11.
            About his respect for the written word, problems of
        working in a foreign language, his recent work, and his
        career.

*1429   AVRIL, CLAIRE. "François Truffaut: La Tendresse." Nice-
        Matin (5 May).
            Listed in the card files at the Centre de documentation
        cinématographique (see entry 1501).

1430   CADOT, ELIZABETH. "François Truffaut: 'Eteignez la lumière.'"
        France-Soir (24 Apr.).
            Short interview, on the occasion of the television debut
        of Adèle H, on the problems of financing it and recommenda-
        tions for viewers.

1431   CHAMPLIN, CHARLES. "A Close Encounter with the Energetic
        Truffaut." Los Angeles Times (1 Jan.):24.
            About his four recent projects. Useful contrast between

1978

        life and art (life goes downhill). Concern for final fif-
teen minutes of a film.

*1432   DOUIN, JEAN-LUC. "Deux réalisateurs devant la caméra."
Télérama, no. 1461 (14 Jan.):72–74.
        Listed in the card files at the Centre de documentation
cinématographique (see entry 1501).

*1433   DUPRAT, FRANÇOIS. "François Truffaut nous parle de La Chambre
verte." Famille chretienne (27 Apr.).
        Listed in the card files at the Centre de documentation
cinématographique (see entry 1501).

1434   "François Truffaut." Écran 78, no. 69 (15 May):57–58.
        Six terse paragraphs on the ideas behind The Green Room.
Like other collaborations with Jean Gruault, it is a love
story, this time between two people who interreact with the
dead "as aggressively and passionately as with the living."

1435   "François Truffaut." Cinéma Français, no. 19:35–40.
        Interview on acting, on The Green Room and Love on the
Run, and how and why he made them.

1436   "François Truffaut Talks about His Dual Role of Actor and
Director." Continental Film Review 25, no. 7 (May):24–25,
43.
        Also about The Green Room, French cinema, his working
methods.

1437   GASPERI, ANNE de. "François Truffaut: La Mort, ma voisine,
mon amour." Le Quotidien de Paris (30 Mar.).
        Series of very short statements about The Green Room,
most repeated elsewhere except for comment about his book
on acting.

1438   LACHIZE, SAMUEL. "François Truffaut se refuser d'oublier."
L'Humanité Dimanche (7 Apr.).
        Contains his strongest statements on death in The Green
Room.

1439   LAPORTE, CATHERINE, and HEYMANN, DANIELE. "Confessions of an
'Out' Filmmaker." Atlas World Press Review 25, no. 6
(June):30–31.
        Translated and excerpted from L'Express (see entry 1440).

1440   _____. "François T." L'Express, no. 1392 (13–19 Mar.):76–84,
87.
        A lengthy interview about The Green Room, its six-year
gestation, careful scripting, and his role as Davenne. With

a professional actor, the film would have been like a letter
composed by a secretary on an electric typewriter; with him
it was more personal, like a handwritten note. Translated
in Atlas (see entry 1439).

1441 MONTAIGNE, PIERRE. "Les Mystères de La Chambre verte." Le
Figaro (25-26 Mar):23.
It is not a psychological film; Julien is Adele H's lit-
tle brother.

*1442 NATTA, ENZO. "I vivi e i morti." Osservatore Romano 118, no.
99 (29 Apr.):6.
Listed in French xx Bibliography.

*1443 PANTEL, MONIQUE. "Dix questions a F. Truffaut." Play Boy
(Paris), (May).
Reference provided by Truffaut.

1444 _____. "Truffaut: 'Je ne supporte pas l'oubli!'" France-Soir
(1 Apr.).
Truffaut challenges the label pudique and distinguishes
between his character in The Green Room and himself.

1445 PARANAGUA, PAULO ANTONIO, and LAZLO, MICHEL. "'On tourne les
films qui nous hantent': Entretien avec François Truffaut."
Rouge (Paris) (8 Apr.).
A good general discussion, though not a lengthy one, with
a special section looking back at his critical work.

1446 PEREZ, MICHEL. "François Truffaut: Le Cinéma, l'amour et la
mort." Le Matin de Paris (29 Mar.).
The Green Room is termed a fairy tale and a musical comedy without dancing or singing, and is compared to other
films.

*1447 PHILIPPE, CLAUDE-JEAN. "Entretien avec François Truffaut."
Le Cinéma des Cinéastes (9 Apr.).
Referred to in review of The Green Room by Laurent Cugny,
Cinématographe (Summer 1978).

1448 STERRITT, DAVID. "Film Is the Act of Going Forward."
Christian Science Monitor (27 Nov.):20-21.
Film ("the art of unfolding like music") is contrasted
to novels (the pleasure of "progressively deeper analysis").
On the dual themes of survival and communication and on
making Jules and Jim to show his mother he understood.

1449 TREMOIS, CLAUDE-MARIE. "J'aimerais que des psychanalystes
m'explique mon film." Télérama, no. 1473 (8 Apr.):80-82.

1978

> Deals with The Green Room, how the script developed, the function of Massigny and the mute boy, death and the cult of the absolute.

1450   "Trois fois Truffaut. . . ." Le Film Français, no. 1644 (24 Sept.):12-13.
> On his acting in Close Encounters, writing about actors, and directing Man Who Loved Women.

1451   VAINES, COLIN. "Truffaut's Encounters." Screen International (1 Apr.):10.
> On acting in his own films and in Close Encounters.

1979

1452   ALLEN, DON. "Truffaut: Twenty Years After." Sight and Sound 48, no. 4 (Autumn):224-28.
> Invaluable source of information dealing with Truffaut's antagonism to parody and documentary and his preference for "first-person confidential tone," spoken commentary, and solitary characters. He admits he is less experimental than he used to be, but still sees films as aesthetic problem-solving exercises. Ends on why he avoids politics.

1453   ANON. "Truffaut Apprehensive about Film Retrospective." New York Times (20 Feb.):sec. C, p. 6.
> Brief note in which Truffaut compares the retrospective to "one's first surgical operation." Doinel has not matured much because "the social roles we play are an extension of childhood--a lot of childhood remains in him, and that's true of many men."

1454   CARCASSONNE, PHILIPPE; DEVILLERS, MICHEL; and FIESCHI, JACQUES. "Entretiens avec François Truffaut." Cinématographe, no. 44 (Feb.):58-63.
> On technical matters: editing and pacing, color, and music. Truffaut comments more on Shoot the Piano Player than any other film. The interview is probably most interesting because Truffaut divides his career into three periods (the first period ending with Fahrenheit 451, the second with Day for Night, the third with Love on the Run), makes two different distinctions between kinds of films (based on what unifies a film or on how the theme emerges), and compares films to political discourses.

1455   CHAMPLIN, CHARLES. "20 Years of Truffaut." Los Angeles Times (2 Feb.):Calendar sec., pp. 1, 22.
> Career overview built on quotations by Truffaut as part

of an announcement about the AFI retrospective. According
to Annette Insdorf, the Los Angeles area newspapers carried
several interesting interviews with Truffaut. Students and
scholars with access to them are recommended to check.

1456   HENDRICKSON, PAUL. "Life at 24 Frames a Second." Washington
       Post (22 Feb.):1-2.
          An interview/article with Truffaut in the lobby and res-
       taurant of the Watergate Hotel. Remarks on Renoir and on
       his own youth and his parents' reaction to The 400 Blows.

1456a HIGHAM, CHARLES. "François Truffaut." In Celebrity Circus.
       New York: Dell Publishing Co., pp. 333-39.
          Reprint of entry 1393.

1457   KOWINSKI, WILLIAM. "François Truffaut: The Man Who Loved
       Movies." Rolling Stone, no. 293 (14 June):43-44.
          Profile that includes quotes by Truffaut on women and
       love, on his debt to Hitchcock, and on Godard.

1458   LACOMBE, ALAIN. "Truffaut sur Renoir." L'Express, no. 1441
       (24 Feb.):24.
          Brief statements by Truffaut on Renoir's influence on
       and contribution to filmmaking. These are excerpts from a
       radio interview.

1459   MONTAIGNE, PIERRE. "Truffaut accuse la télévision." Le Figaro
       (23 Jan.).
          His tastes remain unchanged, though he regrets being too
       severe on Ford, too gentle on Preminger. He laments con-
       stricting of industry due to television.

1460   POLLOCK, DALE. "Truffaut Re Renoir, Hitchcock, 'Man' vs
       'Situation' Interest." Variety (28 Feb.).
          Quotes from an informal Hollywood press conference.

1461   "Renaissance du cinéma américain." Le Film Français, no. 1768
       (supplement-10 May):1-2.
          Lengthy comments on the current state of the U.S. film
       industry.

1462   SWEENEY, LOUISE. "Truffaut: Obsessed with Film." Christian
       Science Monitor (13 Mar.):sec. B, pp. 1-4, 12-15.
          Contains the best questions and answers of all the AFI-
       inspired interviews. On joy and agony of filmmaking, his
       radiant versus his dark films ("My normal routes are the
       dramatic comedies"), women, writing, visiting Los Angeles,
       and some of his favorite books and music.

1980

1463 BOUJUT, MICHEL. "Je suis un cinéaste de l'extreme-centre."
Les Nouvelles Littéraires, no. 2754 (18 Sept.):45.
On The Last Metro.

1464 BUCKLEY, TOM. "Truffaut Recalls When Nazis Were in Paris."
New York Times (14 Oct.):sec. C, p. 5.
Background information on The Last Metro.

1465 DANEY, SERGE; TOUBIANA, SERGE; and NARBONI, JEAN. "Entretien
avec François Truffaut." Cahiers du Cinéma, no. 315 (Sept.):
7-17 and no. 316 (Oct.):21-35.
This two-part interview begins with the confession that
"the more I work, the less I have to say about my work."
And the questions and answers bear this out; there is not
much that is new or compellingly stated, though the interviewers attempt to cover everything. Part one deals with
Truffaut's tactic of alternation, his relations with
American studios, and his opinions on French production,
on Hitchcock, Cahiers, Godard, acting, and the theme of be-
longing. Part two focuses more on Truffaut's comments about
other directors (Bergman, Chaplin et al.) and films, and on
contrasting his views with Godard's--especially on acting,
words, and character.

1466 "François Truffaut parle de Dernier Metro." Amis du Film/
Cinema et Télévision, no. 294 (Nov.):16-17.
Brief account of the ideas that went into the making of
The Last Metro.

1467 "L'Histoire d'un théatre parisien pendant l'Occupation."
L'Avant-Scène du Cinéma, no. 254 (15 Oct.):61-62.
A brief account of the origin of The Last Metro.

*1468 [Interview]. Cinéma Français, no. 33:4-8.
Listed in BFI card file.

1469 "Interview met Truffaut: 'Filmen is een vak vol angst.'"
Skoop 16, no. 10 (Dec.-Jan.):14-15.
In Dutch; mostly on The Last Metro.

1981

1470 DUSSAULT, SERGE. "Truffaut: Un Oscar qui tomberait pile."
La Presse (Montreal) (21 Feb.):sec. C, pp. 1, 14.
Truffaut underwent two days of nonstop interviews for
the Canadian premiere of The Last Metro. This one is more

career-oriented than the one in Le Devoir (see entry 1472)
and involves redefining ideas (on improvisation, directing,
sentimentality, working in America) from a more mature
position.

1470a   EDER, RICHARD. "Truffaut and the Enigmatic Woman." New York
Times (11 Oct.):sec. D, pp. 19, 24.
   Comments on The Woman Next Door, during which he contrasts his films with American films ("I take sentiments to
the end instead of enterprises"), men with women, and sentimental relations with social ones.

1470b   GILLAIN, ANNE. "Reconciling Irreconcilables: An Interview
with François Truffaut." Wide Angle, no. 4 (n.d.):26-37.
   Truffaut talks at some length about virtually all of his
major films and in refreshingly novel ways. Topics pursued
include the importance of the film's story line, the use of
fairy tales, his indirect style, the influence of Lubitsch,
and his reliance on previous films by himself and others.

1471   INSDORF, ANNETTE. "How Truffaut's The Last Metro Reflects
Occupied Paris." New York Times (8 Feb.):sec. B, pp. 21,
28.
   Background information that includes Truffaut's strongest
antiauteur statement.

1472   PETROWSKI, NATHALIE. "Le Dernier Metro: C'est une symphonie
du compromis, dit François Truffaut." Le Devoir (Montreal)
(21 Feb.):17, 32.
   This film is about, and all films involve, a "symphony
of compromises." Also on critics and political films.

VII. Other Film-Related Actvity

<u>PRODUCER OR COPRODUCER</u> (through Les Films du Carrosse)

1473   <u>Paris nous appartient</u> (1959). Dir.: Jacques Rivette.

1474   <u>Le Testament d'Orphée</u> (1959). Dir.: Jean Cocteau.

1475   <u>Le Scarabée d'or</u> (1960). Dir.: Robert Lachenay.

1476   <u>Anne la bonne</u> (1961). Dir.: Claude Jutra.

1477   <u>La Fin du voyage</u> (1961). Dir.: Michel Varesano.

1477a   <u>La Vie d'insectes</u> (1962). Dir.: Jean-Claude Roché.

1478   <u>Tiré au flanc</u> (1962). Dir.: Claude de Givray.

1479   <u>Mata-Hari, Agent H-21</u> (1965). Dir.: Jean-Louis Richard.

1480   <u>Deux ou trois choses que je sais d'elle</u> (1967). Dir.:
        Jean-Luc Godard.

1481   <u>L'Enfance nue</u> (1968). Dir.: Maurice Pialat.

1482   <u>Ma nuit chez Maud</u> (1969). Dir.: Eric Rohmer.

1483   <u>La Faute de l'Abbé Mouret</u> (1970). Dir.: Georges Franju.

1484   <u>Les Lolos de Lola</u> (1976). Dir.: Bernard Dubois.

1485   <u>Ce Gamin, la</u> (1977). Dir.: Renaud Victor.

1485a   <u>Un beau mariage</u> (1982). Dir.: Eric Rohmer.

<u>WRITER</u>

1486   <u>A bout de souffle</u> (1960). Dir.: Jean-Luc Godard. Written in 1955, this treatment interested several people, but was not marketable until the success of <u>Les Quatre Cents Coups</u>, after which Godard used Truffaut's script as the basis for his first feature-length film.

1487 <u>Charlotte et son Jules</u> (1961). Dir.: Jean-Luc Godard.
   Truffaut helped to write the dialogues in 1959. Uncredited.

1488 <u>Tiré au flanc</u> (1962). Dir.: Claude de Givray.
   Coscriptwriter.

1488a <u>Une gros tête</u> (1963). Dir.: Claude de Givray.
   Coscriptwriter and writer of dialogues with Eddie Constantine. Uncredited.

1489 <u>Mata-Hari, Agent H-21</u> (1965). Dir.: Jean-Louis Richard.
   Coscriptwriter.

<u>ACTOR</u>

1490 <u>Le Coup de berger</u> (1957). Dir.: Jacques Rivette.
   Briefly as passerby.

1491 <u>Les Quatre Cents Coups</u> (1959).
   Truffaut appears fleetingly in the rotor, the spinning carnival ride, that Antoine takes while skipping school. Truffaut got on the ride to reassure the nervous Léaud.

1492 <u>Tiré au flanc</u> (1962). Dir.: Claude de Givray.
   As prisoner in one scene.

1493 <u>L'Enfant sauvage</u> (1970).
   As Dr. Jean Itard.

1494 <u>La Nuit américaine</u> (1973).
   As Ferrand, the director of the film-within-the-film.

1495 <u>L'Histoire d'Adèle H.</u> (1975).
   Hitchcock-type cameo as a soldier who turns to look at Adèle.

1496 <u>L'Argent de poche</u> (1976).
   Hitchcock-type cameo as car driver acknowledged by girl mailing a postcard.

1497 <u>Close Encounters of the Third Kind</u> (1977). Dir.: Steven Spielberg.
   As Claude Lacombe.

1498   L'Homme qui aimait les femmes (1977).
       Hitchcock-type cameo as a man dressed like the main charac-
       ter, who turns to stare at the women gathering for the
       funeral.

1499   La Chambre verte (1978).
       As Julien Davenne.

1500   Truffaut has appeared on several television broadcasts (in
          French and for the BBC in England), a few of which have
          been transcribed and printed in various film journals.
          Some of his radio interviews have been preserved on records.
          (See the list of "Documents télévisés" and "Documents
          sonores" in Dominique Fanne, L'Univers de François Truffaut,
          p. 199 [see entry 249]). He also appeared in the 1975 docu-
          mentary film on Nicholas Ray entitled I'm a Stranger Here
          Myself by David Halpern, Jr., where he describes his admira-
          tion for Johnny Guitar. In 1980 he was the subject of an
          AFI "Dialogue on Film." He answers questions through inter-
          preter Annette Insdorf put to him by students at the AFI
          Center for Advanced Film Studies. The four-part seminar is
          available on videotape.

       Note

          Joseph McBride in an interview in Film Comment (entry 1415)
       indicates that Truffaut was an extra in René Clement's Le
       Château de Verre. Though both Godard and Truffaut visited the
       set of the film for a half-day, only Godard was "recruited at
       the last minute as an extra" by their friend Pierre Kast who
       was assisting the director. Godard and Jacques Rivette appear
       very briefly in the film -- but not Truffaut.

VIII. Archival Sources

1501   Centre de Documentation Cinématographique.
        360 McGill St., Montreal, Quebec H2Y 2E9. Telephone:
        (514) 873-6617 or 6753. Pierre Allard, Librarian
            Open: 1-4 P.M., Tues.-Fri. (Because of financial con-
        straints, the friendly, French-speaking staff has been re-
        duced and operating hours trimmed. The CDC is at press
        time seriously considering a move to the Cinémathèque
        Québécoise.)
            Contains one of the best collections of film books and
        periodicals (in many languages and especially French) in
        North America. All published Truffaut scripts. Stills
        for most films, clipping files on all films and Truffaut.

1502   National Film, Television and Sound Archives
        395 Wellington, Ottawa, Ontario K1A ON3.
        Ms. Vosikovska, Librarian
        Open: 9-5, Mon.-Fri.
            Screenplays: the published ones. Stills from many of
        his films and of Truffaut himself. Books: most of the
        major monographs and "a majority of the articles from in-
        ternational film periodicals." Clippings: from major
        Canadian sources and some American.

1503   The Ontario Film Institute
        Ontario Science Centre, 770 Don Mills Road, Don Mills,
        Ontario M3C 1T3. Telephone: (416) 429-4100.
        Gerald Pratley, Librarian
            Screenplays for the Doinel films, Jules and Jim, Day for
        Night, and Adèle H. Stills for all the films. Clipping
        files on all films, press kits for Jules and Jim, Soft Skin,
        and the films from Gorgeous Kid through Small Change.

FRANCE

1504   Centre National de la Cinématographie
            Service des archives du film, 78390 bois D'Arcy. Telephone:
            460-20-50.
            Nicole Schmitt, Chief of the Documentation Section
                Despite my requests, I never received a list of specific
            Truffaut films held here.

1505   La Cinématheque Française
            82, rue de Courcelles, Paris, 8e, France.
                No response to requests for information.

1506   Institute des Hautes Études Cinématographie
            92 Champs Elysees, Paris, 8e, France.
                35mm prints of Love at Twenty, The Green Room, and Love
            on the Run; 16 mm prints of 400 Blows and Jules and Jim.
            Scripts for all films but Soft Skin and Love on the Run.
            Stills for all through Gorgeous Kid, plus The Green Room
            and Love on the Run. Reviews and essays on Truffaut.

GERMANY

1507   Deutsches Institut für Filmkunde
            6200 Wiesbaden-Biebrich, Schloss. Telephone: 0 61 21/6
            90 74-75.
            Eberhard Spiess, Director
                No Truffaut films or scripts. Photos, press releases,
            program notes, and reviews of the films, plus articles on
            Truffaut in newspapers and film periodicals.

1508   Stiftung Deutsche Kinemathek
            Pommernallee 1, 1000 Berlin 19 (West). Telephone:
            3036-232 and 234.
            Heinz Rathsack, Director
                35 mm prints (German version) of Shoot the Piano Player
            Jules and Jim, Fahrenheit 451 (with German and French sub-
            titles).

GREAT BRITAIN

1509   British Film Institute
            127 Charing Cross Road, London W C 2H OEA.
                Scripts for all films except Bride Wore Black, Two
            English Girls, Gorgeous Kid, and Small Change. Extensive
            periodicals collection and clipping files.

Archival Sources

1510   Margaret Herrick Library
       Academy of Motion Picture Arts and Sciences
       8949 Wilshire Boulevard, Beverly Hills, Calif., 90211.
       Telephone: (203) 278-4313.
       Open: 9-5 Mon., Tues., Thurs., Fri.
          Scripts for the Doinel films, Jules and Jim, Wild Child,
       Day for Night, and Adèle H. Stills for all but Bride Wore
       Black and Man Who Loved Women. Press kits for over one-
       third of the films. Reviews and essays by and on Truffaut.

1511   Charles K. Feldman Library
       The American Film Institute
       501 Doheny Road, Beverly Hills, Calif. 90210. Telephone:
       (213) 278-8777.
       Anne G. Schlosser, Librarian
       Open: 9-5:30, Mon.-Fri.
          Scripts for Doinel films, Jules and Jim, Wild Child, Day
       for Night, and Adèle H. Press kit for Stolen Kisses. Clip-
       ping files for all beginning with Mississippi Mermaid (1969).
       Transcripts of seminars at the AFI on 30 Dec. 1975 and
       28 Feb. 1979.

1512   The UCLA Film Archive
       University of California, Department of Theater Arts,
       1438 Melnitz Hall, Los Angeles, Calif. 90024. Telephone:
       (213) 825-4142.
       Marsha Goodman, Archivist
          35 mm prints of Stolen Kisses and Wild Child; 16 mm print
       of Antoine et Colette.

1513   Archives of the Performing Arts
       University Library, University of Southern California,
       Los Angeles, Calif. 90007. Telephone: (213) 743-6058.
          "All of the standard (and most of the unusual) books on
       Truffaut and an extensive film journal collection." No
       films. Published scripts for 400 Blows, Jules and Jim,
       Wild Child, Adèle H. Stills for Day for Night.

1514   Film Study Center
       Museum of Modern Art, 11 West 53rd Street, New York, N.Y.
       10019. Telephone: (212) 956-4212.
       Charles Silver, Supervisor
       Open: 1-5, Mon.-Fri. By appointment only.
          35 mm prints of 400 Blows, Shoot the Piano Player, Jules
       and Jim, and Soft Skin. Stills from all of the films.
       Clipping files on all of the films and on Truffaut.

1515   Theater Collection
          Library of the Performing Arts at Lincoln Center, New York
          Public Library, 111 Amsterdam Avenue, New York, N.Y.   10023.
          Telephone: (212) 799-2200.
          Open: noon-8:00 P.M., Mon. and Thurs.; noon-6:00 P.M.
          Tues., Wed., Fri., Sat.
             Scripts for the Doinel films, Jules and Jim, Two English
          Girls, and Day for Night. Stills for most films through
          Man Who Loved Women. Press kits for Bride Wore Black and
          Stolen Kisses. Extensive clippings files on each film and
          on Truffaut.

1516   Film Department
          International Museum of Photography, George Eastman House,
          900 East Avenue, Rochester, N.Y.   14607. Telephone:
          (716) 271-3361.
          Open: By appointment well in advance.
          Contains 35 mm print of 400 Blows dubbed in English.

1517   Motion Picture Section
          Prints and Photographs Division, Library of Congress,
          1046 Thomas Jefferson Building, Washington, D.C.   20540.
          Telephone: (202) 426-5840.
          Open: 8:30-4:30, Mon.-Fri. Viewing facilities available
          to serious scholars by appointment well in advance.
             16 mm print of Jules and Jim; 35 mm prints of films from
          Soft Skin through Day for Night except for Two English Girls.

1518   Wisconsin Center for Film and Theater Research
          Film and Manuscripts Archive, The State Historical Society
          of Wisconsin, 816 State Street, Madison, Wis.   53706.
          Telephone: (608) 262-0585 or 262-3338.
             16 mm prints of Les Mistons, 400 Blows, Shoot the Piano
          Player, Jules and Jim, and Antoine et Colette. Dialogue
          transcripts of Bride Wore Black and Mississippi Mermaid.
          Stills from Shoot the Piano Player through Stolen Kisses.
          Press kits for Bride Wore Black and Wild Child.

IX. Film Distributors

1519   Cinema Concepts, 1805 Berlin Turnpike, Wethersfield, Conn. 06109.   (203) 529-0575.
      Stolen Kisses (videotape--sale)
      The Man Who Loved Women (videotape--sale)

1520   Cinema 5, 595 Madison Ave., New York, N.Y.   10022. (212) 752-3200.
      Stolen Kisses
      The Man Who Loved Women

1521   Clem Williams Films, 2240 Noblestown Rd., Pittsburgh, Pa. 15205.   (412) 921-5810.
      Fahrenheit 451

1522   Corinth Films, 410 E. 62nd St., New York, N.Y.   10021. (212) 421-4470.
      Such a Gorgeous Kid like Me

1523   FACSEA, 972 5th Ave., New York, N.Y.   10021.
      L'Histoire d'eau

1524   Festival Films, 4445 Aldrich Ave. S., Minneapolis, Minn. 55409.   (612) 822-2680.
      Les Mistons (sale)
      Shoot the Piano Player (sale)

1525   Films, Inc., 733 Green Bay Rd., Willmette, Ill.   60091. (312) 256-6600.
      The 400 Blows
      Shoot the Piano Player
      Jules and Jim
      Soft Skin
      Two English Girls
      The Story of Adèle H.
      Small Change

1526   Images Motion Picture Library, 2 Purdy Ave., Rye, N.Y. 10580.
        (914) 381-2993.
        Les Mistons

1527   Macmillan Audio Brandon, 34 MacQuesten Parkway S., Mount Vernon,
        N.Y. 10550.   (914) 664-5051 or (800) 431-1994.
        Shoot the Piano Player
        Fahrenheit 451

1528   Modern Sound Pictures, 1402 Howard St., Omaha, Nebr. 68102.
        (402) 341-8476.
        Fahrenheit 451

1529   New World Pictures, 11600 San Vincente Blvd., Los Angeles,
        Calif. 90049.
        The Story of Adèle H.
        Small Change
        The Green Room
        Love on the Run

1530   Roa's Films, 1696 N. Astor St., Milwaukee, Wis. 53202.
        (414) 271-0861.
        Fahrenheit 451

1531   Swank Motion Pictures, 393 Front St., Hempstead, N.Y. 11550.
        Soft Skin
        Fahrenheit 451
        Bed and Board
        Such a Gorgeous Kid like Me
        Day for Night

1532   Twyman Films, 329 Salem Ave., Dayton, Ohio 45414.   (513) 222-
        4014 or (800) 543-9594.
        Fahrenheit 451
        Bed and Board

1533   United Artists 16, 729 Seventh Ave., New York, N.Y. 10019.
        (212) 575-4715.
        The Bride Wore Black
        Stolen Kisses
        Mississippi Mermaid
        The Wild Child

1534   Universal 16, 445 Park Ave., New York, N.Y. 10022.   (212) 759-
        7500.
        Fahrenheit 451

1535   Viewfinders, P.O. Box 1665, Evanston, Ill. 60204.   (312) 869-
        0600.
        Les Mistons
        Antoine and Colette

1536   Warner Bros. Non-Theatrical, 4000 Warner Blvd., Burbank,
        Calif. 63166.
        Day for Night

1537   Westcoast Films, 25 Lusak St., San Francisco, Calif. 94107.
        (415) 362-4700.
        Fahrenheit 451

                                CANADA

1538   Astral Films Ltd., 720 King St.W., Toronto, Ont. M5V 2T3.
        (416) 364-3894.
        Bed and Board
        Such a Gorgeous Kid like Me

1539   Bellevue Film Distributors Ltd., 277 Victoria St., Toronto,
        Ont. M5B 1W2. (416) 593-2049.
        Love on the Run

1540   New Cinema Enterprises, 35 Britain St., Toronto, Ont. M5A 3V8.
        (416) 862-1674.
        Les Mistons
        The 400 Blows
        Shoot the Piano Player
        Jules and Jim
        Stolen Kisses
        The Man Who Loved Women
        The Green Room

1541   New World Mutual Pictures of Canada Ltd., 124 Merton St.,
        Toronto, Ont. M5S 2Z2. (416) 486-5535.
        The Story of Adele H.
        Small Change
        Love on the Run

1542   Pacific Cinematheque, 1616 W. 3rd Ave., Vancouver, BC. V6J 1K2.
        (604) 732-5322.
        Shoot the Piano Player

1543   Pallas Films, 696 Yonge St., Suite 900, Toronto, Ont. M4Y 2A7.
        (416) 961-1064.
        Jules and Jim

1544   Prima Film Inc., 1594 St. Joseph St. E., Montreal, P.Q.
        (514) 521-1189.
        Two English Girls

1545   United Artists Corporation Ltd., 2180 Yonge St., Suite 800,
        Toronto, Ont. M4S 2B9. (416) 487-5371.
        The Bride Wore Black

Mississippi Mermaid
The Wild Child
The Story of Adele H.
Small Change
The Man Who Loved Women
The Green Room

1546　Universal Films, 2450 Victoria Park Ave., Willowdale, Ont.
　　　M2J 4A1.　(416) 491-3000.
　　　Fahrenheit 451

1547　Warner Bros. Distributors Ltd., 70 Carlton St., Toronto, Ont.
　　　M5B 1L7.　(416) 922-5145.
　　　Day for Night

X. Appendix

A list of the films screened by the American Film Institute during the Truffaut retrospective: 19 February to 30 March 1979. According to the AFI Program, they represent "a selection of films admired by François Truffaut as critic. They have been chosen from his book, My Life in Films [sic] and other sources, and the final selection was made with his approval."

Citizen Kane (1941), Orson Welles.

The Rules of the Game (1939), Jean Renoir.

Trouble in Paradise (1932), Ernst Lubitsch.

Gentlemen Prefer Blondes (1953), Howard Hawks.

Hollywood or Bust (1956), Frank Tashlin.

Johnny Guitar (1954), Nicholas Ray.

Foolish Wives (1921), Erich von Stroheim.

The Quiet Man (1952), John Ford.

Kiss Me Deadly (1955), Robert Aldrich.

The Honeymoon Killers (1970), Leonard Castle.

The Mystery of Kaspar Hauser (1975), Werner Herzog.

Tristana (1970), Luis Buñuel.

The Criminal Life of Archibaldo de la Cruz (1955), Luis Buñuel.

Summer Interlude (1950), Ingmar Bergman.

I Confess (1953), Alfred Hitchcock.

Appendix

The Wrong Man (1957), Alfred Hitchcock.

Duel (1972), Steven Spielberg.

Fingers (1978), James Toback.

Notorious (1946), Alfred Hitchcock.

La Marseillaise (1937), Jean Renoir.

Zero for Conduct (1933), Jean Vigo.

L'Atalante (1934), Jean Vigo.

Shadow of a Doubt (1943), Alfred Hitchcock.

Marnie (1964), Alfred Hitchcock.

My Night at Maud's (1969), Eric Rohmer.

The Big Sleep (1946), Howard Hawks.

Verboten (1958), Samuel Fuller.

The Naked Dawn (1955), Edgar G. Ulmer.

Toni (1935), Jean Renoir.

Casque d'Or (1952), Jacques Becker.

Day of Wrath (1943), Carl Th. Dreyer.

A King in New York (1957), Charlie Chaplin.

The Magnificent Ambersons (1942), Orson Welles.

The Night of the Hunter (1955), Charles Laughton.

Rebecca (1940), Alfred Hitchcock.

Ugetsu Monogatari (1953), Kenji Mizoguchi.

The Girl Can't Help It (1956), Frank Tashlin.

To Catch a Thief (1955), Alfred Hitchcock.

Dial M for Murder (1954), Alfred Hitchcock.

Touch of Evil (1958), Orson Welles.

My Life to Live (1962), Jean-Luc Godard.

Appendix

The Testament of Orpheus (1959), Jean Cocteau.

Sunrise (1927), F. W. Murnau.

Orphans of the Storm (1922), D. W. Griffith.

It Should Happen to You (1954), George Cukor.

The Lady Vanishes (1938), Alfred Hitchcock.

Young and Innocent (1937), Alfred Hitchcock.

All the President's Men (1976), Alan Pakula.

Author Index

Abitan, Guy, 328
Adair, Gilbert, 21, 408, 1397
Adler, Melanie, 1403
Adler, Renata, 10, 162, 187
Ajame, Pierre, 142, 435, 1215, 1280
Albera, François, 159
Alion, Eves, 387
Allen, Donald, 188, 284, 1452
Allombert, Guy, 6, 8, 102
Almendros, Nestor, 414a, 1183a
Alpert, Hollis, 4, 6, 11-12, 14
Amiel, Mireille, 13-14, 16
Andrew, Dudley, 388
Andrews, Colman, 1428
Arbois, Janick, 15, 18, 1252
Archer, Eugene, 1202
Armes, Roy, 122, 202-203, 227
Aucuy, Jean-Marc, 26, 67
Aumont, Jean-Pierre, 329, 1166
Aurel, Jean, 601
Avril, Claire, 1429

Baby, Yvonne, 13, 123, 228, 1190, 1203, 1216, 1237, 1253, 1281, 1301, 1340, 1348-1349, 1366
Baigneres, Claude, 1350
Balaban, Bob, 389
Ballerini, Etienne, 1385
Barbera, Alberto, 330
Barron, Fred, 1386
Bayer, William, 262
Bazin, André, 454, 458, 461-462, 507, 984, 999, 1060, 1118, 1122, 1134, 1139, 1147, 1151, 1156, 1174-1175
Beaulieu, Janick, 331
Beazley, Mitchell, 1183

Bechtold, Charles, 358
Becker, Jacques, 790, 1089, 1129
Bellone, Julius, 204
Bellour, Raymond, 435, 1232
Belmans, Jacques, 238, 285
Benayoun, Robert, 8, 68
Benichou, Pierre, 1317
Bernard, Luc, 1351
Beylie, Claude, 2, 9-10, 13, 18-20, 22, 1352, 1367, 1405
Billard, Ginette, 27
Billard, Pierre, 6-11, 14-15, 18, 22, 40, 70, 1191, 1217, 1238, 1250, 1254, 1282
Bitsch, Claude, 864
Blakely, Richard, 332
Blanchard, Anne-Marie, and Blanchard, Gerard, 409
Bluestone, George, 143
Bobker, Lee, 189
Bockris, Victor, 1387
Bohn, Thomas W., 303
Bohne, Luciana, 333
Boland, Bernard, 22, 359
Bologna, Barbera, 304
Bonitzer, Pascal, 390
Bontemps, Jacques, 144
Borde, Raymond, 41, 57, 69
Bory, Jean-Louis, 6-8, 10-12, 15-16, 18, 21
Boujut, Michel, 391, 410, 1463
Bourla, Alain, 1353
Boyum, Joy Gould, 230
Braucourt, Guy, 12, 17-18, 20, 305, 1318-1319, 1341
Braudy, Leo, 164, 239, 306, 334, 360, 392, 455, 1124, 1355,

1361

Breen, James, 6, 91
Brodtkorb, Paul, 124
Brody, Alan, 231
Bromwich, David, 286, 465
Buache, Freddy, 8, 69
Buckley, Tom, 1464
Burch, Noel, 28
Buscombe, Edward, 263
Butcher, Maryvonne, 42
Byron, Stuart, 361

Cadieu, Martine, 1239
Cadieux, Fernand, 43
Cadot, Elizabeth, 18, 1430
Canby, Vincent, 11-13, 15-23,
    205-206, 232, 264, 307
Capdenac, Michel, 11-13, 17-18,
    1270
Capelle, Anne, 1255
Carcassone, Philippe, 362, 1454
Carlesimo, Cheryl, 426a
Carroll, Kathleen, 10, 13-14,
    17-21, 1368
Cast, David, 233
Castonguay, Pierre, 43
Casty, Alan, 265
Cezan, Claude, 1256
Chabert, Louis. See Truffaut,
    François
Chabrol, Claude, 680-682, 736,
    963, 993
Champagne, Roland A., 363
Champlin, Charles, 1431, 1455
Chancel, Jacques, 1342
Chapier, Henry, 9-10, 13-15, 20-
    21
Charensol, Georges, 7, 13, 15-16,
    18
Chauvet, Louis, 5, 8, 14-15
Chazal, Robert, 8, 18, 20-22
Christophe, Jean-Baptiste, 208
Ciment, Michel, 16, 240
Clarisse, Patrick, 1406
Clarity, James, 1407
Clouzot, Claire, 241-242
Clurman, Harold, 18-21
Cocks, Jay, 10, 14-19, 287
Coffey, Barbara, 288
Coleman, John, 6, 8-11, 13-14,
    16-17, 19

Collange, Christine, 1282
Collet, Jean, 5, 7, 13, 16, 18,
    22, 71-73, 125-126, 166-167,
    207, 243-244, 266, 335, 365,
    393, 465, 1218, 1233, 1285
Colpart, Gilles, 6, 18-19, 21
Combs, Richard, 12, 16-17
Comolli, Jean-Louis, 11, 127,
    147, 168, 1272
Conley, Tom, 366
Copeland, Roger, 367
Corbin, Louise, 4, 9, 11
Cornand, André, 11, 14-15
Coté, Guy, 43
Cotet, Jean, 44
Courtade, Francis, 394
Cowie, Peter, 10-11, 17, 309
Crisp, C. G., 245
Crist, Judith, 8-9, 11-14, 16-20,
    169
Croce, Arlene, 45
Croes, Marcel, 87
Crowther, Bosley, 4-9, 368
Cuif, François, 1420
Cukier, Dan, 87, 1219, 1354
Cumbow, Robert, 18, 335a
Curtelin, Jean, 46, 69

Dadoun, Roger, 148
Daney, Serge, 22, 209, 310, 1465
Darrach, Henry B., 47
Dawson, Jan, 10-16, 289
de Baroncelli, Jean, 4-6, 8-12,
    14-18, 21, 435
de Bongnie, Jean, 1406
Degand, Claude, 246
de Gasperi, Anne, 1411, 1422,
    1437
de Givray, Claude, 1260
de Gramont, Sanche, 1303
Delahaye, Michel, 74, 128, 149,
    170
Delain, Michel, 15, 22-23, 247
Delmas, Jean, 9, 20-21, 1408
de Monferrand, François. See
    Truffaut, François
Denby, David, 13, 15, 234, 267,
    287, 447, 1105
DeNitto, Dennis, 311
Desjardins, Aline, 1370
Devillers, Michel, 21-22, 1454

Dickstein, Morris, 392
Doniol-Valcroze, Jacques, 16, 30, 538, 1080
Douglass, Wayne J., 416
Douin, Jean-Luc, 18, 1432
Dubbs, Chris, 333
Dudinsky, Donna, 1389
Dupont, Claude, 1390
Duprat, François, 1433
Durgnat, Raymond, 58, 75, 92
Dussault, Serge, 1470
D'Yvoire, Jean, 2, 488

Eder, Richard, 336, 1470a
Eidsvik, Charles, 395
Elsaesser, Thomas, 210
Engel, Andi, 1275
Estrin, Barbara L., 396
Eyquem, Olivier, 369

Falk, Quentin, 1410
Fanne, Dominique, 248-249
Farber, Manny, 76, 235
Faurecasten, Jacques, 129
Fell, John L., 312
Fields, Sidney, 1391
Fieschi, Jacques, 20, 23, 103, 308, 1421, 1454
Flatley, Guy, 1321
Flaus, John, 93
Flores, Sam, 464
Fox, Joan, 77
Franchi, R. M., 84, 1220-1221
Frenais, Jacques, 370
French, Philip, 9, 150
Fry, Nicholas, 444
Fulford, Robert, 290

Garrigou-Lagrange, Madeleine, 78
Gary, Romain, 104
Gauteur, Claude, 1392
Gelmis, Joseph, 9, 1240
Genêt, 48, 171
Gerlach, John, 250
Gessner, Robert, 211
Gill, Brendan, 6-7, 9
Gillain, Anne, 417, 1470a
Gilliatt, Penelope, 9-10, 12, 16, 22, 212, 435
Gilling, Ted, 251
Gilson, René, 6, 1259

Girard, Pierre, 1372
Glaessner, Verina, 19, 1379
Godard, Agathe, 1373
Godard, Jean-Luc, 4, 31, 110, 172, 447, 1068
Gold, Sylviane, 1412
Goldsher, Art, 337
Goodman, Walter, 338
Gottesman, Ronald, 1116
Gow, Gordon, 8-9, 11, 14-15, 17, 1356
Graham, Peter, 8, 95-96, 173, 1200
Greenspun, Roger, 18-19, 97, 105, 213, 465
Gregor, Ulrich, 291, 371
Grenier, Cynthia, 32, 49
Grenier, Richard, 23, 1392a
Gryn, Jo, 87, 1219, 1354
Gussow, Mel, 18, 313, 1374

Hale, Wanda, 8-9, 11, 1241
Harcourt, Peter, 418, 465
Hartung, Philip, 4, 6, 8, 10-11
Haskell, Molly, 19-20, 23, 292, 314
Hatch, Robert, 4-6, 8, 10-18, 20-23
Hauptman, Ira, 372
Hayman, Ronald, 1357
Henderson, Brian, 411
Hendrickson, Paul, 1456
Herman, William, 311
Herrmann, Bernard, 373
Hess, John, 268-269, 293
Heymann, Daniele, 1439-1440
Higham, Charles, 1393, 1456a
Hinault, Gerard, 159
Hirsh, Allan, 412
Holland, Norman, 50
Hollo, Anselm, 468
Houston, Beverle, 255, 271
Houston, Penelope, 6, 8-11, 15, 17, 59, 79, 98, 174, 180
Hovald, Patrice, 1286, 1325
Hudson, Christopher, 13-14, 17

Insdorf, Annette, 19, 22, 398, 413, 418a, 1178, 1182, 1471
Irish, William, 1183b

Jacob, Gilles, 8, 11, 106, 111, 151, 1273-1274, 1291
James, Clive, 152
Jamet, Dominique, 1263
Jean, Raymond, 6, 80, 112
Jeancolas, J. P., 252
Jebb, Julian, 18, 22, 253, 465
Johnson, Lincoln F., 294
Johnson, William, 457, 1125
Jolivet, Nicole, 1399
Jones, Shirley, 315
Jordan, Isabelle, 214

Kael, Pauline, 6, 11, 14-15, 17, 20, 81, 113, 131, 175, 215, 270, 316, 339-340, 419
Karkosch, K., 295
Kast, Pierre, 60
Kauffmann, Stanley, 4-7, 10-17, 19-23, 153, 236, 317, 341, 374, 419a
Kestner, Joseph, 254
Kinder, Marsha, 255, 271, 399
Kissel, Howard, 16-20, 1375, 1423
Klein, Gillian Parker, 342
Klein, Michael, 114, 256, 296, 343, 375, 420
Klieb, Werner, 1292
Knight, Arthur, 9-10, 176, 435
Kostelanetz, Richard, 297
Kowinski, William, 1457
Kreidl, John Francis, 376
Kroll, Jack, 19, 21, 344
Kummer, Elke, 1275

Labro, Philippe, 1244, 1284
Lachat, Pierre, 145
Lachenay, Robert. See Truffaut, François
Lachize, Samuel, 8, 1438
Lacombe, Alain, 1458
Lane, Harlan, 345
Langley, Lee, 1264
Langlois, Gérard, 11, 191-192, 1293, 1333
Laporte, Catherine, 377, 1439-1440
Laurans, Jacques, 346
Lazlo, Michel, 1445
LeFanu, Mark, 298

Lefebvre, Jean-Pierre, 7, 82
Lefevre, Raymond, 5, 18, 1249
Leger, Guy, 1194
Lellis, George Patrick, 347
Lemery, Christine, 459
Lennon, Peter, 132, 1276
Leonard, John, 318
Lewin, Linda, 459
Lewis, Marshall, 84, 1220-1221
Leyda, Jay, 1421a
Lindsay, Michael, 193
Lipkin, Steven N., 378
Loubiere, Pierre, 1334
Lyndon, Neil, 272

McBride, Joseph, 273, 1394, 1414-1415
McCarthy, Todd, 1415
MacDonald, Dwight, 4-6, 115, 194
McDougal, Stuart Y., 426b
MacKillop, I. D., 8, 177, 319
Magnan, Henry, 116
Magny, Joel, 19, 216, 379, 400
Maillet, Dominique, 308, 1376, 1400, 1424
Malcolm, Derek, 12-13, 15, 17-19, 1335
Malina, Martin, 1377
Mallow, Suni, 1378
Malson, Lucien, 217
Manceaux, Michele, 1195, 1234, 1245, 1307
Mannoni, Olivier, 1425
Manvell, Roger, 133
Maraval, Pierre, 308
Marcabru, Pierre, 5-8
Marchilli, Massimo, 380
Marcorelles, Louis, 4-5, 24-25, 33, 51, 61, 1205, 1212, 1227
Mardore, Michel, 4, 14, 23, 1228
Martin, Marcel, 5, 14, 16, 22, 52, 236a, 299, 401, 1265
Martin, Paul-Louis, 134, 154
Mast, Gerald, 381
Mauriac, Claude, 4, 6, 8-9, 11, 13, 15, 17, 435
Mayhew, Leonard, 473
Mekas, Jonas, 2, 4, 7, 53
Melville, Jean-Pierre, 135
Michaud, Jean, 1232
Michaud, Paul, 1386

Michimoto, Lindsay Ryoko, 401a
Millar, Gavin, 11-15, 17-18, 20,
   179, 195
Millie, Robert, 159
Milne, Tom, 7-10, 13, 17-18, 83
Mithois, Marcel, 1246
Mohrt, Michel, 9, 18-20, 257
Monaco, James, 300, 348-349, 402,
   421, 1179
Montaigne, Pierre, 18, 1441,
   1459
Morgan, Ted, 18, 382
Morgenstern, Joseph, 10-11, 218,
   435, 1206
Mosk, 13-14, 16-18, 20-21
Moussy, Marcel, 427-428
Murray, Edward, 403

Narboni, Jean, 1273, 1465
Natta, Enzo, 1442
Ney, Joanna, 1395
Nichols, Bill, 14, 1159
Nightingale, Paul, 320
Nowell-Smith, Geoffrey, 118
Nusser, Richard, 1294

Oakes, Philip, 1396
Oudart, Jean-Pierre, 196, 219
Oxenhandler, Neal, 107, 301

Pantel, Monique, 14, 22, 1416,
   1426, 1443-1444
Paranagua, Paulo Antonio, 1445
Parinaud, André, 920, 1196, 1308
Paul, William, 197
Pays, Jean-François, 450
Pearson, Gabriel, 62
Pechter, William, 14-15, 18
Perez, Michel, 11, 17, 22-23,
   1446
Perret, Jacques, 1358
Petit, Chris, 1379
Petrie, Graham, 220, 274, 422
Petrowski, Nathalie, 1472
Philippe, Claude-Jean, 1266,
   1447
Pilard, Philippe, 119
Pilon, Jean-Claude, 43
Poague, Leland A., 350
Pollock, Dale, 1460
Porcile, François, 120, 351, 404

Powell, Dilys, 4, 6, 9-10, 12,
   14-15, 17
Prédal, René, 14, 22, 178, 302,
   352

Queval, J., 487
Quigley, Isabel, 4, 6, 8
Quinson, René, 9-11

Rayns, Tony, 1359
Recassens, Gerard, 198
Reed, Rex, 11, 17, 19
Regent, Roger, 8-12, 15-18, 20-21
Reisz, Karel, 179
Renaud, Tristan, 10, 15, 258
Rey, Pierre, 1197
Rhode, Eric, 10-11, 54, 62, 85,
   435
Rich, Frank, 18-20, 22
Richardson, Joanna, 315
Rivette, Jacques, 2, 4, 447, 480,
   539-541, 597, 679, 694, 790,
   931, 953, 963, 1003, 1089,
   1112, 1129, 1194
Robinson, David, 2, 9, 14
Rode, Henri, 1214, 1230, 1247,
   1277
Rohmer, Eric, 482, 542, 700, 1139
Romi, Yvette, 1296
Ronder, Paul, 1235
Rosenthal, Stuart, 17, 1380
Ross, T. J., 275
Ross, Walter, 221
Rouault, Beatrice, 222
Rouch, Jane, 34
Rouchy, Marie-Elisabeth, 423
Roud, Richard, 6, 8, 14-15, 17-18,
   20-21, 55, 99, 155, 180, 223
Roudinesco, Elisabeth, 321
Roulet, Sebastian, 1297

Sadoul, Georges, 4, 6-9, 35, 1198
Salachas, Gilbert, 8, 10, 14, 36,
   63, 198, 1334
Salis, Rene, 87
Samuels, Charles, 12, 15, 17,
   383, 1345, 1360
Sand, Luce, 11, 13, 1298
Sarris, Andrew, 5-6, 8-11, 13-17,
   19-20, 22, 84, 86, 136, 181,
   224, 276, 435, 1089, 1278

Sawyer, Paul, 156
Schickel, Richard, 9, 11-15, 23, 259
Schlesinger, Arthur Jr., 6, 20, 22
Scott, Adrienne, 230
Scott, Helen G., 443, 452, 468
Sequin, Louis, 7, 353
Serceau, Michel, 17, 225, 283
Shatnoff, Judith, 10, 100
Sherer, Maurice. See Rohmer, Eric
Siclier, Jacques, 8, 19, 22, 64-65, 137
Simeral, Fred, 405
Simon, John, 18-20, 157, 237, 260, 277
Simsolo, Noel, 1336
Sobchack, Thomas, and Sobchak, Vivian C., 424
Sobieski, Monique, 1299, 1309, 1337, 1346
Sofer, Micha, 159
Solomon, Stanley, 138
Spiegel, Alan, 354
Spoto, Donald, 1427
Stakerlee, Neal, 1267
Stanbrook, Alan, 101
Staples, Donald E., 158, 226
Stein, Elliott, 19, 21, 23
Sternberg, Jacques, 182
Sterritt, David, 18-22, 1417-1418, 1448
Stoller, James, 108
Stromgren, Richard, 303
Swados, Harvey, 183
Sweeney, Louise, 9, 11-13, 16-17, 1338, 1381, 1462

Tailleur, Roger, 37
Tallenay, Jean-Louis, 4, 6, 20, 38, 1310
Tanner, Carlon Lee, 184
Tarantino, Michael, 322
Taylor, John Russell, 14, 109, 140
Taylor, Stephen, 121
Tecklenburg, Walter, 145
Teisseire, Guy, 15, 1382
Thevenon, Patrick, 18, 1401
Thiher, Allen, 384, 414

Thirard, Pierre-Louis, 10, 15, 21
Thomas, Pascal, 1362
Thomas, Paul, 323, 385, 1311
Thompson, David, 324, 355
Tillier, Maurice, 1248, 1313
Tinter, Adeline R., 425
Topor, Tom, 1383
Torok, Jean-Paul, 66
Toubiana, Serge, 1465
Tremois, C. M., 22-23, 1199, 1314, 1339, 1363, 1384, 1402, 1449
Truffaut, François, 427-1189a
Turim, Maureen, 278
Tyler, Parker, 89, 160

Vaines, Colin, 1451
Van Wert, William, 325
Veillot, Claude, 12-13, 200, 1282, 1315
Veuillot, Jean-Louis, 185
Von Bagh, Peter, 163

Waddy, Stacey, 1269
Wall, James M., 279-280
Walsh, Moira, 7, 13-14
Warren, Jean-Paul, 1249
Weber, Eugen, 39
Weightman, J. G., 56
Westerbeck, Colin, 12-13, 15-17, 356, 406, 426
Wheelock, Alan S., 326
Whitebait, William, 2, 4-5
Wildenstein, Pierre, 1200
Williams, Alan, 327
Williams, Linda Paglierani, 386
Wilmington, Michael, 281
Winsten, Archer, 9-14, 16-17, 21, 1208, 1300
Wood, Robin, 201
Wunderlich, Hans-Jürgen, 282
Wylie, Andrew, 1387

Yost, Elwy, 407
Young, Vernon, 6, 8-10, 261

Zaagsma, Frank, 186
Zeleny, M., 17, 283
Zimmerman, Paul, 12, 14, 17

Film-Title Index

A bout de souffle, 51, 56, 62,
153, 349, 445, 1037, 1068,
1114, 1199, 1249
Adieu Philippine, 1064
Affair in Trinidad, 484
Ali Baba, 512, 628
L'Amant de Lady Chatterly, 629
Amants, Les, 1013–1014
Amants de la Villa Borghese, Les,
513
Ambassador's Daughter, The, 799
L'Ami de la famille, 895
Amis, Les, 1187
Amis pour la vie, 762
L'Amour á la ville, 896
L'Amour á vingt ans. See Antoine
et Colette
L'Amour aux champs, 514
L'Amour d'une femme, 515
L'Amour en fuite, 22, 410, 417–
419, 475, 1435, 1453
Anastasia, 473, 897
And God Created Women, 768, 791,
980
Animal Crackers, 516
Anne and Muriel. See Les Deux
Anglaises et le continent
Antoine et Colette, 7, 71, 108,
220, 245, 249, 284, 322,
330, 349, 352, 365, 397,
448, 452
L'Argent de poche, 19, 331, 339,
346, 363, 365–366, 381, 385,
397, 404, 419, 466, 468,
471, 1399, 1400, 1402, 1405,
1407–1408, 1411, 1415, 1417
Aristocrats, Les, 632, 671

Around the World in 80 Days, 902
Arsene Lupin, 465, 764, 899
Artists and Models, 774, 869
Assassins du dimanche, Les, 765,
867
Assassins et voleurs, 465, 900,
927
Attack!, 766, 888, 966
Auntie Mame, 1045
Autumn Leaves, 798
Aventures de Till l'Espiegle, Les,
767

Baby Doll, 465, 901, 958
Bachelor Party, The, 912
Bad Seed, The, 473, 825
Baisers volés, 11, 166, 188, 197–
198, 201, 213, 215, 218, 220,
224, 236–237, 244–245, 249,
259–260, 284, 290, 322, 330,
340, 349–350, 352, 361, 365,
397, 448, 452, 1287–1288,
1293, 1296–1297, 1303, 1313,
1319, 1333, 1360, 1389, 1400,
1405
Ballon rouge, Le, 465, 769
Bandit, The, 770
Barefoot Contessa, The, 465, 658–
659
Battle Cry, 642
Beau Serge, Le, 993, 1024
Bed and Board. See Domicile
conjugal
Beggars' Opera, The, 586
Belle Fille comme moi, Une, 16,
240, 284, 287, 317, 319, 330,
349, 365, 397, 1130–1131,

1351, 1363–1364, 1367, 1379, 1381, 1386, 1400
Belle Otero, La, 524
Bigger Than Life, 465, 889, 924, 951
Big Heat, The, 511
Big Knife, The, 465, 687, 691, 965
Birds, The, 433, 465, 1069
Black Shield of Falworth, The, 637
Blinkity-Blank, 465, 661
Bonjour Tristesse, 465, 983, 986
Brave et le temeraire, Le, 909
Breathless. See A bout de souffle
Bride Wore Black, The. See La Mariée était en noir
Brigadoon, 772
Broken Lance, 708

Caine Mutiny, The, 587
Calabuig, 911
Carmen Jones, 559, 720
Carrosse d'or, Le, 568
Cas du Dr. Laurent, Le, 914
Casque d'or, 1073
Cause for Alarm, 517
Celui qui doit mourir, 473, 902
C'est arrive à Aden, 772
Cette sacrée famille, 486
Chambre verte, La, 21, 390, 393, 400–401, 404, 406, 408, 414a, 419–420, 424, 472, 1433–1441, 1444, 1446–1447, 1449
Charlotte et Veronique, 991
Cheri Bibi, 648
Chiens perdus sans colliers, 649
Citizen Kane, 465, 809, 1046, 1116, 1165
City Is Dark, The, 531
Close Encounters of the Third Kind, 336, 374, 377, 389, 1404, 1407, 1417, 1450–1451
Club des femmes, 776
Colline 24 ne repond pas, La, 653
Comicos, 654
Comte de Monte-Cristo, Le, 656–657
Condamné à Mort s'est echappé,

Un, 465, 778, 781, 848
Confession, 850
Couronne noire, La, 489
Courte tête, 923
Court Martial of Billy Mitchell, The, 779

Dames du bois de Boulogne, Les, 465, 564
Day for Night. See La Nuit américaine
Dead Line, 491
Decameron Nights, 522
Defi, Le, 1033
Dernier Metro, Le, 23, 426a, 476, 1463–1464, 1466–1467, 1469
Desert Rats, 518
Des gens sans importance, 783
Destination Gobi, 473, 667
Deux Anglaises et le continent, Les, 15, 242–243, 248, 253, 254, 256, 267, 284, 292, 298, 317, 330, 349, 353, 365, 383, 397, 414a, 456, 1117, 1120, 1123, 1128, 1340, 1344, 1349, 1352, 1357, 1362, 1367, 1370–1371, 1380–1381, 1386, 1389, 1400
Deux ou trois choses que je sais d'elle, 1090–1091
Dial M for Murder, 662
Divine, 1027
Doigts dans la tête, Les, 465, 1147, 1153
Domicile conjugal, 14, 216, 221, 244–245, 249, 270, 284, 317, 322, 330, 349–350, 352, 365, 397, 414a, 448, 452, 1318–1320, 1328, 1333, 1336, 1360
Dommage que tu sois une canaille, 670
Dossier noir, 672
Double destin, 673
Dragées au poivre, 1066
Dr. Cyclops, 493, 1125
Droles de bobines, 674
Du Rififi chez les hommes, 473, 675–676

East of Eden, 624, 803

Egyptian, The, 635
8½, 465, 1067
L'Enfant sauvage, 13, 200, 206-
    207, 209, 212, 214, 217,
    219-220, 222, 225, 234, 244-
    245, 249-250, 255, 259, 284,
    308, 317, 330, 335a, 345,
    349, 365, 381, 397, 405,
    414a, 422, 449-451, 459,
    1107-1108, 1113, 1121, 1304,
    1306, 1310-1312, 1315, 1317,
    1321-1322, 1326-1327, 1329-
    1330, 1335, 1338-1339, 1360,
    1370, 1376, 1400
Enfants d'Hiroshima, Les, 537
Espions, Les, 919-920
Eternal Female, The, 526
Etoiles ne meurent jamais, Les,
    932
Evades, Les, 683
Executive Suite, 615

Face in the Crowd, A, 465, 940
Fahrenheit 451, 9, 122, 126-129,
    131, 134, 139, 141, 143,
    146-147, 149-150, 152, 154,
    169, 175, 177, 211, 220, 245,
    249, 261, 273, 275, 284, 328,
    330, 349, 365, 397, 437-441,
    457, 460, 1085, 1215, 1248,
    1253, 1255, 1258-1259, 1262-
    1267, 1269, 1272, 1286, 2192-
    1293, 1297, 1303, 1320, 1358,
    1360, 1424
Fanatiques, Les, 894
Far Country, The, 702
Fear Strikes Out, 1023a
Feathered Serpent, The, 465, 503
Femme d'à côté, La, 23a
Femme diabolique, Une, 794
Femmes interdits, 546
Feu follet, Le, 473, 1074
Fifth Victim, The, 775
Fille d'amour, 547-548
Five, 508
Flight to Tangier, 622
Follies Bergeres, 934
Foreign Intrigue, 787
Four Hundred Blows, The. See
    Les Quatres Cents Coups
Fourth Man, The, 505

French Can-Can, 609, 689, 720
Frenzy, 465, 1127
From Here to Eternity, 612
Future vedette, 690

Gants blancs du diable, Les, 1188
Garden of Evil, 523
Gentlemen Prefer Blondes, 465,
    561
Giant, 936
Girl Can't Help It, The, 473,
    908
Girls, Les, 1005
Glen Miller Story, The, 520
Goha, 988
Gorgeous Bird like Me, A. See
    Une Belle Fille comme moi
Grand Bluff, Le, 937
Grande Illusion, La, 1007, 1149
Grande Jeu, Le, 555
Grandes Familles, Les, 1008
Great Dictator, The, 465, 996
Green Room, The. See La Chambre
    verte
Guerra de Dios, La, 556, 558

Hallelujah!, 684
Harpe Birmane, La, 473, 938
Heroes sont fatigues, Les, 692
High and the Mighty, The, 436
L'Histoire d'Adèle H., 18, 308,
    313-316, 330, 333, 335a,
    337-338, 341-344, 351, 356,
    365, 375, 382, 392, 396-397,
    404, 414a, 418a-419, 469,
    1158, 1163, 1397-1398, 1400-
    1403, 1409-1410, 1418, 1424,
    1430
Histoire d'eau, Une, 3, 220, 223,
    245, 249, 284, 330, 349, 397,
    430
Hold-Up, 1009
Hollywood or Bust, 473, 982
L'Homme à l'impermeable, 939
L'Homme qui aimait les femmes,
    20, 358-359, 364-365, 369-
    370, 379, 398-399, 404, 419,
    470, 1416-1417, 1420-1422,
    1424, 1426, 1450
Hondo, 528
Hot Blood, 898

Houdini, 523
House of Bamboo, 822
How to Marry a Millionaire, 534
Huis clos, 696
Human Desire, 665
Hussards, Les, 698

Il Bidone, 687, 858
Infidels, Les, 565
L'Inspecteur aime la bagarre, 942
It Should Happen to You, 465, 545, 616
I Vitelloni, 566
I Was an American Spy, 636

Jeanne au butcher, 701
Je reviendrai à kandara, 943
Jet Pilot, 1000, 1019
Joe MacBeth, 813, 869
Johnny Guitar, 465, 627, 706, 1142, 1271, 1301
Jules et Jim, 6, 67, 69, 73-74, 78, 80, 82, 84-85, 87, 89, 92-93, 97, 100, 107, 112-113, 122, 125, 153, 160, 181, 190, 194, 220, 224, 230-231, 245, 249, 255, 261-262, 284, 292, 311, 328, 330, 349, 365, 384, 392, 395, 397, 407, 414-414a, 423, 426a, 432, 444, 453, 1215-1217, 1219-1221, 1226, 1229, 1246, 1271, 2178, 1303, 1340, 1344, 1360, 1368, 1380, 1448
Jungle, La, 944
Juvenile Passion, 473, 1030

Killer Is Loose, The, 465, 886
King in New York, A, 465, 967
King of the Khyber Rifles, 582
Kiss Me Deadly, 465, 678, 866

Land of the Pharoahs, 748, 790
Last Act, The, 688
Last Frontier, The, 773
Last Metro, The. See Le Dernier Metro
Last Time I Saw Paris, The, 782, 869
Lifeboat, 818, 869

Life of Her Own, A, 499
Little Boy Lost, 518
Lola Montes, 465, 709, 713, 819, 826, 858, 946
Long Gray Line, The, 645, 726
Long Wait, The, 584
Love at Twenty. See Antoine et Colette.
Love Me or Leave Me, 465, 851
Love on the Run. See L'Amour en fuite
Lucky Me, 634
Lumiere d'en face, La, 820
Lure of the Wilderness, The, 593

Maison de plaisir, La, 573
Mam'zelle Nitouche, 574
Man Alone, A, 808
Manche et la belle, Une, 948
Manderson Affair, The, 510, 575
Man from Laramie, The, 695
Man in the Dark, The, 500
Manteau, Le, 576
Man Who Knew Too Much, The, 807
Man Who Loved Women, The. See L'Homme qui aimait les femmes
Man Who Never Was, The, 941
Marguerite de la nuit, 823
Mariage et bébé, 1033
Mariée est trop belle, La, 824
Mariée était en noir, La, 10, 159, 163, 167, 185, 187, 195, 220, 224, 237, 244-245, 249, 260-261, 275, 284, 330, 349, 365, 397, 1089, 1270, 1273-1274, 1281, 1285-1286, 1293-1294, 1298, 1300, 1303, 1313, 1360
Marque, La, 1015
Marseillaise, La, 1089a
Mata Hari, Agent H-21, 117, 1803
Mauvaises Rencontres, Les, 465, 643, 712, 735, 893
Meilleure Façon de marcher, La, 1160
Meilleur Part, La, 827
Men at War, 922
Mississippi Mermaid. See La Sirène du Mississipi
Mistons, Les, 2, 24, 120, 122, 175, 220, 245, 249, 284, 294,

330, 349, 365, 394, 397, 405,
431, 1200, 1215, 1228, 1270,
1293
Mogambo, 519
Mon Oncle, 878, 990, 1012
Monsieur Ripois et le nemesis,
580-581
Monstre, Le, 950
Mouton a cinq pattes, Le, 519
Mr. Arkadin, 465, 829
Mulatresse, La, 714
Mummy's Hand, The, 501
Muriel, 465, 1075
Mystère Picasso, Le, 830

Naked Alibi, 522
Naked Dawn, 630, 687
Naked Jungle, The, 517
Napoleon, 465, 655, 715
Never Let Me Go, 583
Niagara, 492
Night of the Hunter, 465, 831,
1148
Night People, 639
Nous, les femmes, 585
Nuite américaine, La, 17, 264,
266, 271, 277, 283-284, 286-
287, 289, 296, 317, 319-320,
326, 329-330, 340, 349, 353,
361, 365, 397, 416, 460,
464, 1366-1369, 1371, 1374-
1376, 1378-1380, 1383-1384,
1386, 1388-1389, 1395, 1405,
1420
Nuit et broulliard, 788, 844,
1222

Oasis, 716
Oeil pour oeil, 906
L'Or de Naples, 717
Ordet, 465, 643, 832

Pain vivant, Le, 719
Papa, maman, ma femme, et moi,
835
Paris--Canaille, 836
Parisienne, La, 981
Paris nous appartient, 1003,
1022, 1056
Paris--Palace Hotel, 837
Passion, 640

Paths of Glory, 465, 1028
Patrouille de choc, 956
Pays d'ou je viens, Le, 838
Peau Douce, La, 8, 102-103, 115,
118, 121-122, 124-125, 147,
153, 157, 194, 220, 233, 245,
249, 261, 284, 307, 330, 349,
365, 397, 434, 1072, 1232,
1236-1237, 1239, 1241-1242,
1245-1246, 1248, 1271, 1303,
1360, 1376, 1379
Pete Kelly's Blues, 839
Petit Carrousel de fete, Le, 841
Peur, La, 743, 847
Phfft!, 730
Picnic, 465, 815, 849
Pistonne, Le, 1110
Pointe courte, La, 465, 852-853
Pot--bouille, 955
Prince Valiant, 582
Printemps, l'automne, et l'amour,
Le, 733
Prisoner, The, 677
Prix de la peur, La, 856
Psycho, 436
Pushover, 636

Quai des blondes, 595-596
Quatre Cents Coups, Les, 4, 25,
29, 36, 42, 45, 50, 54, 69,
92, 122, 125, 156, 194, 220,
245, 249, 255, 262, 284, 294,
308, 322, 330, 349, 352, 365,
368, 384, 392, 397, 403, 405,
414, 427-429, 447-448, 452,
455, 1040, 1042, 1190-1191,
1193, 1195-1196, 1198, 1200-
1201, 1206, 1208, 1213, 1215,
1228, 1246, 1270-1271, 1279,
1303, 1307-1308, 1360, 1370,
1390

Racers, The, 647
Rainmaker, The, 933
Rançon de plaisir, La, 734
Ransom, 962
Rear Window, 465, 686
Rebecca, 528
Rebel without a Cause, 799, 843,
858
Regle du jeu, La, 465, 481

Repris de justice, 740
Return to Paradise, 598
Richard the Lion-Hearted, 526
Rififi, 569
Ring of Fear, 633
River of No Return, 582, 599
Robinson Crusoe, 601
Roman Holidays, 620
Rose Tattoo, The, 871
Rouge est mis, Le, 968
Rouge et le noir, Le, 603-605

Sait--on jamais, 970
Salaire du peche, Le, 971
Salauds vont en enfer, Les, 872
Sang et lumières, 606
Saskatchewan, 633
Scarface, 790
Searchers, The, 855
Secret d'Hélène Marimon, Le,
    607-608
Secret de Soeur Angele, Le, 874
Senechal le magnifique, 972
Seven Brides for Seven Brothers,
    745
Seventh Seal, The, 912
Seven-Year Itch, The, 465, 821,
    876
Shadow of a Doubt, 618, 1077,
    1086
Shoot the Piano Player (or: The
    Pianist). See Tirez sur le
    pianiste
Silken Skin. See La Peau douce
Silver Chalice, The, 640
Si Paris nous était conte, 810,
    877
Sirène du Mississipi, La, 12, 196,
    208, 220, 234, 236-237, 245,
    249, 253, 260, 284, 307, 330,
    349, 365, 397, 412, 1102-
    1103, 1104, 1115, 1295, 1301-
    1302, 1314, 1322, 1336, 1356,
    1360
Small Change. See L'Argent de
    poche
Snows of Kilimanjaro, The, 502
So Big, 473, 579
Soft Skin. See La Peau douce
S.O.S. Norohna, 975
Stalag 17, 465, 494

Star is Born, A, 639
Stolen Kisses. See Baisers volés
Story of Adèle H., The. See
    L'Histoire d'Adèle H.
Such a Gorgeous Kid like Me. See
    Une Belle Fille comme moi
Sudden Fear, 496
Summer Madness, 756

Tamango, 1032
Tempête sur la mer, 613
Temps des assassins, 879, 891
Testament d'Orphée, Le, 1078
Tête contre les murs, La, 1004
Tirez sur le pianiste, 5, 43, 58-
    60, 62-63, 66, 69, 77, 81,
    84, 87, 92, 105, 113, 122,
    125, 153, 179, 204, 220, 224,
    239, 245, 249, 255, 284, 311,
    330, 334, 349, 360-361, 365,
    384, 392, 397, 414, 446,
    1049, 1124, 1202-1203, 1205,
    1213, 1215, 1219-1221, 1234,
    1246, 1271, 1278, 1303, 1347-
    1348, 1354-1355, 1360, 1361,
    1454
Titanic, 638
To Catch a Thief, 465, 643, 711
Toit, Le, 880
Toni, 869, 881
Touchez pas au Grisbi, 614, 619
Touch of Evil, 465, 1018
Tour de Nesle, La, 465, 626, 752
Toute la ville accuse, 882
Traversée de Paris, 788, 883-884,
    888
Triporteur, Le, 947
Trois font la paire, Le, 978
Trou, Le, 1055, 1062
Trouble in the Store, 602
Trouble with Harry, The, 858-859,
    864
Twelve Angry Men, 954
Twenty-Three Paces to Baker
    Street, 892
Two English Girls. See Les Deux
    Anglaises et le continent
Typhon sur Nagasaki, 979

Under Capricorn, 618, 1077, 1086
Untamed, 640

Vacances portugaises, 465, 1079
Vera Cruz, 465, 644
Verboten, 1053
Versailles, 611
Versailles en couleurs, 757
Vie, Une, 985
Viel Homme et l'enfant, Le, 465, 1092
Vierges, Les, 1185
Village magique, La, 759
Vincent, François, Paul et les autres, 465, 1144, 1189
Violents, Les, 1035
Visite, Une, 1, 1215, 1336
Vivre sa vie, 1061

Voyage en Italie, 760

War and Peace, 802
Wild Child, The. See L'Enfant sauvage
Wild One, The, 543
Witches of Salem, The, 974
Woman Next Door, The. See La Femme d'à côté
Written on the Wind, 465, 930
Wrong Man, The, 465, 864, 904

You Only Live Once, 1034

08/15, 642

Auteur Index

Aldrich, Robert, 465, 664, 668, 678, 687, 691, 729, 761, 766, 796, 846, 866, 888, 966, 1011, 1026

Allegret, Marc, 629, 690, 754

Allegret, Yves, 574, 716, 788, 827, 935

Antonioni, Michelangelo, 480, 588, 630, 896

Astruc, Alexandre, 630, 643, 687, 712, 735, 893, 985

Audiberti, Jacques, 1057, 1189a, 1271

Autant-Lara, Claude, 603-605, 650, 788, 817, 823, 858, 883-884, 888, 903, 918, 1013, 1022

Bazin, André, 659, 857, 906, 973, 984, 1041, 1060, 1104, 1118, 1122, 1134, 1147, 1151, 1156, 1175, 1356

Beaudine, William, 465, 503-504

Becker, Jacques, 465, 512, 529, 538-539, 591, 614, 619, 628, 764, 899, 1055, 1062, 1073, 1184

Bergman, Ingmar, 804, 912, 1017, 1024, 1136-1137, 1272

Bernard-Aubert, Claude, 910, 956, 1038

Berri, Claude, 465, 1092, 1110, 1186, 1272

Blain, Gerard, 465, 1187

Boetticher, Budd, 465, 885, 973

Bogart, Humphrey, 465, 587, 731, 929, 1141

Boisrond, Michel, 772, 788, 981

Bresson, Robert, 465, 564, 742, 771, 778, 781, 788, 848, 904, 913, 1170

Brooks, Richard, 491, 782, 869, 1024

Buñuel, Luis, 465, 529, 555, 601, 737, 788, 868, 1156, 1238, 1250, 1272

Capra, Frank, 465, 533, 1167

Carné, Marcel, 741, 788, 838

Chabrol, Claude, 465, 993, 1024

Chaplin, Charlie, 465, 483, 741, 860, 967, 996, 1133, 1139, 1168

Ciampi, Yves, 557, 692, 979

Clair, René, 482, 588

Clement, René, 465, 580-581, 888, 1031

Clouzot, Henri-Georges, 804, 830, 868, 919-920, 964

Cocteau, Jean, 465, 564, 926, 1078, 1336

Cukor, George, 465, 499, 533, 545, 616, 639, 1005

Dassin, Jules, 473, 569, 675-676, 681-682, 902, 1050

Daves, Delmer, 583, 617, 772

Dean, James, 465, 795, 803, 812, 1154, 1387

Delannoy, Jean, 625, 649, 723, 816, 868

de la Patelliere, Denys, 632, 671, 964, 971, 1008

de Sica, Vittorio, 650, 717, 833,

880
Doillon, Jacques, 465, 1145, 1153
Dreyer, Carl, 465, 643, 832,
    1119, 1156
Duvivier, Julien, 788, 875, 879,
    891, 939, 955

Fellini, Federico, 465, 566, 687,
    753, 793, 896, 981, 1067,
    1424
Ford, John, 465, 519, 645, 703–
    704, 726, 741, 855, 1132
Franju, Georges, 447, 1004, 1040
Fuller, Sam, 465, 527, 822, 1053

Gance, Abel, 465, 509, 529, 538,
    588, 610, 626, 655, 679, 715,
    752
Germi, Pietro, 804, 988, 1024
Godard, Jean-Luc, 430, 445, 465,
    991, 1037, 1061, 1068, 1081,
    1090–1091, 1099, 1114, 1272,
    1296, 1321, 1380, 1387, 1465
Guitry, Sacha, 465, 611, 810,
    877, 900, 927, 969, 978,
    1172, 1176

Hathaway, Henry, 465, 492, 523,
    582, 647, 892
Hawks, Howard, 465, 561, 592,
    742, 748, 790, 1088, 1129,
    1272, 1393, 1403
Hitchcock, Alfred, 433, 435–436,
    465, 528, 589, 618, 643, 650,
    662, 680, 686, 693, 711, 736,
    741–742, 804–807, 818, 843–
    844, 858–859, 864, 869, 904,
    963, 1020a, 1063a, 1069,
    1077, 1086, 1127, 1129, 1156,
    1162, 1181–1182, 1238, 1250,
    1272, 1318, 1356, 1393, 1465
Hossein, Robert, 835, 858, 872
Hughes, Ken, 813, 850, 869
Huston, John, 705, 814, 1272

Ichikawa, Kon, 473, 889, 938

Joffé, Alex, 698, 765, 867, 894

Kast, Pierre, 465, 1079
Kautner, Helmut, 630, 687, 801,

889
Kazan, Elia, 465, 624, 803, 901,
    940, 958, 961
King, Henry, 502, 582, 640
Kinoshita, Keisuke, 473, 1013,
    1033
Kubrick, Stanley, 465, 1020a,
    1028

Lamorisse, Albert, 465, 769, 804
Lang, Fritz, 465, 511, 665, 723,
    775, 1034
Laughton, Charles, 465, 831, 1148
LeChanois, Jean-Paul, 526, 683,
    759, 834, 914
Leenhardt, Roger, 529, 754, 800,
    858
LeRoy, Mervyn, 473, 825
Litvak, Anatole, 473, 897
Logan, Joshua, 465, 815, 849, 887
Lubitsch, Ernst, 465, 533, 1098,
    1178, 1318–1319, 1333, 1336,
    1405
Lumet, Sidney, 465, 954

MacCarey, Leo, 742, 1318, 1333
MacLaren, Norman, 465, 661, 840
Malle, Louis, 465, 1013–1014,
    1074
Mankiewicz, Joseph, 465, 658–659,
    873
Mann, Anthony, 520, 695, 702,
    773, 922
Mann, Delbert, 871, 912, 992
Melville, Jean-Pierre, 473, 504,
    788
Mizoguchi, Kenji, 473, 817, 888
Mulligan, Robert, 465, 1023a

Nakahira, Yasushi, 473, 1030
Negulesco, Jean, 534, 593, 638

Ophuls, Max, 465, 529, 694, 709,
    713, 738, 819, 826, 858, 905,
    931, 946, 949, 1020, 1025,
    1027

Pinoteau, Jack, 518, 895, 947
Preminger, Otto, 465, 538, 559,
    582, 599, 720, 779, 865, 868,
    986

Ray, Nick, 465, 627, 706, 799, 843, 858, 889, 898, 924, 951, 1142

Renoir, Jean, 454, 458, 465, 481, 529, 538, 540–541, 567–568, 597, 609, 665, 689, 718, 720, 722, 741, 788, 842, 869, 881, 907, 953, 965, 1007, 1089a, 1097, 1112, 1122, 1129, 1134, 1143, 1146, 1149–1150, 1177, 1238, 1250, 1272

Resnais, Alain, 465, 788, 804, 844, 862–863, 1075, 1076a, 1272

Rivette, Jacques, 465, 862, 1003, 1022, 1056

Robson, Mark, 598, 730, 804

Roché, Henri-Pierre, 7, 15, 432, 444, 453, 456, 1069a, 1120, 1123

Rossellini, Roberto, 465, 529, 542, 585, 600, 699, 701, 721, 743, 760, 763, 847, 1046a, 1070, 1088, 1129, 1171, 1238, 1250

Rozier, Jacques, 465, 1064

Sautet, Claude, 465, 1144, 1189

Sirk, Douglas, 465, 503, 930

Sturges, Preston, 529, 533, 646, 1156

Tashlin, Frank, 473, 774, 869, 908, 982

Tati, Jacques, 465, 529, 697, 878, 990, 999, 1012, 1024, 1318

Ulmer, Edgar G., 465, 630, 687, 770

Vadim, Roger, 465, 768, 788, 791, 970, 980, 1048, 1321

Varda, Agnes, 465, 852–853, 1046a

Verneuil, Henri, 519, 589, 783, 788, 837, 948

Vidor, Charles, 465, 528, 851

Vidor, King, 684, 802

Vigo, Jean, 465, 1256

von Sternberg, Joseph, 465, 846a, 1001, 1019

Welles, Orson, 465, 804, 809, 829, 1018, 1046, 1116, 1165, 1174, 1272, 1296, 1393

Wilder, Billy, 465, 494, 821, 876, 1272

Wise, Robert, 473, 518, 579, 615, 667

Wyler, William, 620, 811

Copyediting directed by Ara Salibian
Text formatted and produced by Diane Dillon
Camera-ready copy typed by Ann Condon
        on an IBM Selectric
Printed on 60# Bookmark, an acid-free paper,
        and bound by Braun-Brumfield, Inc.
        of Ann Arbor, Michigan.